100
answers to
100 questions

to ask before

You say

"I Do"

ask
· discover ·
live smart

100
answers to
100 questions

to ask before
You say
"I Do"

Christian
LIFE
A STRANG COMPANY

Most CHRISTIAN LIFE products are available at special quantity discounts for bulk purchase for sales promotions, premiums, fund-raising, and educational needs. For details, write Christian Life, 600 Rinehart Road, Lake Mary, Florida 32746, or telephone (407) 333-0600.

100 Answers to 100 Questions to Ask Before You Say "I Do"

Published by Christian Life
A Strang Company
600 Rinehart Road
Lake Mary, Florida 32746

www.strang.com

Scripture quotations marked CEV are from the Contemporary English Version, copyright © 1995 by the American Bible Society. Used by permission.

Scripture quotations marked GNT are from the Good News Translation, Second Edition. Copyright © 1992 by the American Bible Society. Used by permission.

Scripture quotations marked THE MESSAGE are from *The Message: The Bible in Contemporary English*, copyright © 1993, 1994, 1995, 1996, 2000, 2001, 2002. Used by permission of NavPress Publishing Group.

Scripture quotations marked NIV are from the Holy Bible, New International Version. Copyright © 1973, 1978, 1984, International Bible Society. Used by permission.

Scripture quotations marked NAS are from the New American Standard Bible, Updated. Copyright © 1960, 1962, 1963, 1968, 1971, 1972, 1973, 1975, 1977, 1995 by the Lockman Foundation. Used by permission. (www.Lockman.org)

Scripture quotations marked NLT are from the Holy Bible, New Living Translation, copyright © 1996, 2004. Used by permission of Tyndale House Publishers, Inc., Wheaton, IL 60189. All rights reserved.

Cover design by Whisner Design Group, Tulsa, Oklahoma

Copyright © 2008 by GRQ, Inc.
All rights reserved

ISBN 10:   1-59979-275-3
ISBN 13:   978-1-59979-275-0

BISAC Category: Religion/Christian Life/Love & Marriage

First Edition

08 09 10 11 12—9 8 7 6 5 4 3 2 1

Printed in the United States of America

Don't excite love,
don't stir it up,
until the time is ripe—
and you're ready.

Song of Solomon 8:4, THE MESSAGE

Contents

Child's Play: If You Want Children, How Many Do You Want, and How Will You Raise Them

Right on the Money: Your Financial Philosophy

Talk to Me: Communication and Conflict

Introduction

There's nothing sweeter than a wedding. Friends and family don their wardrobe finery, muster their best behavior, and get together to witness the union of a starry-eyed couple. It's a magical day.

With all of the pomp and pageantry that go into a wedding, couples spend months or even years planning their special day. The bride scours magazines in search of the perfect gown. Bridesmaids scout out a dress that will work for a wide variety of ages, body shapes, and sizes—and the guys need something to wear, too! Then there are the flowers, the music, the scripture readings, the vows, and the format of the service. And of course, there are the reception menu and entertainment to consider. The investment in time and money can be staggering.

So much time is spent planning the wedding that couples forget there is going to be a marriage after the honeymoon is over. Marriage is so much more than the bells and whistles of the ceremony; it is a commitment to one person for the rest of your life.

Your decision to marry will be among the biggest you will ever make, and it requires thoughtful consideration. It seems terribly unromantic, but being in love isn't a big enough reason to get married. A satisfying marriage is as much about compatibility as it is about passion; many a marriage has ended in disaster because of irreconcilable differences.

The questions to follow are designed to help you explore all aspects of compatibility. There are thought-provoking queries about family background, lifestyle, hopes and dreams, money, and sexual compatibility. Some of these questions might seem awkward at first, but discussing them as a couple will help you hone in on your reasons for marrying and set you on the road to marital bliss.

> *Marriage should be honored by all.*
> Hebrews 13:4 NIV
>
> *There is no more lovely, friendly,*
> *or charming relationship, communion,*
> *or company, than a good marriage.*
> Martin Luther

question

Why are you getting married?

Walking down the aisle is probably the single most important decision you will ever make in your lifetime. The question is, why do you want to marry this particular person at this particular moment in time? The bride and the groom will come to the altar with different expectations based on how marriage was modeled by their parents. What is your motivation behind saying "I do"?

answer

A couple needs a solid reason for getting married. In God's eyes, marriage is serious business. Marriage is a sacred union that should be entered into seriously.

There are good reasons for tying the knot, but there are also some bad ones. Are you getting married just because all of your friends are? Are you getting married because your parents want you to? Do you think marriage will provide you with financial or emotional security? Are you lonely or faced with an unplanned pregnancy? By themselves, these are not valid reasons to get married. The problems in your life won't disappear the moment that gold band is slipped onto your finger.

Obviously you want to marry someone with whom you share common interests and enjoy spending time. But marriage isn't just about playing house or hanging out. By saying "I do," you will be making a lifetime commitment. You need to be sure you are truly in love with your partner—along with their good and bad qualities—and not just in love with the romantic notion of a wedding. Marriage is about physical and spiritual intimacy.

Through prayer and a great deal of soul-searching, you can be confident this is the one person God has created for you.

worth thinking about

▶ **Now is a great time** to compile a premarital checklist. Are you emotionally ready for this kind of commitment? Can you see yourself with this person fifty years down the road?

▶ **Avoid the temptation** to take a quick trip to the altar. The engagement period was designed to help a couple get to know each other better, and a longer engagement can be helpful for financial reasons and is often helpful for social as well as personal reasons.

▶ **Both the bride** and the groom need to be on board and ready for the marriage. This is no time to succumb to peer pressure or to strong-arm the other.

> At the beginning of creation God "made them male and female." "For this reason a man will leave his father and mother and be united to his wife, and the two will become one flesh." So they are no longer two, but one. Therefore what God has joined together, let man not separate.
>
> Mark 10:6–9, NIV

2

question

Do you truly trust each other?

You probably like your future mate and are attracted to, have fun with, and appreciate the person he or she is. But can you honestly say you have a forever kind of love? Do you love each other deeply and have a level of trust that is beyond reproach? Do you respect each other for who you are? Once the giddiness of new love wears off and the honeymoon is over, you need something deeper than infatuation for your marriage to withstand the storms a lifetime of togetherness will bring.

answer

Love, trust, and respect are the foundational pillars of any successful relationship, whether it is a romance, family relationship, friendship, or business association. Where there is trust, there is stronger commitment, understanding, and loyalty.

To trust someone means you have confidence in his or her character and faith in your relationship. Many marriages fail because there is a profound breach of trust, a concern over infidelity, a lack of truthfulness, or a question about integrity. Make sure you trust your future spouse implicitly—and he or she reciprocates that trust—or you will have trouble down the road.

Respect is a concept that is not only difficult to define in modern culture, but one that is even harder to see in action. The old sayings "Respect your elders," "Respect authority," and "Respect life" seem to have fallen by the wayside. To respect someone means you recognize that person's worth and value. True respect requires humility and should be a two-way street in your marriage.

One of the best ways to show love and respect to each other is to develop great listening skills. The Golden Rule says, "Do unto others as you would have them do unto you." If you practice that in your marriage, it will be a happy one!

worth thinking about

▶ **One of the** traditional wedding vows is "to love and to cherish." Think about what that means, and make sure you can repeat those vows without reservation.

▶ **In order for others** to respect you, you must first respect yourself. Self-respect comes from appreciating who God made you to be and knowing how important you are to Him.

▶ **Trust is a critical** element of faith. The Bible teaches that trusting God brings peace because He always keeps His promises. Apply the same principles to your marriage.

> *Love is patient and kind. Love is not jealous or boastful or proud or rude. It does not demand its own way. It is not irritable, and it keeps no record of being wronged. It does not rejoice about injustice but rejoices whenever the truth wins out.*
>
> 1 Corinthians 13:4–6, NLT

3

question
▼
Do you both expect the same things?

Couples sometimes get married but don't understand that they're on the same team. There's no "her team" or "his team." They're in it together. They're on the same team with the same goals. The trouble is, couples often get married with different expectations. Living up to your own expectations is hard enough; living up to someone else's is nearly impossible!

answer
▼

Not only do you need a valid reason for getting married in the first place, but before you sign your names on the marriage license, you should also have a clear understanding of what you both hope to get out of the arrangement. As a bride or a groom, what are your expectations about life as a couple?

You've probably heard the saying that opposites attract. In many ways that's true; differences bring an element of excitement to a marriage. God often brings two people together to balance each other out. He pairs an introvert with an extrovert, for example. Two shy people might make for a quiet household!

But the one thing you must have in common is what you expect from married life. For one of you, married life may be all about sexual experimentation, but for the other it is about companionship. One of you might long for the pitter-patter of dozens of little feet, but the other might envision a sophisticated, double-income couple throwing lavish parties.

Men and women often have different notions of what postnuptial life should be like. Unfulfilled expectations will chip away at the foundation of your marriage. Candidly answer the question "What do I really expect from our marriage?" Be careful not to say what you think your partner wants to hear. Be honest with each other. Once you understand what your expectations are, you are much better suited to meet those needs.

worth thinking about

- ▶ A marriage is more difficult to pull off than a wedding. Take some of the time you would otherwise spend on choosing china patterns and honeymoon destinations to discuss your future hopes and dreams.

- ▶ Have realistic expectations. Life isn't all cake and caviar; it's mortgage payments, morning breath, and dirty laundry. Plan on good times and bad.

- ▶ If you determine you have some differences in marital expectations, don't just automatically cancel the reception hall. This is a time for discussion and not rash decisions.

If you paint in your mind a picture of bright and happy expectations, you put yourself into a condition conducive to your goal.
Norman Vincent Peale

4

question

Are you ready for a lifelong commitment?

The number of people making and keeping commitments is on a steep decline in this country. It used to be the norm for people to work their entire careers for the same company. If they bought Fords, they always bought Fords. If they got married, they stayed married. But these days it's easy to change employers, switch brands, and swap spouses. Are you prepared to spend the rest of your life, day in and day out, with the same person?

answer

There are going to be things that drive you crazy about your spouse, especially the first few years: the strands of hair in the sink, the underwear lying in a heap on the floor, that delightful snore you snuggle up to every night. It doesn't matter how perfect you think your spouse is, there are going to be times when you get annoyed. The achievement of any goal requires commitment. The question is, do you think your love is deep enough and your commitment strong enough to make it for the long haul?

There will be challenges ahead, some of them small and manageable, but some will seem impossible to overcome. That's why you promise to love and cherish each other in sickness and in health, for richer for poorer.

Otherwise, at the first sign of trouble you'd bolt and look for greener pastures.

Despite popular current opinion, marriage is not disposable. When you stand before God and witnesses and say your vows, you are promising to stick by each other until "death do you part." This is a nonnegotiable, no-matter-what kind of deal, not a casual affair you enjoy until something better comes along. Your marriage is a contract that not only is legally binding, but also is irrevocable in the eyes of God. So make sure you're willing and excited to spend the rest of your days together.

worth thinking about

▶ **Take a look** at how your future spouse has handled other commitments: jobs, promises, previous relationships, bills. If there are red flags, it would be wise to question your intended's ability to commit.

▶ **As you grow** old you will both change physically, emotionally, intellectually, and spiritually and may evolve into different people. Be prepared to love the whole person, inside and out.

▶ **The most important** question isn't "Can you live with this person for the rest of your life?" but rather, "Can you live without this person?"

This is what GOD commands: When a man makes a vow to GOD or binds himself by an oath to do something, he must not break his word; he must do exactly what he has said.

Numbers 30:1–2, THE MESSAGE

5

question

Is this the right time?

Every time you see each other you catch your breath and get a clenching feeling in your chest. Your heart pounds, and your palms start to sweat. You're not having a heart attack; you're in love. After you've been together for a while, it occurs to you that it's time to get married. But as they say, timing is everything. Is this the right time to walk hand in hand into the future?

answer

In many parts of the world, marriages are arranged, or at least expected, by a certain age. In the United States, for the most part, young people follow a fairly well-traveled road to matrimony. You grow up, graduate from high school, go to college or get a job, get married, and have babies.

If you have a solid relationship, marriage often feels like the logical next step. But there are factors that must be considered before taking the leap. First, do you have time to be married? Chances are you're busy working and have an active social life and family obligations. Lack of time and busy schedules negatively impact marriages in many ways, so make sure you are ready for the time commitment marriage deserves.

Second, can you afford to be married? Not to be a spoilsport, but you can't live on love alone. Money certainly isn't everything, but being married does take a bank account. Make sure you have something in yours.

Third, are you ready to be married? Passions aside, marriage is a huge step and a massive commitment. Know what you're getting into, or spend more time getting to know each other first.

worth thinking about

▶ **Get married** when you want to get married, not when you feel like you should. Don't allow peer or family pressure to get in the way of your own best judgment.

▶ **Consider waiting** until you are out of school before getting married. The stresses of a wedding and new marriage will add to the burden of an already challenging course load.

▶ **Many Christian couples** get married earlier than non-Christian couples because they do not want to engage in premarital sex. Marriage is about more than sex, however, so make sure you are mature enough to handle the responsibility of living on your own and making a lifelong commitment.

There's an opportune time to do things, a right time for everything on the earth: a right time for birth and another for death, a right time to plant and another to reap, a right time to kill and another to heal, a right time to destroy and another to construct.
Ecclesiastes 3:1–3, THE MESSAGE

Can you spend the rest of your life together?

Don't marry the person you think you can live with; marry only the individual you think you can't live without.

James Dobson

6

question

▾

What will be different after the wedding?

A wedding is often a surreal experience filled with fairy-tale memories and indulgent extravagances. But marriage is real life. Chances are good that married life will be different from the utopia you may have pictured. You'll both figure out what the other's hot buttons are and how not to push them, but it may take a while. What will be different about how you relate to each other after the ceremony?

answer

▾

Everything and nothing. That sounds like a politician's answer, but it's true. How your relationship changes will depend in large part on circumstances. You may already know some of your mate's idiosyncrasies, but there will definitely be some surprises in store. Behaviors you thought were endearing before marriage—like the way your sweetheart clips toenails—are going to grate on your nerves later on.

Face it. The heartthrob or beauty queen who could do no wrong will be gone, and the real person will be on the loose. Okay, so that's an exaggeration, but the fact is that your dream date may not be the same after the wedding. You are going to see all aspects of your spouse, not just the dinner-and-a-movie persona. You'll see what your spouse looks like in the morning. Your spouse will know how you talk and act when things don't go right and patience wears thin.

The most awkward part of the marital transition to discuss is your sex life. If you are anticipating a high level of sexual activity, there's a good chance that level will decline once the pressures of life set in. Your relationship will change in a drastic way.

But the part of your relationship that will change the most is your love for each other. It will grow deeper as you discover the mysteries of life together.

worth thinking about

▶ **People are getting** married progressively later in life and are bound to be more set in their ways. Be flexible and learn the art of negotiation; your way of doing something isn't the only way.

▶ **Married life means** more togetherness than ever. Everyone needs alone time and personal space, even newlyweds.

▶ **As you get older** and more settled, the days of your carefree youth will fall away as your level of responsibility increases. Even though life isn't all fun and games, don't take it too seriously, either.

> *You can never be happily married to another until you get a divorce from yourself. A successful marriage demands a certain death to self.*
>
> Jerry McCant

7

question

What are the biggest hurdles?

Life doesn't come with a script or a crystal ball, so you never know quite what to expect around the next corner. As the Bible says, you are not even promised tomorrow. One thing you can count on is that your life will have its share of troubles. As a married couple you will face hurdles as unique as you are. Knowing where the potential obstacles lie in the road before you will save heartache and anguish later on.

answer

You need to always be aware that each day will bring both good and bad. That's the nature of life. Don't allow the negatives to affect your outlook. Look with confidence toward your future together. It's probably easier to talk about being positive than to actually be positive. One way to keep your focus is to be prepared for the challenges that might come up.

Each couple will have their own set of hurdles to jump over as they navigate through marriage. Oftentimes it's the little things that cause the most trouble; when the big things arise you find the depth of character to dig down deep and handle them. The most common problems can be placed in the following categories: communication, overcoming adversity, identity, and daily life.

Undoubtedly there will be heartache ahead: jobs will be lost, loved ones will die, and your love will be tested. But God designed marriage so you could walk through life together; He binds you with love so you don't bottom out in life's potholes. You need to truly open your soul to your partner.

The best way to know what your biggest hurdles will be is to ask the people you trust, your friends and family. They can see your strengths and weaknesses objectively and will give you sound advice. It is better to confront problems ahead of time than wait for the top to blow.

worth thinking about

- ▶ **Before you get married**, you need to be certain you agree on major life issues—things like family, spirituality, lifestyle, fidelity—or are at least open to discussion.

- ▶ **The best way** to manage adversity is to stay grounded in your faith. A strong prayer life and time in the Bible will keep your heart open to God's will for your life.

- ▶ **Torn allegiances** can pose a significant problem. Work, friends, and family can all take a bite out of your marriage and your relationship with God. Set your priorities.

> *Consider it all joy, my brethren, when you encounter various trials, knowing that the testing of your faith produces endurance. And let endurance have its perfect result, so that you may be perfect and complete, lacking in nothing.*
>
> James 1:2–4, NAS

8

question

How can you divorce-proof your marriage?

Nobody signs a marriage license with the intention of some day signing a divorce decree. But with half of all marriages failing, this topic is a serious one that needs to be addressed. As a result of these staggering statistics, half the people considering marriage today come from broken homes while the other half come from two-parent families. Based on your family background, you and your love could have different experiences with marriage longevity.

answer

There is probably no extended family that has not been touched by divorce. Divorce has no demographic profile; it impacts young and old, rich and poor, black and white. Religious people get divorced more than nonreligious people do. Divorce is an equal opportunity home wrecker. The breakdown of a marriage is a heartbreak to those involved.

The key is prevention. That's why you are reading this book, to get to know each other from the inside out before you make a lifelong commitment. It is critically important to make a decision about marriage based on serious discussion and reflection rather than just going with your gut. Postponing or even canceling a wedding is far less harmful than rushing into a partnership that will have destructive impact years down the road.

If your parents divorced when you were growing up, this question might be painful at first, but it is important that you share how the breakup impacted you emotionally. Talking about it will give you and your intended a renewed commitment to each other.

The best way to prevent a divorce is to acknowledge your marriage vows and understand that divorce is not an option. Once the covenant is sealed, you need to make a commitment to love, honor, and cherish each other for the rest of your lives, working hard to make the marriage work.

worth thinking about

▶ **In order to** have a happy marriage, you must keep Christ at the center of your relationship. Just as the church submits to Christ, submit to each other.

▶ **If you are dealing** with feelings of guilt from a previous marriage, remember that there is nothing that is beyond God's forgiveness and nothing you can do will separate you from His unconditional love.

▶ **One of the best** ways to prevent divorce is to never take each other for granted. A treasured and appreciated spouse is a faithful spouse.

> "I hate divorce," says the LORD God of Israel. "I hate it when one of you does such a cruel thing to his wife. Make sure that you do not break your promise to be faithful to your wife."
>
> Malachi 2:16, GNT

9

question

Are you two really soul mates?

If you are considering getting married, you love your partner, are compatible, and enjoy being together. As you contemplate marriage you are probably wondering, *Is this really the one?* Of all the people in the world, is this the one person with whom you share a kindred spirit?

answer

If you give God the reins, He will bless your marriage. But for your marriage to be happy, you need to pick the right partner. The only way you will know if your betrothed is right for you is by praying about it and asking God for guidance. If your intended is in fact the right one, you'll know it because God will give you peace about your relationship.

A relationship between soul mates is often described as one that feels like it was meant to be. Soul mates have a sense of familiarity and harmony between them that brings out the best in both. You can foster those qualities by putting in some time and effort.

First and foremost, you will need to commit to putting your future spouse's happiness above all else. Just as you will want to bring blessings to your spouse, a good spouse will also bring blessings to you. Make it a practice to give these blessings by doing thoughtful and unexpected kindnesses for each other.

Cultivating emotional, spiritual, and physical intimacy will also enhance your spousal harmony. Spending time together and sharing your dreams, fears, joys, and sorrows on the deepest level will not only draw you closer, but will also encourage that spirit of oneness God desires for all married couples.

worth thinking about

▶ **Always seek** God's advice before a big decision. You may think you have sound judgment, but God's thoughts are not your thoughts, and His ways are not your ways.

▶ **The concept** of a soul mate as your exact match is a nice one, but not practical. If you are waiting for perfect chemistry, you'll be waiting a long time. Any worthwhile relationship takes hard work and understanding.

▶ **If your relationship** develops in the presence of God, you will form a bond stronger than you ever imagined possible.

> *In marriage, being the right person is as important as finding the right person.*
> Wilbert Donald Gough

question

What is your concept of a good marriage?

If you were to ask this question separately of men and of women, you'd likely get different answers. The men would be more likely to reply, "Amazing sex, and lots of it!" while the women would say, "Unconditional love, good communication, and someone who'll take out the trash." Good marriages come in many varieties. The two of you need to share what your ideal marriage looks like so you'll be on the same matrimonial page.

answer

People spend a lot more time planning a wedding than they do planning their marriage, so this is going to be a tough question. Unfortunately, there is no marriage rule book, and you will need to have some thoughtful discussions on this topic.

People have different ideals based on their family backgrounds, previous relationships, and self-perceptions. Some people have much higher standards than others. If your childhood home had a chaotic atmosphere to it, you might have different expectations than someone whose family home exuded peace and stability.

How do you define a good marriage? The most logical way to answer this question is by looking at some positive role models, couples you know who have great marriages. Ask them what qualities make for wedded bliss.

The Bible identifies ingredients like faithfulness, commitment, sacrifice, understanding, love, communication, and mutual submission. A good marriage should be like your relationship with Jesus, the ultimate Bridegroom.

worth thinking about

▶ **There will be** many times during the course of your marriage when you will need to look at things through your spouse's eyes rather than your own. True love is selfless.

▶ **One of the quickest** ways to destroy a good marriage is to take your spouse for granted. People often treat strangers better than the ones they love the most. Constantly strive to make your life partner feel special and loved.

▶ **Remember that** you don't have to agree on everything. Sometimes it's okay to agree to disagree.

> *May our dependably steady and warmly personal God develop maturity in you so that you get along with each other as well as Jesus gets along with us all. Then we'll be a choir— not our voices only, but our very lives singing in harmony in a stunning anthem to the God and Father of our Master Jesus!*
>
> Romans 15:5–6, THE MESSAGE

question

11

Do you stand to gain by getting married?

This question is terribly businesslike and unromantic, but it is probably one of the most important of all. It is time to make a list of pros and cons regarding your impending nuptials to make sure you wind up with more items in the pro category. If the biggest advantage you can come up with for getting married is that you'll be able to file a joint tax return, you should probably reconsider your game plan.

answer

Back in the days of pioneers and wagon trains, getting married wasn't a luxury. It was a do-or-die necessity. Men needed wives to cook and clean and bring little farmhands into the world, and they sometimes resorted to mail-order brides. Women needed husbands to provide for them financially and protect them because they had few other options for supporting themselves.

Things are different now, and marriage isn't a necessity for survival. As you put together your list of pros and cons, here are some things to get your brain waves humming:

Advantages of getting married include companionship, financial stability, children, legitimate lovemaking, better insurance rates, and someone to come home to at the end of the day. Disadvantages might include sharing your finances, more responsibility, a loss of independence, and someone to answer to.

Think about what this relationship will cost you emotionally, professionally, and financially. Are you expected to sever ties with family or friends because they either don't approve of the marriage or your intended is jealous? Do you expect the woman's role to be that of a stay-at-home housewife or do you expect her role to be that of a career woman? Do you both agree on what is expected of the woman and of the man in the marriage?

Luke 9:25 says, "What do you benefit if you gain the whole world but are yourself lost or destroyed?" (NLT).

worth thinking about

- ▶ **Not all gains** and losses are equal; having someone to grow old with may be far more desirable, for example, than being able to file a solo tax return.

- ▶ **Everyone has** a different set of priorities, so don't feel obligated to include what you think you *should*. This can be a confidential exercise, so be honest.

- ▶ **Love outweighs** all other reasons. If you are desperately in love with your sweetheart and can't imagine life without him or her, get married. But go into the marriage with both eyes wide open.

> We may think we are doing the right thing, but the LORD always knows what is in our hearts.
> Proverbs 21:2, CEV

question

▼

How well do you know each other?

The eyes are the windows to the soul, or so the ancient wisdom goes. If you are considering marriage, the two of you have no doubt been doing quite a bit of eye gazing. You may get an idea about a person's character by looking in the eyes, but you need to know a lot more than that if you are going to spend your entire lives together. Do you really know your future mate inside and out?

answer

▼

Imagine the emotions you would experience if you learned your spouse not only had been married before, but also had children you knew nothing about from that marriage. Sadly, this scenario is not that far-fetched; investigative reporters cover stories like this all the time.

It's nearly impossible to really know someone before you live together. Human beings are multifaceted creatures. Most people have multiple personalities—one for work, one for family, one for buddies, and another for one's sweetheart. The real person is a composite of all these personalities.

How well do you really know your future spouse? Here's a chance to test your knowledge. See how many of these questions you can answer: Favorite color? Most prized possession? Most cherished memory? If stranded on a desert island, what one book would be brought along? If your future spouse had one day left to live, how would it be lived?

While this isn't *The Newlywed Game*, and you won't get any fabulous prizes for getting the most correct answers, this little exercise will give you an idea of just how well acquainted you are with each other.

worth thinking about

▶ Clues about a person's true self can be found by observing simple behavior in everyday situations: driving, dining in restaurants, interacting with family. How does your intended interact with waitresses or other drivers stuck in rush-hour gridlock? Does a different person emerge in times of stress?

▶ Do you recognize your future mate's hot buttons? Knowing these ahead of time will help you avoid conflict.

▶ A little mystery can be fun and unpredictable. A lot of mystery can be dangerous.

> *When two people relate to each other authentically and humanly, God is the electricity that surges between them.*
> Martin Buber

13

question

What do you know about previous relationships?

Over the years, you may have had some wonderful romantic relationships and many others you'd like to erase from your memory banks. But unfortunately, there are no do-overs. Good or bad, everyone carries around baggage from previous relationships. Like it or not, those entanglements contribute to who you are today. Guilt and regret can be serious burdens, and they can potentially impact your future as a married couple. Have you delved into your betrothed's romantic history?

answer

The more appropriate question might be, what do you and your spouse-to-be *need* to know about each other's previous relationships? Does it really matter whom you dated before you met each other? Dredging up the past is more likely to cause problems in your relationship than to solve them. Learning about your significant other's love life could put a whole new spin on things and cause jealousy, resentment, and avoidable comparisons. Sometimes the truth hurts.

Together, the two of you should agree on what you will share about your respective pasts and how candid you will be. If you decide to talk about it, be sure to discuss how much of it you are willing to put behind you. Sidestep the temptation to bring up old dating relationships in the heat of an argument.

There are times, of course, when asking about previous relationships is necessary. Past behavior is a great predictor of future behavior. Nearly half of the people who get married now are on round number two. If you or your intended has been married before, it is important that you talk about why the previous marriage failed so you can avoid stepping on the same land mines. Discuss things like child support and alimony so there are no surprises.

Bottom line: your past is important, but it is not nearly as important as your future together.

worth thinking about

- ▶ **Should you find out** that your loved one has been badly wounded in a former relationship and has a deep-seated need for assurance, make it a point to express your love often.

- ▶ **Jealousy can be** like a cancer; it can eat away at your relationship bit by bit. If your partner has been romantically involved with someone else in the past, don't focus on it or let it destroy your future.

- ▶ **Forgive yourself** for your own mistakes and failed relationships. To build the future with your new partner, you must first let go of the past.

> *Forget what happened long ago!*
> *Don't think about the past.*
> Isaiah 43:18, CEV

14

question

Will anything in the past affect your marriage?

You might not be too eager to consider this question about the past for fear of what might be disclosed, but it is critical that you do so. Is there anything secretly tucked away in the past that could have future repercussions in your marriage?

answer

If either of you has had significant events or experiences in your history that could seriously impact your joint future, it's time to spill the beans. Not all skeletons need to come out of the proverbial closet, but those that could jeopardize your marital success do need to be exposed. Stressful, traumatic experiences leave scar tissue, and if not properly dealt with, they could have lifelong implications.

Some of these life-changing experiences might include the death of a loved one, divorce (your own or your parents'), physical or sexual abuse, being the victim of a crime, bankruptcy, previous marriage or annulment, a criminal record, a child given up for adoption, or previous addictions (pornography, gambling, drugs, alcohol).

Many of the deepest, darkest secrets were results of sin in more foolish days. No one is perfect; everyone is simply a work in progress. But each day is a new beginning, a chance to wipe the slate clean and start a new chapter. Paul's example in Philippians 3:13 (NIV) is a good one to follow: "Brothers, I do not consider myself yet to have taken hold of it. But one thing I do: Forgetting what is behind and straining toward what is ahead."

Talking about a huge event will be hard, but bearing the secret will be even harder. Many choose not to talk about their checkered pasts for fear of rejection. But if there are things that will impact your marriage, they need to be disclosed.

If you can, find a way past the issues, deal with their ramifications, and then move forward rather than harboring resentment. True love should be unconditional, just like God's love.

worth thinking about

▶ **No matter what** you've done, it can be forgiven.

▶ **If you made** some serious mistakes in your youth, make sure you seek expert advice to minimize their influence on your future. Wise counsel may be invaluable.

▶ **If your partner** confesses something that you find difficult to accept, consider getting professional help. A counselor or trusted member of the clergy may be able to help you.

> *Though your sins are like scarlet, I will make them as white as snow. Though they are red like crimson, I will make them as white as wool.*
>
> Isaiah 1:18, NLT

15 question

How are your families of origin different?

Differences can be charming. Differences can be attractive. But if your in-laws are completely different from your own family, you may experience some serious frustration down the road. Even if you grew up in the same region and have the same ethnic heritage, your families may still be worlds apart. Does it really matter if your families are completely different? After all, you're not marrying them. Knowing how your families differ and what they have in common will be helpful down the line.

answer

Actually, you *are* marrying your spouse's family. It's a package deal. Philosopher Henri Frédéric Amiel wrote, "To marry unequally is to suffer equally." While this statement must be considered in the context of a time when marriages did not occur between people of different classes, there is still some validity in it. Couples raised in significantly different socioeconomic environments will have trouble connecting on a variety of issues, from finances to diet. If your family subsisted on macaroni and cheese while your beloved's family dined on duck a l'orange, there may be some culture shock once you start playing house.

Each family has its own personality. If yours is large and boisterous, your only-child future partner might feel out of sorts and a little threatened at family get-togethers.

There is a lot of territory you can cover, so ask questions, sit back, and observe. What are your family traditions? How do you celebrate holidays? How does your family show affection to one another? What activities do you enjoy doing as a family? Do the family members seem to care about one another? How do you deal with anger? Understanding where your spouse comes from will help you know where you are going.

worth thinking about

▶ **Family differences** will become glaringly apparent at holidays, especially Christmas. Some families concentrate on the celebration itself, while others focus on bestowing lavish gifts. You'll need to find some middle ground.

▶ **At first**, the unique qualities of your spouse's family might drive you a little crazy, but give it some time. You will find you are enriched by embracing new ways of doing things.

▶ **When considering** your differences, pay particular attention to how values, ethics, and morals are expressed. Having disparate views in these areas will be the biggest stumbling block in your marriage.

> You and your families will feast in the presence of the Lord your God, and you will rejoice in all you have accomplished because the Lord your God has blessed you.
>
> Deuteronomy 12:7, NLT

Do you like your future in-laws?

Cherish your human connections—
your relationships with
friends and family.

Barbara Bush

question

How do the ways you were raised differ?

Upbringings can be as different as night and day, oil and water, vanilla and chocolate. Both you and your mate have been shaped into who you are today by lifetimes full of events and people. By default, the likelihood is strong that you and your mate have some significant differences in how you were raised. What you really need to know is how those differences will affect your future as a married couple.

answer

Was yours a traditional two-parent home or was it something less conventional? Single-parent and blended households present unique challenges. The environments in which the two of you were raised could also be in contrast. Growing up on a farm is different from growing up in a metropolitan condominium. Your childhood activities, responsibilities, chores, and worldviews could be a mismatch.

Probably the most consequential difference in how you were raised revolves around your folks' style of parenting. Were they overly permissive, or were they dictators; were they quick to show affection, or were they standoffish?

Their style will greatly impact your style should you decide to become parents. Don't simply dismiss these differences; take them to a counselor for advice on how to avoid turning them into "irreconcilable" differences.

Differences can become problems if they cause arguments, so it is better to address them from the get-go. You need to agree on the big things, like your home environment and religious values. Sit down and talk about some of the characteristics laid out above and how you will address them in your own marriage.

worth thinking about

- ▶ **Even if you can't** identify with or don't approve of the way your loved one was raised, remember that you fell in love with the result of that upbringing. Without it, your intended would be a different person.

- ▶ **Rather than** focusing on the differences in how you were raised, focus on how these differences will enhance your own future marriage. You have an opportunity to pick and choose the best aspects of your childhoods.

- ▶ **If you or your** mate was raised in a household fraught with violence, anger, and addiction, get help in dealing with this, and be patient with each other.

> *The sun has its own beauty, the moon another beauty, and the stars a different beauty; and even among stars there are different kinds of beauty.*
> 1 Corinthians 15:41, GNT

17

question

What was your childhood like?

The early environment shapes the adult. Since most personality traits are formed early on, talking about the key events in your lives will help you understand each other. Adults who had wonderful childhoods may be more eager to create new memories with their own families. On the other hand, childhood might bring back painful feelings.

answer

The U.S. Census estimates that more than one-third of all children are latchkey kids who go home from school to an empty house. If that was your situation, be frank about how that made you feel. Were your relationships with your parents and siblings strained and bitter, or were they fun-loving and affectionate? Did you feel loved unconditionally? The bonds developed in your formative years will carry over into your marriage and into your own parenting.

Life-changing events, both positive and negative, will skew the impressions of your childhood. Unfortunately, people often remember bad experiences more easily than good ones. Do you recall only family fights, failed tests, broken hearts, losses of loved ones, or the mistakes made?

You can make a point to invest more time in reflecting on the good things that happened when you were a kid. Maybe it was a special family vacation at the beach, night games with your best friends, a blue-ribbon achievement, or your junior prom. Maybe it was enough just knowing how much your parents loved you.

If you have painful childhood memories, consider seeking professional assistance from a trusted pastor or counselor. You may have things you need to deal with before getting married.

worth thinking about

▶ **One great way** to trigger your childhood memories is to flip through a few photo albums. Besides, your future mate would love to see your braces and bad haircuts!

▶ **Talk about your** most embarrassing moment. If you can't tell the love of your life, whom can you tell? No doubt, it will be good for a few laughs.

▶ **A child is God's** most precious gift. Yet children are suffering needlessly all over the world. As a wedding gift to each other, consider sponsoring a child. The impact you make on that young life will have eternal rewards.

> *Anyone who welcomes a little child like this on my behalf is welcoming me. But if you cause one of these little ones who trusts in me to fall into sin, it would be better for you to have a large millstone tied around your neck and be drowned in the depths of the sea.*
>
> Matthew 18:5–6, NLT

18

question

Are there any diseases or serious illnesses?

Each person is a unique combination of genetic ingredients. Eye color, height, hair color, and other characteristics are passed down from one generation to the next. Perhaps your family is known for dimples or a particularly strong jawline. Unfortunately, diseases are also passed down through the generations. Knowing what lurks in the shadows of your family health history may one day prove invaluable.

answer

Some researchers believe that nearly all human diseases are genetic. According to the National Institutes of Health, more than four thousand diseases such as sickle-cell anemia and cystic fibrosis are known to be genetic and to be passed on in families. The potential to develop conditions like heart disease, cancer, alcoholism, Alzheimer's disease, and mental illness can also be inherited.

Based on the risk factors they are born with, some people are at greater risk than others for inheriting deadly diseases. So what happens if you find out your betrothed's health profile is dotted with red flags? You needn't stop the wedding if you find out your future spouse comes from a bad gene pool, or sweat profusely when you repeat the in-sickness-and-in-health vow during your ceremony.

Everyone has blips in his or her DNA. But knowledge is power. If you know you are predisposed to heart disease, for example, eating sensibly and exercising regularly can be significant preventives. Having a genetic blueprint will be beneficial.

Nowadays, genetic counseling is available for a wide range of potential problems.

worth thinking about

▶ When they grow up, many adopted children seek their birthparents to find out about their family medical history. If one of you is adopted, consider looking for yours. If your birth parents' medical information is unavailable, genetic testing might be a viable option.

▶ Fully disclose your personal and family health histories, both physical and mental.

▶ For a wonderful resource on conducting your own family health profile, go to www.geneticalliance.org and select Family Health History. The Genetic Alliance is a coalition of more than six hundred advocacy organizations serving twenty-five million people affected by one thousand conditions.

> *My illness must have caused you some trouble, but you didn't hate me or turn me away because of it. You welcomed me as though I were one of God's angels or even Christ Jesus himself.*
> Galatians 4:14, CEV

19

question

What about your parents and siblings?

Whoever said that blood is thicker than water obviously understood strong family relationships. For some people, however, the bonds of friendship are tighter than those with parents or siblings. Strained parental relationships and animosity sometimes carry over into adulthood. Most families, on the other hand, are tight. Before you say "I do," talk about the state of affairs in your family unit.

answer

Weddings can be stressful events. Not only do you have to pick out the flowers, music, attire, and menu, you also have to decide who to invite, who the attendants will be, and what the seating chart at the head table will look like. There are numerous opportunities for social missteps if you don't know the terrain. If there is bad blood between your loved one's parents or between certain siblings, for example, you'll want to know that before Mendelssohn's "Wedding March" begins.

Sibling rivalry has existed since there have been families; it runs rampant throughout the Old Testament. First there were Cain and Abel. Then along came Jacob and Esau. And then came Joseph and his brothers, the latter being one of the earliest records of a troubled family. Families are a hodgepodge of temperaments and personalities. When you put a variety of children together in a close environment with all of them vying for the attention of their parents, there are bound to be problems.

Sitting around the Thanksgiving dinner table could be awkward for a new spouse, so fill in the gaps for your future mate. Who doesn't get along with whom and why? It always helps to have a network of extended family to love and support you through the peaks and valleys of life. As you grow up and older, bygones become bygones, and you learn to appreciate your relatives.

worth thinking about

▶ Have you been accepted as a capable adult, or do you slip back into your child mode as soon as you walk in the front door of your parents' house?

▶ You can still have a strong relationship with your parents after you get married, but remember, your mate is not your parent.

▶ If your sibling stole the love of your life back when you were twelve, it's time to get over it. No parent is perfect, either; in fact, it's a pretty tough job to be a parent. You messed up a few times, too. Forgive and forget. Life is short.

> God places the lonely in families; he sets the prisoners free and gives them joy. But he makes the rebellious live in a sun-scorched land.
>
> Psalm 68:6, NLT

question

▼

What about the family of your future spouse?

Every family includes people with quirky idiosyncrasies, unusual philosophies, and irritating habits that aren't visible on the surface. Sometimes you can't see the less-attractive side of someone until you get to know the person better. Since you won't see your relatives all the time, does it really matter if you like the family of your spouse-to-be? You not only bring yourselves to the marriage, you also carry along your entire clan. Will frustrating family dynamics cause unmanageable friction in your marital bliss?

answer

▼

As you get ready to walk down the aisle, remember that when you marry your sweetheart, you also marry the family. Most likely you'll be spending time with those folks for decades to come, so you need to figure out a way to live with their faults, just as they will have to live with yours. One of the most disconcerting thoughts is realizing that along the way your beloved may have picked up some annoying family traits!

What should you do if members of your new family rub you the wrong way? To put it bluntly, deal with it. Most of the time your exposure to your in-laws will be in small doses, so try to bite your lip and walk the high road. One of the beautiful things about being married is that you have a built-in oasis of escape—your own place. At the end of the day, the annoying relatives live somewhere else.

When little frustrations develop into real problems, keep the dialogue with your spouse open and honest, and don't let feelings of resentment fester. Your in-laws may push your buttons, but remember that they are your future spouse's family, and you owe it to your intended to be a team player. Conversely, if the trouble is with your family, be objective and see both sides, but be supportive of your spouse. That's the person you go home with every night.

worth thinking about

- ▶ You don't have to be best friends with your new family, but you do need to get along.

- ▶ Even though your future mother-in-law may make you crazy, remember that she raised the one you adore. Give her credit for turning out a great product.

- ▶ Everybody has at least one personality trait that's admirable, even your in-laws. Sometimes it's hard to find, but do some digging. Keep in mind that you aren't always 100 percent lovable, either.

> *If anyone does not provide for his relatives, and especially for his immediate family, he has denied the faith and is worse than an unbeliever.*
> 1 Timothy 5:8, NIV

21 question

What do you like and dislike about each other?

Most people were brought up being told that if you can't say something nice about someone, don't say anything at all. So to intentionally tell the love of your life that you don't like a persistent personal characteristic might be a little tough. There are bound to be some things about your sweetheart that you dislike, of course, but hopefully there are far more things you love. Here's your chance to get it all out on the table.

answer

What's the point of having this conversation? It isn't intended to be a rant session. Rather, it should affirm your love by sharing what you like and pointing out some annoying habits. Most of the things that bother you are going to be minor, but letting them fester might create friction.

One thing you learn when dealing with people is that you begin these kinds of conversations with the positives. You are contemplating marriage with this person for many reasons, so there should be far more check marks in the plus column than in the minus column. Maybe you really appreciate the way your sweetheart relates to little children, for example. Be sure to point out what draws you to each other now, and continue to point out these attributes throughout your marriage.

There is a time and a place for constructive criticism. But the key word is *constructive*. This is clearly not the time to call attention to especially worrisome character flaws. If you are aware of too many of them, you should reconsider your impending nuptials. This is the time for sharing how much a particular behavior bugs you. Be gentle. It's counterproductive to inflate your irritation or exaggerate your sweetheart's supposed flaws. It's still true that easy does it.

worth thinking about

▶ **When you first** start this conversation, especially the "dislikes" portion, you both are liable to be defensive and may disagree completely with each other's assessments. But remember, this is how you are perceived, not how you necessarily intend to behave.

▶ **Learning which** of your habits annoy your future mate will do no good unless you make some changes. Make a conscious effort to modify your behavior.

▶ **This model** is also a great one to use at work, with friends and family, and particularly with children.

> *Listen to good advice if you want to live well,*
> *an honored guest among wise men and women.*
> *An undisciplined, self-willed life is puny;*
> *an obedient, God-willed life is spacious.*
> Proverbs 15:31–32, THE MESSAGE

22 question

Do you love each other the way you are?

Can you say, without equivocation, that you love your future spouse "as is"? Do you embrace all the good points and bad points, faults and foibles? If being brutally honest, few can answer that question in the affirmative. Given the option, there are probably things you'd like to change about your mate. Perhaps the question should be rephrased a bit: do you love almost everything about each other?

answer

You show your love for God by how you treat others. There is no place better to demonstrate that than in your marriage.

The truth is, no person can ever love unconditionally without demands or expectations, because human beings are flawed. Many people have visions in their heads of what the ideal marital partner should look like, and they try to mold the one they love into that person.

But for marriage to work, you must embrace your spouse-to-be, not your makeover version, as is. Don't think that if you could change your intended you would suddenly be happy and everything would be perfect. Having a hidden agenda to change your partner once you are married will bring you nothing but frustration and disappointment. What you see is what you get.

Genuinely loving your spouse means embracing your spouse's freedom to be the person God created. Loving people means allowing them to be who they are—faults and all—and still loving them. True love equals acceptance.

When you are able to do that with your sweetheart, you'll find that grace to be reciprocal. Eventually it will be given back to you in even greater measure.

worth thinking about

▶ **You don't fix** things by fixing your partner. If your relationship is in trouble, you might need to be the one to change.

▶ **God loves you** unconditionally. His love is not based on what you do or who you are. It is important to model that kind of reciprocal love to your future spouse.

▶ **As the years** go by, you and your mate will change. When you find you have trouble loving your spouse through thick and thin, ask God to grant you the serenity to accept the things you cannot change.

Hang my locket around your neck, wear my ring on your finger. Love is invincible facing danger and death. Passion laughs at the terrors of hell. The fire of love stops at nothing—it sweeps everything before it. Flood waters can't drown love, torrents of rain can't put it out. Love can't be bought, love can't be sold— it's not to be found in the marketplace.

Song of Songs 8:6–7, The Message

23

question

Are there any personal habits that concern you?

A habit is a pattern of behavior that can be either good or bad. You might have the commendable routine of running a couple of miles before work every morning, or the less-admirable tendency to down an entire pot of coffee for breakfast. Are there things your future spouse habitually does that make you anxious? How about you? Are there things you do that might worry your future partner? Now is the time to express those concerns because the behavior will likely worsen with time.

answer

Bad habits include destructive behaviors like drug abuse, immoderate drinking, sexual indiscretions, tobacco use, gambling, unhealthy eating habits, poor hygiene, and a sedentary lifestyle. Less obvious, but often equally damaging, habits include gossip, laziness, lying, excessive worry, and complaining. Even running the two miles before work in the morning can be a bad habit if it takes precedence over your marriage.

Be aware that old habits die hard, and sometimes they don't die at all. Don't think your habits will automatically go away without diligent effort. As you grow older, lifestyle habits can seriously impact your health, and the two of you want a long and healthy marriage. Bad habits can also define one's entire life if not properly resisted. Depending on what it is, even one bad habit can be too much.

Working through these issues can be a relationship-building experience. If you are both out of shape, make losing weight fun by working out together. If you are both smokers, set a New Year's resolution to quit together and hold each other accountable.

Without God, it is easy to get caught up in a cycle of bad habits if the focus is on yourself rather than on Him. If you have developed a pattern of behavior you are not proud of, lean on your loved one's shoulders and ask God to purge the behavior from your life.

worth thinking about

▶ **Even though** you hold each other accountable, personal responsibility is the key to overcoming bad habits.

▶ **Ask yourself** if you can live with the consequences if you don't say anything about your mate's worrisome habit. If the answer is no, speak up now!

▶ **Studies show** it takes twenty-one days to form a habit. Try replacing a bad habit with a healthier alternative for three weeks and see how much better you'll feel. Perhaps a personal challenge between the two of you will get the ball rolling.

> *Any act often repeated soon forms a habit; and habit allowed, steady gains in strength. At first it may be but as a spider's web, easily broken through, but if not resisted it soon binds us with chains of steel.*
>
> Tryon Edwards

question

Do you have the same views on gender roles?

The proper roles of men and women can be an inflammatory topic in today's society. Nowadays, you're exposed to strong opinions running the gamut from feminism to traditionalism. In your marriage, will the husband and wife be on equal footing? Who will be the primary breadwinner? Who will have the central responsibility for child care, housecleaning, and cooking? Have you and your significant other discussed your expectations for your roles within your union?

answer

The roles husbands and wives assume are usually influenced by several factors, including family background, cultural expectations, and income level. Don't assume you have agreement on what roles you will play in your future marriage—you need to lay out your expectations in black and white.

One of the biggest stumbling blocks for many couples is whether you will both work or if one of you will financially support the other. Another area that needs to be addressed is the chain of command in your household. The Bible clearly delineates the roles of husbands and wives in Ephesians 5:22–23: "A wife should put her husband first, as she does the Lord. A husband is the head of his wife, as Christ is the head and the Savior of the church, which is his own body" (CEV).

After you get married, you will each evolve into your natural roles. One of you will probably do the bulk of the laundry, and the other will take out the trash. One of you will do the majority of the cooking, and the other will do the yard work. Personal preference plays a stronger part here than tradition.

There is no one-size-fits-all answer to the issue of gender roles. What really matters is what the two of you want in your marriage, not what happens in the house next door.

worth thinking about

▶ **It is difficult** to do everything well. One can't be a career person, gourmet cook, auto mechanic, and gardener and expect to be at the top of their game in every area. Have realistic expectations.

▶ **As in most** businesses, there needs to be one CEO with ultimate responsibility. The Bible says it is the husband's role to be the spiritual head of the household.

▶ **Be sure to consider** your gifts and talents. If the bride has a degree in accounting, she should probably handle the family finances. If the groom is a chef, perhaps the kitchen should be his domain.

> *Wives should always put their husbands first, as the church puts Christ first. A husband should love his wife as much as Christ loved the church and gave his life for it.*
> Ephesians 5:24–25, CEV

25

question

Are you comfortable with ambition?

Reaching the pinnacle of success is what drives many people. They'll sacrifice anything to get their name on the top of the organizational chart. To others, career success isn't everything; they are more concerned with the little things in life and in being of service to humankind. More often than not, these two philosophies clash. If you are interested in saving the whales while your spouse is more interested in saving for retirement, you may have major discord on the horizon.

answer

There are two different kinds of ambition—personal and professional. Both have admirable qualities, but they also have the propensity to be abused. One can have a personal ambition to run a marathon or go on a mission trip. While these goals are definitely worthwhile, if you are constantly away from your family running a race or in a foreign land doing service work, you've taken it too far.

Where many get into trouble is with professional ambition. Careers play a huge role in American lives. Lifestyle, amount of free time, vacations, and friendships are dependent upon income. Highly ambitious people are often consumed with their jobs and work excessive hours. They bring work home with them—mentally at least—but they also bring home a larger paycheck.

It may not seem like a big deal now, but contradictory levels of ambition will lead to huge frustration and finger-pointing later on. If one partner is highly driven and the other is extremely laid-back, resentment will build up over time. It's best to come to agreement at the outset and determine what your priorities are as a couple.

Many people start out their careers focused on making as much money as possible. As time goes on, however, that kind of achievement is often not enough. It's not uncommon for those folks to make a career about-face during midlife and opt for a job that more clearly matches their passions and purpose. Why wait until then?

worth thinking about

▶ Prioritize your life this way and you will be a success no matter what you do: (1) God, (2) family, and (3) work.

▶ Being overly ambitious is ill-advised, but so is the other extreme. Sometimes opportunity comes knocking, but you still have to open the door.

▶ A happy home life should be the ultimate result of your ambition. Do you live to work or work to live? Simplifying your life may increase your overall satisfaction.

> *Make it your ambition to lead a quiet life, to mind your own business and to work with your hands, just as we told you, so that your daily life may win the respect of outsiders and so that you will not be dependent on anybody.*
>
> 1 Thessalonians 4:11–12, NIV

Can you live with your mate's imperfections?

There is no perfect marriage, for there are no perfect men.

French Proverb

26

Are you a jealous person?

Jealousy can be detrimental to one's well-being. You can be jealous of people with nicer homes, fancier cars, and better jobs; the list goes on and on. Jealousy is such serious business that it is addressed in the Ten Commandments. Nobody wants to admit to being jealous, yet most people match the classic description from time to time.

answer

In the framework of marriage, jealousy can be extremely damaging. You can be jealous of how much time your sweetheart spends with friends or family, and you can be jealous of your mate's job.

The most damaging offshoot of jealousy is when one in the relationship believes the other to be unfaithful. Unmerited suspicion can cause a great deal of distress in a relationship, and when it gets out of control, it can break up families.

Unfortunately, our culture breeds envy, so you need to find ways to eradicate or at least minimize it before it gets a firm hold on you. For starters, quit comparing your financial situation with that of others. Everyone has different purposes and different gifts, so don't assume you should have the same toys that your friends and neighbors have.

Next, avoid comparing your relationship with those of your friends. Every romantic pairing is different, and all have their strengths and weaknesses.

Finally, have the confidence that your spouse-to-be is trustworthy and will remain faithful to you. Trust each unless there is good reason to doubt.

Remember, the best way to keep jealousy at bay is to be grateful for what you have and to focus on what's really important in life.

worth thinking about

- ▶ **Take an honest** look at your previous relationships. Has either of you had the tendency to display hurtful jealousy in the past? Since history tends to repeat itself, ask yourself what you could do differently this time.

- ▶ **Jealousy can often** be a symptom that you are lacking in self-esteem. Just because you want to spend time with friends and family doesn't mean you love each other any less.

- ▶ **It is common** for people to have working relationships with members of the opposite sex. They volunteer together, attend church together, and go to school together.

> Let us conduct ourselves properly, as people who live in the light of day—no orgies or drunkenness, no immorality or indecency, no fighting or jealousy. But take up the weapons of the Lord Jesus Christ, and stop paying attention to your sinful nature and satisfying its desires.
>
> Romans 13:13–14, GNT

question

▼

Are you a morning person or a night owl?

It starts out innocently enough. Most couples meet in their younger days when they can take on the world with little shut-eye. Pulling an all-nighter doesn't even afford bragging rights because all your friends are doing it, too. So you meet that special someone, fall in love, and decide to get married. But that decision may be based on one essential false premise. It isn't until you've set up house that you discover your honey is actually an early bird!

answer

▼

After marriage, it will be helpful if the two of you are on similar schedules. Not to say that you need to go to bed at the same time, but you at least need to be in the same part of the day! Scientific research has shown that everyone is simply cut from different cloth. Whether someone is a night owl or an early bird is actually driven by biology rather than personality. People's body clocks are wired differently; the reason you are raring to go at midnight when your partner has already been in bed for hours is based on something called your circadian rhythm.

Having mismatched rhythms can have profound implications for your marriage. Mismatched couples tend to have less time for conversation and leisure activities and experience more conflict. Part of the reason for the added friction is that they have sex less frequently than those on similar schedules. On a positive note, you will probably have an easier time adjusting to married life in the beginning because you'll have a little more alone time.

If you and your betrothed are polar opposites in this respect, you'll need to learn to be understanding. Work hard at trying to find common ground, and as time goes on, your cycles will start to mesh.

worth thinking about

- ▶ **If possible**, plan to coordinate your rhythm to your partner's by adjusting your schedule a little at a time. Be patient, and resist the temptation to judge each other based on your own preferences.

- ▶ **Some people** love stimulating conversation as they're making their morning coffee, but others aren't so perky.

- ▶ **Everyone needs** alone time. Being on different schedules will provide that. It will also be a benefit later on if you opt to have children. A night owl is a natural for the 2:00 a.m. feeding.

> *The Kingdom of God is like a farmer who scatters seed on the ground. Night and day, while he's asleep or awake, the seed sprouts and grows, but he does not understand how it happens. The earth produces the crops on its own. First a leaf blade pushes through, then the heads of wheat are formed, and finally the grain ripens.*
>
> Mark 4:26–28, NLT

question

Do you agree on health and fitness?

You can hardly channel surf without coming upon at least one program geared to the health-conscious. Yet the Centers for Disease Control reports that the prevalence of obesity has doubled over the last twenty-five-year period. There are three kinds of people in this country: those who are crazy about exercising, those who do it grudgingly because they think they have to, and those who look forward to jumping on a treadmill about as much as getting a root canal. Where do you fit in?

answer

National attention is focused on health and fitness. In addition to eating poorly, people are turning into couch potatoes or cyber addicts. Exercise is going by the way-side. The Bible, however, commands people to honor God with their bodies because they are His temple.

Exercise offers myriad benefits, including increased metabolism, a sense of well-being, lower cholesterol, and a reduced risk of heart disease and diabetes. When you stay fit and at a healthy weight, you feel better about yourself and are often more interested in sex.

One of the greatest benefits of maintaining a healthy lifestyle is that you can enjoy more time together. But staying in shape is easier if you both are committed to it. You don't have to do the old standby forms of exercise; you can be creative: take a kickboxing class, learn how to salsa dance, join a kickball league, play Dance Dance Revolution, or go on a hiking vacation.

Discuss how the two of you will maintain a healthy balance in your future marriage. If you don't eat right and exercise for yourself, do it for your spouse-to-be and enjoy a long, happy, and healthy life together.

worth thinking about

▶ **Do either of you** have bad behaviors like smoking, excessive alcohol consumption, or binge dieting that concern you? Be sure to come up with a plan before you get married so the behaviors don't become a problem later on.

▶ **Establishing good** diet and exercise habits now will help you live healthier lives and will help set the stage should you decide to have children.

▶ **If one of you** prefers a steady diet of fast food and the other favors homemade vegetarian fare, you might be a tad bit incompatible. Discuss how you will handle this once you start cooking for two.

> *Don't you know that your body is the temple of the Holy Spirit, who lives in you and who was given to you by God? You do not belong to yourselves but to God.*
> 1 Corinthians 6:19, GNT

question

▼

What role should friends have?

God intends for your spouse to be your soul mate, lover, and best friend—but is there a place in your marriage for outside friendships, too? Chances are that bride and groom enter into a marital relationship bringing along a number of other relationships, with both family and friends. Because of the nature of marriage, however, those friendships need to be restructured and reprioritized.

answer

▼

Friendships should be an important part of your life rather than an afterthought because, after all, your spouse can't be expected to meet every one of your needs. You need friends to walk alongside to help maneuver the maze of life with you and to have some fun!

Friends can help you celebrate your victories, mourn your losses, and build your faith. As a Christian it's essential to surround yourself with other believers; God puts people in your life to keep you accountable and keep you walking along the right path.

Who should these friends be? Be selective about whom you choose to hang out with. Focus on friends in the same life stage you're in, especially another couple. If you're lucky, all four of you will get along. There may be room for only a few really good friends rather than a whole group of them. It's all about quality not quantity; choose like-minded, positive people who will enhance your life. Your spouse should take top priority.

Have a candid discussion early on about what role friends will play in your marriage, how much time you'll spend with them, and how you feel about each other's current friends. If your spouse doesn't like your friends, don't be defensive. Instead, take a look at those relationships through fresh eyes.

worth thinking about

▶ **Authentic friendships** go below the surface and are characterized by sacrifice, loyalty, and commitment. True friends don't tell you only what you want to hear; they also tell you what you need to hear. Their opinion could be a godsend as you ponder your future marriage.

▶ **Friendships with** members of the opposite sex exert unique pressures and problems. Discuss with your spouse-to-be how you feel about that situation.

▶ **Spouses can** feel jealous and left out by the history you share with your friends. Be sure to fill in the gaps by sharing stories and including your spouse in your conversations.

> *If you fall, your friend can help you up.*
> *But if you fall without having a friend*
> *nearby, you are really in trouble.*
> Ecclesiastes 4:10, CEV

question

Where are you going to live?

After the honeymoon is over, you'll need a place to hang your hat. Where you will live is a huge decision because it will have repercussions on where you work, where you go to church, and where your children will go to school. Not only must you choose where you will locate geographically, but you will also need to decide what type of housing will work best for you. Will it be a house, townhome, apartment? Will you rent, own, mooch off your parents?

answer

People used to buy one house and stay there their entire lives. Folks are more transient now; in fact, according to the U.S. Census Bureau, 14 percent of Americans move from one neighborhood to another each year. Even though it is easier to move than ever before, it is still a hassle, so a possible move warrants serious discussion.

How do you decide where to lay down roots? First, you need to decide what kind of surroundings best suit you. You might long for a log home in the woods, but your mate is more drawn to big-city living. If you don't find some middle ground, one of you is going to be unhappy.

Once you decide on your style of living, it's time look for a neighborhood. Consider the following: safety, affordability, proximity to work, church alternatives, recreation spots, and where your friends live. You will also need to determine what type of home you prefer and whether you are going to rent or own. Ultimately, building ownership equity is preferable to paying rent, but sometimes that's just not an option right out of the chute.

Whatever you decide, bear in mind that a house isn't just a physical dwelling. Your home should be your sanctuary, your own little slice of heaven here on earth. Create a pleasing environment and start building memories.

worth thinking about

▶ **Find a balance** between renting something inexpensive and renting a dump. On the other hand, don't be house poor and bite off more than you can chew. To be conservative, your housing payment should be no more than 28 percent of your income.

▶ **Consider the length** of your commute—both ways and at rush hour. Some people like to be close to work, and others like to be far enough away so they can't go in on snow days.

▶ **How close do** you want to be to your families? Living too close can be a hindrance to your independence, but you still want a convenient location.

> *The LORD puts a curse on the homes of the wicked, but blesses the homes of the righteous.*
> Proverbs 3:33, GNT

31

question

How will you spend your free time?

God didn't intend for you to work 24-7! Take time to refresh your body and soul and have a little fun. Even the Creator of the universe rested on the seventh day. If you both work, the majority of your waking hours will be spent doing something other than nurturing your relationship. All work and no play will make your marriage dull, so find enjoyable ways to make the most of your limited free time.

answer

The pace of life has become frantic; it's no wonder people have precious little time for their spouse. If you ask divorced couples why their marriages failed, many of them will tell you that they just drifted apart. Staying connected in your marriage means you have to be intentional and make time for each other. You schedule everything else in life, why not time for each other?

Your ideal use of free time might be dropping a solitary line in the nearby river, while your sweetheart might crave the nightlife at a dance club. You will need to find a way to meet halfway to satisfy both your desires: go fishing for one date, but go dancing for the next.

While you clearly need alone time, you should also strive for plenty of time enjoying life together. Consider developing a mutual hobby. Along with your partner, make a list of ten activities you enjoy or would like to try. Then see if anything matches up. If one of you says camping and the other says reading, there's no reason you can't both win—read at the campsite!

The key is to be random and spontaneous. So many times couples settle for the tried-and-true dinner and a movie, but you can't do much bonding whispering in a dark theater. Be creative!

worth thinking about

▶ **Nurture intimacy.** Sex is certainly part of it, but intimacy comes in several forms. Be affectionate. Go on long walks holding hands, and kiss often.

▶ **If you are beat** after a long day at the office, have daytime dates. Every once in a while, have a weekday lunch at home or at a restaurant. You'll go back to work with a whole new attitude!

▶ **Take a fitness** or enrichment class together: photography, ballroom dancing, language, gardening, or golf, for example. It will be win-win for both of you.

> You have six days in which to do your work.... In six days I, the LORD, made the earth, the sky, the seas, and everything in them, but on the seventh day I rested. That is why I, the LORD, blessed the Sabbath and made it holy.
>
> Exodus 20:9, 11, GNT

question

What about volunteer obligations?

Volunteering can be incredibly rewarding. But a person can overdo it and become ineffective and burned out. It's important to choose your causes carefully and not just say yes to every possible opportunity. Serving others is a beautiful thing, but only if you do it with joy in your heart. You both may be entering marriage with a plateful of volunteer obligations. What are you planning to continue, what will you have to let go, and what new opportunities are out there?

answer

Christians have a God-ordained obligation to pitch in and serve others with their time and talents. The concept of giving back in some sort of volunteer service is an important component of a full life. That service will look different for different people. It might be teaching Sunday school, chairing a youth fund-raiser, or singing in the choir at church. The community has far more needs than volunteers, so use your imagination.

If you are looking to get more involved, see if your congregation has a spiritual gifts class or something similar that will identify what you are good at. These classes will not only help you identify your talents, but they will also direct you to the proper spot on the organizational chart where you can get plugged in.

Volunteering doesn't mean you have to attend constant meetings or give up an inordinate amount of your free time. Churches need people with a variety of skill sets: bookkeeping, cooking, gardening, teaching, acting, writing, organizing, and sewing, to name a few. Friendly people of all persuasions will find the perfect place to help.

How about coaching a youth sports team through community education, serving on the city council, or making sandwiches at a local homeless shelter? Your volunteer efforts will make you feel good.

worth thinking about

▶ **To increase** your together time as a couple after the wedding, volunteer as a pair. Working on a joint project will give you something new to talk about around the dinner table.

▶ **As you volunteer** in the community, either before or after you take your vows, be certain to reflect your faith in the most positive light. Be a good sport, watch your language, and be considerate of others.

▶ **Don't be afraid** to say no. Rather than taking on every opportunity, which will take too much time away from your loved one, increase your effectiveness by choosing those tasks best suited to you.

Faith by itself isn't enough. Unless it produces good deeds, it is dead and useless.
James 2:17, NLT

question

How much alone time do you each need?

Even though you are a couple, it is important to remember that you are also still individuals. You both need to grow, learn, and develop as people. That means you needn't feel you must be perpetually joined at the hip and spend every waking moment together. In fact, when you first move in together after you are married, you will probably crave a place to be alone—too much bonding can wear you out!

answer

When you first started dating, you longed to do anything together because you simply wanted to hang out. You probably even agreed to participate in activities you didn't really like just so you could be together. After you get married, occupying the same space doesn't have to be as intentional because you'll be living together. Sometimes you need to feel comfortable going it alone. Absence does make the heart grow fonder.

Of course, everyone has different thresholds. You may find that you need more or perhaps less private time than your sweetheart. Be honest about your own needs with the understanding that craving some time alone doesn't mean you love each other any less. If you are feeling smothered and need some time just for you, simply speak up. Giving each other personal space is important. It'll make living together in close quarters a lot easier.

As a Christian, the most important aspect of having alone time is spending it with God. Everyone is so busy doing this or that and running from appointment to appointment that quiet time with God is often neglected. Yet being still before God is one of the most critical aspects of the Christian life, so make sure you and your future spouse are able to break away from your time together to study and pray separately.

worth thinking about

▶ **After you** are married, be sure to recognize the importance of nurturing yourself. You will need to make time to take a walk, read a book, relax in a hot tub, or just stop and smell the roses and listen to the birds sing.

▶ **Understand that** maintaining your friendships is also an important component in a happy marriage. Your future spouse can't possibly fulfill all of your needs.

▶ **The transition** from being two singles to being husband and wife can be a tricky one, particularly if you have lived on your own for any length of time. Once you are living together, you'll need to be sensitive enough to notice when it's time to back off.

> *Marriage is that relation between man and woman in which the independence is equal, the dependence mutual, and the obligation reciprocal.*
> Louis K. Anspacher

34

question

What role will your extended families have?

Like it or not, your future in-laws will become your family, too, once you don that wedding ring. As with any other group of people, there are going to be some people you like, some people who rub you the wrong way, and some people you just can't stand. When you get married you begin a new chapter in your life. It's time to set boundaries pertaining to your families. The hard part is arriving at an agreement with your spouse about where to draw the line.

answer

For some reason, the mother-in-law has forever been the butt of jokes. Some mothers-in-law may seem like unwelcome meddlers at times, but it's hard for them to sever that umbilical cord. Your future mother-in-law has known and loved your sweetie much longer than you have. The same applies to your future father-in-law. He has been the authority figure for most of your sweetheart's life. It's hard for him to set that role aside as soon as the ceremony ends. But as you enter the ranks of old married couples, your own mom and dad and your in-laws should become more like peers or friends than authority figures.

It's time to have a heart-to-heart with your mate about how your respective families will fit into your new life as a married couple. Here are a few ideas:

It can be difficult to stand up to a parent and set limits, but if you and your mate present a united front, your chances of success are much greater. If you don't want Mom and Dad showing up on your doorstep unannounced at an awkward moment, for instance, respectfully request they call first.

You'll also need to offer guidelines regarding your privacy. Certain subjects should be taboo with the relatives, subjects like your sex life, finances, and health. Make sure everybody is on the same page about when it's okay to call.

worth thinking about

▶ **Your extended family** will be a huge blessing. You will gain a whole new circle of people to love and care for you and one that will greatly enrich your life.

▶ **If you have** a serious dislike for your in-laws, don't despair. Distance can be a great mediator. Simply minimize your exposure. Anyone can grin and bear it for the duration of a family holiday.

▶ **Establishing boundaries** is especially tough if you live with your parents after the wedding. You'll have a hard enough time feeling independent, so set some ground rules with them up front.

> *Be kind and merciful, and forgive others,*
> *just as God forgave you because of Christ.*
> Ephesians 4:32, CEV

question

▼

How will you handle family holidays?

Some family holidays bring to mind a Norman Rockwell painting with a loving family gathered around the piano singing Christmas carols. But some family gatherings are quite stressful, complete with flaring tempers and fighting children. Most families fall somewhere in the middle—a little sentimentality mixed in with a little awkwardness. With two separate families and too many things to celebrate, how are you going to manage the holidays?

answer

▼

Holidays can be nerve-racking, especially Christmas when people attend too many parties, spend too much money, eat too much, and are altogether too busy. As sons add wives, and as daughters add husbands, family dynamics change. Most of the time it all works out great, but everyone has to be on good behavior.

After you are married, you will have to figure out how you are going to handle two Christmases, two Easters, and two Thanksgivings. Trying to do turkey dinner at two family tables is just too grueling, and it will ultimately backfire and ruin your holiday. The best advice is to alternate: do Thanksgiving with the groom's family one year, and with the bride's family the next. Another option is to host a holiday dinner at your home and invite the relatives from both families.

If it's necessary to celebrate with both families, see if one of them is willing to be flexible and celebrate on a different day. Perhaps your Easter Sunday can become Easter Saturday instead. Likewise, if they are in the same town, celebrate Christmas Eve with one family and Christmas Day with the other.

One great way to manage the tasks of the holidays is to take turns hosting and have every household contribute to the meal. That way neither mom has to be the one with the clean house and all the goodies, and every other year one can put her feet up for a change.

worth thinking about

▶ **There's an old** Scottish proverb, "Better bend than break." Ultimately, the best way to manage family holidays is to compromise.

▶ **Plan to create** your own favorite holiday memories by starting new traditions. Buy a special ornament each Christmas, or say a special prayer at Thanksgiving.

▶ **To save both** time and money on family birthday parties, consider consolidating the festivities into a monthly or quarterly celebration.

> *Call a truce, then, to our labors—let us feast with friends and neighbors, and be merry as the custom of our caste; for if faint and forced the laughter, and if sadness follow after, we are richer by one mocking Christmas past.*
>
> Rudyard Kipling

▼

What will be the spiritual foundation of your marriage?

▼

My family and I are going to worship and obey the LORD!

Joshua 24:15, CEV

question

How do you feel about animals?

Are you a cat person or a dog person? Believe it or not, pets can be a touchy subject with some couples. Some people adore feline friends even though they are stand-offish, persnickety, and shed like crazy. And dogs? They drool, bark, and smell bad, but their owners still love them. Now that you are thinking of getting married and moving in together, you need to discuss whether a furry friend will also be part of your family.

answer

Sharing your home with a four-legged friend can be life-enriching. They are accepting and loyal, and they provide wonderful companionship and joy. You can learn a lot about life by watching a dog or cat.

While it's easy to fall in love with a fluffy kitty or a cuddly puppy, it's important to remember that either is also a huge responsibility. Both of you need to be up for it. There are a number of things to consider. Not only do pets require time and attention, but they are also costly and require a long-term commitment; some dogs and cats can live as long as fifteen to seventeen years. Pets are not disposable. You also need to have space for one.

Having a large dog in the middle of a city is not fair; large dogs need room to run and a place to relieve themselves.

One other important consideration is your lifestyle. Having a pet will definitely hamper your social life to some degree; you can't always go out for dinner after a long day at work because Fido will be crossing his legs waiting for you at home. Spontaneous weekend getaways will also be more challenging.

Before you decide on a pet, visit an animal shelter. There you'll see scores of animals that were cast off because the owners either didn't have the time or didn't know what they were getting into. Bringing a pet home that you're not prepared to love is not something you want to do.

worth thinking about

▶ **Birds, rodents,** reptiles, amphibians, and fish can also be fun pets. A goldfish won't have sweet puppy breath, but it won't leave a surprise on the carpet, either.

▶ **If your intended** really wants to have a pet and you really don't, consider a pet that can live outdoors.

▶ **If you already** have a pet, decide what will happen when you get married. It may come to a choice between the one you love and your cat, particularly if there is an allergy problem.

> *All things bright and beautiful, all creatures great and small, all things wise and wonderful, the Lord God made them all.*
> Cecil F. Alexander

37

question

Do you share the same faith?

The United States is a churchgoing nation. According to Barna Research, 90 percent of all Americans believe in God, and 90 percent of those individuals classify themselves as Christians. There are about as many Christian denominations as there are flavors of ice cream, all with unique theological nuances. Some couples never get around to talking about their beliefs about God until they are planning the wedding. But since your faith is such a huge part of who you are, it warrants a much deeper conversation.

answer

Different religious practices can cause strain on a marriage, particularly during life passages such as birth, marriage, and death. If you and your spouse-to-be were raised in different denominations, consider how that will impact your marriage. If you have deep-seated roots in a particular denomination, it may be difficult for you to migrate to a different one.

If you both were brought up in Christian churches but in different denominations, there's no reason you can't work that out. What matters is that you embrace the core tenets of Christianity—don't get too bogged down in the doctrinal details. Obviously you are going to have to determine which church you will be married in and whether or not you will worship together. Ideally, you can come to an understanding so that you can practice one religion together.

Whether you are Baptist or Methodist, Lutheran or Pentecostal, Episcopal or Catholic, what matters is that you put God at the center of your marriage and that your beliefs about Jesus, salvation, and heaven agree.

worth thinking about

- ▶ Whether you both worship in the same branch of Christianity or different ones, consider taking a class together on the core tenets of the faith. That will spur a great deal of discussion.

- ▶ There may be a time down the road when children will enter the picture. You will want to have settled on one single denomination so they don't have mixed messages. Visit a variety of churches together and see what feels right for you.

- ▶ A nondenominational church might be a good fit if you both come from different traditions.

> *Do not try to work together as equals with unbelievers, for it cannot be done. How can right and wrong be partners? How can light and darkness live together?*
> 2 Corinthians 6:14, GNT

38

How important is God to your everyday life?

According to surveys, the majority of people believe in God. But how they live out their beliefs varies widely. For many people, faith is at the core of their being and is the foundation for living. For other people, faith is relegated to a secondary status and shows itself only during times of crisis or holidays. How large a role does God play in your life, and how does that match up with your loved one's relationship with God?

answer

You may share a strong faith in Christ and have devoted your lives to Him, but you probably also demonstrate your faith in different ways. This is influenced by several things, including which denomination you were raised in, your ethnic heritage, and the part of the country in which you grew up. Some Christians are private and stoic about their relationship with God, while others are more obvious and boisterous. What really matters is that you share the same fundamental Christian beliefs. A devout Christian will adhere to God's commandments, will be actively involved in church, will perhaps attend a small-group or Bible study, handle money with an eye on stewardship, and treat others differently than someone who does not embrace those beliefs. More directly, they will have submitted their lives to Christ.

Faith is passed along from generation to generation; plan now to build a household of faith that you can one day pass along to your own offspring.

Faith in Christ should be an integral part of your daily lives. Keep in mind, however, that everyone is not at the same place on their spiritual journey, and you must respect that. Everyone grows and develops spiritually at different rates and in different ways.

worth thinking about

- ▶ Has there been a time in your life where you found it hard to believe in God? Discuss with your intended if you have ever lost your faith and what impact that had on your life.

- ▶ As you grow up and prepare to leave the nest, you may want to worship and express your faith slightly differently than your parents do. That's fine as long as the core message of the Bible is the focus.

- ▶ A marriage grounded in Christ will help you in the good times and in the bad. As you prepare to marry, discuss how you will seek God in all aspects of your marriage.

> *Without faith it is impossible to please God, because anyone who comes to him must believe that he exists and that he rewards those who earnestly seek him.*
>
> Hebrews 11:6, NIV

question

How will you practice your faith together?

You will probably enter your marriage with certain religious practices in tow. It is also likely that in some ways those practices will be different from those of your spouse. Since marriage is the melding of two disparate lives into one, you will have the incredible opportunity to incorporate faith into your relationship. Faith can be expressed in many ways; together the two of you should determine how your beliefs will intersect your daily lives.

answer

To experience personal growth you have to step out of your comfort zone. In a new marriage, you'll be stepping outside the lines on a daily basis. Your spiritual life is no different. In order to grow spiritually, you must look at the world with the wide-eyed wonder of a child.

There are many conspicuous ways to live out your faith—attending worship services, doing volunteer work, or saying grace at the table. It's the less-public demonstrations of faith that will truly resonate. How do you choose to spend your free time? Are your entertainment choices pleasing to God? How much of your hard-earned money makes it into the offering plate each Sunday? One of the best ways of showing your love for God is by giving sacrificially.

Couples also benefit from doing Bible study together. This can be a private study for just the two of you or with a small group or both. These will be the people who will pray for you and hold you accountable.

By far the most important aspect of the Christian faith is a strong prayer life. The Bible says, "Pray without ceasing" (1 Thessalonians 5:17, NAS). One of the best things a couple can do to promote a strong marital foundation is to pray together. At first it might seem awkward, but in time your prayer life will become rich and meaningful.

worth thinking about

▶ Find a Bible study at church for couples who are in the same life stage you are. You'll find it to be an uplifting time of growth and camaraderie.

▶ Get in the habit of saying grace before every meal, whether you are at home or at a restaurant.

▶ At some point you may need to determine how you will incorporate your faith into parenting. How will you teach your children about God in the confines of your home?

> *If you refuse to serve the LORD, then choose today whom you will serve. Would you prefer the gods your ancestors served beyond the Euphrates? Or will it be the gods of the Amorites in whose land you now live? But as for me and my family, we will serve the LORD.*
>
> Joshua 24:15, NLT

40

question

What religious practices are important to you?

If you really think about it, you probably do a whole number of things in your life that are based on faith traditions. Maybe those practices revolve around only births, deaths, and weddings, or perhaps your faith plays a much larger role in your life. Either way, if a particular ritual is important to you, make sure your would-be spouse knows about it.

answer

Expressions of faith show up in various settings, such as infant or believer baptism, confirmation, and funerals. You may have definite opinions on what should take place at those events. You also see them in full force at holidays: at Lent when you give something up as a sacrifice, at Christmas when you read the Christmas story before opening gifts, or at Thanksgiving when you take turns giving thanks around the dinner table.

Being a devoted follower of Christ involves expressing your faith in outward and tangible ways, such as attending worship services, taking Communion, or being part of a Bible study, for instance.

But there is so much more to being a Christian. You have the privilege of talking directly to God, so take Him up on the offer. A regular devotion or quiet time will reap huge rewards as you navigate through this obstacle course called life. A consistent prayer life will keep you grounded and focused on what is most important. Many believers take their quiet time a step further by going on an annual solitary retreat for more focused prayer and fasting.

Unless they give you cause for concern, be respectful of your prospective mate's faith practices. Who knows, you might want to try them yourself.

worth thinking about

▶ **Some spiritual practices** by their nature stir up controversy. For instance, the church is divided on whether infants should be baptized or dedicated. Certain activities, like speaking in tongues or snake handling, also make for lively discussion.

▶ **Mission trips** are another great way of being like Jesus with skin on that more people should consider. You don't need to commit your entire life, but a short-term project might give you a taste.

▶ **Tithing, or giving** 10 percent of your income to the church, is also a way of practicing your faith in a material way.

> Jesus is always waiting for us in silence. In this silence He listens to us; it is there that He speaks to our souls. And there, we hear His voice. . . . In this silence we find a new energy and a real unity.
>
> Mother Teresa

41

question

How important is spirituality to you?

In a culture where so many marriages fall apart, getting married can be a real leap of faith. Lack of commitment, selfishness, and sexual sin are certainly a few of the key reasons for the dismal statistics, but so is a lack of the proper focus. True happiness is elusive without God. He loves you more than you can possibly imagine, and His love is completely unconditional. Will God be at the center of your marriage, or will He be on the sidelines?

answer

In the eyes of God, people can be truly successful only if they lean on Him. The life of a Christian requires complete dependence on God, but as people maneuver through the pitfalls of life, it's easy to forget that and for people to think they can do a better job of running things than the Creator can.

There's no question that focusing on God in a marriage can sometimes be tough duty. It's too easy to get so caught up with work, with your relationships, with parenting, and with all of the hustle and bustle that you forget all about Him. Oftentimes, God comes to the forefront only when people find themselves at a crossroads. If you think that praying, worshiping, and studying take too much time, know that in the long run, going to God first will save countless headaches later on.

A marriage partnership with uneven spiritual goals would be problematic. Decide together what role God will play in your marriage, and find a place where you both are comfortable. Then continue the dialogue as you share your spiritual struggles and triumphs.

Deciding now to have God at the center of your marriage doesn't mean the rain won't fall and life will always be a breeze, but with Him as your navigator, you will be able to weather any storm.

worth thinking about

▶ To be truly fulfilled, you must first discover your purpose and discover God's plan for you. In order to have the best result, though, you need to consult the building plans—the Bible—and speak daily with the Architect.

▶ As you become more in-tune with God, the opportunities He places in your path will be more recognizable.

▶ You have a choice each morning—you can start out the day with a grateful heart and positive attitude, or you can plan to be miserable.

Anyone who listens to my teaching and follows it is wise, like a person who builds a house on solid rock. Though the rain comes in torrents and the floodwaters rise and the winds beat against that house, it won't collapse because it is built on bedrock.
Matthew 7:24–25, NLT

42

question

Will you attend worship services together?

You were created to worship. Worship can be quiet and reverent, or it can be loud and upbeat. The perfect church service is probably a thoughtful mixture of both. There isn't a right way or a wrong way to worship or a one-size-fits-all recipe for the ideal church service. The key is to find a place where you are touched by the experience. Ideally, you should worship together. There's nothing quite so forlorn as a husband or a wife sitting alone in a pew.

answer

You'll find all kinds of styles out there, from reflective hymns to joyous hand-clapping worship. How do you know which congregation is right for you? Beyond the atmosphere of the place, there are a few other things you should consider before settling on a church.

Do you want to be a big fish in a little pond or a little fish in a big pond? Churches come in all shapes and sizes, from ten members to ten thousand. What is the ideal size for you? Then take a look at the programs the church offers. Pick a congregation that is rich in activities for adults—you'll find everything from Bible studies to bowling.

What is the preaching like? Most people can remember sitting in a service and being subjected to a painfully boring message. Not everyone is gifted in public speaking, so choose clergy you can listen to and learn from.

What is the feel of the place? Is it serious and stuffy? Fun and alive? Whatever the style, you should get something out of it. Do you want a place where people dress up, or one where jeans are the norm?

Wherever you end up, it is important that you and your significant other attend services together because you will be a family.

worth thinking about

▶ A church is like a big circle of friends, and you tend to choose a place where the people are similar to you. It's good to branch out, but you still want to blend.

▶ If you and your prospective mate have differing opinions on what church should be like, why not alternate? One week go to a church that makes your sweetheart happy, and the next week attend your favorite.

▶ You don't need to go to church to have faith. A person can worship God standing on the street corner or walking in the woods. But worshiping with other believers is important.

> Come, let us praise the LORD! Let us sing for joy to God, who protects us! Let us come before him with thanksgiving and sing joyful songs of praise. For the LORD is a mighty God, a mighty king over all the gods.
> Psalm 95:1–3, GNT

question

How involved will you be at church?

If you wanted, doing church could be a full-time gig. There are services on Sunday mornings, sometimes Sunday nights, and often midweek. You can take classes virtually any evening, get involved in Sunday school, help with the youth group, be part of the worship team, mow the lawn, wash the dishes, and do men's ministry, women's ministry, or even prison ministry. Whew! It wears you out just thinking about it. So with all of those choices, how involved will you be, and how will your involvement impact your marriage?

answer

Think in terms of baby steps. While getting involved is important, life is one big balancing act. You can't be a successful career person and the deacon of every ministry at your church. Something has to give. If you give too much of your time at church or in the community, you won't be able to devote the quality time your spouse-to-be deserves.

Being involved in a congregation puts you in contact with others who have similar beliefs. If you are new to a community, this is especially important because making friends becomes more difficult as you grow older. Once you are married you will need to find strong friendships with other Christian couples.

Being involved in church keeps you on track spiritually and facilitates continued learning about your faith. Finding your niche in church will allow you to give back just a little to God. Consider it a big thank-you gift. When you were a child, the world seemed to revolve around you and your wants and needs. Well, now that you are an adult, reality strikes. Other people are important, too, and some of them need help more than you can imagine. Through various ministries you will be able to serve your community.

worth thinking about

▶ **Remember the old adage** that says if you want something done, ask a busy person to do it? You don't necessarily want to be that person, so practice saying no in front of the mirror.

▶ **You and your prospective** mate need to agree on how involved in the church you are going to be. It won't fly if one of you spends every other night behind church walls while the other one stays home alone and watches reruns.

▶ **Christians are** instructed to be the light of the world. If you are fraternizing with only church acquaintances, you can't share your faith with those outside the sanctuary.

> *If one of you wants to be first, you must be the slave of the others—like the Son of Man, who did not come to be served, but to serve and to give his life to redeem many people.*
> Matthew 20:27–28, GNT

question

How much money will you donate?

Ultimately, everything you have comes from God. You may earn the money that buys your groceries and your car and pays your mortgage, but God is the One who gave you the job in the first place. Because you are merely a steward of His property, it's only right that you give back God's share. Helping those less fortunate should not be considered a hardship or even a particularly noble gesture. It is simply an obligation. The question is, how much is the right amount to allocate for charitable giving?

answer

Generosity is a learned behavior. If you grew up with parents who had deep pockets when it came to charitable causes, you will much more likely be magnanimous yourself. Giving is part of who you are now and who you will be as a couple.

The Bible says to tithe 10 percent of your income to the church. If you go through your budget and take a look at your assets and liabilities, you may have some anxiety about allocating one of every ten dollars you earn to charity. If you can't see a way to do it and still make ends meet, you may be living beyond your means.

Not only should you give generously at church, but there are thousands of worthwhile causes out there that survive only through the kindness of donors just like you. You don't need to be a rich benefactor. Any financial gift will be greatly appreciated.

Giving sacrificially can be a tremendous act of faith, but God blesses those who give generously.

worth thinking about

▶ **You are called** to support the local church, but there are also many worthwhile causes. If you give to charities, make sure the bulk of your donation goes directly to those in need rather than to administrative costs. Visit www.give.org for more information.

▶ **Forgoing one latte** a week will provide the funds necessary to sponsor a destitute child in a third-world country.

▶ **God wants** you to be a cheerful giver, not one who is bullied into giving a certain amount. Be prayerful about how much you should give, and then discuss it with your future mate. You both need to agree when it comes to the checkbook. Rather than doing your household budget and then seeing what you have left over for your tithe, put it as the first item on your spreadsheet.

> *"Bring the whole tithe into the storehouse, that there may be food in my house. Test me in this,"* says the Lord Almighty, *"and see if I will not throw open the floodgates of heaven and pour out so much blessing that you will not have room enough for it."*
> Malachi 3:10, NIV

45

question
▼
What is your sexual history?

This question is a catch-22. There are sound arguments in support of discussing your previous sexual partners with your intended, and there are convincing arguments against it. Some would argue that what you don't know can't hurt you, and that knowing about previous relationships will produce nothing but hurt feelings. How are you and your spouse-to-be going to cover this sensitive topic? Are you going to fess up or let sleeping dogs lie?

answer
▼

God's preference is that people abstain from sex before marriage. Yet according to the Centers for Disease Control, 47 percent of high school students have had sexual intercourse, 14 percent of them with four or more partners. These days the old cliché should probably say, "What you don't know *can* hurt you." This is as much a question about health as it is about morals. If your partner once led a promiscuous lifestyle, you may be at risk of contracting a life-threatening disease. This is no longer a nice-to-know; it is a need-to-know.

Some people believe that what happened in the past should stay there. Undoubtedly, talking about your sexual histories will be uncomfortable. If one of you has more sexual experience than the other, feelings of jealousy and anger are likely to surface. If you have had sexual partners and your prospective mate hasn't, you may feel a certain amount of regret and shame and prefer not to dredge that up. Likewise, if you are inexperienced you may feel some performance anxiety. But if you truly love each other, your sexual relationship will grow and develop and become something entirely unique.

What's done is done. The two of you are considering making a commitment to each other that will last a lifetime. In some respects, you need to forgive and forget and focus on building your relationship going forward. Remember that most people would like a few do-overs.

worth thinking about

▶ **Guilt and regret** are heavy burdens that could impact your future together. God promises to remove the guilt of all who seek His forgiveness, and He will give them a fresh start.

▶ **After you are married,** don't compare the lovemaking prowess of your new spouse with your previous love interests, either verbally or in your private thoughts. Every relationship is different.

▶ **Particularly painful** sexual experiences will have an impact on your intimacy with your spouse. Be sure to deal with issues stemming from abuse or sexual indiscretions before you go on your honeymoon.

God wants you to be holy and completely free from sexual immorality.
1 Thessalonians 4:3, GNT

question

Is romance as important as sex?

answer

Romance should last a lifetime.

Billy Graham

question

Will you be comfortable with sexual love?

Marriage is so much more than sexual intimacy. A good marriage is the uniting of two best friends, two potential parents, and two lovers. Sex is certainly a big part of the equation. After you say "I do" and walk off hand in hand to start your new life together, will you be ready to take on this completely personal aspect of your relationship?

answer

Several factors come into play when determining your sexual comfort zone. For starters, how do your parents deal with marital intimacy? What has your sweetheart's experience been like? Much of your sexuality is based on your upbringing. Those raised in exceptionally conservative households may feel a sense of shame because they were told sex is dirty. They may initially have a hard time giving themselves permission to respond sexually, but it will come in time.

Self-esteem also plays a huge role in your sexual identity. If you feel bad about your appearance, for example, you'll find it more difficult to bare your body. Self-image is more of a problem for women, but it isn't uncommon among men.

Men and women seem to be worlds apart when it comes to sex. For men, it is often just a matter of physical release, where for women sex is based more on intimacy. These differences can be frustrating. If a woman doesn't get enough affection, she shuts down sexually. If a man doesn't get enough sex, he has a difficult time being touchy-feely.

While discussing sex with your future spouse can be awkward, it is absolutely necessary for a healthy and satisfying marriage bed.

worth thinking about

▶ **Are you affectionate** with each other? Sex is more than the physical act itself; sex is holding hands, kissing, caressing, and hugging, too. It is about demonstrating love.

▶ **God designed** sex not only for procreation, but also for recreation. Within the confines of marriage, lovemaking provides a profound level of intimacy with another human being and enhances your sense of well-being through the release of endorphins.

▶ **As a couple**, do you respect each other's boundaries? This will become even more important as you become sexually intimate.

> *Your lips cover me with kisses; your love is better than wine. There is a fragrance about you; the sound of your name recalls it. No woman could keep from loving you. Take me with you, and we'll run away; be my king and take me to your room. We will be happy together, drink deep, and lose ourselves in love. No wonder all women love you!*
> Song of Songs 1:2–4, GNT

question

What are your expectations?

From lingerie commercials to Top 40 songs to block-buster movies, the sensuality-hyped secular culture makes it look like everybody is having red-hot sex all the time. With the legitimacy a marriage license brings, you'd think married couples would be dancing in the dark every night. They're not. *Newsweek* reports that married couples actually have sex just over once a week. That's probably not what most newlyweds have in mind. What do you expect, a liaison twice a day or something a bit less ambitious?

answer

You and your partner definitely need to agree on this one. One key to great sex is communication, so talk about your expectations, your fears, your desires, your concerns, and your fantasies.

Be careful not to order wedding invitations based solely on the chemistry you share. A marriage can't be based on sex alone, because the passion will most certainly wane. Don't expect the honeymoon phase of your relationship to march on through the years. As you learn more and more about each other's wants and desires, you'll learn that sometimes quality is far more important than quantity.

Sexual expectations can differ not only in the frequency of your trysts, but also in the form taken. One of you may be more open to experimentation, whereas the other may be more traditional. After you are married you will have a lifetime of intimacy, so be creative. At the same time, avoid doing anything that will upset your partner.

In real life, a healthy and mutually fulfilling sexual relationship is not what you see in Hollywood or in the magazines. It is an amazing bond between a man and a woman that will grow deeper over the years. There may be fewer fireworks as time goes on, but the glow will still be there.

worth thinking about

▶ **The man's physical** needs are generally not the same as the needs of the woman. Plan to validate your partner's needs rather than expecting your sweetheart's needs to be exactly like yours.

▶ **A satisfying** sex life is a result of a satisfying relationship once you are married, not the other way around. If you don't nurture your partner's physical or emotional needs, those hot summer nights aren't going to happen.

▶ **Marriage is** give-and-take. If you and your spouse-to-be have different sexual expectations for marriage, don't throw in the towel; learn how to compromise.

Bless your fresh-flowing fountain! Enjoy the wife you married as a young man! Lovely as an angel, beautiful as a rose—don't ever quit taking delight in her body. Never take her love for granted!
Proverbs 5:18–19, THE MESSAGE

48 question

What if your level of desire is unmatched?

When people's sex lives are going great, they don't give it much thought. But when sexual encounters are few and far between, it seems that's all they can think about. At one point or another, it happens to every married couple. Sex experts estimate that one out of every three couples struggles with mismatched sexual desire. It's baffling, but partners rarely have the same sex drive at the same time. Your relationship needs to be strong enough to work through that.

answer

When one partner is dissatisfied because the other is disinterested, the entire intimate relationship will suffer, and you both will feel hurt, rejected, and lonely. If a sexual wall is allowed to build up, there will likely be less affection and marital flirting as well, and tempers will smolder. Getting angry will only create a bigger rift between you.

If one's partner seems to lose interest in sex, the other should try not to cast blame. Instead, the problem needs to be identified. There are many reasons why people suffer a loss of libido. Lack of sleep, too much stress, hormonal issues, depression, anger, and certain medications are common culprits.

Even though you have not yet said "I do," you need to consider the possibility that at some point in your marriage your sex drives might be incompatible. How will you handle that? Something to consider: if your partner's level of desire diminishes, you'll need to work a little harder at the romancing portion of your relationship; it will be time to practice the art of seduction. Create an atmosphere that is conducive to lovemaking. Have candlelit dinners, slow dance in front of a crackling fire, watch a romantic movie holding hands. If you can afford it, take a romantic vacation and get away from it all for a few days.

worth thinking about

▶ **If you are** overloaded with commitments beyond your marriage, you won't have much energy left over at the end of the day. Stress does a real number on your sex drive.

▶ **Remember that** it takes two to tango. As difficult as it is, God encourages you to serve your spouse, sometimes whether you're in the mood or not.

▶ **If you focus** on building the level of nonsexual intimacy before you are married, things will fall into place once you are husband and wife.

> *The marriage bed must be a place of mutuality—the husband seeking to satisfy his wife, the wife seeking to satisfy her husband. Marriage is not a place to "stand up for your rights." Marriage is a decision to serve the other, whether in bed or out.*
>
> 1 Corinthians 7:3–4, THE MESSAGE

question

▼

Can you share your sexual likes and dislikes?

People like to think that loving their spouses and work-ing hard at their marriages will be enough to maintain happiness, even if their sex lives are less than ideal. But intimacy definitely matters. Some couples find out after the wedding that they are sexually incompatible, either because of a mismatched libido or because they enjoy different sexual activities. Just as some people like salty and some people like sweet, you may find after your honeymoon that what turns you on in the bedroom dif-fers from what turns your mate on.

answer

▼

Marriage is a labor of love. Unfortunately, the subject of sex is a sore point in many marriages. In the honeymoon phase, lovemaking is frequent and enthusiastic. As time goes by it develops a different character, which can be frustrating. For a variety of reasons, you may have dry spells where you are seemingly incompatible.

This topic is extremely uncomfortable for most couples. You certainly don't want to make your beloved feel bad. Who wants to be critiqued about a bad performance and then suffer a bruised ego? God designed the sexual rela-tionship in marriage for two reasons: children and pleasure.

Once you are married, you'll need to learn how to tell your spouse what you like and dislike in bed. If something feels great to you, speak up. If your mate does something you don't like, you'll need to say it in a loving way to cushion the blow. Whatever you do, don't wait decades to tell your spouse you don't like something. What a sad waste of time.

According to a study mentioned in *Newsweek*, married couples have sex an average of 68.5 times a year. If you make it to your golden anniversary, that means you will probably have had sex a grand total of 3,425 times!

worth thinking about

▶ **A fulfilling sex life** is a trial-and-error process that evolves over time. Your partner isn't psychic, so you need to tell each other what you need.

▶ **Your emotional needs** affect your sexual relationship. If something is bothering you, it will show up in the bedroom.

▶ **Sexual compatibility** is important, but not as important as good communication. If the channels of communication are open, you will feel free to talk about what you like and dislike in lovemaking.

> *If we exalt money, status, or sex above the Word of God, we are living in idolatry. Every time we inwardly submit to the strongholds of fear, bitterness, and pride, we are bowing to the rulers of darkness. Each of these idols must be smashed, splintered, and obliterated from the landscape of our hearts.*
>
> Francis Frangipane

50

Do you share the same views on fidelity?

Ironically, studies from Barna Research show that born-again Christians have the highest rate of divorce. This may be because they are less likely to engage in premarital sex and then find that their postnuptial physical relationship is disappointing. Or maybe the faithful just have higher standards and can't overlook serious lapses in judgment and infidelity. Whatever the reason, the two of you need to concur when it comes to marital commitment.

answer

In biblical days, adultery was looked upon so negatively that guilty couples were put to death. Now it's almost as if true monogamy has fallen by the wayside. Society has developed a casual attitude toward sex.

The definitions of what constitutes fidelity have blurred. A kiss, a hug, a lingering look, a casual arm around some other person, something more. . . . Are these instances of infidelity? Perhaps you may think it "depends." Loosened definitions fit easily into today's society, but they're likely to end up hurting the one you love.

Internet chat rooms and phone sex lines make committing adultery in your heart only a mouse click or phone call away. Pornography is available online, in magazines, and on TV. Does that really constitute cheating even though you can't physically touch the other person? The Bible says it does: "Anyone who looks at a woman and wants to possess her is guilty of committing adultery with her in his heart" (Matthew 5:28, GNT).

No matter what phraseology you use, your marriage vows will undoubtedly say something about forsaking all others. When you make that promise in front of friends and family, you are making a divine covenant with God as well. If you can't keep your promise, don't get married.

Marital faithfulness provides an unparalleled forum for developing a resilient spiritual bond that would be utterly destroyed by an extramarital affair.

worth thinking about

▶ **What will you** do if one of you is attracted to someone else? What would you do if one of you actually strayed? Many marriages survive and thrive despite infidelity, but many are on the fast track to the divorce court.

▶ **Strengthen your marriage** by giving your heart, soul, and body to your mate. Putting each other on the top of your priority lists will keep your eyes from wandering.

▶ **The consequences** of adultery are long-lasting and severe. When you have an affair, there is a complete breakdown of trust that may never be restored.

> *The man who commits adultery is an utter fool, for he destroys himself. He will be wounded and disgraced. His shame will never be erased.*
> Proverbs 6:32–33, NLT

question

Will you use birth control?

Whether to use birth control is a critical question, because it is conceivable you could find yourselves expecting before your wedding gift thank-you notes are even in the mail. The two of you need to have a frank discussion and determine when and if you are prepared to bring a child into the world. If you're just not ready for diapers and baby food, you'll need to take steps to prevent an unplanned pregnancy.

answer

The matter of contraception has been a controversial one among Christians for years. Some Christians believe it is a sin to ever use birth control because doing so would disobey God's mandate in Genesis 1:28: "Be fruitful and multiply" (NAS). Other Christians believe they should have no restrictions on whether or not to use birth control.

What does the ultimate authority have to say on the subject? There is no question that God's primary purpose for marriage is to have children. It is also clear that God considers children to be a great blessing. Yet the Bible does not state irrefutably that Christians cannot use birth control. Since the Scriptures are silent on the matter, you must search your own heart.

If you decide you are going to use birth control, do your homework on the options. The most reliable methods of preventing pregnancy are birth control pills, injections, implants, IUDs, and sterilization. Latex condoms for men and diaphragms with spermicide are less effective.

Natural family planning is also an option, but it requires considerably more diligence. For this method to work, you must abstain from sex on those days the woman can become pregnant.

worth thinking about

▶ Sex within marriage is pure and honorable, even when conception can't occur. Lovemaking fosters a level of intimacy that can be achieved in no other way.

▶ While children are definitely a treasure, not everyone is wired to be a model parent. Before bringing a vulnerable baby into the world, make sure you can handle it.

▶ Before starting on a birth control program, be sure to investigate any potential side effects. Birth control pills, for example, can cause weight gain, depression, and high blood pressure, and they have been linked to one form of cervical cancer. Natural planning has no negative side effects.

> Those who live as their human nature tells them to, have their minds controlled by what human nature wants. Those who live as the Spirit tells them to, have their minds controlled by what the Spirit wants. To be controlled by human nature results in death; to be controlled by the Spirit results in life and peace.
>
> Romans 8:5–6, GNT

52

question

How important is romance to you?

It's an age-old argument. Most women think men are sorely unromantic, while the guys think their female counterparts are overly sentimental. If your idea of a perfect marriage involves cozy dinners and candlelight while your spouse-to-be envisions a quick roll in the hay, you may be incompatible in the romance department. If romance is more important to one of you than to the other, it would be helpful to get your expectations out in the open and save frustration later on.

answer

This one shouldn't be too tough to figure out. If your partner is romance-challenged, you have probably already seen the warning signs. The funny thing is, many women who complain that men lack romance make few romantic gestures themselves. It often seems that married partners both want to get rather than to give.

Being romantic isn't just about doing big things like taking exotic vacations or dining at expensive four-star restaurants. Romance is often all about the simple and unexpected small gestures that have a big impact. Being romantic is about making your sweetheart feel special— and that doesn't have to cost a penny.

Here are a few ideas for raising your romance aptitude:

Snuggle up on the couch and watch a romance movie. Compose sweet little love notes for each other and hide them in the other's pocket. Put a flower on your sweetheart's seat. Take a picture of yourself on your cell phone and send it to your sweetie in the middle of a workday with an "I love you" text message.

All couples celebrate occasions like Valentine's Day, birthdays, and anniversaries. Why not be a little creative with some obscure occasions like National Hugging Day (January 21), National Chocolate Ice Cream Day (June 7) or Kiss and Make Up Day (August 25)?

worth thinking about

▶ To master the art of romance, do something sweet for your love every day for one entire month. You'll find you are more creative than you ever thought possible!

▶ Some people are uncomfortable with public displays of affection. If your loved one falls into that category, be considerate. Talk about it. You may find over time it becomes more acceptable.

▶ Being romantic is an investment. Practice learning the language of romance now so you'll be fluent when you get married.

> If we want the advantages of love, then we must be willing to take the risks of love. And that requires vulnerability. Of course, we can refuse this path and trod another one devoid of openness. But the toll on such a road is extremely high.
>
> Charles Swindoll

question

Is your love enough to sustain you?

Right now it is probably hard to imagine that the excitement and passion you feel for each other could ever die down, but for most couples that is a near-certain fact of life. The honeymoon phase will eventually end, but that doesn't mean the best part of your marriage is over, unless your love is based on lust alone. Do you have what it takes to make it for the long haul?

answer

True love is so much more than sex; it is compassionate and selfless companionship. True love means being there through the good times and the bad and loving and cherishing each other. That is the secret of a successful marriage, certainly not just an enthusiastic sex life.

Falling in love is characterized by a stomach-churning, palm-sweating euphoria, and it is only the first stage of a deep and abiding love. It is impossible to stay in that stage throughout your entire marriage. What starts out as infatuation must evolve for marriage to survive for the long haul.

In her famous sonnet, Elizabeth Barrett Browning defined the bond of true love like no other: "How do I love thee? Let me count the ways. / I love thee to the depth and breadth and height / My soul can reach, when feeling out of sight / For the ends of Being and ideal Grace."

That is the kind of love you must strive for in your marriage. Ask yourself if you can picture yourself waking up next to that person for the rest of your life. Can you love that person no matter what comes along? No matter what happens or what is said? No matter who or what may cast doubt in your heart? Can you refuse to give in to negativity? Can you love that person as Christ loves you? If you cannot honestly say you love each other with that kind of passion, you will incur trouble down the line.

worth thinking about

▶ As your love for each other matures, it will become more about building a life together and less about libido. Just because your passion fades with time doesn't mean you aren't still in love with each other.

▶ If it is true, your love will develop into something full and beautiful—a love so strong that it is beyond your wildest dreams.

▶ If you base your love on sexual attraction alone, you will be bitterly disappointed. While that chemistry is critical to a happy marriage, it is not the most important factor. You need more.

May your fountain be blessed, and may you rejoice in the wife of your youth. A loving doe, a graceful deer—may her breasts satisfy you always, may you ever be captivated by her love.
Proverbs 5:18–19, NIV

question

▼

What are your household priorities?

Marriage is all about establishing your own household as a couple from two separate homes. Making it a happy one means paying attention to some rather mundane details, things like scrubbing toilets and doing laundry. Because you each come from a different family of origin, your household priorities—the things that really matter to you the most—could be different. It's time to talk about your household hot buttons.

answer

▼

Your home will be so much more than simply where your heart is. It will be where you sustain yourselves physically, emotionally, and spiritually, and where you will kindle the flame of your passion. Unless you will be bringing along a personal butler, that means there are things that need to be done whether you choose to live in a house or an apartment.

In order to send frustration on a detour, it is best to declare from the get-go what really matters to each of you when it comes to your humble abode. Will your house be just a place to crash, or do you picture seeing it on the cover of *House Beautiful* magazine? Must it always pass the white-glove test, or do you like more of the lived-in look? How about the yard? Is maintaining an impeccable yard important to you?

These are all things you need to discuss and agree to, but there are no right or wrong answers. If you plan on making your home truly your castle, substantial investments in both time and money will be required, and something else will have to give. After all, nothing happens by itself.

Perhaps the early stage of marriage isn't the time to focus too much on your place of residence. Focus instead on nurturing your relationship, enjoying your time together, and having some fun!

worth thinking about

▶ **One way** to get the discussion going is to share what went on in your family household growing up. What household tasks did your parents agree on or argue about? Explore how you can handle these same issues.

▶ **You need** to know what really matters to each other. If you are angry because the floors are dirty, it will needlessly hinder your intimacy.

▶ **Have realistic** expectations rather than aiming for perfection. As your level of responsibility increases, you will have job, volunteer, and social obligations that will need to come first.

> *Home—that blessed word, which opens to the human heart the most perfect glimpse of Heaven, and helps to carry it thither, as on an angel's wings.*
> Lydia M. Child

55

▼

What about the cleanliness of your home?

Once you grow up and get a place of your own, you need to learn how to take care of it. Cleaning is about more than just picking up your stuff; you actually need to remove the dirt. Now that's not a fun concept to a lot of people, but it is a necessity. Where do you draw the line? Does your place need to be spotless or merely presentable? How do you and your spouse-to-be match up with regard to your needs for cleanliness?

answer

▼

If having a tidy place isn't critical to you but is to your mate, you need to find a way to make it work. The best strategy is to clean smart and focus on prevention. When you get ready to move in together, get rid of the things you don't use rather than moving the junk from place to place. Then be organized. Everything should have its place, and actually be put there.

Pick up after yourself daily. Don't wait for dishes and dirty clothes to pile up. But even if you keep everything put away, you will still have to clean. Clean one room at a time in a pattern, carrying your supplies with you wherever you go, and you will get out of there more quickly. Playing motivational music will also make it more fun.

Many couples hire a housecleaner to take care of the cleaning. There are several good reasons to hire a professional: you hate to clean, you'd rather play, you are bad at it, or you are sensitive to cleaning solvents. Another very good reason for hiring someone else to clean is that the two of you choose to spend your free time pursuing creative avocations such as woodworking, painting, or quilting. If you fall into one of those categories and can afford it, hiring a cleaning service even once a month will make your life more pleasant.

worth thinking about

▶ Set yourself up for success and invest in good cleaning tools and a powerful vacuum. Get a big tote tray of some kind to carry all your supplies.

▶ Simplify your supplies. There is no need to buy fancy cleaners for every surface in your house. Many professionals carry light-duty glass cleaner, multisurface cleaner, heavy-duty degreasing cleaner, and dusting spray.

▶ Rather than cleaning your entire home in one fell swoop, assign duties to specific days of the week. You may want to keep a chart on the refrigerator to show this.

> When an evil spirit leaves a person, it travels through the desert, looking for a place to rest. But when the demon doesn't find a place, it says, "I will go back to the home I left." When it gets there and finds the place empty, clean, and fixed up, it goes off and finds seven other evil spirits even worse than itself.
>
> Matthew 12:43–45, CEV

Who will do the household chores?

Marrying is easy, it's the housework that's hard.

Author Unknown

56 — question

Whose responsibility is what?

Once you have your own place, there is going to be a long list of things you need to do to maintain it. There will be yard work to do, toilets to plunge, sinks to unclog, and perhaps mounds of snow to shovel. Even apartment dwellers have maintenance projects. If you wait for your superintendent to fix every little thing that needs fixing, it's going to drive you crazy. The question is, would either of you consider yourself a Mr. or Ms. Fix-it?

answer

Gender roles fly out the window when it comes to home maintenance because not everyone is handy around the house. Hopefully your betrothed or you are gifted in this area, because there is work to be done. Since you need to be good stewards of the gifts God bestows on you, someone is going to have to keep things in working order.

If you don't receive one for a wedding gift, be sure to pick up a book or two on home maintenance. There are manuals for do-it-yourselfers of all levels of experience and enthusiasm. Being able to perform small repairs yourselves can save you some serious money, but the DIY approach works only if you know what you're doing. Remember, time is money, so just because you can do it doesn't mean you should. Why bother fixing something when you can just pick up the yellow pages and call an expert? Because it costs money, that's why. Some basic things you should be able to do by yourself.

Despite your best intentions, sometimes you need to call in the heavy artillery and bring in a professional. If you find yourself either unable or unwilling to fix it yourself, know what you're doing. An unethical contractor may sense your inexperience and take advantage of your naïveté.

worth thinking about

▶ Superstores like Home Depot and Lowe's often have free seminars on how to do typical household projects. Take advantage of their expertise rather than trying to figure it out solo.

▶ It is important that you have the right equipment to get the job done. A good-quality tool kit, lawn-care tools, and snow shovels are must-haves.

▶ Big household projects are more fun when they are done together. If you want to plant a garden, put on your gloves and do it together. If the walls need painting, put on some fun music and get to it.

> *God's various gifts are handed out everywhere; but they all originate in God's Spirit. God's various ministries are carried out everywhere; but they all originate in God's Spirit. God's various expressions of power are in action everywhere; but God himself is behind it all.*
> 1 Corinthians 12:4–6, THE MESSAGE

57

question

How will you divide household chores?

Merriam-Webster's defines the word *chore* as a "difficult or disagreeable task." The term might engender less-than-fond memories of long-ago Saturday mornings cleaning up your childhood bedroom. Well, chores don't go away just because you are an adult. They actually grow legs and multiply. Your marriage should be a partnership on all fronts, including housework. How will the two of you manage the upkeep that lies before you?

answer

It's important to be proactive when it comes to your household chores in order to prevent hurt feelings and animosity later on. For starters, you need to determine if you are going to split the work evenly, or if one of you will shoulder the brunt of it. The division will rest in large part on your outside job responsibilities and volunteer commitments. If one of you works outside the home and the other doesn't, the one at home should clearly take on more of the household chores. That doesn't mean, however, that the breadwinner should be off the hook entirely.

If you both work, you'll need to find a way to divvy up the work equitably. The best way to do that is to make a list of the household chores that need to be done and how often. Cover all the bases: daily chores like making the bed, cooking, doing the dishes, emptying the dishwasher, managing the laundry, and taking out the garbage; periodic chores like changing the oil, mowing the lawn, and shoveling the driveway. Then mark off the things you each absolutely hate doing. Hopefully your lists of hateful chores will be different and you can help each other out. If you both despise the same tasks, you will need to do some negotiating. Perhaps you can rotate the least liked jobs on a monthly basis.

worth thinking about

▶ Be clear about your desired standard of living. A certain degree of disorder might be your preference but not your mate's. If you can't find middle ground, you may need to consider hiring outside help.

▶ Rather than tackling really big jobs on your own, do them together. You can commiserate with each other later.

▶ If you find your list of chores is ridiculously long, reprioritize. Doing so will help you determine how you'll manage after the wedding. Are there things that can be eliminated to save time and money? Being organized will also minimize your workload.

> *Whatever you do, work at it with all your heart,*
> *as working for the Lord, not for men, since*
> *you know that you will receive an inheritance*
> *from the Lord as a reward. It is the*
> *Lord Christ you are serving.*
> Colossians 3:23–24, NIV

58

question

How will you allow for style differences?

It's sad but true—couples can sleep together, vacation together, and play together, but when it comes to working together there can be a serious personality clash. It's like the old tortoise-and-hare analogy. You might be quick out of the gate and rush through your chores, but your sweetie may be slow and methodical and ultimately do a better job. Coming from two separate households it's likely you'll do things differently. How will you navigate that?

answer

Once you start living together after marriage, the way your partner does things might drive you crazy. But you need to be flexible and allow for personal style. The two of you will fold towels, match socks, load the dishwasher, and make the bed differently—and that's okay. Neither way is wrong, just different.

This can be a tough thing to accept, but your way of doing things isn't necessarily the only way. What you don't want is a my-way-period mentality. Rather than complaining that your spouse-to-be uses a mop with a disposable cleaning cloth to wash the kitchen floor rather than getting down on hands and knees as you do, be grateful that the floor is getting cleaned. If you absolutely must have something done a certain way, do it yourself.

Here's the trick. If you see something that bothers you about the way your mate works and you feel that you absolutely must intercede, do one of two things: count to ten, take a deep breath, and talk about something completely off-topic; or turn around and walk away. Whatever you do, don't be bossy.

By being open to new ways of doing things, you may make some great discoveries.

worth thinking about

- ▶ **Be considerate** of each other's body clock if you're an early riser and your spouse-to-be isn't.

- ▶ **If you are** getting married after living on your own, you will both undoubtedly be set in your ways to some extent. That means the melding of your unique housekeeping styles will be more pronounced.

- ▶ **You may have** different opinions on the products that should be used to maintain your home. If it's not a big deal to you, give in.

> What you do in your house is worth as much as if you did it up in heaven for our Lord God. We should accustom ourselves to think of our position and work as sacred and well-pleasing to God, not on account of the position and work, but on account of the word and faith from which the obedience and the work flow.
>
> Martin Luther

59 question

What about grocery shopping, cooking, and cleanup?

Eating is one of life's simplest pleasures. It just goes to show you how cool God is. After all, the human diet could still consist of manna morning, noon, and night as it did for the Jews in the Book of Exodus. The tough part is, unless you have a personal chef, you are going to need not only to cook for yourselves, but also to do the grocery shopping and clean up your culinary mess. Who will do the food-related chores at your place?

answer

When you first get married there's a good chance you'll be on a pretty tight budget. You don't need to go as far as buying a freezer full of meat or a thirty-six-roll economy pack of toilet paper to save a buck, but you will probably need to stretch your food dollar. Bottom line is this: you need to buy things you want, but save money when you can.

You should discuss who will do the big weekly or biweekly shopping. Designate the one who is least annoyed by the process. Back in the day, most grocery stores bagged your purchases for you, but that service has gone the way of full-service gas stations. If you get stressed as you scramble to bag up your groceries while other customers wait impatiently in line, the job might not be for you.

Once the groceries are home, who is going to cook them up into a palatable meal? Many newlyweds have little experience in the kitchen other than boiling some pasta and heating up a jar of marinara sauce. Now that you have your own kitchen and can cook what you want, you might find you really enjoy making culinary masterpieces.

Most people agree that the worst part of cooking is cleaning up afterward, and the more complicated the dish, the messier your kitchen will be. But this one is easy: if you ate the meal, you probably should help clear the wreckage.

worth thinking about

- ▶ **Cooking together** is romantic. If you don't get a good one for a wedding present, be sure to invest in a few cookbooks. Who needs a fancy French restaurant when you can re-create a bistro menu at home?

- ▶ **It can be frustrating** if your sweetheart cooks you a beautiful meal and then has to face cleanup duty alone. Be thoughtful and pitch in.

- ▶ **Some people** love to grocery-shop. Decide who will do the bulk of your shopping or if you'll do it together.

> *Jesus replied, "I am the bread of life. Whoever comes to me will never be hungry again. Whoever believes in me will never be thirsty."*
> John 6:35, NLT

question

How do you feel about eating out?

Only a few decades ago, it was considered a treat for a family to eat at a restaurant, and such extravagances were often limited to special occasions. In this new millennium, that has certainly changed. According to the National Restaurant Association, the average household expenditure for food away from home in 2005 was $2,634, or $1,054 per person. That's a huge number. Once you are married, what allotment of your hard-earned greenbacks will go to satisfying your appetites at eating establishments?

answer

The first thing you need to determine is how you feel about home-cooked meals versus convenience foods versus dining out. There are plenty of advantages to eating in. The most obvious is cost. A meal of cheeseburger and fries at a casual sit-down restaurant will run you somewhere between five and eight dollars. You can probably make the same thing at home for about a dollar. And for the same price, you could have a steak or an orange roughy fillet instead.

You certainly can't ignore the issue of nutrition. While restaurants—even the fast-food variety—offer more health-conscious options today than ever before, most menus are still laden with sodium and fat, and the portion sizes are far too large.

Now that you are on your own, it's time to be bold, branch out, and try something other than takeout and macaroni and cheese. Cooking doesn't mean microwaving a frozen dinner or reading the directions on a boxed entrée. Cooking can be fun, nutritious, and economical.

You may not be a top chef right off the bat, but give it a try. There are few things that say "I love you" more than a scrumptious meal made from scratch.

worth thinking about

▶ Stretch your dining budget by splitting meals. Most restaurant portions can easily accommodate that. Besides, then you'll have room for a yummy dessert.

▶ Planning your weekly meals in advance will reduce the temptation to order a last-minute large pepperoni with extra cheese. Be sure to put a slow cooker on your gift registry wish list; using it in the morning will allow you to eat as soon as you walk in the door.

▶ Choose restaurants that serve dishes you won't make at home. Ethnic cuisine is a great choice. Save restaurant trips for special occasions, and then really go for it.

> *He Himself is the fuel our spirits were designed to burn, or the food our spirits were designed to feed on. There is no other.*
>
> C. S. Lewis

61

What if one is a slacker?

In your planning, you've compiled your to-do list and divvied up the chores. If you've set the stage properly and both been involved—and in agreement—about the division of household duties, there will be a stronger likelihood of compliance. There is still the possibility, however, that your future mate will let you down. If you don't do your schoolwork, you fail. If you don't meet your deadline at work, you get fired. What will the fallout be in your marriage if one of you doesn't hold up one's end of the bargain?

answer

The Book of Proverbs makes it clear that being willing to work hard and do your best is an important aspect of successful living. Those who are lazy waste good resources, desire things but refuse to work for them, and are more likely to experience poverty.

Nobody likes a slacker. What will you do if you unwittingly marry one? Rather than just getting mad, you will need to try to figure out why your mate isn't doing the chores. Is it because of sheer laziness? Or is the task too difficult? Don't assume that your sweetheart knows how to do something.

Plan ahead to be proactive. Here are some ways to help: Don't take for granted the tasks that your partner accomplishes. Give a compliment for a job well done. That will do more to inspire your sweetheart than nagging ever will. One sure way of getting your spouse-to-be to quit doing housework is to criticize the way it's been done. Positive works. Negative doesn't.

If either one of you bears the responsibility for chores and the other refuses to do so, you need to have a candid discussion. If there is still a stubborn refusal, know that there isn't much you can do about it. But there are two things you can do: lower your standards, or hire an outside party to do the work.

worth thinking about

▶ **If you see** aspects of your prospective spouse's life that point toward laziness, be wary. If your sweetheart doesn't do the chores living solo, there is a strong likelihood that behavior will continue after the wedding.

▶ **Once you are married,** plan to surprise your spouse by secretly doing all the chores when least expected. If your mate is especially busy with other obligations, cut him or her some slack.

▶ **It helps if you** post the list of chores in the form of a calendar or checklist in a conspicuous spot. It will serve as a constant reminder.

> *Laziness grows on people; it begins in cobwebs and ends in iron chains. The more one has to do, the more he is able to accomplish.*
> Thomas Buxton

62 question

What do you want out of life?

This question is a whopper, and it is probably the most important one you'll ask each other before setting a wedding date. If one of you dreams of raising a brood of children in a small town while the other hopes you will travel to the far reaches of the world as missionaries, you are doomed to failure. Having complementary goals is critical to sustaining a mutually satisfying marriage. At the core, do the two of you want the same things out of life?

answer

Some people are visionaries while others are more practical in their approach to life. Most often, these philosophies are at odds. The two of you need to agree on how you hope to live your lives. Before you can live happily ever after, you must do some private soul-searching about your dreams and goals and whether the one you love will support or destroy them.

To get a handle on your future partner's zest for life, sit down and make a list of all the things you'd like to do before you die. If one of your lists is an amalgamation of bold pursuits like skydiving, bungee jumping, and exotic travel while the other's is much tamer, you will have to find a way to manage that. Otherwise, as the years tick by the frustration will cause insurmountable discontent.

If your ambitions are God-inspired, He will bless them. Where you'll get into trouble is when you try to do things on your own. God's plans aren't always convenient, either. He certainly didn't take the Israelites out of Egypt by the most direct route. Likewise, He may take you on a circuitous journey on the way to accomplishing your dreams. But some goals are worth working and waiting for.

worth thinking about

▶ **If your sweetheart** is more adventurous than you are, that doesn't necessarily mean you shouldn't get married. That's where friends come in. Some activities can be done solo or with a good buddy.

▶ **People's aspirations** change with the passage of time. The key is to share your hopes and dreams with each other and strive to accomplish them together.

▶ **Just because** you get married doesn't mean you cease living. You can be successful in your career, seek adventure, continue exploring, and still be a good spouse.

> *How do you know what your life will be like tomorrow? Your life is like the morning fog—it's here a little while, then it's gone. What you ought to say is, "If the Lord wants us to, we will live and do this or that." Otherwise you are boasting about your own plans, and all such boasting is evil.*
>
> James 4:14–16, NLT

63

What are
your financial
goals?

These days a significant number of couples are waiting until their late twenties and early thirties to get married. When they wed, therefore, they'll be combining households and finances that are already well established. Your incomes will be combined, but so will your debt. No matter what your age, this is the time to review your financial goals and determine how they mesh with those of your future spouse.

answer

Most couples cringe at the thought of discussing finances. If you're honest with yourself, the notion that someone else might have a say in how you spend your money is pretty uncomfortable, especially if you pride yourself on your independence. Yet, as the Bible says, the two shall become one—and that includes your money.

Most people want to have it made financially, but that can mean entirely different things to different people. To you, it may mean not living paycheck to paycheck, while to your betrothed it might mean amassing a small fortune. Money is a means, not an end.

The prudent idea is for each of you to make a wish list of your short-term and long-term goals, complete with timelines, and see where they match up. But a list can go only so far.

Some specifics you should discuss in your goal-planning session include whether or not to create a house fund, if you plan on investing in the stock market, where those funds will come from, how much you need in your emergency fund, and the amount you might want to maintain in your mad-money account for things like vacations and furniture.

worth thinking about

▶ **Workers used** to count on Social Security and pension plans to support their retirement. For the most part, those programs can no longer be counted on. You need to have a plan for your golden years.

▶ **Your goals need** to be realistic, or you won't stick with them. You can always set new ones once you attain the others. Schedule an annual meeting to review your progress.

▶ **A financial planner** is a great partner to help you start off the business aspect of your marriage on the right foot. Referrals from friends and associates are your best option.

Trust in your wealth, and you will be a failure, but God's people will prosper like healthy plants.
Proverbs 11:28, CEV

64

question
▾
What are your career goals?

Since it's unlikely you are going to live off the land in some remote stretch of wilderness, somebody is going to have to earn a living. The focal point of this discussion is how important your careers will be to you as a married couple. Are you both dreaming of reaching the top of the corporate ladder, or are you hoping to work just enough to keep the wolf away from the door?

answer
▾
For many, work is what gives their lives meaning, and what they do for a living is who they are. But what happens when a job is lost and one's self-esteem is wrapped up in work? Like everything else, your career needs to be kept in proper perspective. Many a couple has split up because one or both of them were workaholics. When you are taking your final breath on this earth, you'll be thinking about the ones you are leaving behind and the joys you've experienced with them. At the same time, it is not a sin to be successful and have ambition, unless work becomes your god.

Having a highly demanding job is fine when you are single with limited responsibilities. It is unfair, however, to continue that pace and level of stress when you get married. Being married means having a life together, and that's difficult to do if you're never home.

Rather than waiting until you have a midlife crisis, discuss your options together now. Why not begin your career doing what you love? If you focus on doing something you are passionate about, something that fulfills your God-ordained purpose, you will be happy and successful. Listen to your heart, and the money will follow.

worth thinking about

▶ **Don't just look** at the financial rewards of your or your sweetheart's work; also consider the humanitarian aspects. That doesn't mean either or you needs to be in some form of ministry—your workplace can also be a mission field.

▶ **Before you settle down**, discuss how many hours a week you are comfortable with each other working. You'll also want to explore how business travel would impact your relationship.

▶ **If you anticipate** a career shift or long to go back to college, be sure to include that as part of your financial planning and goal setting.

> *Anything I wanted, I got. I did not deny myself any pleasure. I was proud of everything I had worked for, and all this was my reward. Then I thought about all that I had done and how hard I had worked doing it, and I realized that it didn't mean a thing. It was like chasing the wind—of no use at all.*
>
> Ecclesiastes 2:10–11, GNT

question

What are your hopes and dreams?

Most kids grow up dreaming about being something, maybe a firefighter, an astronaut, a dancer, or a doctor. Some actually grow up to become what they'd envisioned. When you begin your new life together as husband and wife, that doesn't mean you leave your dreams at the altar. This is a great time to share your biggest hopes with your biggest fan. What have you always dreamed of doing?

answer

In the 1989 movie *Field of Dreams*, a dreamer built a baseball diamond in the middle of his cornfield. His family and neighbors thought he'd lost his mind; but he did it anyway, and some amazing things happened. A life without dreams is a life devoid of meaning and purpose.

God and family must always be your top two priorities, but there is also room in your life for some goals of your own. The biggest advantage of having dreams after you're married is that you have a built-in cheerleader.

Never feel that your dreams are silly or unattainable. As an unknown sage once said, "You cannot stuff a great life into a small dream." So why not dream big? Many a writer, an entrepreneur, or a performer goes for it and makes it big. Why should your dreams be any different?

Your dreams don't have to be about seeing your name in lights or winning a medal. Perhaps you dream of having a large family or running a marathon. Maybe you've always seen yourself living in a wilderness paradise. Whether big or small, if your dream is in line with God's will, it isn't impossible.

Talk it all over with your sweetheart, and work to make your dreams come true. Together you can do it.

worth thinking about

▶ Be careful that your dreams aren't one-sided; support your future mate's dreams as well.

▶ Some level of risk is inherent when pursuing your dreams, either financial or on a personal level. Don't let unreasonable ideas put your family at risk.

▶ If you have a dream in your heart that has been brewing for years, and if your future mate agrees, there is no time like the present to begin making it a reality. Just as a business does when launching a new product, come up with a plan and a timetable. Sometimes opportunity only knocks once, so be sure to open the door.

> *Give a man a dollar and you cheer his heart.*
> *Give him a dream and you challenge his heart.*
> *Give him Christ and you change his heart.*
> *Then the dollar and the dream become*
> *meaningful to him, and to others.*
>
> C. Neil Strait

Do you support each other's hopes and dreams?

If you can imagine it you can create it. If you can dream it, you can become it.

Arthur Ward

66

question

What are your future plans?

Sounds like a question you'd get at a job interview, doesn't it? Potential employers need to be confident that your short-term and long-term goals synchronize with their overall business strategy. If they don't, you won't get the offer. Likewise, you and your spouse-to-be need some semblance of harmony regarding where you want to be in the next decade. Otherwise, the two of you will wind up on different paths. What do you hope to be doing down the road?

answer

Admittedly, it's tough for some people to imagine what they'll be doing tomorrow let alone in the next decade, so this one will certainly stimulate some conversation. While there's no such thing as a crystal ball, you can still put some thought into what you hope to be doing at five- and ten-year intervals.

In five years you could be experiencing some career success, have several little ones running around, and own a starter home. In ten years you could have earned several promotions, have those same kids in the throes of adolescence, and be on home number two clear across the country. Your lives could be taking decidedly different turns.

This question is about more than physical location, although that is certainly important. It's about goals—if one of you wants to start a business, go back to school, and take a trip around the world, for example, it will take some careful planning and agreement.

The problem is that even the most carefully laid plans can go topsy-turvy on you when life gets in the way. As the years go by, God may have a completely different plan for you than you do for yourself: "'I know the plans I have for you,' declares the LORD, 'plans to prosper you and not to harm you, plans to give you hope and a future'" (Jeremiah 29:11, NIV).

worth thinking about

▶ **Planning is good**, but you also have to be flexible enough to roll with the punches. A plan B is not such a bad idea, either.

▶ **Some couples** have an annual meeting to assess how they're doing on their goals. But keep in mind that too much in life is already overplanned. Leave room for the Holy Spirit to work.

▶ **What is your dream** job? Thinking about that now will help you develop the skill set to make it a reality one day.

> *Rest in this—it is His business to lead, command, impel, send, call, or whatever you want to call it. It is your business to obey, follow, move, respond, or what have you. . . . The sound of "gentle stillness" after all the thunder and wind have passed will be the ultimate Word from God.*
>
> Jim Elliot

67

What are your plans for buying a home?

Homeownership is a wonderful by-product of the American dream. Most people long for a place of their own where they can call the shots. You've probably heard it said that renting is like throwing away money. There's definitely some truth to that. But that doesn't mean you need to take the plunge before you and your finances are ready. How do you know when the time is right to ditch the apartment and start building some equity?

answer

There are many great reasons for buying a house: you want a yard, you have pets, you need more privacy, or simply because you want a good investment. A house also has some disadvantages. For one, there's no superintendent to maintain the property; you're on your own. A house can be great until you wake up one morning, there are twelve inches of snow on the ground, and someone has to get out and shovel.

It's time to consider purchasing a home when you meet the following criteria: you have a reliable source of income, you plan to stay in the area at least five years, you have a solid credit score and manageable debt, and the economic outlook in the area is healthy.

Where people get into trouble is in buying more than they can afford. You should commit to a place only if the payment—including mortgage, taxes, insurance, utilities, phone, and maintenance—comes in at less than 28 percent of your net spendable income (income after tithes and taxes are deducted).

For some people, ownership means a condominium or a townhome instead, which often have community features like pools and tennis courts and have staff to manage things like snow removal, lawn care, and garbage hauling.

worth thinking about

- ▶ **Don't start looking** for a house until you have built a solid nest egg to cover a large down payment, closing costs, inspection fees, and moving expenses.

- ▶ **Consider starting** with a fixer-upper and then sell it for a profit. Follow this process with a larger home until you can pay cash for the one you really want.

- ▶ **If you go** for your dream house from the get-go, you'll put a definite cramp in your lifestyle. Vacations and entertainment will move to the background in favor of household expenses. That could cause undue stress on your relationship.

> If GOD doesn't build the house, the builders only build shacks. If GOD doesn't guard the city, the night watchman might as well nap. It's useless to rise early and go to bed late, and work your worried fingers to the bone. Don't you know he enjoys giving rest to those he loves?
>
> Psalm 127:1–2, THE MESSAGE

68

question

▼

When do you want to retire?

It probably seems strange to discuss retirement at the same time you are in the process of planning a wedding. When you are in your twenties and thirties, you don't need to have your golden years all planned out, but you should at least explore your thoughts on the subject to make sure you have similar philosophies. Realistically, when would you like to retire, and how are you going to make that happen?

answer

▼

A secure, comfortable retirement is every worker's goal. Achieving it is much easier with some thoughtful planning. Surprisingly, however, only 42 percent of Americans have calculated how much they need to save for retirement. In 2005, of those who had 401(k) plans available, 25 percent of them didn't even participate, according to the U.S. Department of Labor.

These days, the average American spends eighteen years in retirement. Experts estimate that you'll need approximately 70 percent of your preretirement income to maintain your standard of living when you stop working, so you'd better start saving.

Here are some tips: Contribute the maximum amount allowed to your 401(k) plan at work and Roth IRA accounts each year. Buy a modest home that you can pay off rather than carrying a large mortgage. Commit to investing at least 15 percent of your earnings.

Working longer and retiring later may be the key to future financial security. Delaying retirement can boost your Social Security benefits (assuming there are some left when it's time for you to retire). If you were born in 1960 or later, you will reach full retirement at age sixty-seven. Few people can manage on their benefit checks alone, so instead of retiring completely you might plan to downshift to part-time or cyclical work.

Save as much as you can as early as you can, and you'll be well on your way to a more financially secure retirement.

worth thinking about

▶ **One added** benefit of planning your golden years is that you are more likely to stay together to enjoy them.

▶ **Do you come** from ancestors known for their longevity? Keeping in mind how long you might live will have an impact on your retirement plans.

▶ **God wants you** to be productive your entire life. Rather than ceasing to work completely, migrate toward something less demanding and spend more time volunteering.

> *Divide your investments among many places, for you do not know what risks might lie ahead.*
> Ecclesiastes 11:2, NLT

question

▼

Do you want children someday?

In the past it was assumed that all married couples would one day want to have children. With reliable forms of birth control and shifting social mores, offspring are no longer a compulsory eventuality of marriage. In fact, according to a report by the National Center for Health Statistics, in 2002, 42 percent of childless women ages thirty-five to forty-four were voluntarily childless. How about you? Do you and your intended see a family in your future?

answer

▼

In the past, people used to ask newlywed couples how many children they were going to have. Now, that same couple would just as likely be asked *if* they are going to have children. Many couples are childless by choice.

There are many reasons people choose not to have children. Some prefer to focus on their career or their spouse. Some have health issues that would either impact their ability to parent or could be passed along to their offspring. Still others remain child-free because they had an unhappy childhood.

Whatever the reason, rampant hormones known as "baby fever" can cause a change of heart in even the most stalwart DINKs (double income, no kids) and turn them into mommies and daddies. Procreating is part of your DNA.

One can't ignore the fact that producing children is one of the primary purposes of marriage. The human body was designed for that purpose; otherwise there would be an on/off switch on your reproductive system.

Children will change your relationship with each other and alter your lifestyle irrevocably. Yet children are a tremendous blessing from God.

worth thinking about

▶ **Think past today** and envision what your old age would be like without children and grandchildren surrounding you. It could be lonely, particularly if your spouse precedes you in death.

▶ **The decision** to have children is one you must make together with your spouse-to-be before the wedding. You have to agree; if one of you wants them and the other doesn't, someone could be bitter for years.

▶ **Genetic testing** can help you know if there are any hereditary conditions you might pass on to your unborn children.

> *Children are a gift from the LORD; they are a reward from him. Children born to a young man are like arrows in a warrior's hands. How joyful is the man whose quiver is full of them! He will not be put to shame when he confronts his accusers at the city gates.*
>
> Psalm 127:3–5, NLT

70

question
▼
When do you want to start a family?

It's one thing to agree that someday you want to bring a little bundle of joy into the world; it's another thing entirely to figure out when the time is right. Besides getting married, the decision to start a family is the most important one you will ever make. Are you hoping to have your family tree planted by the time you unpack from your honeymoon, or would you rather wait for the perfect time years down the road?

answer
▼
Having a baby changes a marriage in profound ways. Most noticeably, your amount of responsibility will increase exponentially until those carefree days of doing what you want when you want will all but disappear. You'll have new bills to pay and new mouths to feed. Instead of just loving your spouse, you'll adore your offspring as well.

Becoming a parent brings with it a multitude of emotions. On the positive side are joy, excitement, wonder, happiness, and satisfaction. On the not-so-positive side are fear, anger, frustration, and jealousy. All of those feelings rolled together make parenthood the greatest adventure you will ever experience. Parenthood is far more than a biological process. When you have a child you give your heart away.

It's best to wait a few years before conceiving so that you have time to be a couple before you become a family. Be prepared not to succumb to peer or family pressure; plan to wait until you are ready, not jump into parenthood just because other people tell you it's time.

Having said that, you need to know that there is no such thing as the ideal time to have children. If you wait until your job is going well, your bills are paid, your marriage is stable, and you are mature enough to handle the responsibility, you'll probably never have children.

worth thinking about

- ▶ **While children** are a tremendous blessing in a marriage, many couples also experience a decrease in marital satisfaction due to a marginalized sex life when babies come along.

- ▶ **Waiting too long** will make you an older parent who may not have the stamina for your children. You want people to think you are the parent, not the grandparent.

- ▶ **Men produce sperm** their entire lives, but women's fertility begins to decline after about the age of thirty. Late pregnancies carry an increased possibility of fetal abnormalities.

Every child born into the world is a new thought of God, an ever fresh and radiant possibility.
Kate Douglas Wiggin

71

question

What is your ideal family size?

It may seem rather premature to discuss how many children you want before you even walk down the aisle, but you at least need to be in the same ballpark on your ideal family size. If one of you wants six or seven and the other is thinking you'll be happy with one or two, that may cause some grumbling. So what'll your family be like? Will you parent an only child or a battalion?

answer

These days, it's unusual to meet couples with extremely large families. Back in the day, however, larger families were more commonplace—farmers needed farmhands, birth control was less reliable, and most women were stay-at-home wives and mothers.

You may think you want a dozen children now, but once you experience the joy of dirty diapers and spit-up, you might downsize your original estimate. There are some disadvantages to a large family. The biggie is added expense. You need to be able to afford children. It might not seem that babies put much of a dent in the household food budget, but wait until they are teenagers. Obviously, the larger the family, the larger the home will need to be. Vacations and gift-giving will also be impacted.

Now for the disadvantages of a smaller family. Children from larger families have built-in playmates, whereas an only child can be lonely. There is always excitement in the air, a sense of camaraderie and belonging with a larger family, and an only child can sometimes feel cheated later in life after the parents are gone when there are no brothers and sisters. Finally, if you ask people who grew up with siblings how they felt about that experience, most of them would have had it no other way.

worth thinking about

▶ **Whatever you decide**, you want to make sure you are able to give your children the love and attention they deserve.

▶ **If you are miles** apart on how many kids you want, it only seems fair that the voice of whoever will have the primary responsibility for child care carry a little more weight.

▶ **The number** of children you want will be determined in large measure on how large your own family was. People from large families beget large families of their own.

Children, do what your parents tell you. This is only right. "Honor your father and mother" is the first commandment that has a promise attached to it, namely, "so you will live well and have a long life." Fathers, don't exasperate your children by coming down hard on them. Take them by the hand and lead them in the way of the Master.

Ephesians 6:1–4, THE MESSAGE

72

question

▼

What if you can't have children?

Modern reproductive advances like intrauterine insemi-nation, in vitro fertilization, and a plethora of powerful medications have brought the joys of parenthood to countless couples who otherwise wouldn't have been able to conceive. Still, there are many who are not able to have biological children of their own. How would the two of you handle it if you wanted children but couldn't produce your own? Would your commitment be strong enough to endure the heartbreak of infertility? Would you be open to adoption? These are just a few of the things you need to explore on this topic.

answer

▼

According to the National Center for Health Statistics, 2.1 million married couples are infertile (10 percent–15 percent of couples in childbearing years). By definition, *infertile* refers to those women who are unable to get pregnant and those men who cannot impregnate a woman after at least one year of trying.

The stress involved in not being able to conceive causes anger, depression, anxiety, sexual dysfunction, and social isolation. Both men and women experience a profound sense of loss when they find out they cannot have their own biological children—a grieving process of sorts. These feelings can put a serious strain on a marriage.

Having your own biological offspring is not the only way to be a parent. There are thousands of children in need of a loving home. There are many options for adoption, both international and domestic.

There are some problems inherent in adoption. After a great deal of effort, an adoption can fall through; there may be unknowns about a child's genetic background; or there could be issues related to abuse or neglect.

Successful adoption requires the buy-in of both parents. It can be a time-consuming, frustrating, and expensive process, but you can really save a life while enriching your own.

worth thinking about

▶ Before you get married you both may want to schedule an appointment for a complete physical examination to see if you are able to have children.

▶ Some family members may throw out strong opposition to an adoption. While this would be your own decision, family conflict could put undue stress on your future marriage.

▶ Having children is not a critical success factor for a happy marriage or a fulfilling life. God does not bless everyone with children, but gives some a different purpose.

> *Children are the hands by which we take hold of heaven.*
> Henry Ward Beecher

question
▼
How will children change your life?

Parents-to-be often say things like this at baby show-ers: "We're so excited about the baby, but we don't plan on changing our lifestyle too much." Yeah, right! Those are great goals to have, but the fact of the matter is, once you have a baby, your priorities and your relation-ships change. How will things change in your forthcom-ing marriage after you bring home your first bundle of joy, and are you willing to make those sacrifices?

answer
▼

For starters, once you have a family, your time will no longer be your own to do what you please. You won't even be able to sleep when you want to. Your spontane-ity will take a beating, because you certainly won't be able to just pick up and go at the drop of a hat. Your din-ing habits will also change. Romantic evenings spent din-ing on fine French food will be replaced by grabbing hot dogs cut up into bite-size pieces.

It's sad to say, but despite your best efforts, your sex life will also change. Those private interludes between husband and wife will become fewer and farther between. By the time you get the kids in bed and have a few minutes to yourselves, you'll be too tired to fool around.

Now don't panic, you'll still be able to have some fun in your life; you'll just have to make some modifications. You can still go out to dinner, though. You will simply have to take the baby along or plan ahead and get a sitter. You can still go on vacation, but it might be to Walt Disney World instead of Acapulco for a while. You can still have a healthy sex life, but you may have to do some scheduling.

Children not only change your life, but they also change how you view life. They upend your priorities. For your future marriage to work, you both have to be ready for the changes.

worth thinking about

▶ Regular dates are critical to marital satisfaction. Plan to go out to dinner alone sometimes, preferably at a place with cloth napkins. Never forget that you were a couple first.

▶ Once you have children, your perspective will be different. Maintaining a spotless home won't matter as much as playing choo-choo with little Johnny.

▶ While mothers are most often the primary caregivers, fathers also play substantial roles in raising children. That's why it's important that both of you agree on when it is time to start your family.

> *Children are not casual guests in our home. They have been loaned to us temporarily for the purpose of loving them and instilling a foundation of values on which their future lives will be built.*
>
> James Dobson

74

question

Will you both continue working?

Depending upon how you were raised, you may have different opinions when it comes to mixing career and family. If you were raised in a traditional one-career family where your mom stayed home to raise the children, that may be your dream as well. If, on the other hand, both of your parents worked, you will be more inclined to have a two-career family of your own when the time comes. Where do you and your intended stand on the issue of working versus staying at home?

answer

There seems to be a constant tug-of-war on the subject of working mothers. All you have to do is look at the broadcast schedule of popular talk shows to see a lively debate. Unfortunately, having one parent stay home is not an option for many families. In the United States, the majority of mothers have outside jobs.

There are pros and cons about combining work and child rearing. The pros include greater financial flexibility, daily adult interaction, and intellectual stimulation. Some of the cons include missing out on key childhood milestones, more day-to-day stress, and a sense of feeling conflicted.

Ideally, one of you should stay home and care for your own kids. According to a survey done by Pew Research Center, only 21 percent of working mothers say full-time work is the ideal situation for them; 60 percent would rather work part-time; and 19 percent would prefer not to work at all. More and more women are opting to stay home.

The primary caregiver does not have to be the woman. As of 2004, the U.S. had an estimated 5.5 million stay-at-home parents. While the vast majority were women (5.4 million), there were 98,000 full-time dads.

worth thinking about

► **When the time** comes, calculate the cost of working to see if it makes fiscal sense. Consider expenses such as child care, increased income taxes, gas and vehicle maintenance, parking, lunch, work clothing, dry cleaning, and so forth.

► **There is no scientific** evidence that children are harmed when their mothers work. According to the American Academy of Pediatrics, a child's development is most influenced by the emotional health of the family and the quality of child care.

► **Two-career couples** are often so busy that they have little time for a social life or each other. That can cause resentment to build over time.

Anyone who neglects to care for family members in need repudiates the faith. That's worse than refusing to believe in the first place.
1 Timothy 5:8, THE MESSAGE

question

What is your philosophy on discipline?

Children will challenge you in ways you can't even begin to imagine. They will make you angry, try your patience, push your buttons, and test the limits. And you will love them anyway. Fighting about the best forms of discipline is right up there with fighting about money and sex for married couples. What do you think is the right way to correct kids?

answer

It is the job of parents to provide love and support, but also discipline. There's no doubt that teaching your kids right from wrong is the hardest part of being a parent. Up until about the 1970s, physical punishment was common and children were routinely spanked. But social mores have changed, and for the most part, such forms of punishment are frowned upon.

The Bible is clear that it is your job as parents to mold your children into respectable adults. "My child, don't reject the LORD's discipline, and don't be upset when he corrects you. For the LORD corrects those he loves, just as a father corrects a child in whom he delights" (Proverbs 3:11–12, NLT).

What is unclear is exactly how to correct them, and that is cause for serious debate. The American Academy of Pediatrics recommends that parents avoid spanking in lieu of other forms of punishment, including consequences, withheld privileges, and time-outs.

It is imperative that you discuss this issue thoroughly before getting married. If your spouse-to-be was paddled as a child, he or she may be predisposed to doing the same thing with your own kids. If you were merely given time-outs when you were naughty, you may be vehemently opposed to physical punishment. At the first sign of offspring misbehavior, your tempers could flare.

worth thinking about

▶ **Your views** on discipline may change abruptly once you see the cherubic face of your firstborn. Likewise, you may chuck your pacifist views after witnessing your child's first temper tantrum. It is impossible to know how you will react until you actually become a parent.

▶ **Since there is** no test or formal rule book, parenting skills are developed by trial and error. Prayer is your biggest ally.

▶ **You don't want** to be a bully, but being a wishy-washy parent will also do your children a disservice. Be firm, fair, and consistent.

> *Correct your children, and they will be wise; children out of control disgrace their mothers.*
> Proverbs 29:15, CEV

Will you make good parents?

There is no friendship, no love, like
that of the parent for the child.

Henry Ward Beecher

76 question

What part will spirituality play?

Most couples learn early on that it's easier to produce a child than it is to raise one. Not only must you provide for their physical needs—food, shelter, and clothing—but you must provide for their spiritual needs as well. Your job is to be their role models of faith. In order to have a happy and tranquil home, faith must be an integral part of everyday life. How do you and your intended anticipate incorporating faith into the raising of your own children someday?

answer

Parenting is undoubtedly one of the most frightening—and important—endeavors you will ever undertake. It will be your job as parents to nurture the faith of your children and help sustain it as they mature. Here are some ideas for doing that. Make prayer a family thing: pray before every meal, and encourage your kids to pray for everyday events and relationships. Incorporate God talk: Talk about God as casually as you talk about the weather.

All the tips and tricks in the world are pointless if you don't focus on Christ. "Come near to God and he will come near to you" (James 4:8, NIV). Without question, the best offensive weapon in your parenting arsenal will be prayer; it impacts the parenting journey more than all the support groups and parenting books combined.

If you're willing to do whatever it takes to build a solid Christian family, look no further than your heavenly Father. He will provide you with all the tools you need if you put Him at the center of your home. Parenting is a hard job, but it's one of the most rewarding jobs in the world.

worth thinking about

▶ **Parenting is all** uncharted territory; you learn as you go. Don't expect to be an expert the minute you and your spouse get home from the hospital with your newborn.

▶ **Discuss any denominational** differences before you have children. Do you agree on infant baptism or dedication? How important do you consider religious instruction? Do you plan to take your child to the church nursery and then later to Sunday school?

▶ **Once you are** getting ready to start a family, consider taking a parenting class. Parenting classes are available through local communities and online.

> *You must love the LORD your God with all your heart, all your soul, and all your strength. And you must commit yourselves wholeheartedly to these commands that I am giving you today. Repeat them again and again to your children. Talk about them when you are at home and when you are on the road, when you are going to bed and when you are getting up.*
>
> Deuteronomy 6:5–7, NLT

▼

What family quirks will you discontinue?

Hopefully you grew up in an idyllic setting with parents who were crazy about you and siblings who deeply respected you. But chances are there were some family quirks you'd just as soon not repeat in your own family. While you are shaped by your family upbringing, you don't necessarily have to duplicate it. What you need is a plan to change the things you didn't like about your own family—or don't like about your intended's family—or you will be liable to repeat them in your own.

answer

▼

Parenting style comes from who you are, what you know, and what you've experienced. Children generally rationalize, walk, talk, communicate, and treat others the way their parents did. They also come with a similar set of values. Patterns of behavior are passed down, both the good patterns and the bad, so if you aren't careful, some of the problems from childhood will seep into your future marriage.

Many family units are brimming with admirable qualities like unconditional love, mutual respect, and ease in demonstrating affection, but many families have problems. Less-admirable family characteristics like addiction, excessive anger and discipline, lackadaisical and overly permissive parents, strained sibling relationships, lack of spiritual focus, and an atmosphere of confrontation are also sometimes present.

Unfortunately, you may be too close to the situation to be able to objectively analyze your family and look for trouble spots. As you talk with your spouse-to-be about this question, respect his or her feedback and allow for constructive criticism.

Identifying areas of concern is half the battle and is the first step in eradicating these concerns from your future life together. With some hard work, cycles of behavior can be broken and turned into positives. You need a plan of attack and a willingness to work together.

worth thinking about

▶ **The parents** with the biggest advantage are the ones who grew up in healthy, godly households. If that's not you or your intended, you'll have to work harder at getting what you didn't have the first time around.

▶ **As you work** through this question, be sure to be gentle when you discuss the problems within your respective families. Avoid bashing, and be constructive.

▶ **New ways** of relating might be awkward at first, but after a while they will become like second nature.

> *What is past is past. Today we start anew, and what we do today will make our life for tomorrow.*
> William Thomson Hanzsche

78

question

What role will your extended family have?

To answer this question you'll want to describe your ideal vision of the relationship your kids will have with your parents along with the parents of your significant other. In some cultures, extended families play a key role in the upbringing of children, to the point where many all live together. The American family has gotten away from that tradition. Do you want daily contact with your respective families or do you want something more sporadic? What role will your parents play in the lives of your future children?

answer

Obviously, if you are more than a day's drive away, their influence on your family life will be minimal. If they live across the street, however, your relationship will be cozier and potentially more volatile.

When the time comes, involving your family in the lives of your children can be a tremendous blessing. In a sense, your extended family is your safety net—especially the grandparents. Grandparents provide love, financial assistance, attention, and a strong sense of belonging to their grandchildren.

Take advantage of their wisdom. When you first become a parent you will be overwhelmed with insecurities. *What if I make a mistake? What if my kids get hurt? What if I am a terrible parent?*

A close relationship with your extended family would be wonderful, but problems might also arise. Grandparents sometimes have trouble letting go.

You'll definitely need to establish boundaries, but at the same time be sensitive to the needs of your families— especially your parents. Many parents dream of the day they will be grandparents, so don't rob them of that joy.

worth thinking about

▶ Once you have children, you will spend more time with those family members who also have children than with those who don't.

▶ When it comes to disputes between parents and grandparents, it's wise to find common ground. As long as you both have the best interests of the children uppermost in your minds, things will work out.

▶ Some members of your extended families will have undesirable behaviors. That doesn't necessarily mean that a relationship is off-limits. Obviously, there need to be safeguards and boundaries. Be more concerned about safeguarding your children than pacifying your family.

> *Fools are headstrong and do what they like; wise people take advice.*
> Proverbs 12:15, THE MESSAGE

question

What are your current assets and liabilities?

Very few people get a charge out of looking at their balance sheets. Dissecting your assets and comparing them to your liabilities can be depressing, but this is no time to stick your head in the sand. While your decision to marry should definitely not be based on your financial situation, the two of you at least need to know what you are up against when you combine your finances. If there is more red ink on your spreadsheet than black, you have some decisions to make.

answer

Money is understandably a personal issue that can be awkward to discuss before you're married—especially if your financial picture isn't pretty. Since money is one of the things married couples fight about most often, you need to cover some financial territory now. Financial discord is the number one reason for divorce, so this is an important step. You never want to keep secrets once you're married; start divulging your entire financial picture now.

Depending upon your financial aptitude and attitude toward money, there will likely be a painful adjustment period when you combine your finances with your soon-to-be spouse's. It's helpful to go into marriage knowing what you are worth—from a financial standpoint.

Assets are your worldly possessions, the things you own that can be converted into cash. Examples of assets are cash, bank accounts, securities and investments, pensions and retirement plans, life insurance policies, real estate, vehicles, home furnishings, and jewelry.

Liabilities are your debts, or the money you owe. Examples of liabilities are mortgages, auto and other loans, credit card balances, and bills due. Ideally, you have far more assets than liabilities, but it takes a while to build that kind of equity.

Marriage is a partnership, so both of you need to be well informed. Financial ignorance is not bliss.

worth thinking about

▶ Some couples sign prenuptial agreements to safeguard their finances. Since divorce is not an acceptable escape clause from the covenant of marriage, prenuptial agreements only show a lack of trust.

▶ As you look at your possessions, don't forget that God is the giver of all things. You are simply a steward.

▶ To calculate your combined net worth, use documents like credit card, bank, and investment statements. Assess your financial health as a couple.

> *Listen carefully to me, and you will enjoy the very best foods.*
> Isaiah 55:2, CEV

80

Should you have separate checking accounts?

Genesis 2:24 states, "That's why a man will leave his own father and mother. He marries a woman, and the two of them become like one person" (CEV). But does that "oneness" have to apply to money, too? You'll be going to your wedding with two homes, two cars, two sets of family, and two bank accounts. After you are Mr. and Mrs., those things will be comingled. The question is, will you maintain two individual checking accounts or join forces in one?

answer ▼

This question actually pertains to both checking accounts and debit cards. A debit card offers the convenience of a credit card but the limits of cash. This helps you avoid spending money you don't have.

Many married couples have one joint checking account, while others—especially those in which both the bride and groom have been in the workforce for a while—have their own, and possibly even another household account. What's right for you?

There are several problems with sharing one joint account. First, there's the whole who-has-the-checkbook routine, which can be a huge inconvenience. Second, the one who controls the checkbook has a certain degree of power and authority over the other. If you are true marriage partners, that could cause some hurt feelings.

It is important for both of you to have some financial freedom. That means you have some of your own discretionary money to spend. Having some of your own funds helps you feel like you haven't given yourself up completely in order to be married. With that in mind, it is advantageous to have separate accounts. However, you still need to be held accountable and make sure you live within your budget. Don't hide your spending from your spouse-to-be, or you will lose trust.

worth thinking about

- ▶ If you are shopping for a checking account, be sure to find out if there is a minimum balance, a limit on how many checks you can write, if there is overdraft protection, and how much the bank charges for overdrafts.

- ▶ Sharing one joint checking account will encourage you to work toward your goals together. There will be a greater sense of sharing and mutual accountability.

- ▶ If you have a checking account, it is important that you reconcile it every month. Good software programs can help you do that in a flash.

> *A devout life does bring wealth, but it's the rich simplicity of being yourself before God. Since we entered the world penniless and will leave it penniless, if we have bread on the table and shoes on our feet, that's enough.*
>
> 1 Timothy 6:6–8, THE MESSAGE

81

question

How will you handle spending decisions?

The New Testament addresses the subject of money more than any other subject besides the kingdom of God. The message is clear that people are to treasure relationships more than things. Still, you are in the world, which means you need to earn money to survive. It's in the spending of money where trouble begins. Once you're married, there will be two of you dipping your hands into the household's proverbial cookie jar. Which items will get the go-ahead and which will get the kibosh?

answer

Your views on money—how much you love it, how you earn it, and how you spend it—tell a lot about you. How will your money personality jibe with your soon-to-be mate's?

Since you can't possibly run every single purchase past each other once you're married, you will have to decide on a comfortable spending limit. Do you need the other's permission before you spend $50? $100? $500? Keep in mind that if the limit is too restrictive, you will both be more likely to sneak around the limit and hide purchases. You don't want that to happen, but you do need to maintain a modicum of control.

Be careful not to assume that the one making the most money should automatically have a bigger say on how it's spent. You will both be contributing to the marriage, and both should have a voice. Making financial decisions as a team is the healthiest and most amenable approach to money.

On a tight budget you must limit your spending. Decide ahead of time how much you will spend on daily living purchases such as groceries and clothing for the family, and how much you will spend on big-ticket items like furniture and electronics. Then make sure you keep the lines of communication open.

worth thinking about

▶ **Even if you** have separate accounts, you should avoid the "this is mine and this is yours" mentality. Marriage is a partnership, and your money is joint property.

▶ **As you discuss** spending limits and how you will make big spending decisions, remember that you both need to feel comfortable with the guidelines you establish.

▶ **No matter what,** never use money as a weapon. Remember that you aren't children who get an allowance for good behavior. You are both adults who deserve respect. Give each other the benefit of the doubt until you have cause for concern.

> *No one can serve two masters. For you will hate one and love the other; you will be devoted to one and despise the other. You cannot serve both God and money.*
> Matthew 6:24, NLT

82

Who will be responsible for paying the bills?

Managing money is an ugly business. Life would be so much more fun if everything you wanted was free. But since you don't live in that kind of utopia, someone has to make payments and keep Uncle Sam off your back. Who will it be? Keeping your new family financially solvent by paying the bills each month is a critical aspect of a healthy marriage. Who will get the honor of managing the money in your marriage?

answer

It's best to have one person in charge who is the one to actually sit down and pay the bills once a month. This simplifies the process and increases the likelihood that it will get done.

But who should it be? The person who should pay the bills is the one who is able to balance a checkbook and has an affinity for numbers. If you are both the creative type, picking the one who is the most detail-oriented and responsible would be the logical move. Who in the couple is strongest in this area?

Plan to evaluate your system occasionally to make adjustments so that all bills can be paid on time and any adverse effects on your credit ratings can be minimized. Remember that you can always shift responsibilities, but don't plan to do it too frequently. The one who pays the bills should have strong knowledge of your household's payment history.

When it comes time to deal with the IRS, you have a few choices. If you're brave and your taxes are simple enough, you can do your taxes yourself. If the idea of filling out a tax form gives both you and your sweetheart a stomachache, consider hiring an accountant. You will still need to do some record-keeping, however, so you can turn over the appropriate figures to your tax adviser.

worth thinking about

▶ **Managing the household** finances is a huge job, and the one who volunteers to do it should be rewarded. That means the other will need to pick up the slack somewhere else on the to-do list.

▶ **If your income** is steady and predictable, consider streamlining bill payments by setting up automatic payments or online payments with all your creditors. That way you won't have to write many checks out each month.

▶ **To make life** easier when tax time rolls around, be sure to use a good software program to keep track of your expenses.

He is rich or poor according to what he is, not according to what he has.
Henry Ward Beecher

83

question

What do your credit reports look like?

The world revolves around credit: personal credit, business credit, and international credit. Even the United States, the richest nation in the world, borrows money from other countries. As two single people, you each have a credit history—good or bad—that you will be bringing with you to your marriage. That history could have far-reaching implications regarding your financial goals. Do you have any idea what your credit report contains or what your credit score is?

answer

A credit report is a record of your credit activities. It contains information on the credit card accounts and loans you have, their balances, and payment timeliness. It reports if you've ever been sued, filed for bankruptcy, or been arrested. It lists the names of those who have requested your credit report during the past twelve months. It even lists where you've lived and your job history.

Potential creditors use this information to either approve or reject your applications for credit, insurance, a lease, or even employment. A good credit score means it will be easier for you to get a loan at a lower interest rate. A bad one means you might not get that new job or the home you've always dreamed of. Your credit history stays on your report for seven years.

It only makes sense, therefore, to safeguard your credit rating by paying your bills on time and not taking on more debt than you can manage. It also behooves you to review your credit report before you make purchases like houses and cars when you need credit. Check yours and that of your betrothed before you get married.

Unfortunately, errors are not unusual. If you find some, contact your consumer credit reporting agency immediately. If the errors can be substantiated, incorrect data will be removed.

worth thinking about

▶ **You are entitled** to one free credit report every twelve months from each of the three nationwide consumer credit reporting companies—Equifax, Experian, and TransUnion. A report can be requested by going to www.annualcreditreport.com.

▶ **Beware of credit** repair scams. You hear ads all the time on daytime and late-night cable TV for credit repair services. The only things that truly fix your credit problems are time, paying your bills when due, and getting out of debt.

▶ **Be diligent** in correcting errors and improving your credit score.

> *Just as the rich rule the poor,*
> *so the borrower is servant to the lender.*
> Proverbs 22:7, NLT

question

How will you manage your debt?

Barely scraping by from paycheck to paycheck is no way to live. When you live hand to mouth, it takes only one emergency to lose everything. Getting married means you are committed to building a future together, and that includes your financial future. If you are going into your marriage with a substantial amount of debt, you have two choices: you can pay down your debt before you put that ring on your finger, or you can come up with a plan for extinguishing it after.

answer

Many people live far beyond their means and purchase high-priced homes and luxury cars they can't afford. To finance all of this extravagance they accrue frightening amounts of debt.

As you enter into holy matrimony, you need to discuss what you are going to do about your existing debt. Will you each be responsible for handling the debt you are bringing with you, or will it become a joint problem? Ideally, you should clean up your balance sheet before the wedding so that you have one less stress to worry about as newlyweds.

If you are in financial trouble, there are some things you can do. To begin, prioritize your debt by first paying off the credit cards with the highest interest rates, and then focus on the payments that are most critical and can get you in the most trouble if you default.

Second, contact your creditors and work out modified payment plans. If you are forthcoming with them, they are usually eager to help. You can also seek the advice of a reputable credit counseling agency; but do your homework before signing up. Finally, you can consider debt consolidation, which would lump all your debt into one easy payment. Avoid bankruptcy at all costs.

Once you are married, start off on the right foot by agreeing to a budget and sticking to it.

worth thinking about

▶ **If you can't pay** for a purchase in cash, you shouldn't make the purchase at all. Don't spend what you don't have. You will spend less if you pay in cold, hard cash.

▶ **Pay down** your debt by having a sale and liquidating some of your expensive toys, or sell your spiffy new car and buy a more modest used one instead.

▶ **Call your credit** card companies and request a lower interest rate. If you threaten to switch to their competitor, card issuers will often oblige. They'll sometimes even waive late charges and annual fees.

> *Let love be your only debt! If you love others, you have done all that the Law demands.*
> Romans 13:8, CEV

question

▼

How much money will you make together?

In marriage, it shouldn't be "my money and your money," it should be "our money," even if you maintain separate accounts for your spending money. You will be maintaining a household together, so in order to budget properly, you must know what you have to work with. If both of you will be working after the wedding, what will your combined income be? What do you anticipate earning in one year, in five years? Are you upwardly mobile or in a downward spiral?

answer

▼

You should not only determine what your combined income will be at the onset of your marriage, but you should also estimate what your earnings will be in the near future. If you are on the fast track for a promotion, you'll want to take that into consideration when working on your budget. If you are going to be quitting work to go back to school, your income will also be impacted.

It can be especially awkward if the bride makes more money than the groom. Even though most people think of themselves as modern and progressive, deep-seated traditionalism exists. They may not admit it, but many women would love to be supported—at least partially—

and most men have been raised to financially take care of their families.

Some occupations pay more than others no matter what your gender is. That's why it's important to understand your purpose and not just choose an occupation based solely on its earning potential. No matter what your paycheck says, you should do what God has called you to do.

worth thinking about

▶ It may be difficult to pool your finances when you first get married because you've been accustomed to spending without consulting anyone else. Remember that you are building a life together.

▶ Before you can safely plan your wedding, honeymoon, and future living arrangements, you need to know what your income looks like.

▶ Once you ascertain what your combined income will be, you need to figure out if it is enough to handle your expenses. If not, one of you will need to look for a more lucrative job or you may need to lower your standards.

When the LORD your God brings you into the land he swore to your fathers, to Abraham, Isaac and Jacob, to give you—a land with large, flourishing cities you did not build, houses filled with all kinds of good things you did not provide, wells you did not dig, and vineyards and olive groves you did not plant—then when you eat and are satisfied, be careful that you do not forget the LORD, who brought you out of Egypt, out of the land of slavery.
Deuteronomy 6:10–12, NIV

question

What percentage will you each contribute?

Unfortunately, as you grow older the days of looking forward to picking up your mail with great anticipation will grow dim. Instead of receiving letters, greeting cards, and the occasional check, you're more likely to receive bills, bills, and more bills! That means you'll have to devise a plan for paying them. As a couple, will you split them fifty-fifty, or will one of you have the job of paying the majority of the bills while the other focuses on spending money on other things?

answer

There are about as many ways to divvy up the bills as there are bills in the first place. Some couples simply split the bills in half and pay those each month. Others divide bills based on who spent the money, especially when it comes to items like department store statements and personal credit cards. Other couples have one partner pay the utilities and the other pay everything else.

It's much easier to pay the bills based on a percentage. If one partner makes 75 percent of the income, he or she should pay 75 percent of the general household bills, and the remainder should be absorbed by the other partner. It's always best to have one person responsible for paying the bills. Upon receipt of each paycheck, the other automatically deposits the allotted percentage into the checking account of the bill payer. This approach is seamless and foolproof.

Of course, you need to decide what's fair in your own situation. Perhaps you want to handle shared household expenses in the manner outlined above, but you want to pay for your own personal things separately. No one system works for all couples, so discuss your best option and then stick with it. But keep equity in mind. You both need to pay your fair share and not take advantage of your loved one.

worth thinking about

▶ **Be prepared** to revisit this as your circumstances change. Children, job changes, and other events may dictate a modification of your responsibilities.

▶ **The person** who is the primary breadwinner doesn't necessarily have to be the one who actually pays the bills. Pick the person who is the best money manager for that job.

▶ **There will be times** in your marriage when you will find yourselves in a financial valley. Make a pledge now to sit down calmly to strategize about the situation with cool heads and solidarity.

> *Give, and you will receive. Your gift will return to you in full—pressed down, shaken together to make room for more, running over, and poured into your lap. The amount you give will determine the amount you get back.*
>
> Luke 6:38, NLT

question

How do you like to spend your money?

Do you scour the Internet for the best deal on the hottest new video game, or is waiting in line overnight to get concert tickets more your idea of a good time? Do you dream of dining out at a five-star restaurant every night, or is taking in a round of golf more your speed? Everyone has different passions; it's too bad these passions have to cost money. When it comes to spending your hard-earned coin, what do you like to splurge on?

answer

Billy Graham once said, "If a person gets his attitude toward money straight, it will help straighten out almost every other area in his life." In most areas of life, attitude is everything, including how you like to spend your money.

There's nothing wrong with allocating funds for entertainment and material goods; it's all a matter of perspective and moderation. Life shouldn't be all work and drudgery. After your financial obligations are met, you've put some money in savings, and you've tithed, go ahead and spend some money on things that make you happy.

Perhaps the question shouldn't be what you like to spend your money on, but rather how your extravagances are compatible with those of your spouse-to-be. If you have decidedly different interests, you might clash—particularly if the ventures are costly. It's not critical that you always enjoy spending money on the same things, but if you don't have some common interests, bitterness might creep into your relationship. You also need to put your soon-to-be spouse's interests above your own from time to time.

In a recent survey of more than twelve thousand people nationwide, Harris Interactive, a market research firm, asked respondents if they found more happiness in spending money on activities or on acquiring things. Most people chose the experiential purchase. Rather than just buying stuff, build some memories.

worth thinking about

▶ **The Bible says,** "Keep your lives free from the love of money, and be satisfied with what you have" (Hebrews 13:5, GNT). Rather than having the best of everything, consider donating some of your wealth to those who are suffering around the world.

▶ **The rug can** be pulled out from beneath you at any time, so be prudent enough with your money that you don't spend yourself right out of your home.

▶ **Find some fun** ways to spend money together—go on a vacation or start a new hobby rather than going it alone.

> *Do you gain anything if you win the whole world but lose your life? Of course not!*
> Mark 8:36, GNT

88

question

How do you measure financial success?

In this world, success is measured by the size of your bank account, your investment portfolio, or the title on your business card. Success is the recognition you receive, the trophies on your mantel, or the number of cars in your garage. Yet everyone has different definitions of *success* and what it takes for fulfillment. What do you consider being financially successful, and how important is it that you attain financial success?

answer

These days, the prosperity gospel is everywhere—in churches, on television, in corporations, and in bookstores. As a matter of fact, a keyword search for *financial success* on amazon.com brought up more than twenty-four thousand hits.

For some people, being financially successful means having a large Swiss bank account and loads of disposable income. Is that how you measure success? Or are you aiming for something more basic like financial independence and a simpler life? The challenge is that success is in the eye of the beholder—it could mean one thing to you, but something entirely different to your significant other.

Of course, your financial goals as a couple should encourage you to be self-sufficient, to be able to provide for yourselves and your family, to enjoy life, and to have a secure retirement. Discuss what financial success means to you beyond that, and aim for some semblance of agreement.

What often happens is that young people set out on their own with something to prove and dreams to pursue. Then, as life unfolds, their perspectives change and their goals are tempered. Success becomes less about making millions and more about being happy.

Too much emphasis on monetary accomplishment can be dangerous. Abraham Lincoln pointed that out when he said, "Intoxicated with unbroken success, we have become too self sufficient to feel the necessity of redeeming and preserving grace, too proud to pray to the God that made us."

worth thinking about

▶ **True success** is unattainable if you leave God out of the equation.

▶ **Be careful** not to allow your self-esteem to be too intricately woven with financial success. One's true worth comes only from God.

▶ **One measure** of financial success is being able to enjoy life with no debt.

> *Watch out! Be on your guard against all kinds of greed; a man's life does not consist in the abundance of his possessions.*
> Luke 12:15, NIV

question

What is your desired standard of living?

This question is a great offshoot of the last one, because your level of success will determine your standard of living. The term *standard of living* refers to societal quality of life and takes into account such variables as access to goods and services, socioeconomic fluidity, and level of education. Before you march down the aisle, you should have a discussion about how you hope to see your lifestyle take shape.

answer

In the past, a working man could support his entire family on his income. But as societal expectations became loftier and loftier, that became impossible. No longer are families satisfied with only one vehicle and a one-car garage, a modest three-bedroom home, children sharing rooms, all meals at home, and no-frills vacations. Now everything is supersized.

If you and your future mate come from different socioeconomic backgrounds, you may have different expectations. If you grew up in a low-income neighborhood, for example, going to college, earning a decent living, and having a home of your own would likely make you feel successful. If you grew up among the social elite, however, that same outcome would make you feel like a failure. Somehow you will have to come to terms on your goals to make sure they are compatible.

While *standard of living* pertains to quality of life, its definition is rather nebulous. Not only does its meaning include financial aspects, but it also includes things like life expectancy, health, political and religious freedom, and even the climate in which you live. Oddly enough, many people find they have a better quality of life when they slow down and make less money.

worth thinking about

▶ **Nobody plans** to be poor, but bad choices and circumstances can often deal a pretty sorry hand. That's why it is so critical to work hard and plan for your future.

▶ **Success is one** of the things that are tough to quantify. Donald Trump probably thought he was a financial whiz kid many millions of dollars ago. How about Bill Gates? At what moment in his Microsoft career do you think he could look in the mirror and say he'd made it?

▶ **It is your responsibility** to care for those less fortunate: "If anyone has material possessions and sees his brother in need but has no pity on him, how can the love of God be in him?" (1 John 3:17, NIV).

> *The answer's simple: Live right, speak the truth, despise exploitation, refuse bribes, reject violence, avoid evil amusements. This is how you raise your standard of living! A safe and stable way to live. A nourishing, satisfying way to live.*
>
> Isaiah 33:15–16, THE MESSAGE

question

90

Are you a saver or a spender?

Some people spend money like it's going out of style but find they have little to show for it. Others are downright scrooge-like in their spending habits and have a hard time parting with any money. Being an overzealous spender or an overzealous saver can have serious relationship ramifications. Fortunately, most people fall somewhere between these two extremes. How about you and your intended? Do you have similar philosophies when it comes to saving? If not, how are they different?

answer

Perhaps it's not a matter of whether you are a saver or a spender; perhaps it is a matter of degree of where you fall in those categories and where your prospective mate falls. A significant mismatch could eventually precipitate a contest of wills. Being a spender isn't all bad, but having two of them in a marriage can be tough.

Oftentimes, people don't know how much they actually spend. Try this experiment: For one month write down every purchase you make and its cost, from a tiny tin of mints to a new suit. At the end of the month take a look at your list. You'll be surprised to see how just how much you spent in certain categories, and how many of your expenditures were frivolous and unnecessary. The challenge is to minimize those that produce the least value.

Being a strict saver also has its disadvantages. You probably know people who won't spend a red cent on themselves and are always saving for a rainy day. What if that rainy day never comes? Savers are often so focused on the future that they forget to have fun in the present. Being too frugal can cause you to miss out on life and will probably annoy your mate, unless of course your mate is the same way!

Whether you are a saver or a spender, strive for a healthy balance.

worth thinking about

▶ If you are trying to cut back on your spending, reduce the amount of cash you carry around. It tends to disappear easily and leaves no paper trail.

▶ You probably know people who always like to buy the oddest gadgets just to be different and then banish them to the back of the garage after the novelty wears off. Be smart and invest in things you'll use long-term.

▶ Don't save your good china and crystal only for special occasions. Since no one is assured of tomorrow, live a little.

> *It is wonderful to think how men of very large estates not only spend their yearly income, but are often actually in want of money. It is clear, they have not value for what they spend.*
> Samuel Johnson

91

question

▼

Will you create and stick to a budget?

Just hearing the word *budget* induces anxiety in most people, especially those creative self-indulgent types who have trouble staying within the lines. There are zillions of books available on the subject because most people have a hard time managing their own money. Getting married calls for many adjustments, especially financially. A budget can be a great tool to help you get a handle on your income, expenses, and goals. Do the two of you plan on establishing a budget and then living within it?

answer

▼

As much as you may recoil from the thought, it is important to establish a budget, especially when you are just starting out and have more-meager earnings. It just makes sense to pay close attention to your finances so you can get the most for your money. If you want to get past living hand to mouth and enjoy financial security, a budget can help with that. Budgeting isn't just about deprivation; it's all about saving more and spending less.

The first thing you need to do is determine your combined monthly income. Then decide which of your monthly expenses are absolutely necessary and subtract them from your income. These would be items like rent, car payments, parking expenses, and utilities.

From what remains, allocate a certain amount that will automatically go into savings every month without fail. This amount will be based on your short-term and long-term goals. Be realistic because you do not want to tap into that savings account under any circumstances, except perhaps in a life-or-death situation.

Once that's all figured out, give yourself an allowance for discretionary expenses. Creating a budget doesn't have to be a complicated process. It should be simple and flexible and agreed to by both parties.

worth thinking about

▶ A budget should be a fluid document. If you get a raise, reformulate the amount of money you are saving and giving yourself in the form of allowance.

▶ There are some great money-management software tools that make establishing a budget a snap. They'll also help you manage your household finances after that.

▶ Be sure to create an emergency fund and agree on what constitutes an emergency. It should be equal to at least six months' take-home pay.

> Honor the LORD with your wealth and with the best part of everything you produce. Then he will fill your barns with grain, and your vats will overflow with good wine.
>
> Proverbs 3:9–10, NLT

question
▼
Who will provide health insurance?

Health insurance has become a politically charged issue in this country, and for good reason. The number of people without health insurance coverage rose from 44.8 million in 2005 to 47 million in 2006. That's approximately 15.8 percent of the population, according to the U.S. Census Bureau. Unfortunately, more and more employers are cutting back on benefits—or eliminating coverage altogether. Once you are married, what kind of health insurance will you have, and who will provide it?

answer
▼

Health insurance brings peace of mind. Before you get married, review your health insurance options. If you are both covered through work, compare your plans closely to see if it makes sense to have joint coverage through one policy or to maintain separate ones. Many companies cover only the employee and exclude spouses and children, so check the fine print or ask someone in human resources.

With many carriers you have only thirty days after your marriage to add your spouse without providing evidence of insurability, which may mean an unnecessary physical exam after that period, so don't procrastinate.

While you're at it, you should also review your other insurance policies, including auto, long-term disability, and either homeowner's or renter's insurance. You may have some duplication, and adjustments may need to be made based on your combined assets. You'll also need to change your beneficiaries on the policies that require them.

It's disquieting to think about what might happen in the event of your death, but you'll want life insurance to protect those you leave behind.

worth thinking about

▶ **Besides your insurance** policies, you will also need to change the beneficiaries listed on your investment accounts, IRAs, 401(k) plans, and bank accounts.

▶ **If you drop** one of your property insurance policies, make sure you have enough coverage to protect things like jewelry, electronics, and collectibles. You may need separate riders for those items.

▶ **Do your homework** before purchasing life insurance. Seek the advice of a certified financial planner on these decisions and other major investments.

Trust God from the bottom of your heart; don't try to figure out everything on your own. Listen for God's voice in everything you do, everywhere you go; he's the one who will keep you on track. Don't assume that you know it all. Run to God! Run from evil! Your body will glow with health, your very bones will vibrate with life!

Proverbs 3:5–8, The Message

question

Are you open and honest with each other?

Honesty is the cornerstone of any healthy relationship, be it marriage, friendship, or business. Honesty breeds trust and fosters intimacy. Dishonesty, even telling the smallest untruths, can destroy trust and intimacy. At the same time, one has to wonder if honesty is always the best policy when being transparent can hurt the one you love the most. How important will honesty be in your marriage? Should you commit to being completely open with each other no matter what?

answer

Honesty is one of the most basic needs in marriage. Without it, trust cannot be built and total intimacy is infeasible. But if you tell everyone how you feel, no matter what, your relationships will be riddled with friction.

That presents a dilemma. Is being 100 percent truthful with your sweetheart a good idea, or are there times you should avoid spilling your guts? The best policy is probably a combination of the two. You must certainly be open about the big things, but if your partner gets a bad haircut or botches the meat loaf, it's not always necessary to share your opinion.

One of the most difficult things is telling your partner how you feel. Sometimes people aren't completely honest with the ones they love for fear of hurting their feelings. "Love must be sincere" (Romans 12:9, NIV). It is impossible to be sincere if you are always saying what you think your mate wants to hear rather than speaking from your heart. Hoarding your feelings can result in a buildup of resentment and anger until there is an emotional explosion.

worth thinking about

▶ **There is a big** difference between zipping your lip and telling a lie. Dishonesty is highly destructive to a marriage.

▶ **Honesty is a two-way** street. Your partner is more likely to be open and honest with you if you, too, are open and honest and make it easy to share without fear of recrimination. That means holding judgment at bay and really listening.

▶ **If something is** bothering you, your mate will probably know something is wrong. If you hold back, your sweetheart's imagination will likely be far worse than reality.

> *Do not let any unwholesome talk come out of your mouths, but only what is helpful for building others up according to their needs, that it may benefit those who listen.*
> Ephesians 4:29, NIV

question
▼
Are you a good listener?

"Can you hear me now?" has become a well-known saying due to the popularity of an advertising campaign for a wireless company. People often have trouble hearing one another because they are so busy focusing on themselves and their own thoughts. Similarly, a lot of marriages are troubled because husband and wife don't listen to one another. They may have ears that hear, but they don't genuinely listen, which leads to a tremendous amount of frustration. Are you and your betrothed practiced in the art of listening?

answer
▼

Good communication comprises the sending and receiving of clear messages. Unfortunately, men and women often have different ways of communicating. Good communication is a critical component for a strong and healthy marriage. Listening is usually the biggest roadblock. Few people have trouble talking, but listening?

There is a big difference between hearing and listening. If you are actively listening, you should not only be able to repeat what the other says, but you should also be able to communicate the feeling with which it has been shared.

More than half of all communication is nonverbal, so watch facial expressions and gestures, which will give you clues about how your partner is feeling. Body language goes both ways, though, so show you are listening by maintaining good eye contact, nodding, and making affirming sounds.

Listening is one of the best ways to show someone you care. Couples who have taken the time to really learn how to listen have the happiest, healthiest, and most rewarding relationships.

worth thinking about

▶ **Never mentally prepare** a quick response as your partner is talking. If you're busy thinking about what you're going to say next, you can't possibly be paying attention to what is being said.

▶ **It also helps** to clarify what you've heard. The best way to do that is to ask relevant follow-up questions. Don't parrot your partner by repeating exactly what has been said, but rephrase: "What I hear you saying is . . ."

▶ **As you are listening** to your mate, avoid judging. That doesn't mean you have to agree with everything, but be an empathetic listener.

> *Come and listen to my counsel. I'll share my heart with you and make you wise. I called you so often, but you wouldn't come. I reached out to you, but you paid no attention. You ignored my advice and rejected the correction I offered.*
> Proverbs 1:23–25, NLT

question

How do you like to show affection?

Many schools prohibit what teenagers call PDAs, or public displays of affection. You may think that hand-holding and kissing are no longer obligatory once you have a marriage license and sex is morally acceptable, but marital affection is vital for nurturing intimacy. It's common for men and women, husbands and wives, and boyfriends and girlfriends to have different takes on the importance of such endearments. Do the two of you like to show affection in similar ways, or is your relationship bankrupt in the area of affection?

answer

One of the most obvious ways you demonstrate your love for your partner is by showing affection, which is the emotional dimension of love. Depending upon your upbringing, you may feel uncomfortable showing affection in public by hugging, kissing, and sweetly nudging. If your parents were affectionate toward each other in front of the kids, you will be more likely to do the same. Conversely, if your parents had a standoffish relationship, it might be difficult to be joined with a gregarious, touchy-feely mate.

Men and women don't always agree on what constitutes affection. For many guys, it is synonymous with sexual foreplay, but to women, it is far more sentimental. Touching is a central aspect of communication. Your sexual relationship will be about more than the physical act of making love; your relationship will also be about the emotional actions that take place all day long when you caress and hold each other.

If your mate has a strong need for affection but you do not, you will need to try to adjust your tastes to meet that need. Similarly, your mate must respect your need to work at it slowly, and not pressure you. Of course there are other forms of affection besides the physical variety. You can express your love with words, with candy and flowers, with a home-cooked meal, or with silly love notes.

worth thinking about

- ▶ **An important first** step in learning how to show affection is to find out what your significant other likes. Favorite food? Favorite recording artist? Favorite flowers? Favorite movie? Favorite sports team? Favorite author? Favorite weekend activity?

- ▶ **Displays of affection** can be playful, spontaneous, tender, and heartfelt, but a combination of all those forms is best. Keep your special one guessing!

- ▶ **Affection is shown** not only to your romantic partner, but also to your friends, family, and even pets. Learning how to demonstrate affection in all these areas will enrich your life.

> *Affection is responsible for nine-tenths of whatever solid and durable happiness there is in our lives.*
> C. S. Lewis

question

▼

How will you manage conflict?

If you've been dating for any length of time, you have probably already experienced some conflict in your relationship. If you haven't yet, well, get ready for some fireworks. Confrontation is a natural part of every relationship, whether it is with your soon-to-be spouse, with family or friends, or with someone you meet in line at the grocery store. What really matters is how you deal with it. Left on its own, conflict can make or break your marriage. What is your strategy for coping with it?

answer

▼

Marital conflict is a guarantee because everyone is imperfect and peppered with character flaws. You and your sweetheart each have your own wants and desires, and they won't always match up. The key is to deal with your anger rather than letting it go unexpressed until it builds up to the point of bitterness. The most common things couples argue about include finances, sex, work, parenting, and housework, but there are plenty of others. Conflict appropriately handled can actually build a relationship. Left unattended, it can destroy it.

There are several critical rules of engagement when it comes to spousal disagreements. On the front line is keeping things in perspective. Learn how to pick your fights, and learn to let some things go. You also want to make sure you know what you're fighting about and not just having a bad day.

It's easy to get carried away in the heat of the moment, but yelling and screaming will get you nowhere. Focus on the issue, rather than character assassination.

What's the bottom line? You're going to fight, so learn how to fight fair.

worth thinking about

▶ **Fight privately**, never in front of family or friends, and especially not in front of any children. These public displays make everyone uncomfortable and unfairly insert others into your business.

▶ **If you're too** angry to discuss a problem rationally, reschedule. That will give you both time to calm down so cooler heads can prevail. The issue may even resolve itself.

▶ **Abuse is never** acceptable in a relationship, no matter what the issue. To stay calm, have your discussion sitting down. Taking a few deep breaths and counting to ten can keep you from saying something you'll regret later.

If our faith is strong, we should be patient with the Lord's followers whose faith is weak. We should try to please them instead of ourselves. We should think of their good and try to help them by doing what pleases them.

Romans 15:1–2, CEV

97

question

Are you able to agree to disagree?

Couples fight for a variety of reasons. They argue to clear the air, resolve issues, release stress, or just vent. More often they fight about inconsequential things like which way the toilet paper roll should go or whether to fold the towels in twos or threes. Even couples who consider themselves kindred spirits don't agree on everything. It helps if you and your betrothed can come to terms with that and agree to disagree on nonessential issues.

answer

To agree to disagree means you set some irreconcilable differences aside to maintain relational harmony. Christians often disagree about the exact interpretation of scripture, but that doesn't mean the conversation ends. Small groups thrive on that kind of friendly banter.

Believe it or not, you aren't always right, and there isn't always a right way and a wrong way to look at things. There are usually valid points on both sides of an argument, so don't demand that your beloved see things exactly as you do. If you find yourselves constantly fighting about the same issues, take a step back and ponder two things: what is the real issue, and does it really matter?

Some issues don't need to be resolved because they just don't matter much in the grand scheme of things. You may disagree on politics, how things should be done around the house, whether your new car should be pearl or white, or what you should name your new baby. If they don't impact the overall health and happiness of your marriage, let the disagreements go. In order to agree to disagree successfully in your marriage, however, you both need to concur.

One simple commitment will save you countless sleepless nights. No matter what, never go to bed angry.

worth thinking about

▶ **You can disagree** without being disagreeable. A sure sign of a sound relationship is if you can disagree but hold hands while you are doing it.

▶ **Accepting that you** won't agree on everything will help you save your energy for the big battles rather than the little skirmishes. Don't sweat the small stuff.

▶ **When you are** fighting about an important issue, don't interrupt or belittle. Instead, speak in a calm, respectful voice and maintain good manners. Ranting and raving and carrying on accomplish little.

> *Don't pick on people, jump on their failures, criticize their faults—unless, of course, you want the same treatment. That critical spirit has a way of boomeranging. It's easy to see a smudge on your neighbor's face and be oblivious to the ugly sneer on your own.*
> Matthew 7:1–3, THE MESSAGE

98

question

What are your hot buttons?

Children have brought button-pushing to a high art form. They know exactly what to do to make their parents, siblings, friends, and teachers crazy. They can end up sitting in the principal's office or doing a time-out for their trouble. Spouses have a knack for doing the same thing, sometimes innocently and often intentionally, but they don't get detention. The best way to keep the peace in your marriage will be to stay away from those triggers. But first you need to know what they are.

answer

With the pressures of modern life, there are countless things for couples to fight about. A few of the biggies are money, sex, children, household tasks, communication, substance abuse, and the in-laws. Even the holidays can cause angst. Once you're living together, you'll come to know just which of those areas your intended is most sensitive about.

There are enough reasons to argue without needlessly provoking your mate. Honestly, some people relish a good verbal brawl. If you are that person and are tempted to get into it, think about what's motivating your disposition.

If your mate is particularly argumentative, think about what's causing it. Is stress or anxiety a factor? Is someone else the real target but you're the handiest one to take it out on? Are allergies or an illness a part of it? If you can answer yes to any of these questions, it is time to back off and save the discussion for another day.

When you've resolved your differences, learn how to forgive and move on. Holding a grudge is harmful to your spiritual growth as well, and can disconnect you from God.

worth thinking about

▶ If you do end up bickering, ask yourself if you pushed your mate's buttons and think about what you can do differently next time.

▶ Never use sex as a weapon. If you are upset about something else, never use lovemaking as a bargaining chip. That cheapens it. "Husbands and wives should be fair with each other about having sex" (1 Corinthians 7:3, cev).

▶ You can unintentionally push each other's buttons with the language you choose. Emotion-charged words, your tone of voice, and absolutes like *always* and *never* can escalate tensions.

Fools have short fuses and explode all too quickly; the prudent quietly shrug off insults. Truthful witness by a good person clears the air, but liars lay down a smoke screen of deceit. Rash language cuts and maims, but there is healing in the words of the wise.
Proverbs 12:16–18, THE MESSAGE

99

question
▼
What are effective ways to avoid arguing?

Lovers' spats are about as unavoidable as death and taxes. Tensions rise whenever two people live together. And things are certainly far more complicated with a husband and a wife. While arguments can't be completely sidestepped in your future marriage, you can certainly limit their frequency with some forethought and a few helpful tips. Of course, preventing altercations will make for a more harmonious marriage, but how in the world do you accomplish that?

answer
▼

You are going to think this sounds obvious, but the best way to prevent arguments is to be nice. Practice the Golden Rule, and do unto others as you would have them do unto you. Think about what Jesus would do when you are tempted to jump down your sweetheart's throat. Strive to make more nice comments than critical ones. Instead of making excuses, make apologies. And while you're at it, make suggestions rather than demands.

Another key problem-avoidance tactic is to stay connected. If you ask divorced couples why their marriages were not successful, many of them will tell you they drifted apart. That happens because they simply don't spend enough time together. The pace of life has become so frantic that it's no wonder couples have precious little time for each other.

Ironically, resolving conflict is another great way to derail an argument. If you walk away from a disagreement without a resolution, an emotional wall can be built up, and bitterness will fester. If you refrain from talking about your frustrations, they will build momentum until you rupture and lash out in an angry and hurtful way.

Resolve with your intended that you will both focus on strength training for your relationship.

worth thinking about

▶ **Don't play** the blame game. One way to keep a minor problem from escalating into a big one is to avoid making accusatory statements like "You never" and "You always." Those kinds of overgeneralizations are dangerous and will make your mate defensive.

▶ **If you are** really perturbed with each other, give yourselves a time-out. Walk away and calm down before continuing the discussion.

▶ **If your betrothed** is angry, you don't have to automatically pick up that brick and throw it right back. Show your maturity and demonstrate your love by letting your sweetheart be right sometimes.

A man of knowledge uses words with restraint, and a man of understanding is even-tempered.
Proverbs 17:27, NIV

question

How does your family deal with conflict?

Did you grow up in a home where there was constant bickering but little was resolved? Was your home a dictatorship where one parent ruled without question? Were there healthy discussions and peaceful solutions to family problems? Couples have argued about the same issues since the dawn of time, so you will likely have some of the same issues in your own marriage that your parents had in theirs. How did they handle it when the going got tough?

answer

Exploring how your respective families handle confrontations will give you a clue as to how you will naturally approach conflict as a couple. Your parents are your role models, so the way they handled confrontational situations will seem comfortable and normal to you. The following are a few of the unhealthy ways family units deal with conflict.

The avoidance method is a common one. Many people are uncomfortable with conflict, so they pretend it doesn't exist. They don't raise their voices, but instead they make snide comments and dish out the silent treatment. Issues rarely get resolved, and familial intimacy suffers.

The antagonistic approach is even worse. These families yell, call each other names, and fight in front of other people.

The healthiest conflict management strategy is a collaborative one. These family members are good listeners, openly discuss their feelings, and deal with people directly rather than sulking or backbiting.

If you were raised in a family that dealt with conflict in an unhealthy way, you'll want to discuss what changes you'll make before you get married. Anger, abuse, and violence can be a vicious cycle if left unchecked.

worth thinking about

▶ How did you handle conflict with your siblings? Families are a hodgepodge of different temperaments and levels of maturity, so when you put a variety of people together in a close environment, there are bound to be problems.

▶ According to the National Coalition on Domestic Violence, boys who witness domestic violence are twice as likely to abuse their own wives and children.

▶ If you did not have good family role models on how to manage conflict, consider counseling. Not only will developing this valuable skill help you at home, but it will help you in your other relationships as well.

Any kingdom where people fight each other will end up ruined. And a town or family that fights will soon destroy itself.
Matthew 12:25, CEV

The Last Word

By exploring all the questions in this book you have taken an important step in securing a happy future. You have thought about and discussed with your intended some crucial elements of a mutually satisfying marriage. As with any investment, exercising due diligence is necessary before taking the plunge.

Don't be disappointed if you didn't ace the test; there is no such thing as a perfect marriage. It is impossible to be wildly compatible in all areas of your relationship; there will be times when you are completely enamored with each other and other times when the two of you are like oil and water. But hopefully you are well-matched in the key focus areas, those areas that are most likely to cause you to split up later on: money, sex, and communication.

While a rock-solid commitment is vital for a happy marriage, you must also keep Christ at the center of your relationship. As you are walking down the aisle, remember that He is walking right alongside you.

> *Those marriages generally abound most with love and constancy that are preceded by a long courtship. The passion should strike root and gather strength before marriage be grafted on it.*
> Joseph Addison
>
> *The LORD says, "I will guide you along the best pathway for your life. I will advise you and watch over you....So rejoice in the LORD and be glad, all you who obey him! Shout for joy, all you whose hearts are pure!*
> Psalm 32:8, 11, NLT

**Readers who enjoyed this
book will also enjoy**

100 Answers to 100 Questions About God

100 Answers to 100 Questions About God's Promises

100 Answers to 100 Questions About Loving Your Husband

100 Answers to 100 Questions About Loving Your Wife

100 Answers to 100 Questions About Prayer

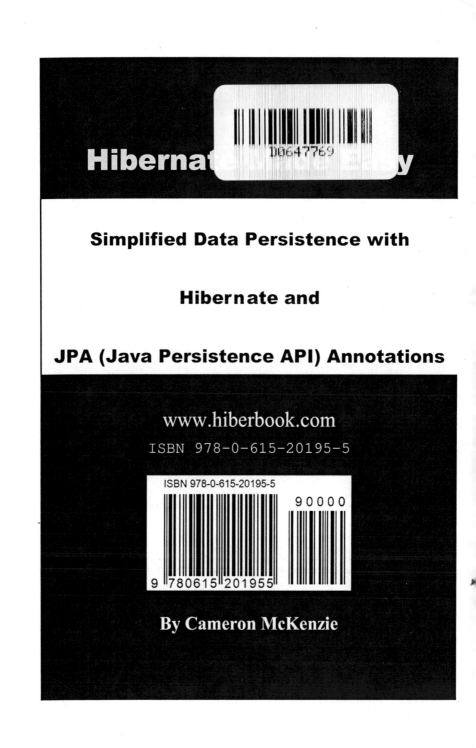

Hibernate Made Easy:
Simplified Data Persistence with Hibernate and JPA Annotations
by Cameron McKenzie

Third Printing (the HibernateUtil fix)

www.hibernatemadeeasy.com
Copyright © 2008 by Cameron McKenzie
Notice of Rights:

Notice of Liability

Trademarks

ISBN 978-0-615-20195-5

Thanks to all the girls at Tim Hortons, especially that cute brunette on drive-thru.

A big thanks to Tun Chang for pointing out the missing HibernateUtil import on page 137! A Tim Hortons coffee is on me, the next time you're on the good side of the border. ☺

And another big thanks to "Amazon Dave," from Ohio, for pointing out the need for clarification on where to put the log4j.properties file. (C:_mycode)

For updates, errratuh, downloads and discussions:
www.hiberbook.com

9

The Required Preamble
About this Book and Stuff

Okay, this is the preamble for the book.

Now, I hesitate to start this book off on a negative note, but one thing I hate is a technology book with a huge preamble. I always feel the need to read preambles, just in case they contain some golden nugget of information that I need to comprehend, lest the rest of the book doesn't make any sense; but usually, pre-ambles don't contain much more than marketing hype, a bunch of information that I already know, and a bunch of other useless information that I have to sift through before I get to the nitty-gritty of how to start using the technology that I'm interested in learning.

Well, I assure you, this preamble is no different than any other useless preamble that you've ever read. If you want to jump right into Hibernate, flip over to the next chapter and start learning. I promise you, this chapter contains nothing pivotal to your intellectual progression as a Hibernate developer. Nor does this preamble contain anything that you need to know in order to start making sense out of the rest of the book. If you want to skip ahead, the only thing you'll miss out on is a quick description of what Hibernate is, all wrapped up inside of the incessant ramblings of a mad man. That's all you'll miss out on, I promise.

I mean, seriously, do I really need to write a 200 page preamble telling you what Hibernate is? It seems that all of the other Hibernate books do, but personally, I just think that's a waste of time. After all, if you actually bought this book, which you obviously did, otherwise you wouldn't be reading this, you probably have a basic understanding of the fact that Hibernate is used to help take the information maintained by your Java programs, and subsequently save that information to a database. And naturally, you would know that Hibernate is good at doing the reverse – that is, taking data from your database, and then seamlessly pulling that data *into* your Java applications. Well, I guess you know it now, regardless, as I've just said it. But my point is, you probably didn't need me to tell that to you in the first place.

And do I really need to tell you how wonderful Hibernate is, or who all the handsome and intelligent people are that are using it? I mean, does it really matter if Hibernate is used heavily by Cisco, or AT&T Labs, or IBM?

If you're reading this book, you're reading it for a reason. Maybe your work has adopted the technology without any input from you whatsoever, and you've got to learn it quickly. If that's the case, you probably don't care who's using Hibernate. Or maybe you're looking for a job, and you've noticed that every good Java related want ad is demanding a certain level of competency with Hibernate. If that's the case, you really don't care that Hibernate is easy to work with, or that it's fairly simple to learn, or that it's implemented in a fairly elegant manner.

If you're reading this book, you're reading it because you need to learn Hibernate, and it doesn't really matter if I tell you how fabulous the technology tastes, or how fragrant the technology smells. If Hibernate really is great, well, you'll figure that out on your own. Maybe you'll love it, maybe you'll hate it, but I'm sure you can make up your own mind on the topic, and you don't need me telling you how I personally believe that Hibernate greatly simplifies the process of managing the persistent state of your Java applications.

No, if you're reading this book, you probably just want to learn about Hibernate, and learn Hibernate quickly, and that's exactly what I want this book to facilitate – the quick, easy, and somewhat fun learning of a very kewl technology – Hibernate.

Well, I guess before I dive into the first chapter, and start discussing how to configure a Hibernate development environment, I should probably do the compulsory discussion about what Hibernate is, so here it goes:

What is Hibernate?

What is Hibernate, you ask? Well, there's a long answers to that, and there's short answers to that. The long answer is covered in the next 400 pages of text. ☺ The short and simple answer? Hibernate makes it easy to save data to, or load data from, a database.

And of course, Hibernate is Java based, and we all love Java. Java's object oriented, it's cross platform, it's fun to code, and it makes you think of that black blood of the soul: Tim Hortons Coffee. Seriously though, Hibernate is real easy, and almost fun to use, especially if you have a bit of a Java background. And it integrates quite naturally into your existing Java programs, too.

What is Java Persistence?

"I keep hearing the term 'Java Persistence.' What does 'Java Persistence' mean?"

When we write Java code, we create objects, and those objects have properties. Here's a simple piece of code. Just by looking at it, I think you can tell what the User's name and password are:

```
User user = new User();      //an object named user is created
user.setName("Cameron");     //name is initialized to Cameron
user.setPassword("n0tte11ing"); //password is initialized to n0tte11ing
```

I think even the uninitiated Java programmer would recognize that we have just created a user named **Cameron** with a password of **n0tte11ing**. We see this type of object creation and property initialization in Java programs all the time. But the problem Java developers always face is figuring out how to take the data associated with their objects and subsequently *persist* it to the database. Basically, persisting the state of your JavaBeans is a challenge, but Hibernate makes the persistence of your Java objects, aka *Java Persistence*, easy.

POJO==Plain Ordinary Java Object == JavaBean = Java Class

Just How Easy is it to use Hibernate?

With a magical and mystical object known as the Hibernate Session, persisting the state of your Java objects is pretty easy. Just look at how readable and understandable the following code snippet is:

```
User user = new User();        //an object named user is created
user.setName("Cameron");       //name is initialized to Cameron
user.setPassword("n0tte1ling");        //password is initialized
Session hibernateSession = HibernateUtil.getSession();
                               //get the magical Hibernate Session
hibernateSession.save(user);       //save the user to the database!
```

The line of code hibernateSession.save(user); saves the state of the user instance to the database. Of course, there's a little bit of plumbing code that needs to go in there to make the whole Hibernate framework work; but setting up that plumbing code really isn't that bad. Overall, Hibernate is real easy to use, fairly easy to set up, and probably the easiest way to manage the persistent state of your domain model objects.

What are JPA Annotations?

JPA (Java Persistence API) annotations greatly simplify persistence programming with Hibernate, but to understand why they're so great, it helps to understand what we needed to do before the introduction of JPA annotations.

The Historical hibernate-mapping.xml File

Hibernate makes persisting the state of your Java objects incredibly simple. However, in order for Hibernate to know where to store your JavaBeans, or how to map the property of a JavaBean to a database column, the developer has to provide a bit of direction to the Hibernate framework. As such, people developing Hibernate based applications in the past had to maintain an unwieldy, monolithic, mapping file that described how to save a given Java object to the database.

So, for example, if you had a class named Tent that had three properties, one called id, one called birthday, and another property called title, you would have to add the following segment to a hibernate-mapping file, and put that mapping file on your Java classpath:

```
<hibernate-mapping>

  <class name="tent.Tent" table="TENT">

    <id name="id" column="id">
      <generator class="native"/>
    </id>
    <property name="birthday" type="timestamp"/>
    <property name="title"/>

  </class>

</hibernate-mapping>
```

Did you hear the one about the guy that went to the psychiatrist, complaining that one night he'd dream that he was a WigWam, and the next he'd dream he was a TeePee? The doctor said he was *too tense*. ☺

POJO==Plain Ordinary Java Object == JavaBean = Java Class

What's wrong with an XML mapping file?

Of course, there is nothing inherently *wrong* with a mapping file, and in fact, thousands of very salacious Hibernate applications that are currently in production use XML mapping files; but having a big XML mapping file, or even many little mapping files, presents a variety of non-lethal, but certainly annoying problems, including the following:

☞ *information about the Java class must be maintained in an external file*

☞ *XML isn't always easy to write*

☞ *with lots of classes, the XML file can become unwieldy and massive*

☞ *errors in one part of the XML file can ricochet all over your Java program*

Anyways, Java 5 introduced a new Java based artifact – the annotation. Basically, an annotation allows you to add detail and information about a Java class, without damaging, disturbing or changing any of the code that is actually found inside a Java class or a Java method. So, instead of using a monolithic mappings file, Hibernate with JPA annotations allows you to completely rid applications of a mapping file, and instead, you can annotate your Java classes like so:

20

A JPA Annotated, Hibernate Entity

```
@Entity
public class Tent {

  private Long id;
  private String title;
  private Date date;

  @Id
  @GeneratedValue
  public Long getId() { return id; }
  private void setId(Long id) {this.id = id;}

  public Date getDate() {return date;}
  public void setDate(Date date) {
    this.date = date;
  }

  public String getTitle() {return title;}
  public void setTitle(String title) {
    this.title = title;
  }

}
```

The **@Entity, @Id and @GeneratedValue** tags you see in the Tent class are JPA annotations, and they replace the need to describe how to persist your Java classes in an external, hibernate-mappings.xml file. Instead of using an external file, each Java class maintains its own mapping information, which is much more natural, and much easier to maintain on a class by class basis. Furthermore, it makes introducing new classes, or even removing persistent classes from your domain model, much, much easier.

If you're using Hibernate, and you have the ability to choose between using annotations or using a hibernate-mappings file, well, it's really not much of a choice. Always use JPA annotations if you have a choice. JPA annotations are much easier to use, easier to maintain, and will help to make your Hibernate development experience a real pleasure.

And that takes us to the whole point of this book. The whole purpose of this book is to show you how to leverage both Hibernate and JPA annotations to simplify your designs and greatly improve the quality of your data-driven, Java based applications.

Creating Some Realistic Expectations

Now, I really want to set an expectation about this book very early on. I hate to disappoint you, but this book is NOT going to cover every single, possible, transcendent, probable, hypothetical or imaginary situation you might encounter in your day to day enterprise programming. I'm sorry, but this book isn't an answer to every single question ever asked about Hibernate. Sorry to disappoint you. ☹

Furthermore, this is not a reference book that will regurgitate every part of the Hibernate or Java Persistence API. For documentation, there are free JavaDoc files you can download from hibernate.org that fairly efficiently, and incredibly accurately, document the technology we'll be discussing in this book.

Books that simply regurgitate existing reference documentation annoy me, and they should annoy you too. I want to teach you how to use Hibernate, and I want to teach it to you as quickly and as efficiently as possible. I want to teach you all of *the most important parts* of the technology, so you can become productive and knowledgeable as quickly as possible. However, I'm not going to cover every single class in the Hibernate API, and I'm not going to document every single annotation in the Java Persistence libraries. If I did that, you'd get bored and lose interest, and with that end, you wouldn't learn anything. As I said before, free documentation exists for Hibernate and JPA. Download it and use it! I know I do. I use it every day. But this book isn't going to regurgitate every little piece of it. I think you as the reader deserve a little bit better than that.

A Tangential Trip Down Memory Lane

You know, when I write a book about technology, I think about that time when I was 16 and my dear old Dad, God bless his soul, took me out for driving lessons. You know what he didn't do? He didn't sit me down and lecture me for an hour about what a car was. *I sorta already knew that.* And he didn't lecture me about all of the neat things you could do with a car. *I'd kinda figured that out too.* No, he took me to an empty parking lot, he put me behind the wheel, he showed me the brake pedal, he showed me the accelerator, he showed me the steering wheel, and he showed me how to put the car into drive. Then he let me drive for a little bit.

From there, he let me gain some speed, he showed me the turn signals, he let me practice, and eventually, we went onto the back streets, and then residential streets, and then we went onto the highway for a bit. Progressively, and one step at a time, my Dad taught me what I needed to know to drive safely and effectively. Eventually, with a bit of practice on my own, I got my drivers license.

But my Dad didn't try to teach me everything there is to know about cars, engines, pavement, bridges and global weather patterns that might affect driving conditions. Some things were never going to be important to me, and there were other things I needed to learn on my own.

I mean, my Dad never taught me the mechanics of the internal combustion engine. If I wanted to be a mechanic, that's something I could learn on my own. My Dad never taught me how to do a burnout, or take a tight corner at an excessive speed. If I wanted to be a stunt driver or a race car driver, those are things I'd have to learn somewhere else. Furthermore, it wouldn't have done me any good to learn those things when I was still trying to master how to shift gears without jack-rabbiting the car. To learn anything, you've got to start with the things that are the most important. Once that is done, you can move into other, more specific areas of concern.

POJO==Plain Ordinary Java Object == JavaBean = Java Class

The way I see it, a technology book should be a lot like learning how to drive a car. This book won't teach you every imaginable aspect of Hibernate. Doing so would not only be impossible to do, but in many cases, it would be a complete waste of your time. On the other hand, this book *will* teach you the most important aspects of Hibernate. This book will teach you, fairly quickly and efficiently, what you need to know to become knowledgeable and productive.

And when I say knowledgeable, I don't mean just in the arena of Hibernate programming. If you read this book, you'll not only gain a fundamental knowledge of how Hibernate works, but you'll also learn some good programming practices and techniques, including a few important design patterns, such as the data access object pattern and the factory pattern. You'll also see how Hibernate can be integrated into a simple, JSP, web-based application. There's a huge amount of information in this book, but again, this is not a reference book, and it's not intended to be the Encyclopedia *Hybernattica*. This book is just intended to be the best book around for helping you to learn Hibernate, and helping you to learn it in a hurry. And to be honest, I think it does a pretty good job at doing that. ☺

A Few Words About Me and my Writing Style

Now, one thing you should know about me is that I self-publish. There are huge drawbacks to that, and a few key benefits, and for me, I think the benefits tend to outweigh the drawbacks.

The drawbacks? Well, my distribution channel is pretty small, and I don't sell a whole whack of books. That makes my per-unit cost pretty high, and as a result, my books cost a bit more than other books on the market. **I always try to sell them directly through amazon.com as an associate seller with a big discount,** but the list price I've gotta charge on Amazon to cover costs *(they take 55%)* is pretty high. That really sucks. ☹

The other drawback is that I don't have a whole list of editors and proofreaders to help me edit the final copy. My friends help me out, that's for sure, and I always edit and reproof my books three or four times before they go to press, but the fact is, there are always typos and other little errors that make it into print.

I always find the typos that make it into the prose quite embarrassing, so if you catch any, please shoot me an email at **typos@cameronmckenzie.com** and let me know about them. You see, the flip-side of self-publishing is the fact that I can quickly make changes to my master manuscript, so if I find a typo or grammatical error, I can fix it and have the correct content into circulation within a month – you'll simply never see that type of responsiveness with the big publishers.

Furthermore, I can add or update the content in my books rather quickly, too. If there's something you'd like to see added or changed, again, I can make that happen. My ultimate goal is to have some really great technical books on the market. If you can help me make that happen, I'd really appreciate it, and so would everyone else that reads my books in the future.

Now as I said, I've never released a book that was free of typographical errors or grammatical mistakes, although I do try. Of course, errors in the prose is one thing, but errors in the actual code in this book is totally another matter. My guarantee to you is that **every line of code in this book is error free,** and will compile as it is written, and I'm willing to put my money where my mouth is on that point.

The $100 Code Error Challenge

I really have no tolerance for programming books that contain errors in their code. I mean, how can someone learn if what they are being taught is wrong? There are a lot of reasons why technical books get riddled with errors in their code, but I don't find any of them acceptable.

My promise to you is that if you find a syntax error in my Java code, anywhere in this book, from this page forward, and you are the first person to inform me of it, I will write you a check for one hundred American dollars. And on top of that, I'll add your name in a special 'thank you' section of the next printing of the book, and say all sorts of great things about you. That's how confident I am that there are no code errors in this book. And to be honest, if there is something in here that's wrong, and you find it, I'll be more than happy to pay. That's my commitment to quality, and to you, the reader. If you can help me improve the quality of this book, I will more than appreciate your help!

Send any errata to: **errata@cameronmckenzie.com**

Good Things You Won't Notice

Along with my commitment to error-free code, there are a few other neat little things about how this book is laid out that I believe will make learning much more enjoyable. For example, I hate books that do this:

```
<?xml version='1.0' encoding='UTF-8'?>
<!DOCTYPE hibernate-configuration PUBLIC
"-//Hibernate/Hibernate Configuration DTD 3.0//EN"
"http://hibernate.sourceforge.net/hibernate-
configuration-3.0.dtd">
<hibernate-configuration>
  <session-factory>
  <property name="connection.url">
  jdbc:mysql://localhost/examscam
  </property>
  <property name="connection.username">root
```

```
  </property>
  <property name="connection.password">password
  </property>
  <property name="connection.driver_class">
  com.mysql.jdbc.Driver
  </property>
  <property name="dialect">
  org.hibernate.dialect.MySQLDialect
  </property>
  </session-factory>
</hibernate-configuration>
```

What was wrong with that? Well, why the heck was that code spread out over two pages? I mean, half of the XML was at the bottom of the previous page, and the other half was at the top of this one. How does that help you learn?

In my opinion, I think branching code over two pages shows a real disregard to the reader. Style and structure of programming code is just as important to understanding it as is the actual content. I truly believe that when you're learning, it's important to see as much of the code as possible, *all on one page*, so your mind can absorb it all. Furthermore, if you're typing along, it's much easier to figure out what you're doing by being able to easily look over the entire code sample without having to flip back and forth between pages. So, when I'm formatting my books, I go to extremes to try and make sure that code snippets are all contained on a single page, and don't needlessly breach a page break. Of course, sometimes code gets so long that it can't possibly fit on a single page, but even then, I try to ensure all the code spans across the same two pages you'd see when you open to a certain page. Basically, I try to make code that breaches a page break *start* on an even page, and *end* on an odd page – that way you can see all of the code at the same time. It's not always possible, but I assure you, I try, and if you're looking for it, you'll notice it. ☺

The other thing I try to do, which you'd probably never notice if I didn't mention it, is that I try to put important images and large code samples on odd number pages. Sounds strange, but people find odd numbered pages, that is, the ones on the right hand side, easier to read. I don't know why, but it's just true –

you'll notice that chapters in technical books usually start on an odd numbered page. It's just a happy place for the brain for some reason.

For example, I've just pulled some HibernateUtil code from later on in the book and put it on the opposite, odd numbered page. Doesn't your brain seem happy just to look at it? Well, maybe not, but apparently, it does make a difference.

Now, the HibernateUtil class on the opposite page also demonstrates another important part of how I like to demonstrate code. I certainly focus on code snippets and methods at times, but somewhere in a chapter, I always like to show *the entire class,* with all of its methods, package and import statements. I just think that leaving anything out, especially when someone is learning a new technology, just isn't right, even if it is just package and import statements. Of course, no good deed goes unpunished, so if you go to Amazon, you'll see all sorts of complaints about how the 7 point font on the package statements is too difficult to read, but I assure you, there is a method to my madness. (Speaking of Amazon, if you do like this book, feel free to write me a 5 star review. Every single one brings a big smile to my face ☺)

As I said, I like to show *the entire class*, and I like to try and put it all on one page (compare that to some other Java programming books you have laying around). To do that, sometimes I have to make the font *in the fairly redundant parts of the Java class* pretty small. So, as I did with the HibernateUtil class on the opposite page, I shrunk the package and import statements. Furthermore, I'll sometimes shrink the verbose header on XML files to a completely unreadable font:

```
<?xml version='1.0' encoding='UTF-8'?>
<!DOCTYPE hibernate-configuration PUBLIC
"-//Hibernate/Hibernate Configuration DTD 3.0//EN""http://hibernate.sourceforge.net/hibernate-configuration-3.0.dtd">
```

Actually, that's a 5 point font, and I don't think I ever really go *that low.* But the point is, if I've already displayed something like this standard XML header, which never changes, in a readable 9 or 10 point font, subsequent times I just might opt to shrink it. I think it's important to keep it in, but at the same time, I'd rather increase the font on the new and interesting parts of the code. It's a balance I'm trying to strike, but I do hope you appreciate the thinking behind it. ☺

Crammed on an Odd Numbered Page

```
package com.examscam;  /* small 7 point font for redundant sutff */
import org.hibernate.Session;
import org.hibernate.SessionFactory;
import org.hibernate.cfg.AnnotationConfiguration;
import org.hibernate.cfg.Configuration;
import org.hibernate.tool.hbm2ddl.SchemaExport;
import com.examscam.model.User;
/* The HibernateUtil class. ☺ */
public class HibernateUtil {
   private static SessionFactory factory;
   public static Configuration
                   getInitializedConfiguration() {
     AnnotationConfiguration config =
                   new AnnotationConfiguration();
/* add all of your JPA annotated classes here!!!*/
     config.addAnnotatedClass(User.class);
     config.configure();
     return config;
   } /* larger font for the important stuff */
   public static Session getSession() {
     if (factory == null) {
       Configuration config =
         HibernateUtil.getInitializedConfiguration();
       factory = config.buildSessionFactory();
     }
     Session hibernateSession =
                   factory.getCurrentSession();
     return hibernateSession;
   }
   public static void recreateDatabase() {
     Configuration config;
     config=HibernateUtil.getInitializedConfiguration();
     new SchemaExport(config).create(true, true);
   }
   public static void main(String args[]) {
     HibernateUtil.recreateDatabase();
   }
}
```

POJO==Plain Ordinary Java Object == JavaBean = Java Class

But we'll cover that later...

Have you ever been working through some code samples in a programming book, and get to some code that for the life of you, won't compile? You've followed all of the steps, copied the code out line for line, debugged it for three frustrating hours, only to give up, read ahead two pages, and then find out that the authors hadn't told you about a jar file you needed, or the authors introduce a piece of code you needed to write *first* before the code that wasn't working would ever compile? I see that all the time, and it annoys the pants off me.

So, my other promise to you is that if you follow the exercises in this book, as they appear, they will all compile as written. Sure, I think there's a spot in chapter 21 where I write a piece of code on one page that won't compile until you also do the code on the next page, but even then, I have huge boxes warning you that both classes must be written to get things to work. I really try hard to ensure that if you follow the examples as they are written, everything will compile and run. I want this book to be a fun experience, not an exercise in frustration.

Oh, and here's another thing I really hate: when technology books introduce a topic, and then say "oh, but we'll cover that later." It's difficult to figure out a good way to teach complex topics like Hibernate, but making a book read like a Visual Basic program that's filled with GOTO statements is not acceptable, and is a disservice to the reader. My personal philosophy is that if you can't take the time to properly explain a given topic, or the reader doesn't have the proper context to fully understand the topic, it shouldn't be brought up at all.

I'm not saying that I'll never, ever, never reference a later section of a book I'm writing, but I really, really, really try not to, and if there's any way to avoid it, I will. I'm not a big fan of GOTO statements, be it in a book *or* in your VB code. ☺

Anyways, I'm starting to bore myself with all of this editorializing. The bottom line is, I really work hard on these books, a great deal of thought goes into them, and I really want you to enjoy them. Now, with all of that said, and this whole preamble going way too long, I think it's time to jump into the fun stuff, and start working with Hibernate!

For more details about the $100 Code Error Challenge, check out:
www.hiberbook.com

Chapter 1
Getting Started

How do you get started with Hibernate?

When I write a book about technology, I like to assume the reader already has their environment set up and ready to go. For example, in my portlet programming book, I jump right into the code, expecting that if someone is reading a book on portlets, they've already got some type of development tool set up to help facilitate their coding. Unfortunately, I just don't feel comfortable doing that with Hibernate. So, we're going to start this book off with a little discussion about all of the things you need to download and configure in order to work through the various examples in this book. Don't worry, there's not *too much* to do. You do need a database, you do need a Java compiler, and you will need to download some files from Hibernate.org, but in the grand scheme of things, it's not really a back-breaking amount of work.

So, without any further ado, here's what you need in order to start working with Hibernate and JPA annotations:

☞ *A JDBC compliant Database. (and the ability to perform the most basic of database administration tasks.) You can't do Java persistence without a database!!!*

☞ *The JDK 1.5 or better, as annotations didn't exist before Java 5 (JDK 1.5 == Java 5. Why? Don't ask!)*

☞ *JDBC Drivers for your Database – that's how Hibernate connects to your database of choice*

☞ *The various jar files and libraries associated with the Hibernate Core and Hibernate Annotations (essentially, you need Hibernate)*

☞ *A properly configured hibernate.cfg.xml file on your runtime classpath.(Don't worry, we'll work on that together when the time comes)*

Step 1: Get a Database!!!

Hibernate is all about persisting the state of your Java components to a database. That's what Hibernate does; it helps Java programmers, in a very natural and object-oriented way, persist their data to a database. And if you want to persist data to a database, well, you obviously need a database.

Now, I don't really care which database you install. Hibernate is database agnostic, and very egalitarian in the fact that it really doesn't care which database you use, so long as your database is JDBC compliant. For the examples in this book, I'm going to use MySQL as the database of choice. You can use DB2, Oracle, Sybase, or any other JDBC compliant database that you like, but for me, I'm going to use MySQL. Why MySQL, you ask? Well, because it's free, and that's a price I don't mind paying. Plus, the installation is a snap, and it comes with some pretty sweet GUI tools for doing basic database administration. If you're not committed to any particular database, MySQL really isn't all that expensive of a download. ☺

My Three Favorite MySQL Components

From mysql.org, I downloaded three key components, namely:
1. The Free (GPL), MySQL Database (**Version 5.0.45**)
2. The Free, MySQL GUI Tools
3. ConnectorJ, the MySQL certified JDBC drivers

As far as installation goes, with MySQL, it's more of an unzipping of files than anything else. I just unzip the database related files into a folder named *C:_mysql*, and I unzip the MySQL GUI tools into a folder named *C:_mysql gui tools*, and voila, MySQL and its complimentary GUI tools are installed.

You'll notice that whenever I create folders, I typically create them with a leading underscore, _. I do this for two reasons:

1. It annoys the hell out of my fellow developers who have to share folders with me or work on my computer. ☺

2. It puts all of my important folders right at the top of the *File Explorer* hierarchy, making things easier to find, and I like looking for things that are easy to find.

Gentlemen...Start Your Database...

Before you can do anything interesting with a database, you need to start it. To start MySQL for example, I just jump in the bin directory and run the **mysql-nt.exe --console** command. Obviously, this is on a Windows XP machine, and dare I say it again, for a MySQL installation. Each database and operating system will have its own unique startup command. If starting up your locally installed database is a mystery, ask for some help from a friend, co-worker or mentor. This is no time to be too proud to recruit some experienced help – if you can't get a database started, you won't be very successful in the world of database persistence.

```
C:\_mysql\bin>mysqld-nt.exe --console
InnoDB: Starting crash recovery.
InnoDB: Reading tablespace information from files...
InnoDB: Restoring possible half-written data pages
InnoDB: buffer...
080103  7:42:57 InnoDB: Starting log scan
InnoDB: log sequence number 0 46441.
080103  7:42:57 InnoDB: Started; log sequence number 0 46441
7:42:59 [Note] mysqld-nt.exe: ready for connections.
Version: '5.0.45-community-nt'  socket: ''  port: 3306  MySQL Community
Edition (GPL)
```

Please, Make This a True Assumption

As I write this book, and prepare to introduce you to the marvelous world of Hibernate, I have assumed that you have successfully installed a database, *any database of your liking*, and have a basic, fundamental idea about how to use it. I like MySQL, but you can use any JDBC compliant database that you want; unfortunately though, I can't give detailed descriptions on how to install and configure every single database in the world. ☹ There are just too many databases out there for me to describe how to install and configure each and every one. However, on a brighter note, once we jump into the world of Hibernate, there really isn't that much database specific configuration that needs to be done, as Hibernate is database agnostic.

POJO==Plain Ordinary Java Object == JavaBean = Java Class

The Shortcomings of Hibernate

Hibernate is pretty amazing, and you'll be astonished at how many neat things it can do when it comes to managing database tables, manipulating data, and persisting the state of your JavaBeans. However, as amazing as Hibernate is, there are certain things that it just can't do. Here's a brief list of some of Hibernate's biggest shortcomings:

1. It won't grab you a Tim Hortons coffee in the morning
2. It won't stop you from making a dumb, drunk phone call to your ex-girlfriend
3. It can't create a database schema for you

Now, all said and done, I think we can learn to live with these three shortcomings. I have my own ways of dealing with the first two, but the third is the one I'd like to deal with right now, namely, the creation of a database schema named *examscam*.

What the Heck is a Schema?

What is a database schema? Well, a schema is where a common set of database tables reside. Think of it as a form of logical partitioning of application related tables within a database.

Different databases may have different colloquialisms for the idea of a schema, but regardless of what it's called, you need a recognizable schema in your database in order for Hibernate to know of which collection of database tables to connect.

A database schema named *examscam* is the umbrella under which all of the tables that we will use in this book will be created and maintained. The schema name *examscam* will be referenced quite a few times throughout this book, and it will also be written in a configuration file or two. If you don't like the schema name of *examscam*, and you decide to give *your* schema a clever little name of your own, just be forewarned that the clever little name you choose will need to be injected into a variety of config files. If you're new to Hibernate, and you want to be safe, just humor me and use the same schema name. I assure you, life, and troubleshooting, will be easier. ☺

36

Quickly Creating a Database Schema in MySQL

Using the MySQL Query Browser GUI Tool, creating a new schema is just two or three simple steps. Each database is different though, and if you're having trouble with yours, you may need to go to the reference material for your database of choice. Or better yet, ask someone in the know, or even post a query on a message board such as the Big Moose Saloon at JavaRanch.com. (I tend to hang out at the ranch quite a bit. ☺)

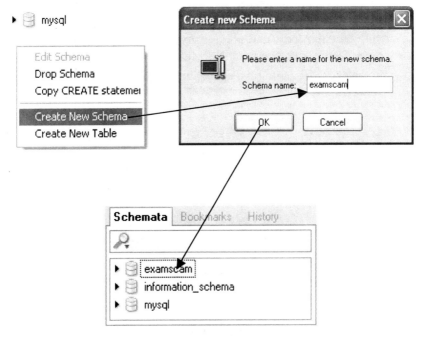

The Create Schema SQL Command

So, database tables must be contained within a schema (schemata? Catalog?). The following is your standard SQL for creating a database schema named examscam, just in case you're one of those freakish people that gets off on command line executions, as opposed to using those *girly-man* GUI tools.

```
CREATE DATABASE `examscam`;
```

Knowing the Database Basics

I know I've said it before, but I want to say it again: I do apologize for not taking you through every piece of minutia with regards to creating a database, and setting up database tables. I mean, I'll always try to provide the SQL required to manipulate a database, but how to execute the provided SQL against *your particular database,* and how to issue commands against *your database,* is a little bit outside the scope of this book.

If you're new to using a database like MySQL or Oracle, or DB2, and you're not comfortable with issuing SQL statements or using the GUI tools that accompany your database, reach out to someone on your team, or someone you know, and get some assistance. Programming is tough enough without having to struggle with getting the basic database schema set up.

Step 2: Installing the JDK–Version 1.5 or Higher

In order to write and run Java code, you need a compiler and a runtime environment. You can get all of that from Sun Microsystems by simply downloading the JDK, aka the Java Development toolKit.

In order to use Hibernate with JPA annotations, you need to have a Java 5 environment or higher, which means your JDK must be at version 1.5 or better. Yes, I know it's called Java **5**, but if you look under the covers, it's really a 1.5 version of the runtime environment. I guess Java 5 just sounded kewler to the people at Sun, so that's what they call it; but don't be fooled, as a Java 5 JRE is really at a JDK version level of 1.5.

For the most part, I use Java 1.6 for the examples in this book, but anything from *Java version 5* and onwards will do just fine.

And a note about downloading the JDK: there are all sorts of Java *'environments'* out there, including the Enterprise Environment, a Micro Environment, and a Standard Edition Environment. Since we just want a basic Java runtime, the Java SE, or Standard Edition, or the Standard Development Kit (SDK), is what you want to download and install.

POJO==Plain Ordinary Java Object == JavaBean = Java Class

Finding the JDK on Sun's Site

In order to get your fingers on the JDK, you have to go to Sun Microsystems's website, at http://java.sun.com, or even http://www.javasoft.com. Both URLs pretty much take you to the same place. There's usually a link on the landing page called 'Popular Downloads,' which will probably change as soon as I finish writing this, but nevertheless, there should be a link on Sun's site that allows you to download Java SE, the Standard Edition. Java SE is what you want.

Now, when you go to the downloads page, you'll see all sorts of links to download JDK 6, or JDK 6u1, or something like that. Java 6 will do just fine, but so will Java 5. If you want Java 5, you'll have to find a link on the page that says "Previous Releases" or something like that. Regardless, you need a Java 5 SE JDK or better to work with Hibernate and JPA annotations, so head over to www.javasoft.com and dig around until you find a link for *J2SE Downloads* or something similar.

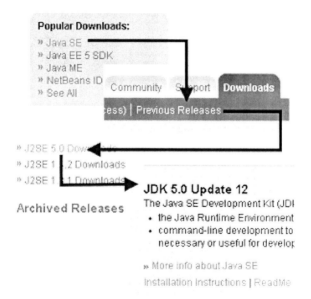

Installing the SE JDK, 1.5 or Higher

Now, when you install the JDK, the installer will ask for an installation directory. On Windows, this usually defaults to C:\Program Files\jdk1.6.0x.x or something crazy like that. I hate that.

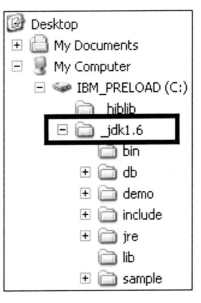

Personally, I recommend you install the JDK into a folder right off the root of C:\, preferably **C:_jdk1.5** if you're using Java 5, or **C:_jdk1.6** if you're using Java 6. I like to have the underscore in there as well, because it puts the JDK right near the top of the folders list when you open up the file system explorer. After I've been working on a computer for a while, there'll be a whole whack of folders branching off the root of C:\ with leading underscores. Those will all be mine. ☺

Using a Proper Development Environment

Now, for this chapter, I'm going to demonstrate the most basic, bare bones environment that is needed in order for you to get Hibernate working and configured properly. To do that, I'm going to assume you have nothing more than the JDK and a text editor to create, compile, and run some Java code. *But for God's sake, get yourself a proper development environment for writing code.* Eclipse is a free Java development environment, and I hear good things about NetBeans as well. Once you start doing some heavy coding with Java and Hibernate, you should be working within a proper, rapid application development environment. It will make your life easier, help you learn Hibernate faster, and allow you to maintain what is left of your sanity for just a little while longer.

41

POJO==Plain Ordinary Java Object == JavaBean = Java Class

Step 3: Add the JDBC Drivers to the Classpath

You can install a Java Runtime Environment (JRE), and you can install a database, and you can code all of the Hibernate or JPA or Java code that you want, but that doesn't help your Java runtime environment connect to your database. In order for a Java program to connect to a database, the Java environment needs access to the appropriate JDBC drivers. JDBC drivers are used by a Java program to connect to the database of interest.

Since every database in the world is different, every database has its own special set of JDBC drivers. For example, after installing MySQL on my own computer, I had to go to mysql.org and download the Connector/J, MySQL JDBC drivers, which were distributed in a jar file named **mysql-connector-java-5.0.8-bin.jar.** This file then needed to be added to the classpath of my Java environment. The last time I checked, DB2 had all of its JDBC drivers packaged in a jar file named db2java.zip. I'm not sure about Oracle or Sybase. The point it, every database has its own special set of JDBC drivers, and it is *your job* to find them, download them, and add them to your classpath.

Since every database is different, I can't possibly describe all the various database drivers that might be required to make your Java environment connect to your particular database. If you're on shaky ground when it comes to figuring out which database drivers you need to use, and where to get those database drivers, ask a friend, solicit help from someone on your development team, or even post a question for help in JavaRanch's Big Moose Saloon (www.javaranch.com). Don't waste too much time fighting battles over where to find your database's JDBC drivers. They're out there – go find them!

An Extra Nugget or Two of Information

When your Java application uses JDBC drivers to connect to a database, it needs a couple of very important pieces of information, namely, the *specific class name* of the JDBC driver which is contained within the JDBC driver archive file (zip or jar), as well as the syntax for the *connection URL.*

For MySQL, the **connection URL** and **JDBC driver class name** looks like this:

```
For MySQL:
JDBC Driver Name: com.mysql.jdbc.Driver
Connection URL: jdbc:mysql://localhost/examscam
```

We don't need to configure these values right now, but it is worth mentioning right now that these values are required, as you usually find these values referenced time and time again in the same place that you download your JDBC drivers.

The *JDBC driver name* will be the fully qualified name of a class file that is contained within your JDBC driver archive file.

The *connection URL* can actually get pretty bizarre. The big thing to note is that the connection URL will contain the name of the database schema you are using, which in this case, is *examscam*. If you're asking someone what your specific connection URL should be, you should phrase it something like this: *"given a database schema named examscam, and my specific database, what would be the syntax of the connection URL."*

Try to figure out the values of these two properties for your specific database, given a db schema named examscam, and write them down here. Then dog-ear this page, 'cuz you'll need it later.

JDBC Driver for MY database:

_____

Connection URL for MY database:

_____

43

Put Your JDBC Drivers on you Classpath!!!

Once you've got your JDBC drivers downloaded and on your workstation, you've got to put them somewhere that your Java runtime can find them. I'm creating a folder named _hiblib, right off the root of C:\ on my hard drive (C:_hiblib, yes, that's an underscore) , and I'm going to place all of my required libraries, such as the hibernate libraries and JDBC drivers, right into this _hiblib folder. Then, when I run my complier or kick off my runtime environment, this folder will be referenced.

The key is that the JDBC drivers must be on the classpath so the Java environment can find them. I'm going to keep things as basic and as egalitarian as possible in my examples, simply using the JDK and the javac compiler to compile my code. Alternatively, if you're developing within a Servlet and JSP environment, you might put the JDBC drivers in the lib folder of the web module. For that matter, if you're working in a production environment, you may actually have the JDBC drivers on the application server's external classpath, so instead of packaging the JDBC drivers in the lib directory of an EJB module or WAR file, you might just link to them as external JAR files, resting securely on the knowledge that you'll be able to link to them at runtime.

How you package your application isn't the biggest concern right now. Right now, the biggest concern is that your Java environment can find your JDBC drivers when Hibernate needs them.

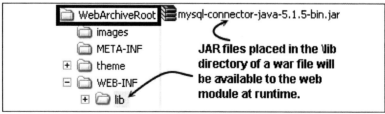

Step 3: Get the Hibernate Libraries

Do you know what this book is called? Well, actually, as I write this, I don't know what it will *actually* be called when it goes to press, but I'm sure the title will be something about doing Data Persistence with **Hibernate** and **JPA Annotations**. Given such a title, it shouldn't surprise you to find out that you're going to need to head over to hibernate.org and download a couple of Hibernate modules, and then add the various libraries that are a part of those modules to the classpath.

For older versions of Hibernate that used the very unsexy XML mapping files, all you needed to download to get things working was the **Hibernate Core**. Indeed, we still need to download the Hibernate Core module from hibernate.org, but since we don't want to mess around with XML mapping files in our applications, --- we want to use *annotations* --- we need to download an additional Hibernate module, namely the aptly monikered **Hibernate Annotations** module. The Hibernate Annotations module will give us access to the very kewl *JPA annotations* that make life so much easier than previous editions of Hibernate that required hours of editing of tedious XML files.

The following versions of the Hibernate Core and Hibernate Annotations were used for this book:

Hibernate Core   **3.2.5.ga 31.07.2007**

Hibernate Annotations   **3.3.0 GA 20.03.2007**

VERY IMPORTANT NOTE!!!

The examples in this book require you to download the Hibernate Core package, and the Hibernate Annotations module as well, from www.hibernate.org

YOU MUST **DOWNLOAD THE HIBERNATE CORE**

YOU MUST **DOWNLOAD HIBERNATE ANNOTATIONS**

You must also have a jar file containing your JDBC Drivers.

The downloaded contents must be extracted to your file system, and all of the jar files contained within that extracted download must be made available to your Java development environment, as well as your Java runtime environment. Adding the contained jar files to the Java CLASSPATH typically does the trick.

POJO==Plain Ordinary Java Object == JavaBean = Java Class

Linking to the Hibernate Jar Files

After downloading and extracting the Hibernate Core module, you will be presented with quite an elaborate directory structure, involving folders named doc, etc, lib and src.

As you can probably guess, the *doc* folder contains a wealth of information, including JavaDoc for the entire set of Hibernate core libraries. For specific information about a given Hibernate component and method, the JavaDoc is the right place to look.

Tutorials and Sample XML Files

The doc folder also contains a tutorial folder, with some sample XML files, namely a sample **hibernate.cfg.xml** file and some sample hbm.xml files.

These files are very fussy about syntax and grammar, so when it comes time to write your own, sometimes borrowing from these sample files is a very good idea.

The All Important \lib Directory

For us right now, the most important folder in the Hibernate Core download is the *lib* directory. This *lib* directory contains most (note *most*, not *all*) of the various jar files needed for running Core Hibernate applications. I really don't care how you do it, but you have to make sure these files are on the CLASSPATH of your JVM.

If you're coding a web based application, you can happily shove these jar files into the WEB-INF\lib directory. If you are running your code directly from the JDK, you can reference this folder using a –CLASSPATH switch; heck, you could even throw these files in the JDK\lib directory if you really wanted, although that would be a pretty heavy hammer to drop. The key point is, you need to be able to link to these jar files at both compile time and runtime. For me, I'm adding them all to the C:_hiblib folder in which I also added my JDBC drivers. I will then reference this folder when I both compile and run my Hibernate code.

Figure 1-1

The Hibernate framework requires quite a sizeable number of jar files to be available to the JVM at both compile time and runtime. Make sure these Hibernate Core jar files, along with the jar files from the Hibernate Annotations module, plus JDBC drivers, are added to the classpath!

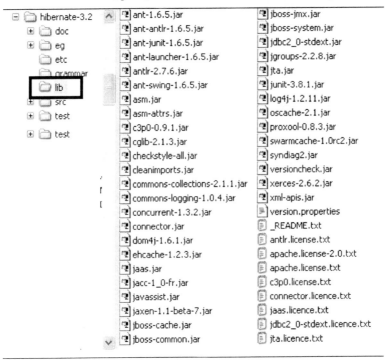

Get the Core Hibernate File – hibernate3.jar

Curiously, out of all of the files contained within the lib directory of the Hibernate Core module download, none of those files actually contain the Core Hibernate API. Bizarre, isn't it?

All of the files in the lib directory of the Hibernate Core download are required files that the Hibernate API needs to link to at runtime. However, the actual byte-code embodiment of the Hibernate Core API is contained within a 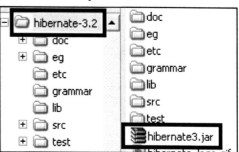 file named **hibernate3.jar**, and that file just happens to be floating around right there in the root of the Hibernate Core download. Look for it right there in the base folder, with the folder itself likely being named something like **\hibernate-3.2**.

Add the hibernate3.jar File to Your Classpath

Again, the core Hibernate API files are in the hibernate3.jar file, so this file must be on the classpath of your runtime and compile time environments. As with the JDBC driver JAR file for your database, and the numerous JAR files that were in the Core Hibernate download's \lib directory, I'm going to copy the hibernate3.jar file into the C:_hiblib directory. If you're following along, I suggest you copy the hibernate3.jar file in there as well. However, regardless of where you put it, make sure it's on the classpath of both your runtime and compile time Java environments.

Getting the Hibernate Annotations Module

I sure hope you enjoyed the various steps associated with getting access to all of the Hibernate Core libraries, because you're going to have to follow pretty much the same steps to acquire the libraries associated with the Hibernate Annotations module.

There are three JAR files contained within the Hibernate Annotations module download that *must* be added to your classpath, namely (*I bet you'll miss one of them*):

1. **ejb3-persistence.jar**
2. **hibernate-commons-annotations.jar**
3. **hibernate-annotations.jar**

Just to keep you off guard, these three JAR files are contained in two different folders of the Hibernate Annotations module download. The \lib directory of the downloaded Hibernate Annotations module contains the *commons* and *annotations* jar files, whereas the ejb3-persistence.jar file is in the root folder of the download, with that root folder most likely being named hibernate-annotations-3.3.0.GA or something creative like that; at least mine was. ☺

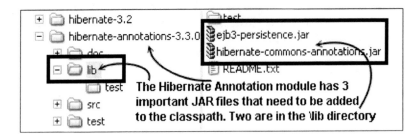

So, take the two JAR files in the \lib directory of the Hibernate Annotations module and throw them in your C:_hiblib folder, or, for that matter, any folder that will make these JAR files available to both your Java compile time and Java runtime environments. I've put all my JDBC drivers and Hibernate Core libraries in the C:_hiblib directory, so I'm going to do the same with the JAR files associated with Hibernate Annotations.

(Before turning the page – which jar file is still missing???)

49

hibernate-annotations.jar

As was mentioned, you need to add *three* JAR files to your classpath in order to use Hibernate with JPA annotations, with those three JAR files being:

1. ejb3-persistence.jar
2. hibernate-commons-annotations.jar
3. hibernate-annotations.jar

The **ejb3-persistence.jar** and **hibernate-commons-annotations.jar** files are found in the \lib directory of the Hibernate Annotations download, while the third file, **hibernate-annotations.jar**, is found in the root folder of the Hibernate Annotations download. This JAR file also needs to be added to your classpath, otherwise you'll run into all sorts of linking and ClassNotFoundExceptions.

To use Hibernate Annotations, the hibernate-annotations.jar file must be on the classpath, along with ejb3-persistence.jar and hibernate-commons-annotations.jar

For me, all of the JAR files my application needs are getting placed in the **C:_hiblib** directory, which I will reference when I compile and run my code.

A Hasty Mistake

By this point, people who are new to Hibernate are getting a little anxious and unruly, as they want to get their environment configured so they can start hacking out some code. Quite often, due to overanxious haste, only one or two of these three required JAR files makes it onto the classpath, causing frustrating errors down the road. Do a double-check, making sure you have added all of the required JAR files to your classpath.

A Look at my Hibernate & JDBC Libraries

After getting my JDBC drivers, Hibernate Core and Hibernate Annotations related JAR files, my C:_hiblib folder, which I'll make sure is available to my Java compile and runtime environments, looks like this:

C:_hiblib	
version.properties	hibernate-commons-annotations.jar
ant-1.6.5.jar	jaas.jar
ant-antlr-1.6.5.jar	jacc-1_0-fr.jar
ant-junit-1.6.5.jar	javassist.jar
ant-launcher-1.6.5.jar	jaxen-1.1-beta-7.jar
antlr-2.7.6.jar	jboss-cache.jar
ant-swing-1.6.5.jar	jboss-common.jar
asm.jar	jboss-jmx.jar
asm-attrs.jar	jboss-system.jar
c3p0-0.9.1.jar	jdbc2_0-stdext.jar
cglib-2.1.3.jar	jgroups-2.2.8.jar
checkstyle-all.jar	jta.jar **MySQL JDBC Driver**
cleanimports.jar	junit-3.8.1.jar
commons-collections-2.1.1.jar	log4j-1.2.11.jar
commons-logging-1.0.4.jar	mysql-connector-java-5.1.5-bin.jar
concurrent-1.3.2.jar	oscache-2.1.jar
connector.jar	proxool-0.8.3.jar
dom4j-1.6.1.jar	swarmcache-1.0rc2.jar
ehcache-1.2.3.jar	syndiag2.jar
ejb3-persistence.jar	versioncheck.jar
hibernate3.jar	xerces-2.6.2.jar
hibernate-annotations.jar	xml-apis.jar

Configuring the hibernate.cfg.xml File

Now, there is one last piece of the puzzle that we must put in place before we can start coding our Hibernate applications and watching the Hibernate framework persist the state of our JavaBeans to the database. That last piece of the puzzle is the appropriate editing and saving of the hibernate.cfg.xml file, which is a special configuration file that tells hibernate where our database is, what database driver to use to connect to our database, what the connection URL is, and any username and password credentials that might be needed to create an authenticated database connection.

Get a Sample hibernate.cfg.xml File!!!

I hate writing XML, especially when I don't have any XML validators checking my syntax and structure as I type. The hibernate.cfg.xml file is a pretty big XML file at the best of times, and trying to write the whole darned thing out by hand is just silly. If you need one, the best thing to do is to get a sample hibernate.cfg.xml file and edit it to suit your particular installation.

If you downloaded the Hibernate Core module, you'd be able to find a tutorial with an src folder in it. This src folder contains a hibernate.cfg.xml file that is used for the sample Hibernate application that comes with the download. Use this file as a template, and make the changes required to suit your own environment.

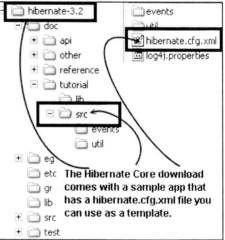

The Hibernate Core download comes with a sample app that has a hibernate.cfg.xml file you can use as a template.

Looking at the hibernate.cfg.xml File

Here's how my hibernate.cfg.xml file is going to look when I get it all edited. As you can see, it's far too big for a Luddite like myself to correctly type out by hand.

```xml
<?xml version='1.0' encoding='UTF-8'?>
<!DOCTYPE hibernate-configuration PUBLIC
"-//Hibernate/Hibernate Configuration DTD 3.0//EN"
"http://hibernate.sourceforge.net/hibernate-
configuration-3.0.dtd">

<hibernate-configuration>
  <session-factory>
  <property name="connection.url">
  jdbc:mysql://localhost/examscam
  </property>
  <property name="connection.username">
  root
  </property>
  <property name="connection.password">
  password
  </property>
  <property name="connection.driver_class">
  com.mysql.jdbc.Driver
  </property>
  <property name="dialect">
  org.hibernate.dialect.MySQLDialect
  </property>
  <property name="transaction.factory_class">
  org.hibernate.transaction.JDBCTransactionFactory
  </property>
  <property name="current_session_context_class">
  thread
  </property>
  <!-- this will show us all sql statements -->
  <property name="hibernate.show_sql">
  true
  </property>
  <!-- mapping files NOTICE WE HAVE NONE-->
</session-factory>
</hibernate-configuration>
```

Editing YOUR hibernate.cfg.xml File

Properly editing your hibernate.cfg.xml file is a pretty important step; after all, if you mess up here, your Java applications will fail when Hibernate tries to connect to your database.

I've tried to prepare you for this next step, as when I talked about downloading the JDBC drivers for your database, I mentioned that it was a good idea to figure out what the **connection url** and **driver name** was for your particular database. With this information in hand, you must edit your hibernate.cfg.xml file to look like mine, with the key differences being that you must provide the username and password for connecting to YOUR database, along with the **connection.url** and **connection.driver_class** property that is appropriate for you. Furthermore, you will need to add a dialect entry for your specific database.

For MySQL, the dialect is set to org.hibernate.dialect.MySQLDialect, which is actually a Java class that comes with the Hibernate Core download. If you are using a database other than MySQL, you'll have to check the documentation to find the dialect class specific to your database, and make the appropriate change in the hibernate.cfg.xml file.

Where do you put the hibernate.cfg.xml file???

Of course, if you're customizing the sample hibernate.cfg.xml file that comes with the Hibernate Core download, you'll have to save the edited file to a more conspicuous place on your workstation.

The hibernate.cfg.xml file not only needs to be on your classpath, but it must also be available to the classloader that runs your Hibernate Configuration, aka *plumbing*, code. This can be achieved by placing it in the root of the src directory where you write your Java code, and make sure it gets copied into the build folder where compiled byte-code gets placed.

Temporarily, **I'm just going to save the hibernate.cfg.xml file in the C:_hiblib folder**. However, when we start writing code, we will make sure the hibernate.cfg.xml file is placed alongside our source and comiled code.

For now, the C:_hiblib folder is a good, temporary spot to place the hibernate.cfg.xml file. However, I'll eventually be moving it into a folder named C:_mycode.

Important Properties of the hibernate.cfg.xml

You'd be amazed at the number of configurable properties that you can define in the hibernate.cfg.xml file. It's worth looking at the documentation that comes with Hibernate to see all of the different settings that are possible. My goal here is not to bore you to death by regurgitating the contents of a Hibernate reference manual, so I'm not going to go over every possible configuration setting. However, here is a little bit more detail about the minimum configuration settings that should exist in any hibernate.cfg.xml file.

connection.url: this is simply the standard URL that any Java application would use to connect to the database of choice. For connecting to a MySQL database on the local machine, with a schema name of examscam, the URL would be:
```
jdbc:mysql://localhost/examscam
```
However, it should be noted that each database is different, and the URL syntax is dependent upon both the database, the schema name, and the database driver being used.

connection.driver_class: a database specific setting, this setting defines the database driver, in the form of a Java class file, used by Hibernate to connect to the database. It should be mentioned that the class file you specify as the driver_class must actually be on the CLASSPATH, or Hibernate will not be able to find it at runtime.

connection.username and **connection.password:** somewhat self-explanatory, you typically need to provide the username and password used for connecting to your database.

dialect: despite all of the best efforts at standardization, every database behaves differently. To try and iron out the various

POJO==Plain Ordinary Java Object == JavaBean = Java Class

nuances between all of the different databases, Hibernate defines database specific dialects. For MySQL, we use :

`org.hibernate.dialect.MySQLDialect`

transaction.factory_class: this is used to specify the class implementing the TransactionFactory interface. For me, I use:

`org.hibernate.transaction.JDBCTransactionFactory`

hibernate.show_sql: this will instruct Hibernate to output the SQL code used whenever it interacts with the database. This is very helpful for both learning how Hibernate works, and when trying to diagnose bugs and problems.

My Complete hibernate.cfg.xml File (Again)

```xml
<?xml version='1.0' encoding='UTF-8'?>
<!DOCTYPE hibernate-configuration PUBLIC
"-//Hibernate/Hibernate Configuration DTD 3.0//EN"
"http://hibernate.sourceforge.net/hibernate-configuration-3.0.dtd">
<hibernate-configuration>
  <session-factory>

  <property name="connection.url">
  jdbc:mysql://localhost/examscam
  </property>

  <property name="connection.username">
  root
  </property>
  <property name="connection.password">
  password
  </property>

  <property name="connection.driver_class">
  com.mysql.jdbc.Driver
  </property>

  <property name="dialect">
  org.hibernate.dialect.MySQLDialect
  </property>

  <property name="transaction.factory_class">
  org.hibernate.transaction.JDBCTransactionFactory
  </property>

  <property name="current_session_context_class">
  thread
  </property>
  <!-- this will show us all sql statements -->
  <property name="hibernate.show_sql">
  true
  </property>
</session-factory>
</hibernate-configuration>
```

And that's it!

So, that's it. I guess it's a bit of work getting all of the various class files that are required to make Hibernate work, and of course, there's a bit of work involved in installing and configuring a database, but I assure you, it's all worth it. Having the Hibernate framework at our fingertips is going to make Java programs that persist data to a database so much easier to write.

And just to review, what were the steps we took to get our environment configured? Well, there were really five, important, top level steps, namely:

☞ *Installing a JDBC compliant Database*

☞ *Obtaining JDBC Drivers for the Database*

☞ *Getting the various jar files and libraries associated with the Core Hibernate and Hibernate Annotations modules*

☞ *Installing the JDK, version 1.5 or sexier*

☞ *Appropriately editing and saving a hibernate.cfg.xml file*

So, what's next?

What's next, you ask? Well, if you think everything is configured, it's time to test to see if it's configured correctly. The next chapter will have you write some kewl Java code that uses Hibernate and JPA Annotations to connect to the database and create some supporting database tables. If it works, everything is configured properly, and we can then dive head first into that empty pool known as database persistence. ☺

Chapter 2
Validating the Hibernate Setup

Okay, so Chapter 1 discussed the basics of setting up a Hibernate environment, including the core configuration steps of:

☞ *installing a database and creating a schema named examscam*

☞ *installing the JDK, version 1.5 or greater*

☞ *downloading the Hibernate Core and Hibernate Annotations libraries*

☞ *downloading the appropriate JDBC driver for your database and placing it on the CLASSPATH*

☞ *appropriately editing the hibernate.cfg.xml file*

Now, once you've done that, you'll probably want to verify that all of those components are integrated together and working properly. Here's what we're going to do to make sure everything is set up and ready to go:

First, we're going to create a simple **User *JavaBean***. Coding and being able to compile this JavaBean, aka ***POJO*** (Plain Ordinary Java Object), will confirm that the JDK has been installed properly. Furthermore, the User ***bean*** will employ some very kewl *Java Persistence API **annotations***, which will verify that the JDK is linking to the downloaded Hibernate and JPA libraries properly. And finally, we're going to tell the Hibernate framework all about the existence of this User JavaBean, and ask the Hibernate framework to create a database table, under the umbrella of the examscam schema, that will support this User

POJO==Plain Ordinary Java Object == JavaBean = Java Class

JavaBean. Yeah, that's right – if you tell Hibernate about a JPA annotated JavaBean, Hibernate can create an underlying database table for you, right there on the fly! If everything goes well, this chapter should result in the creation of a database table, without us ever having to use a database tool to create it!

A Quick Review

Again, here's what we're going to do in this chapter:

☞ *create a JavaBean, aka POJO, aka class, named User*

☞ *annotate the User class with JPA annotations*

☞ *feed the User bean to the Hibernate framework*

☞ *ask the Hibernate framework to create a database table based on the properties of the User class*

Designing The Object Model – Looking Ahead

One of the things I'd like to work towards in the first part of this book is the creation of a simple, JSP based application that manages user information. Given a user, our primitive online application will be able to add, update, delete, search for, and create, new users; the content of which would be persisted to an underlying database. As you could imagine, the core artifact of this online application will be a Java class named *User*, which will map to a database table in our examscam schema that will very uncreatively be named *user. (notice the lower case 'u'?)* With this online, user management application in mind, let's take our first step towards leveraging Java and the Hibernate framework by creating a very simple class named User.

The User class will contain two very simple properties: an id of type Long, and a password of type String. Yes, I know, this is a pretty lame Java class, but that's just fine for right now. The current goal is to create a *simple* class that we can decorate with JPA (Java Persistence API) annotations and subsequently use to validate our development environment, making sure that Hibernate, our database, and all of the required drivers and libraries are linked up and working together properly. Keeping things relatively simple right now is a good thing. ☺

The Un-Annotated User Class

I've placed the User class in a package named com.examscam.model. This is a good place for our domain model classes to go.

```java
package com.examscam.model;
/* The User Class without JPA annotations */
public class User {

  private Long id;
  private String password;

  public Long getId() {
    return id;
  }
  public void setId(Long id) {
    this.id = id;
  }

  public String getPassword() {
    return password;
  }
  public void setPassword(String password) {
    this.password = password;
  }

}
```

This User class may look relatively simple, but rest assured, this simple little class will grow to become the cornerstone of our user management, online, JSP-based, web-application.

POJO==Plain Ordinary Java Object == JavaBean = Java Class

Of Tables and Java Classes

So, as just a bit of a reminder about where we're going in this chapter, let me rehash what we're doing. We have created a simple Java class named User. This Java class has two properties, one of type Long named *id*, and another of

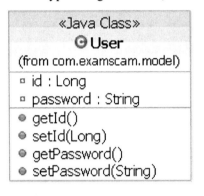

type String that is smartly named *password*. Now, our application is going to have to store and retrieve User information, and in order to do that, we're going to need a database table; one that has columns for both the User's id and the User's password. Essentially, our application must persist the data in the class named User to corresponding columns in a database table.

```
package com.examscam.model;
public class User {
  private Long id;
  private String password;
  public Long getId() {
    return id;
  }
  public void setId(Long id) {
    this.id = id;
  }
  public String getPassword() {
    return password;
  }
  public void setPassword(String password) {
    this.password = password;
  }
}
```

Annotating POJOs with JPA Tags

So, you're probably wondering how Hibernate is supposed to know how to persist the state of a JavaBean, like our User class, to a database. Well, as it stands right now, Hibernate doesn't have a clue about how to persist our User bean. In fact, Hibernate doesn't even know of its existence! If we want Hibernate to know how to persist the state of our User POJO to the database, we must decorate our Java code using special constructs known as JPA, or Java Persistence API, annotations.

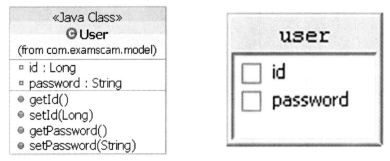

Annotations – New with Java 5!!!

Annotations are a new concept with Java 5, so some legacy Java developers might not be familiar with the concept. Basically, an annotation allows a developer to provide extra information about the code that is being written. For our User class, we will provide a number of annotations, the most important of which will be the @Entity annotation that indicates that the User class is in fact a database related *entity*, whose state Hibernate should persist to the database. This is done by adding a special **@Entity** tag immediately before the class declaration.

Furthermore, we need to tell Hibernate that the User's id field represents a unique primary key. We indicate this by adding the **@Id** annotation before the getter of the id field. Also, since we are relying on our database to generate unique primary keys for us, we need to provide the **@GeneratedValue** annotation as well. Again, we will add the @Id and the @GeneratedValue annotations immediately before the getId() method of the User class.

The JPA Annotated User POJO

```
package com.examscam.model;
import javax.persistence.Entity;
import javax.persistence.GeneratedValue;
import javax.persistence.Id;

@Entity
public class User {
  private Long id;
  private String password;

  @Id
  @GeneratedValue
  public Long getId() {
    return id;
  }
  public void setId(Long id) {
    this.id = id;
  }
  public String getPassword() {
    return password;
  }
  public void setPassword(String password) {
    this.password = password;
  }
}
```

Notice the addition of the JPA annotations to the code, including the @Entity, @Id and @GeneratedValue tags.

The @Entity annotation tells Hibernate that the User class is a persistent entity that needs to have its state persisted to the database. Furthermore, the @Id annotation indicates that the field named **id** in the JavaBean represents a primary key, or unique identifier. Finally, the @GeneratedValue annotation informs Hibernate that when a new entity is persisted to the database, the database will generate a unique primary key for the record; given this generated value, Hibernate will then set the id in the User POJO instance accordingly.

Hibernate Annotations and JPA

One interesting thing to note about these annotations is that they actually come from the Java Persistence API, or JPA. This fact is evidenced by the surreptitiously added set of import statements at the top of the User class:

```
import javax.persistence.Entity;
import javax.persistence.GeneratedValue;
import javax.persistence.Id;
```

The Java Persistence API is not a standard part of the JDK installation or the *core* Hibernate download. As such, being able to use JPA annotations in our code requires the appropriate libraries to be available at compile and runtime. These libraries are available by downloading the Hibernate annotations extension package from hibernate.org. The bytecode embodiment of these annotations and related files are found in the following jar files: **ejb3-persistence.jar, hibernate-commons-annotations.jar and hibernate-annotations.jar.**

If you download the Hibernate Annotations module from hibernate.org, the compressed file you receive will contain these three jar files. Make sure these jar files are on the classpath of your Java development environment.

Annotations and Java 5

Furthermore, annotations are not only a new module for Hibernate, but they are a relatively new concept in the world of Java programming, having been introduced for the very first time in a standard edition with Java5, aka the JDK 1.5. That's a pretty important point, because even if you've downloaded and placed all of the required JAR files on your classpath, if you're not using JDK 1.5 or greater, your annotations are not going to work.

You can always confirm your version of Java by typing in the following command and switch on the command line:

java –version

Here's an example of what you might get as output. Notice that I'm using a flavor of Java 1.6!

```
C:\>java -version
java version "1.6.0_02"
```

POJO==Plain Ordinary Java Object == JavaBean = Java Class

Communicating with the Hibernate Framework

Okay, so you've got yourself a JPA annotated JavaBean named User, and you have all of the required Hibernate Core and Hibernate Annotations JAR files on your classpath, and now you want to use the Hibernate framework in the job of mapping your User POJO to an actual database table. The question is, how do you do it?

JavaBeans and the AnnotationConfiguration

Well, the first thing you need to do to get Hibernate to map the User bean to the database is write some Java code that tells Hibernate to configure itself to be able to handle an annotated JavaBean, which in our case will be the User class. That first requires the creation of Hibernate's AnnotationConfiguration object, which can be easily created by calling the AnnotationConfiguration's constructor.

```
AnnotationConfiguration config =
                new AnnotationConfiguration();
```

java.lang.Object
└ org.hibernate.cfg.Configuration
└ **org.hibernate.cfg.AnnotationConfiguration**

public class **AnnotationConfiguration**
        extends org.hibernate.cfg.Configuration

Similar to the parent Configuration object but handles EJB3 and Hibernate specific annotations as a metadata facility.

An instance of Configuration allows the application to specify properties and mapping documents. Usually an application will create a single Configuration. The Configuration is meant only as an initialization-time object.

                                        --Hibernate API JavaDoc

Telling Hibernate about your Annotated POJOs

After creating the AnnotationConfiguration object, we must add *to it* all of our annotated JavaBeans, which for now is just our lonely, yet stoic, JPA annotated User class.

```
config.addAnnotatedClass(User.class);
```

This *addAnnotatedClass* method call tells Hibernate which JavaBeans to read and manage as persistent objects. For every class you annotate with JPA tags, you must add it as an annotated class to the AnnotationConfiguration object, just as we have done for the User class.

```
public AnnotationConfiguration
        addAnnotatedClass(Class persistentClass)
            throws org.hibernate.MappingException
Reads a mapping from the class annotation
metadata (JSR 175).
  Parameters: persistentClass - the mapped class
  Returns: the configuration object
  Throws: org.hibernate.MappingException
        --a minor regurgitation of the Hibernate API JavaDoc
```

Once we have added all of our persistent, JPA annotated Java classes to the config object, we invoke the *configure()* method of the AnnotationConfiguration instance. This gets the Hibernate configuration object to read the hibernate.cfg.xml file, allowing Hibernate to understand how to access the underlying database, while at the same time, telling the configuration instance to process all of the JPA annotations on any decorated Java classes that have been added to the config.

```
AnnotationConfiguration config =
            new AnnotationConfiguration();
config.addAnnotatedClass(User.class);

config.configure();
```

*Sometimes I'll say config, or configuration object, or config instance when I'm really talking about the AnnotationConfiguration object. ☺

Neat AnnotationConfiguration Stuff

So, now that we've got ourselves a fully initialized AnnotationConfiguration object, what can we do with it? Well, we can do all sorts of neat stuff with it. The AnnotationConfiguration object has the ability to kick off magical objects called *SessionFactories*, which can in turn create even more mystical objects known as *Hibernate Sessions*, which can be used to perform all of the basic CRUD (Create, Retrieve, Update and Delete) operations against the underlying database.

However, for our current purposes, we want to use the AnnotationConfiguration object to create the various tables that are needed to persist the state of our User class to the database. To do this, we leverage the facilities of a special Hibernate component known as the SchemaExport object, whose create method can be passed an AnnotationConfiguration instance, with which the SchemaExport object subsequently connects to the underlying database and generates the various tables required by the Java based object model. All of this can be accomplished by invoking the SchemaExport object's very sensibly named *create* method.

```
new SchemaExport(config).create(true, true);
```

```
org.hibernate.tool.hbm2ddl
Class SchemaExport
java.lang.Object
   └ org.hibernate.tool.hbm2ddl.SchemaExport
```

public class **SchemaExport** extends Object

Commandline tool to export table schema to the database. This class may also be called from inside an application.

--Hibernate API JavaDoc

AnnotationConfiguration Class Diagram

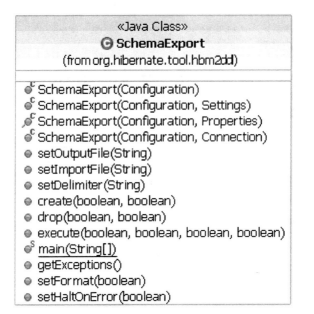

«Java Class»
⊖ **AnnotationConfiguration**
⅋F ARTEFACT : String
⅋F DEFAULT_PRECEDENCE : String
⌀C AnnotationConfiguration()
⌀C AnnotationConfiguration(SettingsFactory)
◉ addAnnotatedClass(Class)
◉ addPackage(String)
◉ createExtendedMappings()
◉ setCacheConcurrencyStrategy(String, String, String, boolean)
◈ setCollectionCacheConcurrencyStrategy(String, String, String)
◉ setPrecedence(String)
◈ addInputStream(InputStream)
◈ buildSessionFactory()
◉ getReflectionManager()

SchemaExport Class Diagram

«Java Class»
⊖ **SchemaExport**
(from org.hibernate.tool.hbm2ddl)
⌀C SchemaExport(Configuration)
⌀C SchemaExport(Configuration, Settings)
⌀C SchemaExport(Configuration, Properties)
⌀C SchemaExport(Configuration, Connection)
◉ setOutputFile(String)
◉ setImportFile(String)
◉ setDelimiter(String)
◉ create(boolean, boolean)
◉ drop(boolean, boolean)
◉ execute(boolean, boolean, boolean, boolean)
⌀S main(String[])
◉ getExceptions()
◉ setFormat(boolean)
◉ setHaltOnError(boolean)

POJO==Plain Ordinary Java Object == JavaBean = Java Class

The SchemaExport Create Method

You will notice that the create method of the SchemaExport object takes two boolean parameters. The first boolean value indicates whether or not you want the generated database creation script to be printed out to the log file. The second parameter indicates whether you want the generated script to be executed against the underlying database. Passing two true values to the create method will cause the database generation scripts to be printed out to the log files, while also triggering the execution of the database creation scripts, which would mean dropping the existing tables in the database, and subsequently recreating them.

```
public void create(boolean script, boolean export)

Run the schema creation script.

Parameters:
script - print the DDL to the console
export - export the script to the database
```

As was mentioned before, the instance of the AnnotationConfiguration object holds all of the information about how to connect to your database, along with all of the information gleaned from the JPA annotated JavaBeans that have been added as annotated classes. With all of this delicious information, connecting to the appropriate database schema and running a database create script really isn't such a difficult endeavor.

```
AnnotationConfiguration config = new AnnotationConfiguration();
config.addAnnotatedClass(User.class);
config.configure();

new SchemaExport(config).create(true, true);
```

70

hibernate.cfg.xml Again

I keep mentioning that the AnnotationConfiguration object reads from the hibernate.cfg.xml file to glean information about how to connect to the database. I just though it'd be polite to show you the hibernate.cfg.xml file again, just so you don't have to flick back to an earlier chapter where it was first defined. Key properties for connecting to the database include the connection.url, the dialect, the driver class and of course, the username and password.

```xml
<?xml version='1.0' encoding='UTF-8'?>
<!DOCTYPE hibernate-configuration PUBLIC
"-//Hibernate/Hibernate Configuration DTD 3.0//EN"
"http://hibernate.sourceforge.net/hibernate-configuration-3.0.dtd">
<hibernate-configuration>
  <session-factory>
  <property name="connection.url">
  jdbc:mysql://localhost/examscam
  </property>
  <property name="connection.username">root
  </property>
  <property name="connection.password">password
  </property>
  <property name="connection.driver_class">
  com.mysql.jdbc.Driver
  </property>
  <property name="dialect">
  org.hibernate.dialect.MySQLDialect
  </property>
  <property name="transaction.factory_class">
  org.hibernate.transaction.JDBCTransactionFactory
  </property>
  <property name="current_session_context_class">
  thread
  </property>
  <!-- this will show us all sql statements -->
  <property name="hibernate.show_sql">true
  </property>
  </session-factory>
</hibernate-configuration>
```

Running the Code

The following snippet of code can be used to not only verify the proper configuration of our Hibernate environment, but when it is executed, it will also connect to our database and create the database related artifacts that are needed to support the persistence of instances of the User class.

```
AnnotationConfiguration config =
                   new AnnotationConfiguration();
config.addAnnotatedClass(User.class);
config.configure();
new SchemaExport(config).create(true, true);
```

The question is, where are we going to put this code? Personally, I like to use JUnit tests to run code, even when I'm just experimenting, as opposed to writing a main method. Using main methods to test code is very 1990's. Still, it's probably the simplest way to run four lines of code, so I'm going to go against my better judgment, and just add a main method to the User class that includes all of the lines of code that we have written that lead to the SchemaExport(config).create(true, true) command. Here's how the main method looks, followed by the entire class definition:

```
public static void main(String args[]) {
  AnnotationConfiguration config =
      new AnnotationConfiguration();
  config.addAnnotatedClass(User.class);
  config.configure();
  new SchemaExport(config).create(true, true);
}
```

Note that compiling and running this main method will also require a few import statements as well:

```
import org.hibernate.cfg.AnnotationConfiguration;
import org.hibernate.tool.hbm2ddl.SchemaExport;
```

```
package com.examscam.model;
import javax.persistence.Entity;
import javax.persistence.GeneratedValue;
import javax.persistence.Id;
import org.hibernate.cfg.AnnotationConfiguration;
import org.hibernate.tool.hbm2ddl.SchemaExport;

@Entity
public class User {

  private Long id;
  private String password;

  @Id
  @GeneratedValue
  public Long getId() {
    return id;
  }

  public void setId(Long id) {
    this.id = id;
  }

  public String getPassword() {
    return password;
  }

  public void setPassword(String password) {
    this.password = password;
  }

  public static void main(String args[]) {
    AnnotationConfiguration config =
                new AnnotationConfiguration();
    config.addAnnotatedClass(User.class);
    config.configure();
    new SchemaExport(config).create(true, true);
  }
}
```

Before Running the User's main Method

Running the main method of the User class should result in the creation of a table named *user* in the *examscam* database schema. Now, one thing you must remember is that Hibernate can create all the tables in the world, but it cannot create the database schema for you. You have to go into the database and actually create the schema yourself, a task that will involve a unique set of steps depending upon the database you use.

Quickly Creating a Database Schema in MySQL

I discussed creating a schema in the previous chapter, but I'll mention it again, just for the sake of posterity. ☺

Using the MySQL Query Browser GUI Tool, creating a new schema is just two or three simple steps. You first select the "Create New Schema" option from the right-click, context menu. In the dialog box that appears, you enter the name *examscam*, and then click 'OK.' Once 'OK' is clicked, your database schema is created!

Each database is different though, and if you're having trouble, you may need to go to the reference material for your particular database, or better yet, ask someone in the know, or even post a query on a message board such as JavaRanch.com.

Compiling the User.java Class

C:_jdk1.6 is where I have installed the JDK.

C:_mycode\com\examscam\model is where I have saved the User.java class.

C:_mycode is where my hibernate.cfg.xml file is located.

C:_hiblib is where I have saved all of the necessary libraries, including the JDBC drivers, required Hibernate Core related libraries and the Hibernate Annotations libraries.

Given this configuration, the following line of code will compile my User.java class.

C:_mycode> c:_jdk1.6\bin\javac -classpath "C:_hiblib*"
C:_mycode\com\examscam\model\User.java

Note: this all appears on one line in the command prompt. The quotes around the "C:_hiblib" directory is required to pick up all of the jar files in the folder.

Running the Compiled User.class

With the User.java class compiled, it is time to run the main method. The User.class will be looking for the hibernate.cfg.xml file, so to avoid an error message such as: *HibernateException: /hibernate.cfg.xml not found.* I have thrown the hibernate.cfg.xml file right into the C:_mycode directory. Given my configuration, the following command will run the main method of the User class:

C:_mycode> c:_jdk1.6\bin
java -classpath "C:_hiblib*";C:_mycode com.examscam.model.**User**

Assuming your hibernate.cfg.xml file is edited properly, and your database is started, the main method of the compiled User class will run, and Hibernate will connect to the database and create the User table.

It should be stressed that this exercise shows you how to compile and run a Java program using the most basic environment possible. With this knowledge, you should be able to obtain a proper, application development tool such as Eclipse, and use it to write, compile, test and run your Java code.

POJO==Plain Ordinary Java Object == JavaBean = Java Class

Output from Running the User.class

Running the main method of the user class sent the following output to my System.out.log file. There's some interesting stuff here, although it's the SQL statement that gets spit out at the end that I find most interesting. Take a look at it:

```
org.hibernate.cfg.annotations.Version <clinit>
INFO: Hibernate Annotations 3.3.0.GA
org.hibernate.cfg.Environment <clinit>INFO: Hibernate 3.2.5
org.hibernate.cfg.Environment <clinit>
INFO: hibernate.properties not found
org.hibernate.cfg.Environment buildBytecodeProvider
INFO: Bytecode provider name : cglib
org.hibernate.cfg.Environment <clinit>
INFO: using JDK 1.4 java.sql.Timestamp handling
org.hibernate.cfg.Configuration configure
INFO: configuring from resource: /hibernate.cfg.xml
org.hibernate.cfg.Configuration getConfigurationInputStream
INFO: Configuration resource: /hibernate.cfg.xml
org.hibernate.cfg.Configuration doConfigure
INFO: Configured SessionFactory: null
org.hibernate.dialect.Dialect <init>
INFO: Using dialect: org.hibernate.dialect.MySQLDialect
org.hibernate.cfg.AnnotationBinder bindClass
INFO: Binding entity from annotated class:
com.mcnz.olgc.data.User
org.hibernate.cfg.annotations.EntityBinder bindTable
INFO: Bind entity com.mcnz.olgc.data.User on table User
org.hibernate.validator.Version <clinit>
INFO: Hibernate Validator 3.0.0.GA
org.hibernate.tool.hbm2ddl.SchemaExport execute
INFO: Running hbm2ddl schema export
org.hibernate.tool.hbm2ddl.SchemaExport execute
INFO: exporting generated schema to database
org.hibernate.connection.DriverManagerConnectionProvider
configure
INFO: Using Hibernate built-in connection pool
org.hibernate.connection.DriverManagerConnectionProvider
configure
INFO: Hibernate connection pool size: 20
org.hibernate.connection.DriverManagerConnectionProvider
configure
INFO: autocommit mode: false  /* continued on next page */
```

76

```
org.hibernate.connection.DriverManagerConnectionProvider
configure
INFO: using driver: com.mysql.jdbc.Driver at URL:
jdbc:mysql://localhost/examscam
org.hibernate.connection.DriverManagerConnectionProvider
configure
INFO: connection properties: {user=root, password=****}
drop table if exists User
create table User (id integer not null auto_increment,
password varchar(255), primary key (id))
org.hibernate.tool.hbm2ddl.SchemaExport execute
INFO: schema export complete
org.hibernate.connection.DriverManagerConnectionProvider
close
INFO: cleaning up connection pool:
jdbc:mysql://localhost/examscam
```

The Results of Running SchemaExport

From the log file that is generated by running the User's main method, you'll notice a few interesting tidbits of information, not the least of which is the following SQL statement:

```
drop table if exists User
create table User (id integer not null
auto_increment, password varchar(255), primary key
(id))
```

Hibernate created this SQL command based on the JPA annotated User class. Furthermore, this was executed against the database using the connection URL of: jdbc:mysql://localhost/examscam, as was defined in the hibernate.cfg.xml file. After executing this code and refreshing the database schema, you should see a new table in the database named *user*, with two fields, an id field, and a password field. Hibernate magically created this table for us. Pretty kewl, eh?

Setting up log4j

You will also notice a little log4j error message in my output:

```
log4j:WARN No appenders could be found for logger
log4j:WARN Please initialize the log4j system properly.
```

This error is due to the fact that Hibernate is using Log4j, and a properties file that Log4j uses to initialize itself cannot be found on the classpath. The Hibernate download contains a sample log4j.properties file you can place on your classpath that will eliminate this error message and subsequently direct logging entries to the System.out log. Alternatively, you can create your own log4j.properties file with the following settings:

```
### direct log messages to stdout ###
log4j.appender.stdout=org.apache.log4j.ConsoleAppender
log4j.appender.stdout.Target=System.out
log4j.appender.stdout.layout=org.apache.log4j.PatternLayout
log4j.appender.stdout.layout.ConversionPattern=%d{ABSOLUTE} %5p %c{1}:%L - %m%n
### set log levels - ###
log4j.rootLogger=warn, stdout log4j.logger.org.hibernate=info
### log JDBC bind parameters ###
log4j.logger.org.hibernate.type=debug
### log schema export/update ###
log4j.logger.org.hibernate.tool.hbm2ddl=debug
```

Make sure the file is named log4j.properties, and is placed on the classpath of both the JVM, and the classloader that creates the AnnotationConfiguration object; for me, the log4j.properties file gets placed in the C:_mycode folder, alongside the all important hibernate.cfg.xml file. Add in this properties file, and then you'll get all sorts of crazy log messages!

Here's another properties file that promises more logging. I haven't tested it out myself, but it looks neat. ☺ Give it a try!

```
##### direct log messages to standard out #####
log4j.appender.stdout=org.apache.log4j.ConsoleAppender
log4j.appender.stdout.Target=System.out
log4j.appender.stdout.layout=org.apache.log4j.PatternLayout
log4j.appender.stdout.layout.ConversionPattern=%d{ABSOLUTE} %5p %c{1}:%L - %m%n
##### direct messages to file hibernate.log #####
log4j.appender.file=org.apache.log4j.FileAppender
log4j.appender.file.File=hibernate.log
log4j.appender.file.layout=org.apache.log4j.PatternLayout
log4j.appender.file.layout.ConversionPattern=%d{ABSOLUTE} %5p %c{1}:%L - %m%n
log4j.rootLogger=warn, file
log4j.logger.net.sf.hibernate=debug
### enable the following line if you want to find DM connection leaks ###
#log4j.logger.net.sf.hibernate.connection.DriverManagerConnectionProvider=trace
### log JDBC bind parameters and prepared statement cache ###
log4j.logger.net.sf.hibernate.type=debug
log4j.logger.net.sf.hibernate.ps.PreparedStatementCache=debug
```

Inspecting the Created Database Table

Digging into some of the GUI tools for MySQL, I can view information about the database table named *user* that was created by Hibernate. While the id and password fields of the User class were of type Long and String respectively, Hibernate knew enough to create these fields in the MySQL database as INTEGER and VARCHAR(45) values.

Furthermore, you will notice that the primary key is defined as a NOT NULL column, along with the option to AUTO INC the primary key as needed. The AUTO INC setting was a direct result of the @GeneratedValue JPA annotation that was defined immediately before the getId() method in the User class.

Column Name	Datatype	NOT NULL	AUTO INC	Flags
id	INTEGER	✓	✓	✓ UNSIGNED
password	VARCHAR(45)			☐ BINARY

Table Name: user   Database: examscam

Columns and Indices | Table Options | Advanced Options

Class to Table Mappings

The promise of Hibernate is to make the job of persisting and managing the state of your JavaBeans easy, or at least, as non-intrusive to your Java applications as possible. As a first pass through Hibernate, we have seen how easy it is to simply decorate a typical JavaBean with some JPA annotations, and have the Hibernate framework consume that JavaBean and subsequently create the underlying database tables that are needed to persist and manage the state of that JavaBean.

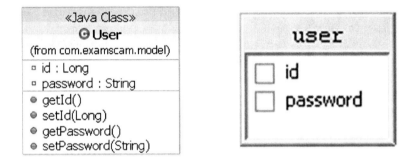

Hibernate really is an amazing, lightweight framework, that allows Java developers to concentrate on their object models, without burdening those same developers with the onerous task of figuring out how to map their JavaBeans to the underlying persistence store.

Chapter 3
Adding Records

Chapter 1 dealt with what was required in order to start working with, and developing, a Hibernate application.

Chapter 2 looked at the Hibernate configuration object that manages JPA annotated JavaBeans, namely the AnnotationConfiguration object. Along with the SchemaExport class, we managed to take a JPA annotated JavaBean and have Hibernate create the underlying database table that is needed to persist the state of instances of the User POJO we created.

The next logical step is to actually look at what is required to take an instance of a JavaBean and actually persist the state of that instance to the database. To do so, we'll have to familiarize ourselves with the following topics:

☞ *creating and initializing the properties of a JavaBean*

☞ *obtaining a Hibernate SessionFactory*

☞ *starting and committing database transactions using the Hibernate Session*

☞ *using the Hibernate API to dictate which instances will be persisted to the database*

These topics will be the focus of this chapter, and once you're done reading it, you'll be familiar with the basic steps that are required to persist an instance of a JavaBean to the database using Hibernate.

Mapping the User Class to the user Table

This chapter will continue with the mapping of the POJO named *User* to the corresponding table in the examscam database named ***user***.

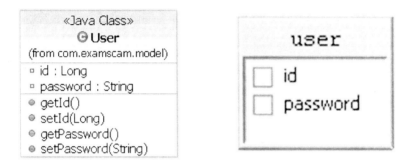

Here's the SQL code that was used to create the user table:

```
drop table if exists User
create table User (id integer not null
auto_increment, password varchar(255), primary key
(id))
```

The User Class

I know I've printed this out before, but I like to make sure that if anyone is jumping into this chapter, they don't have to backtrack page after page to see what we've been up to. For the sake of posterity, here's the User class as we have coded it so far. In this chapter, we'll be building upon the code that already exists inside of the main method of the User class.

The Annotated User POJO

```java
package com.examscam.model;
import javax.persistence.Entity;
import javax.persistence.GeneratedValue;
import javax.persistence.Id;
import org.hibernate.cfg.AnnotationConfiguration;
import org.hibernate.tool.hbm2ddl.SchemaExport;

@Entity
public class User {

  private Long id;
  private String password;

  @Id
  @GeneratedValue
  public Long getId() {return id;}

  public void setId(Long id) {this.id = id;}

  public String getPassword() {
    return password;
  }

  public void setPassword(String password) {
    this.password = password;
  }

  public static void main(String args[]) {
    AnnotationConfiguration config =
                new AnnotationConfiguration();
    config.addAnnotatedClass(User.class);
    config.configure();
    new SchemaExport(config).create(true, true);
  }
}
```

Persisting Data to the Database

So, with the User class coded, we have a fine example of a simple, JPA annotated JavaBean. Furthermore, chapter two showed us how a Hibernate configuration object can read the hibernate.cfg.xml file, ingest a JPA annotated POJO and subsequently connect to a JDBC compliant database and create the various tables needed to support POJO based persistence.

But, how can we get Hibernate to programmatically persist the state of a JavaBean instance to the database? Well, there are a few steps involved, and a few new Hibernate objects will be required, such as the Hibernate Session and the Hibernate SessionFactory, but overall, it's a pretty interesting, relatively easy, and fairly elegant process.

Editing the User's main Method

The main method in our User class creates and configures an AnnotationConfiguration object that is aware of our User class. That's really the first step in doing any type of Hibernate persistence work. In the main method of the User class, we then have Hibernate create the required database tables by calling the create method on a new SchemaExport object. Let's assume that we've already created our database, and comment out the call to the SchemaExport task. After all, we don't want to keep recreating the database every time we run our code. ☺

```
public static void main (String args[]) {

  /*create the configuration object*/
  AnnotationConfiguration config =
                  new AnnotationConfiguration();

  /*make hibernate aware of the User POJO*/
  config.addAnnotatedClass(User.class);

  /*read and process hibernate.cfg.xml and JPA metadata*/
  config.configure();

  /* COMMENT OUT THE SchemaExport CALL */
  // new SchemaExport(config).create(true, true);
}
```

Hibernate & Transient Instances

When an instance of a JavaBean is created in your Java code, the JVM treats it as a free and unfettered spirit. As long as the instance is in scope, its properties can be referenced, and its methods can be invoked. When a JavaBean goes out of scope, it is simply forgotten, and the JVM's garbage collector takes care of the funeral arrangements. In the Hibernate arena, these types of instances are called transient instances, because their existence is evanescent, as Hibernate remains completely ignorant of them.

So, even though the User class may have been added as an annotated class to the Hibernate configuration, the following instance of the User class would be transient in its existence, as Hibernate would be completely oblivious to it, and as such, the POJO's state would never get persisted to the underlying database:

```
public static void main (String args[]) {
  AnnotationConfiguration config =
                   new AnnotationConfiguration();
  config.addAnnotatedClass(User.class);
  config.configure();
  // new SchemaExport(config).create(true, true);

/* This User instance, u, is completely transient. Hibernate
is not aware of it, nor does Hibernate care about it. */

  User u = new User();
  u.setPassword("abc123");


}
/* as the User instance, u, goes out of scope, it is
garbage collected, and its state is not persisted. */
```

The Hibernate Session and the SessionFactory

When a JavaBean is instantiated in your Java code, it is treated as a transient instance, and Hibernate pretty much ignores it. So, the question is, how do you get Hibernate to not only pay attention to your JavaBean, but to manage the persistence lifecycle of the JavaBean as well?

In order to get Hibernate to pay attention to a JavaBean, the instance must *touch*, or become *associated with*, a Hibernate **Session**. The Hibernate Session is without debate, the most magical of all of the Hibernate components. Simply passing a JPA annotated instance, such as an instance of the User class, to the saveOrUpdate method of a Hibernate Session object is enough to pique Hibernate's interest in the JavaBean in question, and get Hibernate to manage all of the instance's persistence. However, the question is, where do we get our hands on a Hibernate Session? Well, as any good 18th century industrialist will tell you, you get things from a Factory, or more specifically in our case, a SessionFactory. ☺

Sessions and the org.hibernate.SessionFactory

The Hibernate SessionFactory is actually extracted from the configuration object through a compound method call, with the first call being to the AnnotationConfiguration object's config() method, and the second to the somewhat self-explanatory buildSessionFactory() method.

```
AnnotationConfiguration config =
            new AnnotationConfiguration();
config.addAnnotatedClass(User.class);
config.configure();
// new SchemaExport(config).create(true, true);
/*The SessionFactory is obtained through the config object*/
SessionFactory factory =
        config.buildSessionFactory();
/* The User instance is still transient and not associated
with any Hibernate Session. */
User u = new User();
u.setPassword("abc123");
```

The SessionFactory is of type **org.hibernate.SessionFactory,** which you may need to import if you're coding along. ☺

Class Diagram for the SessionFactory

«Java Interface»
🛈 **SessionFactory**

- *openSession(Connection)*
- *openSession(Interceptor)*
- *openSession(Connection, Interceptor)*
- *openSession()*
- *getCurrentSession()*
- *getClassMetadata(Class)*
- *getClassMetadata(String)*
- *getCollectionMetadata(String)*
- *getAllClassMetadata()*
- *getAllCollectionMetadata()*
- *getStatistics()*
- *close()*
- *isClosed()*
- *evict(Class)*
- *evict(Class, Serializable)*
- *evictEntity(String)*
- *evictEntity(String, Serializable)*
- *evictCollection(String)*
- *evictCollection(String, Serializable)*
- *evictQueries()*
- *evictQueries(String)*
- *openStatelessSession()*
- *openStatelessSession(Connection)*
- *getDefinedFilterNames()*
- *getFilterDefinition(String)*

The SessionFactory and Resource Allocation

The SessionFactory itself is a fairly resource intensive object to create. In the first few Hibernate tutorials in this book, we'll typically create SessionFactory objects whenever we need them, but in practice, it is imperative to control how often the SessionFactory gets created. Minimizing the number of SessionFactory objects you create can be done by perhaps making the SessionFactory a static variable that is accessed through a Singleton design pattern, or better yet, in a J2EE environment, simply have the SessionFactory bound to, and accessed through, the JNDI naming service of the J2EE application server. You really only need one SessionFactory in any application. Controlling the number of SessionFactory objects that get created, and for that matter, destroyed, will help to minimize unnecessary resource allocations.

On the other hand, the Hibernate *Session*, which is produced by the SessionFactory, is a very efficient object that you don't have to feel guilty about creating *willy-nilly*. A single SessionFactory is great at efficiently pumping out Hibernate Session objects whenever you need them. Limit the number of SessionFactory objects that are created in an enterprise application to one, but feel guilt-free about generating Hibernate Sessions whenever you need them.

Sessions and the org.hibernate.SessionFactory

It doesn't take a genius to figure out that the job of the SessionFactory is to pump out Hibernate Session objects. Obtaining the Session is actually a pretty straight forward endeavor once you have access to the SessionFactory, as you simply have to invoke the factory's getCurrentSession() method.

```
AnnotationConfiguration config = new AnnotationConfiguration();
config.addAnnotatedClass(User.class);config.configure();
// new SchemaExport(config).create(true, true);
SessionFactory factory = config.buildSessionFactory();
Session session = factory.getCurrentSession();
/* a session is around, but the User is still transient! */
User u = new User();  u.setPassword("abc123");
```

Putting the Hibernate Session on Alert Status ☺

Once you have your Hibernate Session all instantiated and ready to go, you need to rattle its cage a little bit and let it know that it is about to be used to perform some database interactions. The **beginTransaction()** method of the Hibernate Session does just that; it essentially puts the Hibernate Session on alert.

After invoking the beginTransaction() method, you do all of your JavaBean stuff, and then pass your JavaBean instances to the save, or update, or saveOrUpdate methods of the Hibernate Session. When all of that is done, you typically see the following compound method call to commit the transaction: **session.getTransaction().commit().**

```
Session session = factory.getCurrentSession();
session.beginTransaction();
✂✂✂
/* Do some sexy JavaBean & POJO stuff in here */
✂✂✂
session.getTransaction().commit();
```

Saving a Simple POJO with Hibernate

So far, we've laid the groundwork for obtaining a Hibernate Session, and we've talked about beginning a transaction, and correspondingly, the method call needed to commit a transaction. But how do we actually get the data contained in our JavaBean persisted to the database? Well, from a Java coding point of view, it is incredibly simple.

Let's think about our User object for a second; it has two properties, one of which is the id, (which through the @GeneratedValue annotation, we have already indicated that it will be generated for us by the database) and a property of type String, named password. To create a new database record representing the state of a User instance, all we have to do is create an instance of the User class, initialize the password field, and then tell Hibernate to save the state of the instance we just created to the database using the saveOrUpdate(Object obj) method call. It's just that easy!

```
Session session = factory.getCurrentSession();
session.beginTransaction();
/* create & initialize your User POJO */
User u = new User();
u.setPassword("abc123");
/* at this point, the User instance is still transient */
/* ask the session to save your POJO to the db*/

session.saveOrUpdate(u);  /*at this point, the User
instance is considered persistent*/

session.getTransaction().commit();
```

Persistent Objects

Once a JavaBean has *touched* by the Hibernate Session, which happens when an instance is passed to the saveOrUpdate method of the Session, the instance **stops being *transient*, and becomes a *persistent object.*** Once a JavaBean has 'touched' the Session within the scope of a transaction, Hibernate will manage the persistent state of that instance, right up until the point that the enclosing transaction is committed.

save, update and *saveOrUpdate*

Notice how we have called the *saveOrUpdate* method of the Hibernate Session. If a JavaBean gets passed to this method, and it has an id, Hibernate will attempt to update the existing, corresponding row, in the database – after all, if an instance has an id, it must have a corresponding representation in the database. On the other hand, if the JavaBean passed to the saveOrUpdate method does *not* have a primary key attached to it, Hibernate will treat the operation as a create invocation, and create a new row in the database.

Hibernate does have separate update and save method calls, but in light of the fact that the functionality of the two is so similar, a combined saveOrUpdate method has been added to the API. Use it, it's much simpler. ☺

---

public void **saveOrUpdate**(Object object)throws HibernateException

Either save(Object) or update(Object) the given instance, depending upon resolution of the unsaved-value checks. This operation cascades to associated instances if the association is mapped with cascade="save-update".

-another shameless regurgitation of the Hibernate API JavaDoc

Basking in the Beauty of Hibernate Persistence

Believe it or not, but as far as the Java programming aspect goes, that's how easy it is to persist a JavaBean instance to the database using Hibernate. You create your JavaBeans just as you normally would, and then you ask the Hibernate Session to save your instances. Next thing you know, once you have committed your transaction, a new record will pop up in your database. It's amazing!

«Java Interface»
Session
getEntityMode()
getSession(EntityMode)
flush()
setFlushMode(FlushMode)
getFlushMode()
setCacheMode(CacheMode)
getCacheMode()
getSessionFactory()
connection()
close()
cancelQuery()
isOpen()
isConnected()
isDirty()
getIdentifier(Object)
contains(Object)
evict(Object)
load(Class, Serializable, LockMode)
load(String, Serializable, LockMode)
load(Class, Serializable)
load(String, Serializable)
load(Object, Serializable)
replicate(Object, ReplicationMode)
replicate(String, Object, ReplicationMode)
save(Object)
save(String, Object)
saveOrUpdate(Object)
saveOrUpdate(String, Object)
update(Object)
update(String, Object)
merge(Object)
merge(String, Object)

```
«Java Interface»
ⓘ Session (continued)
```

- *persist(Object)*
- *persist(String, Object)*
- *delete(Object)*
- *delete(String, Object)*
- *lock(Object, LockMode)*
- *lock(String, Object, LockMode)*
- *refresh(Object)*
- *refresh(Object, LockMode)*
- *getCurrentLockMode(Object)*
- *beginTransaction()*
- *getTransaction()*
- *createCriteria(Class)*
- *createCriteria(Class, String)*
- *createCriteria(String)*
- *createCriteria(String, String)*
- *createQuery(String)*
- *createSQLQuery(String)*
- *createFilter(Object, String)*
- *getNamedQuery(String)*
- *clear()*
- *get(Class, Serializable)*
- *get(Class, Serializable, LockMode)*
- *get(String, Serializable)*
- *get(String, Serializable, LockMode)*
- *getEntityName(Object)*
- *enableFilter(String)*
- *getEnabledFilter(String)*
- *disableFilter(String)*
- *getStatistics()*
- *setReadOnly(Object, boolean)*
- *disconnect()*
- *reconnect()*
- *reconnect(Connection)*

Pulling it all Together in Code

Code Figure 3-1 pulls together all of the code we have discussed so far with regards to interacting with the Hibernate Session and persisting the state of an instance of the User class to the database, all within the confines of a runnable main method. With an appropriately configured hibernate.cfg.xml file, which we created and tested in an earlier chapter, we could run the main method of the User class as a stand-alone Java application, and the code would actually persist an instance of the User class, storing a password of *abc123*, to our database, along with a uniquely generated id for the database row.

Hibernate and JPA Imports

One thing to notice about the code in Figure 3-1 is the collection of import statements before the class declaration. As you can see, we are using an assortment of classes pulled from the Hibernate API's org.hibernate package, along with classes, or more accurately, *annotations*, from the Java Persistence API, which are found in the javax.persistence package.

Java Classes and main Methods

Now I should also point out that I'm not a big fan of using the main method of a Java class for testing purposes. Creating proper tests is not only an art, but it is an extremely important part, if not the most important part, of any enterprise application development endeavor. However, for learning, I think it is important to keep things as simple as possible, especially at the beginning, as we iteratively incorporate more and more complex ideas. For now, testing our code in the main method of a POJO should not be a punishable offence, but good Java developers should make testing frameworks such as JUnit and EasyMock an important ingredient in their daily programming bread. ☺

Code Figure 3-1

```
package com.examscam.model;
import javax.persistence.Entity;
import javax.persistence.GeneratedValue;
import javax.persistence.Id;
import org.hibernate.Session;
import org.hibernate.SessionFactory;
import org.hibernate.cfg.AnnotationConfiguration;

@Entity
public class User {
  private Long id;
  private String password;

  @Id
  @GeneratedValue
  public Long getId() {return id;}
  public void setId(Long id) {this.id = id;}
  public String getPassword() {return password;}
  public void setPassword(String password) {
    this.password = password;
  }
  public static void main(String args[]){
    AnnotationConfiguration config =
                    new AnnotationConfiguration();
    config.addAnnotatedClass(User.class);
    config.configure();
    // new SchemaExport(config).create(true, true);
    SessionFactory factory = config.buildSessionFactory();
    Session session = factory.getCurrentSession();
    session.beginTransaction();
    System.out.println("creating user");
    User u = new User();
    u.setPassword("abc123");
    session.saveOrUpdate(u);
    System.out.println("user saved");
    session.getTransaction().commit();
    System.out.println("transaction successful!!!");
  }
}
```

Running the Application

With all of the Hibernate Core, Hibernate Annotations and JDBC driver JAR files are on your classpath, having properly edited the hibernate.cfg.xml file, having eliminated any compile errors in your code, and having your database up and running, you are ready to test your User class by running its executable *main* method. Running my main method results in the following output:

```
creating Hibernate config
creating user
Hibernate: insert into User (password) values (?)
user saved
log4j:WARN No appenders could be found for logger
(org.hibernate.cfg.annotations.Version).
log4j:WARN Please initialize the log4j system properly.
transaction successful!!!
```

Looking at the Database Results

After running the User class' main method, when I look at the *user* table in my database, I actually see that the state of the User object I created in my Java code has been persisted by Hibernate to the database.

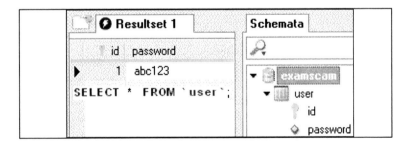

The auto-generated id of the new record is 1, and the password is abc123, which is the value that was hard-coded into the main method of the User class.

Showing SQL in the Output

In the console output generated from running my main method, which is displayed on the previous page, you will notice that I bolded the **insert** SQL statement. This statement was printed out by Hibernate as a result of the hibernate.show_sql property that was set to *true* in the Hibernate configuration file. This is a great property to have enabled during development time, although you should disable this setting in production as this will tend to slow down your application as it swamps your JVM log files with needless SQL verbosity.

```
<property name="hibernate.show_sql">true</property>
```

Setting up log4j

You will also notice a little log4j error message in my output:

```
log4j:WARN No appenders could be found for logger
log4j:WARN Please initialize the log4j system properly.
```

This error is due to the fact that Hibernate is using Log4J, and a properties file that Log4J uses to initialize itself cannot be found on the classpath. The Hibernate download contains a sample log4j.properties file you can place on your classpath that will eliminate this error message and subsequently direct logging entries to the System.out log. Alternatively, you can create your own log4j.properties file with the following settings:

```
### direct log messages to stdout ###
log4j.appender.stdout=org.apache.log4j.ConsoleAppender
log4j.appender.stdout.Target=System.out
log4j.appender.stdout.layout=org.apache.log4j.PatternLayout
log4j.appender.stdout.layout.ConversionPattern=%d{ABSOLUTE} %5p %c{1}:%L - %m%n
### set log levels - ###
log4j.rootLogger=warn, stdout log4j.logger.org.hibernate=info
### log JDBC bind parameters ###
log4j.logger.org.hibernate.type=debug
### log schema export/update ###
log4j.logger.org.hibernate.tool.hbm2ddl=debug
```

Make sure the file is named log4j.properties, and is placed on the classpath of both the JVM, and the classloader that creates the AnnotationConfiguration object; for me, this is the C:_mycode folder, which by the way, is the same place you'll find the hibernate.cfg.xml file.

You will also notice that I have set they **type** attribute to **debug**. With the type setting at debug, rather than info, you will see much more information about the values that are getting inserted into the database by Hibernate.

And that's it! That's how easy it is to persist the state of your JavaBeans to the database using Hibernate and JPA annotation!

Revisiting the hibernate.cfg.xml File

```xml
<?xml version='1.0' encoding='UTF-8'?><!DOCTYPE hibernate-configuration PUBLIC
"-//Hibernate/Hibernate Configuration DTD 3.0//EN" "http://hibernate.sourceforge.net/hibernate-
configuration-3.0.dtd">
<hibernate-configuration>
  <session-factory>
  <property name="connection.url">
  jdbc:mysql://localhost/examscam
  </property>
  <property name="connection.username">
  root
  </property>
  <property name="connection.password">
  password
  </property>
  <property name="connection.driver_class">
  com.mysql.jdbc.Driver
  </property>
  <property name="dialect">
  org.hibernate.dialect.MySQLDialect
  </property>
  <property name="transaction.factory_class">
  org.hibernate.transaction.JDBCTransactionFactory
  </property>
  <property name="current_session_context_class">
  thread
  </property>
  <!-- this will show us all sql statements -->
  <property name="hibernate.show_sql">
  true
  </property>
  <!-- mapping files -->
  </session-factory>
</hibernate-configuration>
```

Chapter 4
CRUD Based Operations

Okay, so, I'm just over the moon that we've got a basic Hibernate environment configured, we've got some code compiled, and we're successfully saving data to our database. Plus, we've effectively used a few JPA annotations in our code as well. All in all, were making good progress, but there's still a long way to go before we can say that we've mastered Hibernate.

This chapter will go beyond the basic *save* functionality we saw in Chapter 3, and take a look at all four of the basic CRUD operations, namely:

☞ *Create Operations (a quick review of chapter 3)*

☞ *Retrieve Operations*

☞ *Updating Functionality*

☞ *Delete and Destroy Functionality*

Interestingly enough, on the topic of data retrieval, there are actually a few different ways that entities can be brought into your application given a unique primary key. This chapter will finish off by discussing these *entity acquisition* options, as we try and shed some light on their differences and benefits.

Create (We've Seen This Before)

All database driven applications revolve around the four basic CRUD operations: **C**reate, **R**ead (retrieve?), **U**pdate and **D**elete (destroy?). In previous chapters, we examined the code that was required to get the Hibernate framework to create a new database record based on an instance of the User class. We're going to start off this chapter by leveraging that knowledge of Hibernate as we create a new class called CrudRunner.

Take a look at the starter code for the CrudRunner on the following page. As you can see, the CrudRunner is a simple Java class with a static create method and a runnable main method. As far as the create method goes, there's nothing new in there. It's the same Hibernate code we saw in the previous chapter when we learned how to save the state of

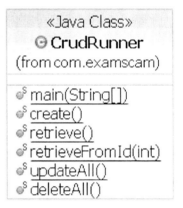

a User instance to the database. As far as the *main* method goes, it just calls the static *create* method.

All That Plumbing Code

All of the plumbing code that has to do with creating a Hibernate AnnotationConfiguration object, which is needed to create a SessionFactory, which is eventually used to generate a Hibernate Session, is *very verbosely* coded in the CrudRunner class. We're going to repeat that stuff ad nauseum in this chapter. Of course, we could always factor it out into a single, reusable method, but we'll save that for another time and place. For now, it's probably a good learning strategy to be further exposed to the fundamental code that's required to get Hibernate to work, so I'm not going to feel the least bit guilty about repeating it over and over again in this chapter.

The CrudRunner Class – First Iteration

```
package com.examscam;
/* Notice the com.examscam package!!! */
import org.hibernate.Session;
import org.hibernate.SessionFactory;
import org.hibernate.cfg.AnnotationConfiguration;
import com.examscam.model.User;
import java.util.*;
public class CrudRunner {
  public static void main(String[] args) {
/* Run all the static methods (currently only 1) */
    CrudRunner.create();
  }
  public static void create (){
/* Create the config object, reading from the
hibernate.cfg.xml file. */
    AnnotationConfiguration config =
                  new AnnotationConfiguration();
/* Make sure all annotated classes are added to the
configuration */
    config.addAnnotatedClass(User.class);
    SessionFactory factory;
/* Obtain the SessionFactory after calling the config()
method of the AnnotationConfiguration instance. */
    factory =
        config.configure().buildSessionFactory();
/* Get a Hibernate Session */
    Session session = factory.getCurrentSession();
    session.beginTransaction();
/* Create and initialize an instance of a JPA annotated
class */
    User user = new User();
    user.setPassword("abc123");
/* Have the instance touch the session and then commit the
transaction */
    session.save(user);
    session.getTransaction().commit();
  }
}
```

Retrieving and Querying Data with Hibernate

So, we should be pretty solid on creating a new record in the database using Hibernate, seeing that we've done it a few times. The next question is: how do we query and see all of that fabulous information that we have previously *stuffed inside* of our database?

Well, querying a database with Hibernate is a little bit more of an involved process than simply creating a new record. I mean, you have to create a special query object, you have to pass some special *Hibernate 'SQL'* to the createQuery method of the Hibernate Session, you have to throw the results of your query into a java.util.List object, and then, after sprinkling in a little Haitian Voodoo, you do a few casts and subsequently inspect the data that Hibernate throws back at you. As I said, querying the database is a slightly more involved process than simply saving the state of a JPA annotated POJO, but don't be intimidated. In the grand scheme of things, pulling information out of a database using Hibernate really isn't all that difficult.

I'm going to add a new static method to my CrudRunner class called retrieve that has all the code in it that's needed to pull all of the records out of the user database table. Take a look at it; we'll debrief it in a moment.

```
public static void retrieve() {
  AnnotationConfiguration config =
                    new AnnotationConfiguration();
  config.addAnnotatedClass(User.class);
  SessionFactory factory;
  factory = config.configure().buildSessionFactory();
  Session session = factory.getCurrentSession();
  session.beginTransaction();
  java.util.List allUsers;
  Query queryResult=session.createQuery("from User");
  allUsers = queryResult.list();
  for (int i = 0; i < allUsers.size(); i++) {
    User user = (User) allUsers.get(i);
    System.out.println(user.getPassword());
  }
  session.getTransaction().commit();
}
```

Debriefing the retrieve() Method

The retrieve method starts off with some redundant and repetitive Hibernate *plumbing code* that basically initializes the Hibernate infrastructure classes and gets our Java program ready to interact with the database. Again, you will notice that a Hibernate **Session** is obtained from the SessionFactory, which itself is built from Hibernate's AnnotationConfiguration object. This Hibernate Session then begins a transaction, which is something we should do every time we interact with our persistence store. Of course, we've seen all of this plumbing code umpteen times before. ☹ Don't worry, we'll eventually look at factoring this repetitive code out into a helper method or HibernateUtil class or something, but for now, we'll leave it in, just for the sake of simplicity.

```
/* your standard Hibernate connection code */
AnnotationConfiguration config =
                    new AnnotationConfiguration();
config.addAnnotatedClass(User.class);
SessionFactory factory;
factory = config.configure().buildSessionFactory();
Session session = factory.getCurrentSession();
session.beginTransaction();
```

Querying the Database

After the Hibernate Session is obtained, we declare an object of type java.util.List, to which we assign the variable name *allUsers*. Basically, when we do a standard, non-unique query of the database, we can expect a result to be returned to us in the form of a java.util.List. The allUsers list will hold the results of our *from User* query.

```
java.util.List allUsers;
```

Say Hello to HQL

Once we have our List for holding the query results, *and this is a pretty important point,* the createQuery method is invoked on the Hibernate Session, with the String *"from User"* being passed in as the argument.

```
/* specifically the org.hibernate.Query */
Query queryResult=session.createQuery("from User");
allUsers = queryResult.list();
```

As you have probably guessed, the literal String "from User", which is passed into the Hibernate Session's createQuery method, is a special type of query statement that is derived from a Hibernate specific query language, HQL. For now, the *"from User"* String can be thought of as the object oriented equivalent of *SELECT * FROM USER.*

```
Query queryResult=session.createQuery("from User");
allUsers = queryResult.list();
```

However, don't be fooled by what may appear on the surface to be a great similarity between standard SQL and the query language used by Hibernate. The Hibernate Query Language, HQL, is actually an object-oriented data query language, meaning that HQL understands object oriented concepts such as association, inheritance, aggregation and polymorphism. HQL is pretty awesome once you get into it, but it is definitely different from SQL. ☺

Execution of the createQuery("from User") method call returns a Hibernate object called a Query. Calling the **list() or iterate()** method of the Hibernate Query object will trigger a database call that will execute the given query, and return a collection of JavaBeans that match the type and criteria of the HQL statement. As you could imagine, the **list**() method of the Query object returns a java.util.List of JavaBeans, whereas the **iterate**() method returns an object the implements the java.util.Iterator interface.

```
allUsers = queryResult.list();
```

Looping through the List

So, when we invoke the list() method on the Query instance, we get a java.util.List in return. I guess the big question is then: **what exactly does this java.util.List contain?**

Well, it contains instances of the User class, representing the data in the underlying user table of the database.

A Subtle Distinction

Now, since the POJO and the database table are both named User, an important little subtlety may have been missed. When the HQL statement references the User, it is actually referencing the Java *class* named User, not the database table named user. This is a subtle but extremely important distinction. You see, we could change the name and location of the underlying database table and infrastructure, but so long as our User class is mapped accurately to the underlying datastore, the HQL query doesn't have to change. You see, our HQL queries are based on our Java classes, and Hibernate translates those HQL queries into the appropriate SQL needed to manipulate the underlying database. Of course, Hibernate does all of those translations behind the scenes, effectively insulating Java developers from any changes that might happen to the underlying database. Awesome, eh?

Looping through the Query Results

Looping through the list, and extracting a User instance out of the List, with a combination of the List's get(int) method and a handy cast, gives us access to all of the User instances returned by the query.

```
for (int i = 0; i < allUsers.size(); i++) {
  User user = (User) allUsers.get(i);
  System.out.println(user.getPassword());
}
```

The CrudRunner's retrieve() Method

Once you have a User instance both extracted from the List and cast into the appropriate type, it is completely up to the you with regards to what you want to do with it. In this example, we simply print out the password of the user instance to the console, which, given the fact that I'm looping through every instance in the List, will provide me the passwords of all of the entities in the user table of the database.

And that's pretty much it! To retrieve data from the database, you simply leverage the Hibernate Session's createQuery method, pass in some HQL, convert the guts of the returned Query object into an easy to use List, and then loop through the collection of POJOs contained in the List. **It's just that easy!**

```
⌘⌘⌘
public static void retrieve() {
  /* your standard Hibernate connection code */
  AnnotationConfiguration config =
                        new AnnotationConfiguration();
  config.addAnnotatedClass(User.class);
  SessionFactory factory;
  factory = config.configure().buildSessionFactory();
  Session session = factory.getCurrentSession();
  session.beginTransaction();
  System.out.println("Querying the whole database...");
  java.util.List allUsers;
  Query queryResult=session.createQuery("from User");
  allUsers = queryResult.list();

  System.out.println("Number of rows: " + allUsers.size());

  for (int i = 0; i < allUsers.size(); i++) {
    User user = (User) allUsers.get(i);
    System.out.println(user.getPassword());
  }
  System.out.println("Database contents delivered...");
  session.getTransaction().commit();
}⌘⌘⌘
```

Retrieving a *Unique Entity* with Hibernate

The retrieve method we just coded dropped a pretty heavy hammer on our database, returning all of the entities in the underlying system via the *from User* HQL query. However, not all queries are interested in obtaining a massive resultset from the database. Quite often, database queries should return either zero or one unique result from the database. Let's explore how we can handle the scenario where a query should, at most, return one, single, unique result from the database.

The primary key of the User, named id, is a unique value that can't be duplicated in the user table. If we were to query the user table on the id alone, we should never receive more than one record in return. So, let's do an HQL query that looks for a User, based on a primary key of a User already added to your database. I'm going to use the id of 1. ☺

A Note About Primary Keys

The retrieveFromId method we are about to create will use HQL and something called variable injection to retrieve a unique entity from the database. The real objective of this method is to explore HQL a little bit deeper, and demonstrate how to handle queries that will only return one or zero results.

However, it should be noted that the Hibernate Session provides two very helpful methods for retrieving a single entity from a database if you know the primary key for the record, with those methods being load() and get(). We'll track those methods down at the end of this chapter. I just wanted to mention that, if you do have a primary key for an entity, there are other, potentially easier ways to retrieve the associated instance with Hibernate.

Variable Injection Queries: Hibernate vs. SQL

When performing a query where the criteria isn't exactly known until runtime, we need to take advantage of HQL's *variable injection* facilities. If you've ever used JDBC and worked with PreparedStatements, you'll notice a number of similarities in the philosophy of how variables are injected into HQL statements, although the syntax between HQL and JDBC statements may be a tiny bit different.

With a JDBC PreparedStatement, a select query against the user table, where the value of the id is not known until runtime, would look something like this:

```
String idVariable;
✂✂✂/*obtain the id from user somehow!!!*/ ✂✂✂
String sqlQuery = "select * from user where id = ?";
PreparedStatement ps = con.prepareStatement(sqlQuery);
/*replace the first ? mark with the value held by the
variable*/
ps.setString(1, idVariable);
ResultSet rs = ps.executeQuery();✂✂✂
```

Notice the SQL code of *select * from user where id = ?"*, with an emphasis on the question mark. When this code is run, the value of the id is not known until runtime, so it must be garnered through the user, or perhaps, from some other part of the program. So, instead of hard coding in a value for the id, you just code the SQL statement with a question mark, ?, in the spot where the unknown value should go. You then code some way to get this value at runtime, substituting the initialized runtime variable for the question mark in the query using one of the methods of the JDBC PreparedStatement object. Once the ? is initialized with a real value, you send the query to the database. That's how JDBC PreparedStatements work. Hibernate is similar, but different. ☺ Let's take a look at how Hibernate would achieve the same result.

Variable Injection with Hibernate

Hibernate uses a syntax that is very similar to that of a JDBC PreparedStatement to perform runtime variable injection with an HQL statement. But while the syntax may be a bit different, the idea is pretty much the same.

Rather than putting a question mark into the Hibernate Query Language String where the runtime variable needs to be inserted, HQL statements typically use a variable name with a preceding colon. This is actually a bit of an improvement over using the old question mark, because you can use real names for where the variables need to be inserted, rather than rhyming off the question marks as you typically do with JDBC PreparedStatements. Here's how our Hibernate query String might look when leveraging the facilities of variable injection:

```
String queryString = "from User where id = :id";
```

This HQL String is then passed to the createQuery method of the Hibernate Session to create a Query object:

```
Query query = session.createQuery(queryString);
```

From there, a setter method on the initialized query object, which I creatively named *query*, is used to substitute the variable, defined in the HQL String as :id, with an actual value. Here, we use an id value passed into the program:

```
query.setInteger("id", idVariable);
```

Once the placeholder in the HQL query has been substituted by our intended variable, we can execute the query:

```
Object queryResult = query.uniqueResult();
User user = (User)queryResult;
```

Once the query is executed, we take the queryResult, which is returned as an Object, and cast it into a User. Once the cast is completed, it's totally up to you what to do with the instance. It's all just that easy!

Returning a Unique Result

A notable difference between the Hibernate code used to obtain a unique result, as opposed to a query that returns multiple rows, is the name of the method invoked on the Hibernate Query object. When you expect a single row to be returned from the database, you invoke the query object's uniqueResult() method. When you expect multiple rows to be returned, you use the Query's list() method.

```
Object queryResult = query.uniqueResult();
User user = (User)queryResult;
```

Let's add a static **retrieveFromId** method to the CrudRunner class that leverages all of our newfound knowledge on the topic of variable injection. The full method that returns a single User instance, given a primary key provided by the calling program, is as follows (note that a primary key of 1 is hard coded into the main method.):

```
XXX
public static User retrieveFromId(int idValue) {
  AnnotationConfiguration config = new AnnotationConfiguration();
  config.addAnnotatedClass(User.class);
  SessionFactory factory;
  factory = config.configure().buildSessionFactory();
  Session session = factory.getCurrentSession();
  session.beginTransaction();
  String queryString = "from User where id = :id";
  Query query = session.createQuery(queryString);
  query.setInteger("id", idValue);
  Object queryResult = query.uniqueResult();
  User user = (User)queryResult;
  session.getTransaction().commit();
  System.out.print(user.getPassword());
  return user;
}
public static void main(String[] args) {
  CrudRunner.create();
  CrudRunner.retrieve();
  CrudRunner.retrieveFromId(1);    /* id of 1 */
}XXX
```

Updating Database Records with Hibernate

So far, we've mastered the 'C' and 'R' of the CRUD acronym. Okay, maybe saying that we've *mastered* them is going a bit far, but we've been exposed to them, and we're getting a good idea of how they work. The next letter we have to tackle is the 'U,' or the *update* operation.

The process of updating a record is fairly simple. All you have to do is get a User object, update some of its information, and then pass that updated User POJO to the Hibernate Session.

For my little example, I'm going to update all of the passwords in the User table, changing all existing passwords to the word *'password.'* So, to do that, I'll first retrieve all of the records from the database in the form of a java.util.List, using the techniques that were mastered when dealing with the retrieve operation. I will then pull the User objects out of the java.util.List, *one at a time*, and call the setter on the User POJO, updating the password of the User instance to the word *'password.'*

```
/* update an instance of the User class */
user.setPassword("password");
```

After updating the User instance, I'll then pass the updated instance to the *update* method of the Hibernate Session.

```
/* pass the updated user to session's update method*/
session.update(user);
```

Of course, nothing is guaranteed to be updated until the transaction is committed, so, once all of the User objects in the java.util.List are updated, the getTransaction().commit() method is invoked on the Hibernate Session.

```
session.getTransaction().commit();
```

111

The *Updated* CrudRunner

Here's the CrudRunner class with the updateAll method contained within. The meat of the create and retrieve methods have been scratched out for the sake of brevity.

```
public class CrudRunner {
  public static void main(String[] args) {
    CrudRunner.create();
    CrudRunner.retrieve();
    CrudRunner.retrieveFromId(1);
    CrudRunner.updateAll();
  }
  public static void create(){ X}X}X }
  public static void retrieve(){ X}X}X }
  public static User retrieveFromId(int idValue) { X}X}X }
  public static void updateAll() {
    AnnotationConfiguration config =
                        new AnnotationConfiguration();
    config.addAnnotatedClass(User.class);
    SessionFactory factory;
    factory = config.configure().buildSessionFactory();
    Session session = factory.getCurrentSession();
    session.beginTransaction();

    java.util.List allUsers;
    System.out.println("Updating all records...");
    Query queryResult = session.createQuery("from User");
    allUsers = queryResult.list();
    System.out.println("# of rows:"+allUsers.size());

    for (int i = 0; i < allUsers.size(); i++) {
      User user = (User) allUsers.get(i);
      System.out.println(user);
      user.setPassword("password");
      session.update(user);
    }

    System.out.println("Database table updated...");
    session.getTransaction().commit();
  }
}
```

save, update & saveOrUpdate

In chapter 2, when we saved a User instance to the database, we used the **saveOrUpdate** method. When we tackled the create method of the CrudRunner, we used **save**. Now that we are updating instances, we are using the **update** method. It's all kinda confusing, and people often wonder which one of the three methods they should use. Basically, when you have an entity that does not have a primary key, and you know that it needs to be saved as a new record to the database, you can use the save() method. A nice thing about the save method is that it returns the primary key generated as the new instance is saved.

---

public **Serializable** save(Object object) throws HibernateException

   Persist the given transient instance, first assigning a generated identifier. (Or using the current value of the identifier property if the assigned generator is used.) *-Hibernate API JavaDoc*

On the other hand, the update() method will do just that, update the database record that is associated with the entity being passed to the method. The method returns void, throws the HibernateException, and expects the entity passed in to have a primary key associated with it.

---

public void **update(Object object)** throws HibernateException

   Update the persistent instance with the identifier of the given detached instance. If there is a persistent instance with the same identifier, an exception is thrown. *-Hibernate API JavaDoc*

Finally, the saveOrUpdate() method intelligently combines the save *and* update functionality, knowing to create a new record for an instance passed in that does not have a primary key, and updating the associated record if the instance passed in does have a primary key associated with it.

---

public void **saveOrUpdate(Object object)** throws HibernateException

   Either save(Object) or update(Object) the given instance, depending upon resolution of the unsaved-value checks (see the manual for discussion of unsaved-value checking). *-Hibernate API JavaDoc*

How to Delete A Record with Hibernate

The final function associated with the acronym CRUD is delete, or destroy; whichever term you prefer. Deleting a record using the Hibernate framework is, in many respects, remarkably similar to the coding of an update, with the exception of the fact that the word *update* gets transposed with the word *delete*.

Once we obtain the Hibernate Session, all we need to do to delete a record is pass an object of the appropriate type to the Session's delete method. Of course, for this example, the appropriate *type* is an instance of the User class. The only really important piece of information the User instance needs to contain is the primary key of the record to be deleted. Once a valid User instance, with an appropriate primary key, is passed to the Hibernate Session's delete method, and a transaction commit is issued, the corresponding record is deleted from the database.

```
Session session = sessionFactory.getCurrentSession();
session.beginTransaction();
User user = new User();
user.setId(2); /*won't work if setId is a private method*/
session.delete(user);
session.getTransaction().commit();
```

Looking at the code above, a delete method that hard codes an id into an instance of a User (which actually shouldn't be possible, because the setId(int) method of the User class *should* be private) isn't a good idea. Actually, arbitrarily picking a primary key out of thin air is a very, very bad idea. But, if a user record with a primary key of 2 does in fact exist within the database, then after the session.getTransaction().commit() method is invoked, the corresponding record in the database would be deleted.

Again, persistent objects should initially be pulled from the database when you want to delete them, as opposed to just arbitrarily picking a primary key out of thin air. A better example might be the following deleteAll method, which looks up all the entities in the user table, and then quite destructively, one at a time, deletes every record in the database. A violent method for sure, but extreme violence is justifiable if it helps us learn. ☺

Deleting Every Database Record with Hibernate

Our CrudRunner has an updateAll method, so why not add a deleteAll method as well? The syntax of the deleteAll method is very similar to that of the updateAll, with the exception of the fact that we call the *delete* method on the Hibernate Session, as opposed to the *update* method.

```
public static void deleteAll() {
  AnnotationConfiguration config =
                        new AnnotationConfiguration();
  config.addAnnotatedClass(User.class);
  SessionFactory factory;
  factory = config.configure().buildSessionFactory();
  Session session = factory.getCurrentSession();
  session.beginTransaction();
  java.util.List allUsers;
  System.out.println("Deleting all records...");
  Query queryResult = session.createQuery("from User");
  allUsers = queryResult.list();

  for (int i = 0; i < allUsers.size(); i++) {
    User user = (User) allUsers.get(i);
    System.out.println(user);
    session.delete(user);
  }
  System.out.println("Database contents deleted...");
  session.getTransaction().commit();
}
```

Again, this method is very similar to the updateAll() method, where we use the Hibernate Session, the createQuery method, and some HQL in the form of the select String *"from User"*. Once the List of query results are returned to us, we hold the results in a java.util.List, and then loop through the List, one entity at a time, extracting our User POJOs out of the list, and issuing a session.delete(user); invocation. Finally, when the looping is complete, the session.getTransaction().commit() method is issued, and our User database table is empty, because we have deleted everything in it. It's just that easy. ☺

The Fabulous, Full, CrudRunner Class:

```java
package com.examscam;
import java.util.List; import org.hibernate.cfg.AnnotationConfiguration;
import org.hibernate.Query;import org.hibernate.Session;
import org.hibernate.SessionFactory; import com.examscam.model.*;
public class CrudRunner {
 public static void main(String[] args) {
  CrudRunner.create();CrudRunner.retrieve();CrudRunner.deleteAll();
  CrudRunner.retrieveFromId(1);CrudRunner.updateAll();
 }
 public static void create() {
  AnnotationConfiguration config = new AnnotationConfiguration();
  config.addAnnotatedClass(User.class);
  SessionFactory factory= config.configure().buildSessionFactory();
  Session session = factory.getCurrentSession();
  session.beginTransaction();
  User user = new User();user.setPassword("abc123");
  session.save(user);
  session.getTransaction().commit();
 }

 public static void retrieve() {
  AnnotationConfiguration config = new AnnotationConfiguration();
  config.addAnnotatedClass(User.class);
  SessionFactory factory= config.configure().buildSessionFactory();
  Session session = factory.getCurrentSession();
  session.beginTransaction();
  Query queryResult = session.createQuery("from User");
  java.util.List allUsers;
  allUsers = queryResult.list();
  for (int i = 0; i < allUsers.size(); i++) {
   User user = (User) allUsers.get(i);
  }
   session.getTransaction().commit();
}
 public static User retrieveFromId(int idValue) {
  AnnotationConfiguration config = new AnnotationConfiguration();
  config.addAnnotatedClass(User.class);
  SessionFactory factory= config.configure().buildSessionFactory();
  Session session = factory.getCurrentSession();
  session.beginTransaction();/*let's hope an id of 1 exists!*/
  String queryString = "from User where id = :id";
  Query query = session.createQuery(queryString);
  query.setInteger("id", idValue);
  Object queryResult = query.uniqueResult();
  User user = (User)queryResult;session.getTransaction().commit();
  return user;
 }
```

116

```
/* Sorry about the small font. I know you need a magnifying
glass to read this. I just have this obsession about trying
to put the entire class, with pretty much all the code, on
one or two pages next to each other, so that you can really
get a good idea of what it looks like. It's supposed to
make things easier for you. ☺ */

 public static void updateAll() {
  AnnotationConfiguration config =
                          new AnnotationConfiguration();
  config.addAnnotatedClass(User.class);
  SessionFactory factory=
                  config.configure().buildSessionFactory();
  Session session = factory.getCurrentSession();
  session.beginTransaction();
  List allUsers;
  System.out.println("Updating all records...");
  Query queryResult = session.createQuery("from User");
  allUsers = queryResult.list();
  System.out.println("# of rows: "+ allUsers.size());
  for (int i = 0; i < allUsers.size(); i++) {
   User user = (User) allUsers.get(i);
   System.out.println(user);
   user.setPassword("password");
   session.update(user);
  }
  System.out.println("Database contents updated...");
  session.getTransaction().commit();
 }
 public static void deleteAll() {
  AnnotationConfiguration config =  new AnnotationConfiguration();
  config.addAnnotatedClass(User.class);
  SessionFactory factory=config.configure().buildSessionFactory();
  Session session = factory.getCurrentSession();
  List allUsers;
  session.beginTransaction();
  Query queryResult = session.createQuery("from User");
  allUsers = queryResult.list();
  for (int i = 0; i < allUsers.size(); i++) {
   User user = (User) allUsers.get(i);
   System.out.println(user);
   session.delete(user);
  }
  session.getTransaction().commit();
 }
}
```

Loading Entities with Hibernate

Now, earlier in this chapter, we looked at the hypothetical example where you had the primary key of an entity, and wanted to query the database and have Hibernate return the unique User instance associated with that primary key. The Haitian Voodoo required to perform that retrieval task looked something like this:

```
✂✂✂

public static User retrieveFromId(int idValue) {
  AnnotationConfiguration config =
                     new    AnnotationConfiguration();
  config.addAnnotatedClass(User.class);
  SessionFactory factory;
  factory = config.configure().buildSessionFactory();
  Session session = factory.getCurrentSession();
  session.beginTransaction();
  String queryString = "from User where id = :id";
  Query query = session.createQuery(queryString);
  query.setInteger("id", idValue);
  Object queryResult = query.uniqueResult();
  User user = (User)queryResult;
  session.getTransaction().commit();
  System.out.print(user.getPassword());
  return user;
}

✂✂✂
```

Taking a primary key, and using it to demonstrate variable injection and the retrieval of a unique entity was very androgologically sound, but the fact of the matter is, if you actually have the primary key of an entity, there is a much easier, or should I say 'a couple

of much easier' ways to retrieve the corresponding entity from the database. We'll demonstrate those ways by coding a few methods into a new class called the LoadRunner. ☺

The LoadRunner Class

The LoadRunner class is going to have a runnable *main* method, and two static methods, named *callGet* and *callLoad*, which will be used to demonstrate the two different ways you can get at an entity given its associated primary key. For now, I've coded in all the redundant code we need to have each method connect to the database, create a session, and start a transaction. I know that all of this Hibernate plumbing code is getting repetitive; we'll factor it out into a HibernateUtil class soon enough. ☺

```
package com.examscam;
import org.hibernate.*; import com.examscam.model.User;
import org.hibernate.cfg.AnnotationConfiguration;
public class LoadRunner {
  public static void callLoad(){
    AnnotationConfiguration config
                = new AnnotationConfiguration();
    config.addAnnotatedClass(User.class);
    SessionFactory factory=
          config.configure().buildSessionFactory();
    Session session = factory.getCurrentSession();
    session.beginTransaction();
    /***** load code will go here *****/
    session.getTransaction().commit();
  }
  public static void callGet() {
    AnnotationConfiguration config
                = new AnnotationConfiguration();
    config.addAnnotatedClass(User.class);
    SessionFactory factory=
          config.configure().buildSessionFactory();
    Session session = factory.getCurrentSession();
    session.beginTransaction();
    /***** get code will go here *****/
    session.getTransaction().commit();
  }
  public static void main(String[] args) {
    LoadRunner.callLoad();
    LoadRunner.callGet();
  }
}
```

The callGet Method

Within the session.beginTransaction() and the session.getTransaction().commit methods, we want to use the Hibernate Session to take a given primary key, and provide our program with the entity associated with that primary key in the database. It's all a pretty simple process. To get an entity from the underlying persistence store, all you have to do is call the Hibernate Session's get method, and provide two arguments: the Java class associated with the entity that your are retrieving, which in this case would be the User.class, and the actual primary key associated with the record. I know that I have a user in the database with a primary key of 1, so the number one will be used to test my methods.

Here's all the code you need to resurrect a User instance from the database using the Hibernate Session's load method:

```
session.beginTransaction();
User user=(User)session.get(User.class, new Long(1));
System.out.println(user.getPassword());
session.getTransaction().commit();
```

And that's about it! You simply call the load method of the Hibernate Session, provide the *class type* and the *primary key* as parameters, and then cast the object that is returned from Hibernate back into the appropriate Java type. From there, you can do just about anything with your JavaBean that you want. In this case, I simply print out the password of the User instance. It's all just so easy.

Now, as I mentioned, there are two ways to pull an entity from the database, one of which is to use the *get* method of the Hibernate Session, and the other way is to use the *load* method. Compare and contrast the following code snippet that invokes the Session's load method to the code snippet that invoked the Session's get method. The difference is subtle, to say the least.

```
session.beginTransaction();
User user=(User)session.load(User.class, new Long(1));
System.out.println(user.getPassword());
session.getTransaction().commit();
```

Hibernate load vs. Hibernate get Methods

Well, if you were to compare the load and get methods of the Hibernate Session, you'd think that they looked pretty darned similar; and you'd be correct, but there are subtle and very important differences.

First of all, the get method hits the database as soon as it is called. So, using the Hibernate Session's get method will always trigger a database hit. On the other hand, the load method only hits the database when a particular field of the entity is accessed. So, if we use the load method to retrieve an entity, but we never actually access any of the fields of that entity, we never actually hit the database. Pretty kewl, eh?

Well, actually, as kewl as the load method might sound, it actually triggers more problems than it solves, and here's why. If you initialize a JavaBean instance with a load method call, you can only access the properties of that JavaBean, for the first time, within the transactional context in which it was initialized. If you try to access the various properties of the JavaBean after the transaction that loaded it has been committed, you'll get an exception, as Hibernate no longer has a valid transactional context to use to hit the database. So, while **this code will work just fine.....**

```
session.beginTransaction();
User user=(User)session.load(User.class, new Long(1));
System.out.println(user.getPassword());
session.getTransaction().commit();
```

..... this code will fail .....

```
session.beginTransaction();
User user=(User)session.load(User.class, new Long(1));
session.getTransaction().commit();
System.out.println(user.getPassword());
```

..... and generate the following error, telling you that since the transaction was committed, there was no valid Session in which a read transaction against the database could be issued:

```
org.hibernate.LazyInitializationException:
could not initialize proxy - no Session
```

So, the big thing to take away from this is that with the load method, you can't really use your loaded JavaBeans after the transaction has been committed, whereas, with the get method you can, because all of the various properties of a JavaBean retrieved through the get method are initialized right away.

Loading Non-Existent Records

An important scenario under which you need to contrast the load and get methods of the Hibernate Session has to do with what happens when you provide a primary key that doesn't actually exist in the database. Well, with the get method, you are simply returned a null object, which is no big deal.

With the load method, there's also no *initial* problem when you provide an invalid primary key to the method. From what you can tell, Hibernate appears to hand you back a valid, non-null instance of the class in which you are interested. However, the problems start when you actually try to access a property of that instance – that's where you run into trouble.

Remember how I said the load method doesn't hit the database until a property of the bean is requested? Well, if you've provided a primary key that doesn't exist in your database to the load method, when it does go to the database for the first time, it won't be able to find the non-existent, associated record, and your code will cough up big time. In fact, looking up a *field* based upon a non-existent primary key with the Hibernate Session's load method triggers the following error:

org.hibernate.ObjectNotFoundException:
No row with the given identifier exists: [User#123]

public Object **get** (Class clazz, Serializable id) throws HibernateException
Return the persistent instance of the given entity class with the given identifier, or null if there is no such persistent instance. (If the instance is already associated with the session, return that instance or proxy.)

public Object **load** (Class theClass,Serializable id) throws HibernateException
Return the persistent instance of the given entity class with the given identifier, assuming that the instance exists. You should **not** use this method to determine if an instance exists (use get() instead). Use this only to retrieve an instance that you assume exists, where non-existence would be an actual error.

-Regurgitated Hibernate API JavaDoc

```
package com.examscam;
import org.hibernate.*; import com.examscam.model.User;
import org.hibernate.cfg.AnnotationConfiguration;
public class LoadRunner {

  public static void main(String[] args) {
    LoadRunner.callLoad();  LoadRunner.callGet();
  }
  public static void callLoad(){
   AnnotationConfiguration config =
               new AnnotationConfiguration();
   config.addAnnotatedClass(User.class);
   SessionFactory factory=
           config.configure().buildSessionFactory();
   Session session = factory.getCurrentSession();
   session.beginTransaction();
    try {
      User user=
         (User)session.load(User.class,new Long(1));
     System.out.println(user.getPassword ());
    } catch (ObjectNotFoundException e) {
      e.printStackTrace();
    }
   session.getTransaction().commit();
/* System.out.println(user.getPassword()); This would
fail!!! */
  }
  public static void callGet() {
    AnnotationConfiguration config =
                new AnnotationConfiguration();
    config.addAnnotatedClass(User.class);
    SessionFactory factory=
            config.configure().buildSessionFactory();
    Session session = factory.getCurrentSession();
    session.beginTransaction();
    User user=
        (User)session.get(User.class,new Long(1));
    System.out.println(user.getPassword());
    session.getTransaction().commit();
    /* no problem!!!*/
    System.out.println(user.getPassword ());
  }
}
```

When to use get? When to use load?

So, after comparing and contrasting the load and get methods, the natural question that arises is *"when do I use the one, and when do I use the other?"* It's a good question. ☺

For the most part, you'll probably use the get method most often in your code. If you ever want to use the JavaBean that you are retrieving from the database after the database transaction has been committed, you'll want to use the get method, and quite frankly, that tends to be most of the time. For example, if you load a User instance in a Servlet, and you want to pass that instance to a Java Server Page for display purposes, you'd need to use the get method, otherwise, you'd have a LazyInitializationException in your JSP.

On the other hand, if your goal is largely transactional, and you are only going to be accessing the JavaBean of interest within a single unit of work that will pretty much end once the transaction is committed, you'll want to use the load method. For that matter, if you want to ensure that the JavaBean of interest is completely in sync with the database when it is used, you'll want to be using the load method as well, as this will ensure the fields of the JavaBean are being loaded in from the database, and are not just being loaded from the memory of the Java Virtual Machine on which you are running.

Furthermore, the load method may be the method of choice **if you know, and are absolutely sure, that the entity you are searching for exists in the database** with the primary key you are providing. If you don't know for sure that an entity bearing your primary key exists in the database, you can use the get method, and check to see if the instance that gets returned from the method call returns null.

Hibernate's get and load methods tend to cause plenty of problems for new Hibernate developers. But with a good understanding of the differences between the two, you shouldn't have any problem avoiding LazyInitialization and ObjectNotFound Exceptions.

Chapter 5
HibernateUtil – Managing the Hibernate Session

One of the most resource intensive components you will bump into in the Hibernate API is the SessionFactory. The SessionFactory is a very important resource, built upon the AnnotationConfiguration object, and responsible for the generation of Hibernate Session objects which are required any time Hibernate is to perform some type of database interaction.

Of course, the Hibernate SessionFactory is not a component you want to be creating over and over again, as we have been doing in all of the examples so far in this book. Instead, you want to strictly manage how SessionFactory instances are instantiated and accessed within your application. While there are many approaches to doing this, perhaps the most common is the implementation of a HibernateUtil class that manages the SessionFactory, while providing other pieces of common functionality that many parts of a Hibernate application might need.

The ubiquitous Hibernate helper class, called HibernateUtil, will be the focus of this chapter, as we create a class that helps by:

☞ *localizing the addition of JPA annotated classes to the AnnotationConfiguration object*

☞ *mitigating access to the Hibernate SessionFactory and Session object*

☞ *providing methods for performing the most common transaction based functions*

☞ *having a runnable main method that can be used to recreate the underlying database*

125

Creating the HibernateUtil Class

Over and over again in this book, we have coded all of the Hibernate plumbing required to perform the most basic of operations. That's not a good practice. Instead, we want to localize the initialization of our Hibernate Configuration, while at the same time, mitigate access to important data layer resources. To do just that, we're going to create a fancy little class named HibernateUtil.

```
package com.examscam;
public class HibernateUtil {    }
```

Now, the most dangerous part of using JPA annotations is doing all sorts of Hibernate code, but forgetting to add all of the annotated classes you are using to your AnnotationConfiguration object. We've only been using the User class, so we've only got one class to add, but you could imagine that as you add classes, it would become dangerously easy to forget to mention an important class when you're doing testing, especially if you're creating the Hibernate SessionFactory from scratch every time. So, one of the first things I like to add to my HibernateUtil class is a simple method that initializes and configures the AnnotationConfiguration object. This becomes the single, central place where all of the JPA annotated classes are added to the configuration, and since the method will actually return the AnnotationConfiguration object, it can be used either to create a new SessionFactory, or do other kewl Hibernate stuff like being passed to the SchemaExport object to recreate the underlying database. Here's how the getInitailizedConfiguration() method looks:

```
public static Configuration getInitializedConfiguration() {
  AnnotationConfiguration config = new AnnotationConfiguration();
  /* add all of your JPA annotated classes here!!!*/
  config.addAnnotatedClass(User.class);
  config.configure();
  return config;
}
```

The Static getInitializedConfiguration() Method

The getInitializedConfiguration() method simply declares, initializes, configures and subsequently returns the ever so useful and important Hibernate Configuration object, of which *AnnotationConfiguration* is a subclass.

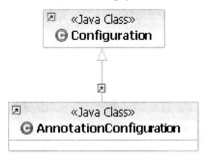

This method becomes the one, single, solitary place in the entire application where all of the JPA annotated Java classes are added to the Hibernate configuration. Remember, even if you decorate your JavaBeans with JPA annotations, if those beans are not added to the Hibernate Configuration object before the SessionFactory is instantiated, well, the Hibernate framework will not be able to manage the persistent state of those JavaBeans. Having JPA annotated classes added to the configuration in one, single, solitary place, is important for managing, maintaining, and iterating over the development of your applications.

```
public static Configuration getInitializedConfiguration(){
    AnnotationConfiguration config
                = new AnnotationConfiguration();
/* add all of your JPA annotated classes here!!!*/
    config.addAnnotatedClass(User.class);
/*Future classes we will be creating. Keep them
commented out for now.*/
    //config.addAnnotatedClass(Snafu.class);
    //config.addAnnotatedClass(FooBar.class);
    //config.addAnnotatedClass(Thing.class);
    //config.addAnnotatedClass(Team.class);
    //config.addAnnotatedClass(Player.class);
    //config.addAnnotatedClass(RightManyCourse.class);
    //config.addAnnotatedClass(LeftManyStudent.class);
    config.configure();
    return config;
}
```

The recreateDatabase() Method

The return type from the getInitializedConfiguration method will be used in two very interesting ways in our HibernateUtil class, with the first devious little usage being to recreate the database. As we have seen before, the SchemaExport class, when passed an initialized Configuration object, can generate a database create script based upon the various JPA annotated classes that have been added to the AnnotationConfiguration instance. From there, it can take that create script and execute it against the database of interest, dropping all the defined tables before recreating them.

The recreateDatabase() method is a very helpful, yet dangerous method, that I like to define in the HibernateUtil class.

```
import org.hibernate.tool.hbm2ddl.SchemaExport;
✂✂✂
public static void recreateDatabase() {
 Configuration config;
 config =
   HibernateUtil.getInitializedConfiguration();
 new SchemaExport(config).create(true, true);
}
✂✂✂
```

The recreateDatabase method can come in especially handy during various application testing routines, where the database is recreated, queries are executed against the database using staged data, and then deleted once the test case has been completed.

If we add a runnable main method to the HibernateUtil class, and call the recreateDatabase() method, we have a nice, single class we can run whenever we want to reinitialize our persistence store:

```
✂✂✂
public static void main(String args[]) {
  HibernateUtil.recreateDatabase();
}
✂✂✂
```

128

Getting the Hibernate Session

With the configuration object initialized, and the recreateDatabase method out of the way, it's time to get deep into the getSession() method of the HibernateUtil class.

If you've done any work with Hibernate, you know that the key to performing database operations is the magical Hibernate Session object. The Hibernate *Session* is a fairly lightweight component, although it is created by a fairly heavyweight, resource intensive component called a *SessionFactory*. Correspondingly, any good Hibernate application should efficiently manage a SessionFactory object, creating it within a method employing a singleton type of design pattern, and subsequently caching the SessionFactory as a static variable. From this static, cached instance of the SessionFactory, we can pump out Hibernate Session objects ad nauseum.

For our HibernateUtil class, we'll implement this singleton design pattern inside the static getSession() method, while at the same time, declaring the SessionFactory as a private, static variable for the class. Here's how it looks:

```
public class HibernateUtil {
✕✕✕
  private static SessionFactory factory;

  public static Session getSession() {
    if (factory == null) {
      Configuration config =
          HibernateUtil.getInitializedConfiguration();
      factory = config.buildSessionFactory();
    }
    Session hibernateSession = factory.getCurrentSession();
    return hibernateSession;
  }
✕✕✕
}
```

```
package com.examscam;
import org.hibernate.Session;
import org.hibernate.SessionFactory;
import org.hibernate.cfg.AnnotationConfiguration;
import org.hibernate.cfg.Configuration;
import org.hibernate.tool.hbm2ddl.SchemaExport;
import com.examscam.model.User;
/* The HibernateUtil class - so far. ☺ */
public class HibernateUtil {
  private static SessionFactory factory;
  public static Configuration
                getInitializedConfiguration() {
    AnnotationConfiguration config =
                new AnnotationConfiguration();
/* add all of your JPA annotated classes here!!!*/
    config.addAnnotatedClass(User.class);
    config.configure();
    return config;
  }
  public static Session getSession() {
    if (factory == null) {
      Configuration config =
        HibernateUtil.getInitializedConfiguration();
      factory = config.buildSessionFactory();
    }
    Session hibernateSession =
                factory.getCurrentSession();
    return hibernateSession;
  }
  public static void recreateDatabase() {
    Configuration config;
    config=HibernateUtil.getInitializedConfiguration();
    new SchemaExport(config).create(true, true);
  }
  public static void main(String args[]) {
    HibernateUtil.recreateDatabase();
  }
}
```

beginTransaction()

With the exception of a few query calls, database manipulations must be done within the scope of a transaction. As a result, client applications must have the ability to both begin a transaction, and subsequently, ask the Hibernate framework to commit any changes that have occurred during the scope of that transaction. To facilitate this in our application, we will allow client applications to begin transactions by creating a publicly accessible beginTransaction() method, along with a corresponding public commitTransaction() method, in the HibernateUtil class.

```
public static Session beginTransaction(){
  Session hibernateSession;
  hibernateSession= HibernateUtil.getSession();
  hibernateSession.beginTransaction();
  return hibernateSession;
}
```

Notice how the beginTransaction() method actually *returns* the Session object. This is simply a helpful little twist that allows a client to both begin a transaction and gain access to the Hibernate Session, all at the same time.

The commitTransaction() Method

Now, in corollary with the beginTransaction() method, the HibernateUtil class needs a commitTransaction() method as well. The commitTransaction() method is relatively straight forward, encapsulating the commit() method call on the Hibernate Session's transaction.

```
public static void commitTransaction(){
  HibernateUtil.getSession()
              .getTransaction().commit();
}
```

Closing the Hibernate Session

Seeing that we have a method to get the Hibernate Session object, it's only polite that we also provide a method to close the Hibernate Session.

This method is pretty simple, as it simply uses the getSession() method of the HibernateUtil class to get the current working session, and then subsequently calls the Session's close method. Having a helper method like this tends to make your final application code look a little bit tidier. ☺

```
✂✂✂
public class HibernateUtil {

  private static SessionFactory factory;  ✂✂✂

  public static void closeSession() {

    HibernateUtil.getSession().close();

  }✂✂✂

}
✂✂✂
```

The rollbackTransaction() Method

Of course, if a transaction is going to begin, and eventually be committed, we have to keep in mind the fact that something might go wrong, and the transaction might need to be rolled back. For this purpose, a good HibernateUtil class should have a helpful little rollbackTransaction method as well.

```
✂✂✂

public static void rollbackTransaction(){
   HibernateUtil.getSession()
             .getTransaction().rollback();
}

✂✂✂
```

Why the extra whitespace?

In the preamble, I mentioned how I like to try to fit entire classes on a single page so the reader can see the entire class at once. Of course, this darned HibernateUtil is going to be too big to put it on just one page. However, I want the whole class to be on the left and right side of a page, so you can see the entire class when you open up the pertinent page of the book. The formatting Gods just weren't on my side in this chapter, so I've had to put a little extra whitespace in to ensure the entire HibernateUtil class fits on the next two pages.

The bottom line? I did it for you. ☺

The Whole Darned HibernateUtil Class

```
package com.examscam;
import org.hibernate.Session;
import org.hibernate.SessionFactory;
import org.hibernate.cfg.AnnotationConfiguration;
import org.hibernate.cfg.Configuration;
import org.hibernate.tool.hbm2ddl.SchemaExport;
import com.examscam.model.User;


public class HibernateUtil {

 private static SessionFactory factory;

 public static Configuration
             getInitializedConfiguration() {
   AnnotationConfiguration config =
             new AnnotationConfiguration();
/* add all of your JPA annotated classes here!!! */
   config.addAnnotatedClass(User.class);
   config.configure();
   return config;
 }

 public static Session getSession() {
   if (factory == null) {
   Configuration config =
       HibernateUtil.getInitializedConfiguration();
   factory = config.buildSessionFactory();
   }
   Session hibernateSession =
                   factory.getCurrentSession();
   return hibernateSession;
 }

 public static void closeSession() {
   HibernateUtil.getSession().close();
 }
         /*** continued on next page ***/
```

```
      /*** continued from previous page ***/

public static void recreateDatabase() {
  Configuration config;
  config =
     HibernateUtil.getInitializedConfiguration();
  new SchemaExport(config).create(true, true);
}

public static Session beginTransaction() {
  Session hibernateSession;
  hibernateSession = HibernateUtil.getSession();
  hibernateSession.beginTransaction();
  return hibernateSession;
}

public static void commitTransaction() {
  HibernateUtil.getSession()
              .getTransaction().commit();
}

public static void rollbackTransaction() {
  HibernateUtil.getSession()
              .getTransaction().rollback();
}

  public static void main(String args[]) {
    HibernateUtil.recreateDatabase();
  }

}
```

Code Without the HibernateUtil Class

So, we've worked our fingers to the bone creating a HibernateUtil class, employing a singleton type of implementation to minimize the creation of SessionFactory objects, while at the same time, making it relatively easy to obtain the magical and highly helpful Hibernate Session object. So, how would the use of the HibernateUtil class look in code? Well, let's take a look at a code sample from a previous chapter:

```
package com.examscam.model;
import javax.persistence.Entity;import javax.persistence.GeneratedValue;
import javax.persistence.Id;import org.hibernate.Session;
import org.hibernate.SessionFactory;import com.examscam.HibernateUtil;
import org.hibernate.cfg.AnnotationConfiguration;
@Entity
public class User {
  private int id;
  private String password;
  @Id
  @GeneratedValue
  public int getId() {return id;}
  public void setId(int id) {this.id = id;}
  public String getPassword() {return password;}
  public void setPassword(String password) {
    this.password = password;
  }
  public static void main(String args[]){
    AnnotationConfiguration config =
                  new AnnotationConfiguration();
    config.addAnnotatedClass(User.class);
    config.configure();
    SessionFactory factory = config.buildSessionFactory();
    Session session = factory.getCurrentSession();
    session.beginTransaction();
    System.out.println("creating user");
    User u = new User();
    u.setPassword("abc123");
    session.saveOrUpdate(u);
    System.out.println("user saved");
    session.getTransaction().commit();
    System.out.println("transaction successful!!!");
  }
}
```

An Improved main using HibernateUtil

As you can see with the code below, when the HibernateUtil class is used, the main method looks much cleaner, with no need to initialize or create an AnnotationConfiguration object. Simplified calls to the HibernateUtil class provides easy access to the Hibernate Session, and it is easy to access important Session functionality such as the beginning and committing of database transactions.

```java
package com.examscam.model;
import javax.persistence.Entity;
import javax.persistence.GeneratedValue;
import javax.persistence.Id;
import org.hibernate.Session; import com.examscam.HibernateUtil;
import org.hibernate.SessionFactory;
import org.hibernate.cfg.AnnotationConfiguration;


@Entity
public class User {
  private int id;
  private String password;
  @Id
  @GeneratedValue
  public int getId() {return id;}
  public void setId(int id) {this.id = id;}
  public String getPassword() {return password;}
  public void setPassword(String password) {
    this.password = password;
  }

  public static void main(String args[]){
    Session session =
            HibernateUtil.beginTransaction();
    System.out.println("creating user");
    User u = new User();
    u.setPassword("abc123");
    session.saveOrUpdate(u);
    System.out.println("user saved");
    HibernateUtil.commitTransaction();
    System.out.println("transaction   successful!!!");
  }
}
```

137

Chapter 6
Column Mappings

Okay, I'm pretty happy about all of the progress we've made so far. Using a fairly simple User class, we've explored all of the basic database operations, looked at some of the fundamental JPA tags we can use to decorate our JavaBeans, and we've even explored some best practices and design patterns through the HibernateUtil class. However, the fact remains that our User class is really starving from a lack of property nutrition. It's time to add some more properties to the User class, and in the process, explore the following topics:

☞ *mapping columns with the @Column JPA Annotation*

☞ *mapping to tables and schemas with the @Table JPA annotation*

☞ *annotating non-persistent properties with the @Transient annotation*

☞ *mapping advanced data types such as dates and large character objects*

139

Adding the LoginName Property

Now, one of the thing you may have noticed about the User example that we have been working with so far is the fact that the name of our table, along with the name of the table-columns, exactly matched the class and property names of the User POJO. There is definitely something to be said for keeping the first few examples simple; However, it's not too often that every database table and column is going map perfectly to the names used in your domain model.

One of the fields I wanted to add to my User JavaBean was a **loginName** field. It just makes sense that a JavaBean named User, that contains a property named password, would also provide some way of maintaining a unique, identifying name for logging a user in. So, I want to add a field, of type String, to my User class, but the column in the User table must be named **login_name**. I know it's not a huge difference, but it is enough to throw the Hibernate framework off a little bit. If the Hibernate framework sees a POJO with an identically named table, or a field in a JavaBean with an identically named database column, well, Hibernate does a great job of doing the Java to database mapping. However, when database and POJO property names do not coincide, you've got to add some new annotations to your JavaBeans.

The @Column Annotation

```
@Column(
  name="columnName";
    boolean unique() default false;
      boolean nullable() default true;
        boolean insertable() default true;
          boolean updatable() default true;
  String columnDefinition() default "";
    String table() default "";
      int length() default 255;
        int precision() default 0;
          int scale() default 0;
)
```

Adding a Column Annotation

One of the great things about Hibernate is that it makes mapping data from your JavaBeans to the database fairly easy, even when changes happen in either your object model, or your data model.

Right now, we have the challenge of mapping a JavaBean *field* named loginName to a *column* named login_name in the database. Well, doing so really isn't all that complicated; it's just a matter of adding the appropriate variable declaration, setters and getters, and finally, adding a special @Column annotation that describes to Hibernate how to perform the field to database column mapping.

```
✂✂✂
import javax.persistence.Column;
@Entity
public class User {
  private Long id;
  private String password;
  private String loginName;
  @Column (name="login_name")
  public String getLoginName() {
    return loginName;
  }
  public void setLoginName(String loginName) {
    this.loginName = loginName;
  }
✂✂✂
```

As you can see, mapping the loginName property to the login_name field in the database is as simple as adding the @Column annotation before the getLoginName() method, and providing the (name="login_name") attribute to the annotation.

Coding for the Updated loginName Field

To take advantage of the new field, all we need to do is add a line of code in the main method of the User class that initializes the loginName property, **user.setLoginName("mj");** We can then commit the transaction to the database.

```
✂✂✂
public static void main(String args[]){
   System.out.println("creating Hibernate config");
   AnnotationConfiguration config =
                   new AnnotationConfiguration();
   config.addAnnotatedClass(User.class);
   SessionFactory factory;
   factory = config.configure().buildSessionFactory();
   Session session = factory.getCurrentSession();
   session.beginTransaction();
   System.out.println("creating user");
   User user = new User();
   /*here is the new stuff!!! The instance is now named
user, just to shake it up a bit. ☺ */
   user.setLoginName("mj");
   user.setPassword("abc123");
   session.save(user);
   System.out.println("user saved");
   session.getTransaction().commit();
  System.out.println("transaction successful!!!");
}✂✂✂
```

Recreating the Database

Of course, if you try to persist the loginName field of the User to the database, you better make sure the user table in the database has a column named login_name, otherwise you'll be seeing an org.hibernate.exception.SQLGrammarException telling you about an unknown 'column name' in the 'field list.' To avoid this exception, you can run the HibernateUtil's main method to recreate the database, or just run this SQL script:

```
create table User (id bigint not null auto_increment,
login_name varchar(255), password varchar(255),
primary key (id))
```

The Newly Inserted User Object

As you can see, when the database is reconfigured to support the login_name field, and the main method of the User class is run, an entry is made into the database that not only includes a unique id and a password, but it also includes a login_name field with the value of "mj" assigned to it.

```
✂✂✂
  User user = new User();
  user.setLoginName("mj");
  user.setPassword("abc123");
  session.save(user);
✂✂✂
```

```
package com.examscam.model;
import javax.persistence.GeneratedValue;
import javax.persistence.Entity;
import javax.persistence.Id;import org.hibernate.Session;
import javax.persistence.Column;
import com.examscam.HibernateUtil;
@Entity
public class User {
  private Long id;
  private String password;
  private String loginName;

  @Column (name="login_name")
  public String getLoginName() {
    return loginName;
  }
  public void setLoginName(String loginName) {
    this.loginName = loginName;
  }

  @Id
  @GeneratedValue
  public Long getId() {return id;}
  public void setId(Long id) {this.id = id;}
  public String getPassword() {return password;}
  public void setPassword(String password) {
    this.password = password;
  }

  public static void main(String args[]){
    Session session=HibernateUtil.beginTransaction();
    System.out.println("creating user");
    User user = new User();
/*here is the new stuff!!! The instance is now named user,
just to shake it up a bit.*/
    user.setLoginName("mj");
    user.setPassword("abc123");
    session.save(user);
    System.out.println("user saved");
    HibernateUtil.commitTransaction();
    System.out.println("transaction successful!!!");
  }
}
```

Further Annotations

As we have seen, when a POJO is marked with an @Entity tag, Hibernate will attempt to persist the POJO to a database table with a matching name. Furthermore, Hibernate will attempt to persist the properties of a JavaBean to similarly named columns in the database table. We saw this functionality when our User POJO was magically mapped to the user table in the examscam database, and the id and password properties in the JavaBean were bewitchingly persisted to database columns with matching names. It was only when a property of the JavaBean, and the corresponding database column, did not match that we were forced to dig into our JPA bag of tricks and pull out the @Column annotation.

Still, as reliable as Hibernate is, sometimes annotating your code, even when it's not explicitly necessary, isn't such a bad idea. It wouldn't kill us to annotate every property in our JavaBean, and it might even make our POJO a little bit more descriptive and readable. We could start by adding column annotations to each of the properties of our JavaBean, not just the loginName.

```
✂✂✂

@Id
@GeneratedValue
@Column (name="id")
public Long getId() {return id;}
public void setId(Long id) {this.id = id;}

@Column (name="login_name")
public String getLoginName() {return loginName;}
public void setLoginName(String n) {this.loginName =n;}

@Column (name="password")
public String getPassword() {return password;}
public void setPassword(String p) {this.password = p;}

✂✂✂
```

@Table Annotation

With out User JavaBean, we simply provided an @Entity annotation before the class definition, and allowed the Hibernate framework to match the User class to a corresponding table in the examscam database. But you can modify this behavior by using the @Table annotation, and providing custom attributes for the table name and database schema.

```
✂✂✂
import javax.persistence.Table;
@Entity
@Table (name="user", schema="examscam")
public class User {
✂✂✂
```

connection.url and the Schema Definition

Up until this point, we have never defined or mentioned the database schema name in our Java code. Just in case you had forgotten, the *examscam* schema name is defined as a SessionFactory property in the connection url entry in the hibernate.cfg.xml file. When the schema property is not explicitly defined using the @Table annotation, the default becomes the schema specified in the connection.url property.

```
✂✂✂
<session-factory>
  <property name="connection.url">
  jdbc:mysql://localhost/examscam
  </property>✂✂✂   ✂✂✂
</session-factory>✂✂✂
```

Note: on some database, you may need to specify a catalog. I know I had to do this when working with a Sybase database.

@Table(name="user", schema="examscam",

                    catalog="examscam_cat")

146

Our Heavily Annotated User Class

```java
package com.examscam.hib.exam;
import javax.persistence.Column;
import javax.persistence.Entity;
import javax.persistence.GeneratedValue;
import javax.persistence.Id;
import javax.persistence.Table;
import com.examscam.HibernateUtil;
import org.hibernate.Session;
import org.hibernate.SessionFactory;
import org.hibernate.cfg.AnnotationConfiguration;

@Entity
@Table (name="user", schema="examscam")
public class User {

  private int id;
  private String password;
  private String loginName;

  @Id
  @GeneratedValue
  @Column (name="id")
  public int getId() {return id;}
  public void setId(int id) {this.id = id;}

  @Column (name="login_name")
  public String getLoginName() {return loginName;}
  public void setLoginName(String loginName) {
    this.loginName = loginName;
  }

  @Column (name="password")
  public String getPassword() {return password;}
  public void setPassword(String password) {
    this.password = password;
  }

  public static void main(String args[]){  ЖЖЖ  }

}
```

Non-Persistent JavaBean Properties

It's not unreasonable to expect that from time to time, a JavaBean will contain some properties that need to be persisted to a database, and some properties that do *not* need to be stored in the database. However, when you mark a POJO with the @Entity annotation, Hibernate will attempt to persist *every* property of the JavaBean. The default behavior of Hibernate is to persist every non-transient and non-static property of a POJO.

However, if your JavaBean has an instance level property that you do *not* want Hibernate to save to the database, you can simply decorate the non-persistent property with a simple little @Transient annotation.

Transient Annotation JavaDoc:

Annotation Type Transient

@Target(value={METHOD,FIELD})

@Retention(value=RUNTIME)

public @interface **Transient**

This annotation specifies that the property or field is not persistent. It is used to annotate a property or field of an entity class, mapped superclass, or embeddable class.

Using the @Transient Annotation

```java
package com.examscam.hib.exam;
import javax.persistence.Column;import javax.persistence.Entity;
import javax.persistence.GeneratedValue;import javax.persistence.Id;
import javax.persistence.Table;
import javax.persistence.Transient;
import org.hibernate.Session;
import org.hibernate.SessionFactory;
import org.hibernate.cfg.AnnotationConfiguration;
import com.examscam.HibernateUtil;

@Entity
@Table (name="user", schema="examscam")
public class User {
  private int id;
  private String loginName;
  private String password;
  private String encryptedPassword;

  @Transient
  public String getEncryptedPassword () {
      return encryptedPassword;
  }
  public void setEncryptedPassword(String ep){
    this. encryptedPassword = ep;
  }

  @Id
  @GeneratedValue
  @Column (name="id")
  public int getId() {return id;}
  public void setId(int id) {this.id = id;}
  @Column (name="login_name")
  public String getLoginName() {return loginName;}
  public void setLoginName(String loginName) {
    this.loginName = loginName;
  }
  @Column (name="password")
  public String getPassword() {return password;}
  public void setPassword(String password) {
    this.password = password;
  }
  public static void main(String args[]){  }
}
```

Non-Persistent @Transient Properties

In the latest iteration of the User POJO's main method, we actually set the encryptedPassword property of the user, and then persist the user to the database. However, as you can see from the resultset, and the underlying database table, the encryptedPassword field is not persisted to the database as a result of it being marked with the @Transient annotation in the User POJO.

```
✂✂✂
public static void main(String args[]){
   Session session=HibernateUtil.beginTransaction();

   System.out.println("creating user");

   User user = new User();
   user.setLoginName("mj");
   user.setPassword("abc123");
   user.setEncryptedPassword("zab012");

   session.save(user);
   System.out.println("user saved");
   HibernateUtil.commitTransaction();
   System.out.println("transaction successful!!!");
}
✂✂✂
```

User Table, User Class, Database ResultSet

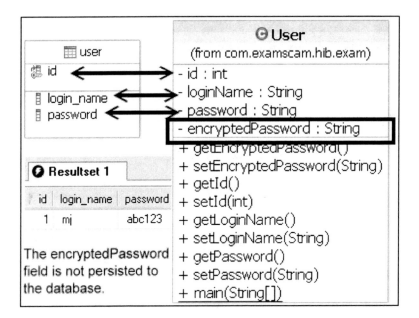

As you can see, when comparing the class diagram of the User to the underlying database table, the encryptedPassword property, which is marked as being @Transient, does not have any representation in the database.

Adding Fields to our User POJO

Our User class is maturing quite quickly, and as such, there are a few more helpful fields I'd like to add to the User JavaBean, namely information about the User's registration date, whether or not the User has verified their registration information, their email address, and finally, the User's last access time. My first step in bringing this vision to fruition is to add the

appropriate, private, instance variables to the User class.

```
private String emailAddress;
private Boolean verified;
private java.util.Date lastAccessTime;
private java.util.Calendar registrationDate;
```

Notice that I have shaken things up a little bit by introducing some new data types. The user will now have an additional String property, a primitive of type Boolean, and two date related variables, one of type Date, and one of type Calendar. To shake things up even more, I should probably tell you that a java.util.Calendar object is actually an *abstract class,* meaning that it can't be directly instantiated in code, but instead, a concrete subclass has to be instantiated instead. See, I told you things would get a bit more complicated. Of course, if we're going to add instance variables, we'll need to add some setters and getters, so if you're following along, you might want to add those in as well. ☺

Helpful Hint:

When declaring instance variables in your JPA annotated POJOs, always use the class type, and shy away from primitive types. I've interspersed both throughout the book, but in production, stick to Long, Integer, Boolean, Character, Float, Double, Byte and Short, as opposed to long, int, boolean, char, float, double, byte and short. With Java 5's autoboxing feature, using the upper-case-letter-leading wrapper classes has been made pretty easy.

Looking at the Annotations

When storing time based information in a database, it can be stored in one of three ways: as a time, as a date, or as a time-date combination known as a TIMESTAMP. If the Hibernate framework sees a time based property, it will be treated as a TIMESTAMP unless you tell Hibernate otherwise. For the instances of the Calendar and Date fields in our User class, we will decorate the getters of our fields with a @Temporal annotation, and use the TemporalType constants to clarify the property as being of type TIME, DATE or TIMESTAMP.

```
@Temporal(TemporalType.TIMESTAMP)
public java.util.Date getLastAccessTime() {
  return lastAccessTime;
}
@Temporal(TemporalType.DATE)
public java.util.Calendar getRegistrationDate() {
  return registrationDate;
}
```

Default @Basic Annotation

The other properties we added, namely the *emailAddress* field and the *verified* field of type Boolean are fairly innocuous, with the exception of the @Basic annotation placed in front of the isVerified() method.

```
@Basic
public Boolean isVerified() {
  return verified;
}
```

The @Basic annotation is pretty much redundant for attributes defined within a JavaBean. Any non-static field that is defined within a JavaBean has an implicit @Basic annotation defined for it by default. We will decorate the isVerified() method with the @Basic annotation, but we will leave the @Basic annotation *off* the emailAddress field to emphasize the fact that @Basic is an optional decoration.

```
package com.examscam.model;
import javax.persistence.Basic;
import javax.persistence.Column;
import javax.persistence.Entity;
import javax.persistence.GeneratedValue;
import javax.persistence.Id;import javax.persistence.Table;
import javax.persistence.Temporal;
import javax.persistence.TemporalType;
import javax.persistence.Transient;import org.hibernate.Session;
import org.hibernate.SessionFactory;
import org.hibernate.cfg.AnnotationConfiguration;
import com.examscam.HibernateUtil;

@Entity
@Table(name = "user", schema = "examscam")
public class User {
  private Long id;
  private String loginName;
  private String password;
  private String encryptedPassword;
  private String emailAddress;
  private Boolean verified;
  private java.util.Date lastAccessTime;
  private java.util.Calendar registrationDate;

  @Transient
  public String getEncryptedPassword() {
    return encryptedPassword;
  }
  public void setEncryptedPassword(String ep) {
    this.encryptedPassword = ep;
  }
  @Id
  @GeneratedValue
  @Column(name = "id")
  public Long getId() { return id; }

  public void setId(Long id) { this.id = id; }

  @Column(name = "login_name")
  public String getLoginName() {
    return loginName;
  }
  public void setLoginName(String loginName) {
    this.loginName = loginName;
  }
          /*****   continued on next page *****/
```

154

```
@Column(name = "password", nullable=false)
public String getPassword() {
  return password;
}

public void setPassword(String password) {
  this.password = password;
}

public String getEmailAddress() {
  return emailAddress;
}

@Temporal(TemporalType.TIMESTAMP)
public java.util.Date getLastAccessTime() {
  return lastAccessTime;
}

@Temporal(TemporalType.DATE)
public java.util.Calendar getRegistrationDate() {
  return registrationDate;
}

@Basic
public Boolean isVerified() {
  return verified;
}

public void setEmailAddress(String emailAddress) {
  this.emailAddress = emailAddress;
}

public void setLastAccessTime(java.util.Date lastAccessTime) {
  this.lastAccessTime = lastAccessTime;
}

public void setRegistrationDate(java.util.Calendar registrationDate){
  this.registrationDate = registrationDate;
}

public void setVerified(Boolean verified) {
  this.verified = verified;
}
public static void main(String args[]){ }
}
```

Testing the New User Fields

As we have updated the User class, it would make sense to add some code to our main method that will initialize the new properties of the User bean. This will then help us test to see if the changes to our User class have made it to the database. Of course, before we can even test our code, we must make sure the database itself has been updated to reflect the changes in our model. There's a couple of ways to sync up the database with our new and improved User class, the easiest of which is to simply run the HibernateUtil.recreateDatabase() method. Of course, if you're more of a sadist, you can always run the following SQL statement:

```
drop table if exists examscam.user
create table examscam.user (id bigint not null
auto_increment, emailAddress varchar(255),
lastAccessTime datetime, login_name varchar(255),
password varchar(255) not null, registrationDate
date, verified bit, primary key (id))
```

With the underlying database updated, a few quick updates to the main method of the User class are in order:

```
public static void main(String args[]){
  Session session=HibernateUtil.beginTransaction();
  User user = new User();
  user.setLoginName("mj");user.setPassword("abc123");
  user.setEncryptedPassword("zab012");

  user.setEmailAddress("mj@scja.com");
  user.setLastAccessTime(new java.util.Date());
  user.setRegistrationDate(
          new java.util.GregorianCalendar());
  user.setVerified(Boolean.FALSE);

  session.save(user);
  HibernateUtil.commitTransaction();
  System.out.println("transaction successful!!!");
}
```

Looking at the Results

After recreating the user table in the database by running the HibernateUtil.recreateDatabase() method, and then running the main method of the User class, you can see that a new record is added to the database, with all of the appropriate fields updated.

Noteworthy additions to the database table are the lastAccessTime field, which being a TIMESTAMP has not only the date, but also the time that the record was saved, as compared to the registrationDate field, which was of type DATE, and only has the actual year, day, and month fields recorded.

	emailAddress	lastAccessTime	login_name	password	registrationDate	verified
1	mj@scja.com	2008-02-05 14:59:57	mj	abc123	2008-02-05	b'0'

DATE vs. TIME vs. TIMESTAMP

It's also noteworthy to point out how the registrationDate column, which is annotated to be TemporalType.DATE, simply gets a year-month-day value, whereas the lastAccessTime column is populated with a full timestamp, including both the day and the time (TemporalType.TIME is the third option which would have simply saved the time, and not the calendar day).

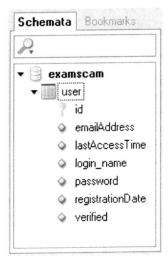

TemporalType.TIMESTAMP is the default if it isn't otherwise specified in your code.

Hibernate Blobs and Clobs (@Lob)

While they won't likely find their way into the User management application I'm building here, it is worth mentioning that any field in a Hibernate POJO can be decorated with the @Lob annotation. This will tell the Hibernate framework to handle the field in question as a large **obj**ect.

Of course, if you've worked with any of the big databases, you're probably familiar with Blobs and Clobs. There is no Blob or Clob annotation to speak of in Hibernate; instead, when Hibernate sees the @Lob annotation, it inspects the Java datatype. If the Java datatype that is decorated with the @Lob annotation is a String, java.sql.Clob, or a big or little sea character array (Character[] or char[]), then the field is typically treated as a database Clob, (or a text type field if Clob is not supported.)

On the other hand, if the Java datatype is a java.sql.Blob, or a byte array (Byte[] or byte[]), well, as you would expect, the field is treated as a Blob.

For databases that don't define a Blob or Clob type, the database dialect decides upon the appropriate way to persist the data. For example, depending upon your version, MySQL will persist Clob fields simply as text columns.

The Hibernate BlobClobber

I've created a silly little class called the BlobClobber, which uses the name game as it maps to a table named *BlobClobBoBob*. ☺ As you can see from the Hibernate generated SQL script below, the byte related fields were mapped to blob types in MySQL, and the character types were simply mapped to text.

```
DROP TABLE IF EXISTS`examscam`.`blobclobbobob`;
CREATE TABLE  `examscam`.`blobclobbobob` (
  `id` int(11) NOT NULL auto_increment,
  `beans` text, `sqlClob` text,
  `witness` text, `ming` text,
  `sqlBlob` blob, `me` blob,
  PRIMARY KEY  (`id`))
```

```
package com.examscam.hib.exam;
import javax.persistence.Column;import javax.persistence.Entity;
import javax.persistence.GeneratedValue;import javax.persistence.Id;
import javax.persistence.Lob;import javax.persistence.Table;
import org.hibernate.cfg.AnnotationConfiguration;
import org.hibernate.tool.hbm2ddl.SchemaExport;


@Entity
@Table(name = "BlobClobBoBob", schema = "examscam")
public class BlobClobber {
  Long id;
  String beans;
  char[] ming;
  Character[] witness;
  java.sql.Clob sqlClob;

  java.sql.Blob sqlBlob;
  byte[] me;

  @Id
  @GeneratedValue
  @Column(name = "id")
  public Long getId() {return id;}
  @Lob
  public String getBeans() {return beans;}
  @Lob
  public byte[] getMe() {return me;}
  @Lob
  public char[] getMing() {return ming;}
  @Lob
  public java.sql.Blob getSqlBlob() {return sqlBlob;}
  @Lob
  public java.sql.Clob getSqlClob() {return sqlClob;}
  @Lob
  public Character[] getWitness() {return witness;}

  public static void main(String args[]) {
   AnnotationConfiguration config =
                      new    AnnotationConfiguration();
   config.addAnnotatedClass(BlobClobber.class).configure();
   new SchemaExport(config).create(true, true);
  }
}
```

blobclobbobob

- [ ] id
- [ ] beans
- [ ] me
- [ ] ming
- [ ] sqlBlob
- [ ] sqlClob
- [ ] witness

Chapter 7
How Hibernate Works

So far, we've been pretty focused on annotating JavaBeans, and invoking methods on some of the core Hibernate classes, such as the Session and SessionFactory objects, to help us perform the basic CRUD operations. However, we haven't really discussed how Hibernate works, or what's going on when a JavaBean touches the Hibernate Session, or for that matter, what happens to instantiated objects when a transaction is committed, or the Hibernate Session goes out of scope. Well, with the experience we've had working with Hibernate, I think it's about time we delved a little deeper into how Hibernate works, and thought a little bit about what exactly is going on when we interact with the Hibernate framework.

Thinking about Transient Instances

Let's start off with the basics. Now imagine you have a JPA annotated User class, and you create an instance of it using the following code:

```
User u = new User();
```

Will Hibernate automatically persist this object, given just this line of code alone? Of course not! When you create an object in your Java code, even if your application does use the Hibernate framework for persistence, the newly created instance will exist only in the memory of the Java program that created it, and Hibernate has nothing to do with it. In fact, there's a special term we use to describe objects in Java programs that have been instantiated, but have not been placed under the spell of the Hibernate Session; such instances are referred to as *transient instances*, as their state is never persisted to the database.

161

From Transient to Persistent

tran·sient   [tran-shuhnt, -zhuhnt, -zee-uhnt] –adjective
1.   not lasting, enduring, or permanent; transitory.
2.   lasting only a short time; existing briefly; temporary: transient authority.
3.   staying only a short time

transient instance: a transient instance is one that is instantiated within a Java program, but is not managed by, or connected in any way to a Hibernate Session. Furthermore, transient objects do not have any existing representation in a database.

Now, if you create an instance of a class in your Java code, and you want Hibernate to manage the persistent state of that object, you have to associate you're newly created instance with the magical Hibernate Session. There are a number of ways to do this, with the easiest probably being to simply pass the Java instance to the saveOrUpdate method of the Hibernate Session.

```
User u = new User(); // transient at this point
session.saveOrUpdate(u); // no longer transient
```

Once an instance of a JavaBean has been associated with the Hibernate Session, it is no longer a transient instance, but instead, becomes what we call a ***persistent object***, and the persistent state of the instance is then managed by the Hibernate Session *for the duration of the transaction.*

Now, that previous sentence was quite a mouthful, especially the part about ***the duration of the transaction.*** You see, whenever you want to perform any of the basic CRUD operations, you must first initiate a transaction, and when you are done, you must close the transaction. Don't let anyone tell you differently; that's the way database operations work.

.

The Transactional Context

As I said, any time you want Hibernate to manage the persistence of your JavaBeans, you must first initiate a transaction, which is just a simple method call on the Hibernate Session.

```
hibernateSession.beginTransaction();
```

Once you being a transaction, you can start associating your POJOs and JavaBeans with the Hibernate Session. If you don't initiate a transaction, you'll get a runtime exception telling you about *no transactional context* being in existence, and at all costs, we want to avoid runtime exceptions.

Now, the really cool thing about Hibernate is the fact that once a transaction has been started, all you have to do is associate an instance with the Session, and then Hibernate will take care of fully managing the persistent state of that instance, right up to and including the point where you commit the transaction. When you finally commit the transaction, the state of all of the POJOs that have been associated with the Hibernate Session will be saved to the database.

The following snippet of code demonstrates the art of beginning a transaction, creating an instance, associating that instance with the Hibernate Session, and then finally, committing the transaction:

```
hibernateSession.beginTransaction();
User user = new User();
hibernateSession.saveOrUpdate(user);
hibernateSession.getTransaction().commit();
```

In this code snippet, a new transaction is created, after which a brand new, unassociated, transient instance of a User is created. This instance is then associated with the Hibernate Session when it is passed as an argument to the saveOrUpdate() method of the session, transitioning the instance from being a transient instance, to a persistent instance.

Affection for the saveOrUpdate Method

Now, I don't actually like the saveOrUpdate method. I mean, I love using it, but I don't really like the name, because I think the name is a little bit misleading, as it implies that an instance that is passed to the method will be saved, or updated, immediately. You see, that's only partly true. Sure, when the saveOrUpdate method is invoked, the instance will eventually have its state persisted to the database, but more happens that just that. The instance in not only queued up for a database save, but the Hibernate Session keeps track of that instance, and if any further changes happen to the instance before the transaction is committed, then those changes to the instance's state will be persisted as well. I'd almost prefer it if the saveOrUpdate method was renamed to something more descriptive like *saveOrUpdateAndAssociateInstanceWithSession*, but then again, I guess there is an upper limit on how long good method names should be. ☺

Take a look at the following code snippet:

```
Session session=HibernateUtil.beginTransaction();

User user = new User();
user.setPassword("abc123");
session.save(user);

user.setLoginName("mj");
user.setPassword("abc123");
user.setEncryptedPassword("zab012");
user.setEmailAddress("mj@scja.com");
user.setLastAccessTime(new java.util.Date());
user.setRegistrationDate(
            new java.util.GregorianCalendar());
user.setVerified(Boolean.FALSE);

HibernateUtil.commitTransaction();
```

Notice that in this code snippet, an instance of the user class is created, the password is set to *abc123*, and then the save method of the Hibernate Session is passed the instance. The call to the save method triggers the following SQL statement to be executed against the database:

```
insert into examscam.user (emailAddress, lastAccessTime,
login_name, password, registrationDate, verified)
values (?, ?, ?, ?, ?, ?)
```

So, when the save method is invoked on the Hibernate Session, the state of the instance, which is really nothing more than a primary key and a password in this example, is persisted to the database. But look at the original code snippet, and see what happens after the save method is invoked. A bunch of other properties of the User instance are modified, and then the transaction is committed. The question is, will these changes to the state of the User instance be persisted to the database, or will the database only contain the primary key and the password once the transaction is committed? Well, in fact, *all of the changes* to the instance that took place even after the save method was invoked on the Hibernate Session will be persisted to the database. As the transaction is committed, Hibernate will issue the following SQL statement against the database:

```
update examscam.user set emailAddress=?, lastAccessTime=?,
login_name=?, password=?, registrationDate=?, verified=?
where id=?
```

You see, that's the great thing about Hibernate: as soon as an instance is associated with the Session, be it through a load, get, update or save invocation, the state of that instance will be managed by Hibernate right up to the point in which the current transaction is committed. Hibernate will keep track of any changes that happen to the instance throughout the course of the transaction, and update the corresponding record in the database accordingly.

Proper Hibernate Coding Practices

I often see developers that are new to Hibernate constantly calling the saveOrUpdate method whenever a set of changes have been made to a POJO. This isn't necessary. You only have to associate an instance with the Hibernate Session once within the scope of a transaction. From that point on, you can do whatever you want to your JavaBean instances. Hibernate will persist the final state of your instance when the current transaction is finally committed.

The following piece of code needlessly calls the saveOrUpdate method after instance variables have been updated. This is totally unnecessary, as the User instance was already associated with the Hibernate Session through the original call to saveOrUpdate.

```
hibernateSession.getTransaction();
User user = new User();
hibernateSession.saveOrUpdate(user);
user.setLoginName("mj");
user.setPassword("abc123");
hibernateSession.saveOrUpdate(user); /*BAD!*/
hibernateSession.getTransaction().commit();
```

With the first call to saveOrUpdate, the instance named u becomes associated with the Hibernate Session. From that point on, you can mess around with the user instance as much as you want, and Hibernate will take care of the persistence. You can initialize, update, change, and modify any instance variable of the user instance that you want, and Hibernate will save the final state of the instance once the transaction has been committed.

```
hibernateSession.getTransaction();
User user = new User();
hibernateSession.saveOrUpdate(user);
user.setLoginName("mj");
user.setPassword("abc123");
hibernateSession.getTransaction().commit();
```

Loading Instances and the Hibernate Session

Of course, the saveOrUpdate method, along with the save method, is great for associating brand new instances with the Hibernate Session, but more often than not, you'll want to pull a previously persisted instance from the database into your Java program, perhaps so you can update the instance and subsequently persist that new information to the database. For pulling existing instances out of the database, while at the same time, ensuring they are associated with the Hibernate Session for persistence management, we use either the *load* or the *get* method of the Hibernate Session.

*Note that the load method is intended to be used **when you know an instance actually exists** in the database. This method actually returns proxy objects that alleviate database hits until transaction commit time, making it a little more efficient. The get method is better used when you don't know for sure if the instance you are loading or getting actually exists in the database.*

Calling the load or get method on the Hibernate Session in order to obtain a persistent object from the database not only provides you access to the instance of interest, **but it also associates that instance with the Hibernate Session**. Take a look at the following code, which obtains an instance of a User through the Hibernate Session.

```
Session hibernateSession = this.getCurrentSession();
hibernateSession.beginTransaction();
User u = (User)hibernateSession.get(User.class, 2);
u.setLoginName("Joey");
u.setPassword("Shabidew");
hibernateSession.getTransaction().commit();
```

Notice that after updating the properties of the instance, namely the loginName and password, that we simply ask the Hibernate Session to commit the transaction, which will in turn, update the database. There is no need to call the saveOrUpdate method after changing the attributes of the instance, because the instance is already associated with the Hibernate Session, and as a result, any changes to the state of the persistent instance will be updated in the database.

Rushing the Update with a flush()

As you know, the Hibernate Session will be keeping track of all of the updates that happen to instances that are associated with it, and as you could imagine, the list of updates that may need to be committed might end up getting quite large. Using the default configuration of Hibernate, you can never be totally sure when the updates will be committed to the database; all you can be sure of is that once the transaction has been committed, the updates have happened. However, if you have some compelling reason to rush the updates, and have them sent immediately to the database, you can call the flush() method on the Hibernate Session.

FlushMode

You can override the default flushing behavior of the Hibernate Session if you so desire. To have more control over how and when Hibernate will flush the changes that the Session is maintaining, you can set the Session's

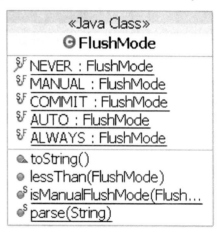

FlushMode. There are five flush modes, although one has been deprecated. They are:

☞ *AUTO – the Session is typically flushed before query execution to ensure query results do not contain stale data*

☞ *ALWAYS – the Session is flushed before every query*

☞ *COMMIT – the Session is flushed when the transaction.commit() method is called*

☞ *MANUAL – the Session is only flushed when the flush() method is invoked on the Session*

There is also a FlushMode of NEVER, although this has been deprecated, and the use of the MANUAL setting is promoted instead.

The opposite of flush()? refresh()?

So, if flush() takes the state of all of the instances in the Hibernate Session and forces a database update, I guess the Session's refresh() method could be considered the flush() method's inverse, as the refresh method is conversely passed a persistent instance, and Hibernate is asked to go to the database and update the already associated instance's properties with the data stored in the database.

For the most part, you won't likely run into too many circumstances where a persistent instance has fallen out of favor with the Hibernate Session, but if you believe such a thing has happened, perhaps due to a set of batch updates that may have been kicked off, or even due to some direct JDBC calls that may have sidestepped the Hibernate Session, well, calling the refresh method just might be required.

Here's the Hibernate API JavaDoc on the Session's refresh() method. Note the warning they give about the appropriate use of the method:

```
public void refresh (Object object)
                         throws HibernateException
```
Parameters: object -a persistent or detached instance

Re-read the state of the given instance from the underlying database. It is inadvisable to use this to implement long-running sessions that span many business tasks.

This method is, however, useful in certain special circumstances:
-- where a database trigger alters the object state upon insert or update
-- after executing direct SQL (eg. a mass update) in the same session
-- after inserting a Blob or Clob

Terminology Review: Transient and Persistent

> **Transient instances** are JavaBean instances that exist in your application, but do not have a representation in the database, and are not associated with a Hibernate Session.
>
> A **persistent instance** is one that not only exists in your application code, but is also associated with a Hibernate Session within the scope of an active transaction, so that when the transaction is committed, the state of that instance will be persisted to the database.

Detached Instances

Okay, so we have a great appreciation for the fact that as soon as an instance has been associated with a Hibernate Session, Hibernate will take responsibility for the persistent state of that object until the current transaction is committed. But what happens after the transaction is committed? For example, take a look at the following code:

```
Session session=HibernateUtil.beginTransaction();
User user = new User();
user.setLoginName("mj"); user.setPassword("aaaaaa");
session.save(user);

user.setPassword("bbbbbb");
HibernateUtil.commitTransaction();

user.setPassword("cccccc")
```

So, if you peeked into the database after running this code snippet, what would the value of the password be for the associated database record? Would it be *aaaaaa*, *bbbbbb* or *cccccc*? The answer is bbbbbb, since the instance is first persisted to the database with the value aaaaaa, then, as the transaction is committed, the password is updated to bbbbbb. But when the final Java based update to the password field is done, there is no open transaction, and Hibernate has no context with which it can update the user's password to cccccc.

After the transaction has been committed, the User instance is said to be a ***detached instance***, because the instance is no longer associated with a Hibernate Session, and no mechanism exists to tie the state of the instance to the database.

Programmatically Detaching Instances

Sometimes you may have an instance whose persistent state is being managed by the Hibernate Session, but then, for some reason, you want to shake that instance free of Hibernate's grasp. If you can't wait for a transaction to commit and have the instance naturally become detached, you can explicitly detach an instance from the Hibernate Session by simply calling the evict method of the Session, just as I do in this following snippet of code:

```
Session session=HibernateUtil.beginTransaction();

User user = new User();
user.setLoginName("mj");
user.setPassword("aaaaaa");
session.save(user);
session.evict(user);
user.setPassword("bbbbbb");
HibernateUtil.commitTransaction();
```

So, after the transaction is committed in this snippet of code, what value would the password column for the user's corresponding database record be? Would it be *null, aaaaaa* or *bbbbbb*? Well, the correct answer is *aaaaaa*.

You see, the instance has its password initialized to aaaaaa, after which it is passed to the save method of the Hibernate Session, and the Hibernate Session does just that – it saves the state of the instance. However, we programmatically evict the instance from the Session, at which point, Hibernate wipes its hands clean of any **further** changes to the User instance. The instance indeed has a representation in the database, but the evict method has detached the instance from its underlying representation, so further changes to the state of the User instance, such as the changing of the password to bbbbbb, are no longer the concern of the Hibernate Session, and such changes are not persisted to the database.

Object Comparisons

Once you start mixing and matching persistent and detached objects within your code, which pretty much any J2EE application will do at some point in time, you will find some not-so-funny, and potentially non-intuitive, problems that come up when you start doing comparisons between seemingly *like* instances.

For example, take a look at the following code that creates two instances, user1 and user2, based on the same, identical, database record. What do you think the output of the code snippet would be?

```
Session session=HibernateUtil.beginTransaction();

User user1 = new User();
user1.setPassword("aaaaaa");
Long id = (Long)session.save(user1);
session.evict(user1);
User user2 = (User)session.get(User.class, id);

System.out.print("The instances are the same: ");
System.out.println( user1.equals(user2));

HibernateUtil.commitTransaction();
```

Since both instances of the User class are based on the same database record, they will have all of their properties set to the same values, which means the two objects are essentially the same, but the comparison of the two objects returns *false*. It's somewhat non-intuitive, but if you know what's going on under the covers of the Java Virtual Machine (JVM), it actually makes sense.

By default, when you compare two instances using .equals(), the compiler simply compares the memory locations of the two instances, as opposed to comparing their actual property values. Since we have two separate instances, we end up having two separate memory locations, and a .equals() comparison returns false. To overcome such situations, a Hibernate best practice is to have all of your JPA annotated classes properly override the inherited .hashcode() and .equals() methods, providing an implementation that makes sense for the class. That way, when two instances with exactly the same state are compared, the actual properties the object contains will be compared, and the compiler will not simply look at the memory locations of objects when performing an equality comparison.

The org.hibernate.NonUniqueObjectException

So, as we have seen, the following code snippet creates two instances, user1 and user2, both of which share the same set of properties, but with the main difference being the fact that user1 becomes a detached object after the evict(user1); method is called, whereas the instance user2 is a persistent object right up until the point that the transaction gets committed. Here's the code:

```
Session session=HibernateUtil.beginTransaction();
User user1 = new User();user1.setPassword("aaaaaa");
Long id = (Long)session.save(user1);
session.evict(user1);
User user2 = (User)session.get(User.class, id);
HibernateUtil.commitTransaction();
```

Now, what do you think would happen if you changed some values in the detached instance, user1, and then tried to use the Hibernate Session to update that instance, considering the fact that user2, an instance that shares its id with user1, is already associated with the Hibernate Session? What would happen if you tried to run the following code:

```
Session session=HibernateUtil.beginTransaction();
User user1 = new User();
user1.setPassword("aaaaaa");
Long id = (Long)session.save(user1);
session.evict(user1);
User user2 = (User)session.get(User.class, id);
user1.setVerified(true);
session.saveOrUpdate(user1);
HibernateUtil.commitTransaction();
```

Well, here's another rule that Hibernate strictly enforces: only one instance of a class with a given unique primary key can be associated with the Session at a time. In this case, if we try to re-associate the evicted user1 with the Hibernate Session, Hibernate will kick out to us a NonUniqueObjectException, indicating that it is already managing an instance that represents that particular database record. So, Hibernate will gladly manage your unique instances, but fundamentally, it is that primary key that makes an object unique, and the developer must be careful not to add a second, non-unique instance of a class to an active Hibernate Session.

A Little Bit About Transactions

One of the things that you should know about a transaction is that it is an all or nothing type of thing. When you start a transaction, you can associate as many instances with your Hibernate Session as you like. Furthermore, you can perform an unlimited number of loads, gets, saves, updates, evictions or refreshes while a transaction is in progress. Hibernate, and the Hibernate Session, will keep track of all of your various method calls and state changes, and finally, when the transaction is committed, Hibernate will persist all of your changes to the database.

However, sometimes, when you are committing a transaction, something can go wrong. There are a multitude of reasons why a database write might fail, be it database deadlocking, or simply a connection timeout. But regardless of why a transaction fails, if a transaction does fail, all of the changes or updates that have taken place within the scope of that transaction are completely rolled back, taking the database back to the state it was in before the transaction was even started. Furthermore, if you have any instances in scope while the transaction failed, those instances will become *detached instances*, because the transaction and the Hibernate Session with which they were associated are both junked, and as such, Hibernate is no longer capable of persisting the state of your data. Furthermore, while data in the database will be rolled back to the state it was in before the transaction was committed, any JavaBeans that are still in scope *will not have their internal state rolled back*, making them out of sync

174

with the database if they did have their state updated during the course of the failed transaction.

Any time we commit a transaction, the possibility of an exception being thrown looms large. As a result, if an exception does occur during the committing of a transaction, it is a best practice to catch the exception, explicitly rollback the transaction, and finally, close the session. Furthermore, since all of the POJO instances have become detached from the database, and are no longer under the Hibernate Session's spell, those instances should be allowed to simply go out of scope and be garbage collected, as they are no longer in sync with the database.

Finally, you can either re-throw the HibernateException, or potentially, throw a custom application exception that will be appropriately handled by an upper application layer, providing an appropriately formatted error message to the end user.

```
try {

  Session hibernateSession = this.getCurrentSession();
  hibernateSession.beginTransaction();

  User u = (User)hibernateSession.get(User.class, 2);
  hibernateSession.evict(u); /* u is now detached */
  u.setLoginName("Joey");
  u.setPassword("shabidew");

  hibernateSession.getTransaction().commit();

} catch (HibernateException e) {

  e.printStackTrace();
  hibernateSession.getTransaction().rollback();
  hibernateSession.close();
  throw e;

}
```

In Summary

So, when we create instances in our Java code, the instance is considered to be a transient instance, which means there is no mechanism in place to manage the persistent state of that instance. However, once we pass a transient instance to the save, update, or saveOrUpdate method of the Hibernate Session, we consider the transient instance to have transitioned into a persistent instance, as Hibernate will begin to manage the persistent state of that object. Any instance associated with the Hibernate Session is said to be a persistent instance.

Saving or updating a JavaBean isn't the only way to get your hands on a persistent instance. JavaBeans that have been loaded into the Hibernate Session, either by a get or load method call, or even an HQL or criteria query, are considered to be persistent instances, and as such, any changes or updates to the state of those instances will be persisted to the database by the Hibernate Session as well.

If you do have an instance that you want to release from Hibernate's control, you can always call the evict method of the Hibernate Session, passing in the name of the instance you want freed from Hibernate's control. When an instance is no longer having its state managed by the Hibernate Session, we call that a detached instance, because while it does have a representation in the database, Hibernate isn't doing anything to keep the instance in sync with the underlying persistence store. In effect, the instance is detached from its corresponding representation in the database.

Of course, when we work with Hibernate, all of our interactions with the database must occur within the scope of a transaction. By default, when we call methods like save or update, we can never be totally sure when the corresponding record in the database is updated – all we know for sure is that once the transaction is committed, all of the changes to any of the persistent instances associated with the Hibernate Session will be saved to the database. Of course, there is always the potential that the act of saving all of the data to the database will fail for some reason, and if that does happen, Hibernate will throw a runtime exception. At this point, there's really not too much you can do, other than roll back the current transaction, and close the Hibernate Session. At this point, all of the instances that were previously under the control of the Hibernate Session become detached objects, and quite likely, are no longer in sync with the database. In such a case, you can always start a new transaction, and try to turn your detached instances back into persistent instances by re-associating them with the Hibernate Session through save or update calls, but in the end, you're probably better off just sending a friendly error message to your client application, and start any request-response cycle over again from scratch.

And that's about it – a quick description of how hibernate works, along with a simple description of what we mean when we talk about transient, persistent and detached objects.

Chapter 8
Finders and Queries

Finders and Queries

One of the fine arts of enterprise programming is figuring out the best way to get all of that information that is currently in your database, out of your database, into your applications, and subsequently displayed back to the user in a manner that is both efficient and effective. Hibernate provides a variety of ways tó extract information from a database, from the simple load and get methods of the Hibernate Session, to HQL, named queries, and even plain old JDBC. This chapter will explore some of the more common ways to query data from the database, including:

☞ *Hibernate Query Language syntax*

☞ *Variable Injection*

☞ *Named Queries*

☞ *Native SQL statements*

The goal of this chapter is to demonstrate the most common mechanisms of performing database queries with Hibernate, helping you to develop a strong foundation of skills upon which you can build.

The Need for a New Query Language (HQL)

Thinking about a time a few years back, I remember when I was creating EJBs and was introduced to EJBQL, the EJB Query Language. My legacy EJBs were working just fine with the loads of SQL that was already in them, so I really didn't understand why I would want to introduce something new into the mix. Of course, looking back, my EJBs were probably a little too database driven, so perhaps it was more of my lack of good design skills that obfuscated the value of EJBQL; but I must say, I wasn't too fond of it when I first saw it.

But if you really do think about it, you will realize pretty quickly that if you're developing Java components, coding in a J2EE environment, and working with an object-oriented model, well, you should probably be thinking about your data queries in an object oriented way. And furthermore, and perhaps even more to the point, since our JPA annotated POJOs effectively *abstract away* the underlying database layer, the fact is, when you are designing your Java based persistence applications, you really can't be sure of what is going to be going on in the underlying database layer at deployment time or runtime.

For example, perhaps you have a JavaBean named User, and that JavaBean has a property named loginName. What is the name of the underlying field in the database? If we are writing SQL statements, the names of the database fields become very, very important, because they must exactly match the column names used in the query. This implies a knowledge of the persistence layer in the application layer, and that makes most good MVC programmers a little antsy.

However, with HQL, as with EJBQL which preceded it, you write your queries based on the properties and names of the Java objects in your domain model. That way, if the names of the underlying tables or columns ever change, your Java applications are not effected – the only thing that has to change is the mappings, or column annotations, but the actual HQL queries remain the same, insulating your Java model from possible changes at the database level. And of course, insulating the Java model from the persistence layer is always a penultimate goal of a good application developer. HQL makes this possible.

Hibernate Query Basics: A Review

As with any other operation in Hibernate involving a database interaction, executing a Hibernate query begins with the program gaining access to the Hibernate Session. The Hibernate Session has a createQuery method that takes any valid Hibernate Query Language String, from which a Query object can be created. A very simple HQL query that would retrieve all User objects from the underlying database would be as simple as the String "**from User**". So, in code, a *select all Users in the database* request would start off looking something like this:

```
Session session = HibernateUtil.beginTransaction();
Query query = session.createQuery("from User");
```

To actually get the results of the query, you simply ask the instance of the query object to return a java.util.List. You do this by invoking the aptly named list() method of the Query instance. The List will simply be a collection of User objects, which you can loop through at your leisure.

```
Session session = HibernateUtil.beginTransaction();
Query query = session.createQuery("from User");
List users = query.list();

for (int i = 0; i < users.size(); i++) {
  User user = (User) users.get(i);
  System.out.println(user.getLoginName());
}
```

Notice how the returned elements in the List are of type User. A quick cast allows us to pull these elements out of the List and start working with all of the yummy properties of the instance.

Selecting specific elements

Notice how the *from User* HQL query returned a grouping of User objects. The *from User* query pulls all of the fields associated with our User class out of the underlying database, and appropriately initializes the corresponding fields of the User instance. In our cheap little code, we simply printed out the user's loginName to prove that everything was working:

```
Session session = HibernateUtil.beginTransaction();
Query query = session.createQuery("from User");
List users = query.list();
for (int i = 0; i < users.size(); i++) {
  User user = (User) users.get(i);
  System.out.println(user.getLoginName());
}
```

If all we were interested in was the loginName, we could have prefaced our find User HQL query with a SELECT element, and selected only the loginName:

String hql = "SELECT loginName from User";

Note though, the result of such a query, where only one parameter is specified, is a list of elements matching the data type of the property. So, in this case, since the loginName property is defined in the User class as a String, the List returned from the query.list() method will be a collection of String objects, not a collection of Users:

```
Session session = HibernateUtil.beginTransaction();
String hql = "SELECT loginName from User";
Query query = session.createQuery(hql);
List names = query.list();
for (int i = 0; i < names.size(); i++) {
  String name = (String) names.get(i);
  System.out.println(name);
}
```

If more than one property is selected, the elements of the returned List are arrays, with the array elements matching the type and order of the elements as they appear in the select portion of the HQL statement.

The HQL where Clause & Unique Results

To narrow down the size of your queries, you'll need to use the irrepressible WHERE clause. To find a User with the loginName of mj, the corresponding HQL query would look like this:

```
String hql="from User where loginName = 'mj' ";
```

Now, assuming the loginName was a unique field in the database, and there could only be one possible row in the database where the loginName was 'mj', there's no point in returning a List via the Query object. Instead, when only one result is expected, we use the uniqueResult() method of the Query class, which returns to the calling program a simple, single, java.util.Object, which can be uneventfully cast into the appropriate object of choice.

Combining the where clause and the uniqueResult() method, our Java code would look something like this:

```
Session session = HibernateUtil.beginTransaction();
String hql="from User where loginName = 'mj' ";
Query query = session.createQuery(hql);
Object o  = query.uniqueResult();
User u = (User)o;
System.out.println(u.getLoginName());
System.out.println("\n\n");
HibernateUtil.commitTransaction();
```

Of course, this particular HQL query hard codes the loginName 'mj' right into the query. This doesn't really make too much sense, as you generally don't know the value you need to look up until runtime. Rather than hard coding values into an HQL query, you'll typically use variable injection instead.

JDBC and PreparedStatements: A Review

When performing a query where the criteria isn't exactly known at runtime, as in the case where we select a record based on the loginName a user provides, we need to leverage HQL's variable injection facilities. If you've ever used JDBC and worked with PreparedStatements, you'll notice a number of similarities in the philosophy of how variables are injected into HQL statements, although the syntax between HQL and JDBC statements is a little bit different.

With a JDBC PreparedStatement, a select query against the user table where the value of the loginName is not known until runtime would look something like this:

```
String loginName;
✂✂✂/*obtain the loginName from user somehow!!!*/ ✂✂✂
String sqlQuery = "select * from user where loginName = ?";
PreparedStatement ps = con.prepareStatement(sqlQuery);
/*replace the first ? mark with the value held by the variable*/
ps.setString(1, loginName);
ResultSet rs = ps.executeQuery();✂✂✂
```

The idea with the above code is that the value of the user's loginName is not known until it is provided to our program, so instead of hard-coding the values into your program, you can code a normal SQL statement with a question mark, ?, in the spot where the unknown value should go. You then code some way to get this value at runtime, substitute the initialized runtime variable for the question mark in the query, and then finally, send the query to the database. That's how JDBC PreparedStatements work! As I like to say, Hibernate is very similar - but different. ☺

Variable Injection with Hibernate

Hibernate uses a mechanism similar to a JDBC PreparedStatement to perform runtime variable injection into HQL statements. The Hibernate syntax is a bit different from standard JDBC code, but the idea is pretty much the same.

Rather than putting a question mark into the Hibernate Query Language String where the runtime variable needs to be inserted, as we might with direct JDBC, a Hibernate best practice is to use a variable name with a colon in front of it, although using the question mark syntax is still possible. Using variable names is preferred, as you can use real names where the variables need to be inserted, rather than numbering off the question marks, like in a JDBC preparedStatement.

Here's how our Hibernate query string might look:

```
String hql = "from User where loginName = :name";
```

This HQL String is then passed to the createQuery method of the Hibernate Session to create a Query object:

```
Query query = session.createQuery(hql);
```

From there, a setter method on the initialized query object, which I creatively named *query*, is used to substitute the variable, which is defined in the HQL String as **:name**, with an actual value. Here, we use a value passed into the program:

```
query.setString("name", loginName);
```

Once the placeholder in the HQL query has been substituted by our intended variable, we can execute the query and obtain a unique result.

```
Object o = query.uniqueResult();
User user = (User)o;
```

Once the query is executed, we take the queryResult, which is returned as an Object, and cast it into a our User type. We can then use the User instance in the application. It's all just that easy!

```
Session session = HibernateUtil.beginTransaction();
String loginName = "mj";
String hql="from User where loginName = :name";
Query query = session.createQuery(hql);
query.setString("name", loginName);
Object o = query.uniqueResult();
User user = (User)o;
System.out.println(user.getLoginName());
HibernateUtil.commitTransaction();
```

ORDER BY and the HQL Alias

Another helpful little token you can add to an HQL statement is the ORDER BY element. Basically, you can specify a specific property of your POJO, and tell Hibernate to sort the results of your query by that property, in either an ascending (ASC) or descending (DESC) manner.

```
Session session = HibernateUtil.beginTransaction();
String hql = "from User as u ORDER BY u.id ASC";
Query query = session.createQuery(hql);
List users = query.list();
for (int i = 0; i < users.size(); i++) {
  User user = (User) users.get(i);
  System.out.println("Hello World");
  System.out.println(user.getLoginName());
}
HibernateUtil.commitTransaction();
```

You will also notice that through a little slight of hand, I used an *alias* in the ORDER BY query. In any HQL query, you can use the word *as* to specify an alias for the class you are querying against. Here, I specified the alias **u**, and when the ORDER BY clause was used, I simply specified the property name using the alias, which equated to **u.id**.

```
String hql = "from User as u ORDER BY u.id ASC";
```

GROUP BY and HAVING

The last two elements of the SELECT query that I haven't talked about are the GROUP BY and HAVING attributes. The results of a query, or aggregate query, can be grouped together using the GROUP BY clause. Furthermore, a logical expression can be provided through the HAVING token of the HQL query as well. Our User class doesn't give us any great scenarios for using the GROUP BY and HAVING tokens, but here's a simple example that effectively demonstrates the syntax. ☺

```
Session session = HibernateUtil.beginTransaction();
String hql;
hql= "from User as u GROUP BY u.id HAVING u.id > 4)";
Query query = session.createQuery(hql);
List users = query.list();
for (int i = 0; i < users.size(); i++) {
   User user = (User) users.get(i);
   System.out.println("Hello World");
   System.out.println(user.getLoginName());
}
HibernateUtil.commitTransaction();
```

Note: setting the hibernate logger to **debug** in your log4j.properties file will provide much more information about your HQL queries. You might even see the values that are used during variable injection if you set the log level from **info** to **debug**, as in the sample below:

```
### direct log messages to stdout ###
log4j.appender.stdout=org.apache.log4j.ConsoleAppender
log4j.appender.stdout.Target=System.out
log4j.appender.stdout.layout=org.apache.log4j.PatternLayout
log4j.appender.stdout.layout.ConversionPattern=%d{ABSOLUTE} %5p %c{1}:%L - %m%n
### set log levels - ###
log4j.rootLogger=warn, stdout log4j.logger.org.hibernate=info
### log JDBC bind parameters ###
log4j.logger.org.hibernate.type=debug
### log schema export/update ###
log4j.logger.org.hibernate.tool.hbm2ddl=debug
```

The log4j.properties file typically goes in the same folder as the hibernate.cfg.xml file, which for us is the C:_mycode folder.

Batch UPDATE Calls with Hibernate

For performing updates and deletes on a large number of records, Hibernate provides a fairly simple batch operation syntax. The syntax is pretty much as follows:

```
( UPDATE | DELETE )
FROM ? EntityName (WHERE where_conditions)
```

So, to change the password on all users who were *lazy and silly* and set their own passwords to the literal string *'password'*, we can issue the following HQL:

```
String hql="update User
            set password = 'abc123'
            where password='password')";
```

This update will effectively change every record that has a password of 'password' to a password of 'abc123'.

One thing to note about performing a batch update or delete is the fact that we do not use the query.list() or query.uniqueResult() methods, but instead, we use the special executeUpdate() method of the Query instance. Very conveniently, this method returns a value of type *int* that tells us how many records were actually effected. Putting all of it together in code would look like this:

```
Session session = HibernateUtil.beginTransaction();
String hql = "update User
            set password = 'abc123'
            where password='password')";
Query query = session.createQuery(hql);
int rowCount = query.executeUpdate();
System.out.println(rowCount + " rows were updated.");
HibernateUtil.commitTransaction();
```

Batch DELETE Calls with Hibernate

Batch DELETE calls with Hibernate are very similar to an update, except there's obviously no need to set any update parameters. So, to delete every user in the database with a name of 'Tim', the HQL DELETE query would look like this:

```
String hql = "delete User where loginName = 'Tim'";
```

And again, the HQL delete query must be sent to an executeUpdate method of the Query object to both run the batch command, and subsequently return the number of rows effected. Here's how a batch delete would look in code:

```
Session session = HibernateUtil.beginTransaction();
String hql = "delete User where loginName = 'Tim'";
Query query = session.createQuery(hql);
int rowCount = query.executeUpdate();
System.out.println(rowCount + " rows were deleted.");
HibernateUtil.commitTransaction();
```

When run, this code would delete every row in the database with the loginName of Tim. Pretty sweet, isn't it?

Hibernate Named Queries

Mingling HQL statements right there alongside your Java code is neither a manageable nor maintainable solution. Instead, it's a best practice to keep all of your HQL queries in a single, manageable location, and invoke those queries by name in your code. To facilitate this functionality, Hibernate leverages the @NamedQuery JPA annotation. To use it, you simply create a class that will contain all of your named queries, and place the @NamedQuery annotation at the top of the class.

```
@NamedQuery(name="user.findByLoginName",
    query="from User where loginName = :name")
```

One thing you should know about named queries is that *the class that defines the @NamedQuery tag must be made part of Hibernate's AnnotationConfiguration object.* Our User class is added to the AnnotationConfiguration object in our custom HibernateUtil class, so we'll add the NamedQuery right before the class declaration of the User.

```
package com.examscam.model;
import javax.persistence.*;
import org.hibernate.Session;
import com.examscam.HibernateUtil;
@Entity
@Table(name = "user", schema = "examscam")
@NamedQuery(name="user.findByLoginName",
    query="from User where loginName = :name" )
public class User {    ✂✂✂    }
```

Once you have defined your @NamedQuery, and the class in which it is defined is loaded into Hibernate's AnnotationConfiguration, you can use this named query anywhere that you access the Hibernate Session.

Calling a NamedQuery in Hibernate

With the class that defines the @NamedQuery annotation made part of the Hibernate Configuration, invoking the NamedQuery is as simple as calling the Hibernate Session's getNamedQuery method, and passing along the query name. From there, you can inject any variables as needed, and then execute the query as per usual.

The following main method implements the *from User where loginName = :name* query in the form of a NamedQuery:

```
public static void main(String args[]){
  String loginName = "mj";
  Session session = HibernateUtil.beginTransaction();
  Query query =
     session.getNamedQuery("user.findByLoginName");
  query.setString("name", loginName);
  Object o = query.uniqueResult();
  User user = (User)o;
  System.out.println(user.getLoginName());
  HibernateUtil.commitTransaction();
}
```

Hibernate and Native SQL

And though our main focus is always Hibernate, it is worth mentioning that you can indeed issue native SQL queries through the Hibernate Session using the Session's createSQLQuery method. You simply pass in a valid SQL String, and Hibernate will return the results in a java.util.List.

Now, one thing to note about native SQL queries is that what gets returned in each element of the List is simply an Object array, containing the datatype to which the queried columns map, as defined by the JPA annotations of the entity class. Furthermore, with a SELECT * query, we would need to know the order of the columns in the database so we can cast the incoming data properly.

The following is an example of a native SQL query that goes against a User database table with id (Integer), email(String), name(String) and password(String) fields:

```
public static void main(String args[]) {
  String sql = "SELECT * FROM USER";
  Session session = HibernateUtil.beginTransaction();
  SQLQuery query = session.createSQLQuery(sql);
  List users = query.list();
  for (int i = 0; i < users.size(); i++) {
    Object[] o = (Object[]) users.get(i);
    System.out.print(((Integer) o[0])); //id
    System.out.print(((String) o[1]));  //email
    System.out.print(((String) o[2]));  //name
    System.out.println(((String) o[3]));//pass
  }
}
```

Chapter 9
The Criteria API

Now, as you may or may not have gathered from reading this book, I'm not a big fan of Query Languages. I mean, it's not that I don't appreciate what they do, it's just that I'm a Java programmer at heart, and writing Java code is what I do best. I'm good with simple SQL, and can bluff my way through a database driven application, but I'm certainly not an SQL master, and when it comes to writing crazy outer joins, or group by statements, well, I'm afraid that my SQL skills are sorely lacking.

So, when someone told me that I could largely eliminate my need to write dry and mundane SQL statements, I have to say that I was more than enthused. I mean, I've always thought that a Java developer should be able to think of the data they need to query in the form of the Java objects that make up their domain model, and I know that HQL tries to bring that dream to fruition, but it wasn't until I started using the Criteria API that I realized somebody had really embraced the idea of object-oriented data access, and had implemented it in a very sound and easy to use manner.

Creating smart, simple, and effective queries is what the Criteria API allows us to do, and as such, using the Criteria API will be the focus of this chapter.

Example Database

The Criteria API allows us to do some very interesting queries, so for the examples in this chapter, I'm going to be executing queries against a user table in the database that contains the following values (Note: I think I messed up Kerri's name - sorry Kerri):

id	emailAddress	lastAccessTime	login_name	password	registrationDate	verified
1	mj@mcnz.com	2008-02-25 14:06:02	mj	abc123	2006-02-01	b'0'
2	mario@scja.ca	2008-01-01 00:00:00	mario	pass	2007-02-01	b'1'
3	avril@scja.com	2008-02-25 14:06:02	sk8trgrl	password	2008-02-01	b'0'
4	getbent@scja.ca	2006-10-05 00:00:00	ridley	mypassword	2006-06-11	b'1'
5	sheehan@princessjava.com	2008-02-25 00:00:00	kerrr	pwd	2008-01-12	b'0'
6	rabbit@princessjava.com	2008-02-25 14:06:02	astra	pwd	2008-02-25	b'0'
7	me@scwcd.com	2008-09-15 00:00:00	cameron	90210	2008-09-12	b'1'
8	stanley@pulpjava.com	2008-02-25 00:00:00	stephen	low	2008-03-15	b'0'
9	ernesto@pulpjava.com	1999-07-26 00:00:00	che	password	1999-04-09	b'1'
10	rabbit@scja.com	2008-02-25 14:06:02	remy	password	2007-06-21	b'0'

I created this database by coding the following into a runnable main method. Feel free to do the same. ☺

```
public static void main(String args[]) {
HibernateUtil.recreateDatabase();
Session session = HibernateUtil.beginTransaction();
{
User u = new User();
u.setLoginName("mj");
u.setPassword("abc123");
u.setEmailAddress("mj@mcnz.com");
u.setVerified(false);
u.setLastAccessTime(new java.util.Date());
u.setRegistrationDate(new GregorianCalendar(2006,01,01));
session.saveOrUpdate(u);
}{
User u = new User();
u.setLoginName("mario");
u.setPassword("pass");
u.setEmailAddress("mario@scja.ca");
u.setVerified(true);
u.setLastAccessTime(Date.valueOf("2008-1-1"));
u.setRegistrationDate(new GregorianCalendar(2007,01,01));
session.saveOrUpdate(u);
}{
User u = new User();
u.setLoginName("sk8trgrl");
u.setPassword("password");
u.setEmailAddress("avril@scja.com");
u.setVerified(false);
u.setLastAccessTime(new java.util.Date());
u.setRegistrationDate(new GregorianCalendar(2008,01,01));
session.saveOrUpdate(u);
}
{
User u = new User();
u.setLoginName("ridley");
u.setPassword("mypassword");
```

```
u.setEmailAddress("getbent@scja.ca");
u.setVerified(true);
u.setLastAccessTime(new java.util.Date());
u.setLastAccessTime(Date.valueOf("2006-10-5"));
u.setRegistrationDate(new GregorianCalendar(2006,5,11));
session.saveOrUpdate(u);
}{
User u = new User();
u.setLoginName("kerrr");
u.setPassword("pwd");
u.setEmailAddress("sheehan@princessjava.com");
u.setVerified(false);
u.setLastAccessTime(Date.valueOf("2008-2-25"));
u.setRegistrationDate(new GregorianCalendar(2007,12,12));
session.saveOrUpdate(u);
}{
User u = new User();
u.setLoginName("astra");
u.setPassword("pwd");
u.setEmailAddress("rabbit@princessjava.com");
u.setVerified(false);
u.setLastAccessTime(new java.util.Date());
u.setRegistrationDate(new GregorianCalendar());
session.saveOrUpdate(u);
}{
User u = new User();
u.setLoginName("cameron");
u.setPassword("90210");
u.setEmailAddress("me@scwcd.com");
u.setVerified(true);
u.setLastAccessTime(Date.valueOf("2008-9-15"));
u.setRegistrationDate(new GregorianCalendar(2008,8,12));
session.saveOrUpdate(u);
}{
User u = new User();
u.setLoginName("stephen");
u.setPassword("low");
u.setEmailAddress("stanley@pulpjava.com");
u.setVerified(false);
u.setLastAccessTime(Date.valueOf("2008-2-25"));
u.setRegistrationDate(new GregorianCalendar(2008,02,15));
session.saveOrUpdate(u);
}{
User u = new User();
u.setLoginName("che");
u.setPassword("password");
u.setEmailAddress("ernesto@pulpjava.com");
u.setVerified(true);
u.setLastAccessTime(Date.valueOf("1999-7-26"));
u.setRegistrationDate(new GregorianCalendar(1999,3,9));
session.saveOrUpdate(u);
}{
User u = new User();
u.setLoginName("remy");
u.setPassword("password");
u.setEmailAddress("rabbit@scja.com");
u.setVerified(false);
u.setLastAccessTime(new java.util.Date());
u.setRegistrationDate(new GregorianCalendar(2007,05,21));
session.saveOrUpdate(u);
}
HibernateUtil.commitTransaction();
}
```

www.hibernatemadeeasy.com

The SQL Insert Statement

For anyone that has their heart set on writing an SQL statement to populate their database with the same data as mine, here's the pertinent SQL statement:

```
INSERT INTO `user`

(`id`,`emailAddress`,`lastAcces
sTime`,`login_name`,`password`,
`registrationDate`,`verified`)
VALUES

(1,'mj@mcnz.com','2008-01-13
14:49:01','mj','abc123','2006-02-01',0x00),
  (2,'mario@scja.ca','2008-01-01
00:00:00','mario','pass','2007-02-01',0x01),
(3,'avril@scja.com','2008-01-13
14:49:01','sk8trgrl','password','2008-02-01',0x00),
(4,'getbent@scja.ca','2006-10-05
00:00:00','ridley','mypassword','2006-06-11',0x01),
(5,'sheehan@princessjava.com','2008-02-25
00:00:00','kerrr','pwd','2008-01-12',0x00),
(6,'rabbit@princessjava.com','2008-01-13
14:49:01','astra','pwd','2008-01-13',0x00),
(7,'me@scwcd.com','2008-09-15
00:00:00','cameron','90210','2008-09-12',0x01),
(8,'stanley@pulpjava.com','2008-02-25
00:00:00','stephen','low','2008-03-15',0x00),
(9,'ernesto@pulpjava.com','1999-07-26
00:00:00','che','password','1999-04-09',0x01),
(10,'rabbit@scja.com','2008-01-13
14:49:01','remy','password','2007-06-21',0x00);
```

The User Class to this Point

Here is the User class, as it has been coded and JPA annotated, up until this point.

Please note that a new, toString() method has been added to the class. This will make printing out information associated with the user much simpler.

```
package com.examscam.model;
import javax.persistence.*;
import org.hibernate.Session;
import com.examscam.HibernateUtil;
@Entity
@Table(name = "user", schema = "examscam")
public class User {
  private Long id;
  private String loginName;
  private String password;
  private String encryptedPassword;
  private String emailAddress;
  private Boolean verified;
  private java.util.Date lastAccessTime;
  private java.util.Calendar registrationDate;

  @Id
  @GeneratedValue
  @Column(name = "id")
  public Long getId() { return id; }
  public void setId(Long id) { this.id = id; }

  @Transient
  public String getEncryptedPassword(){return encryptedPassword;}
  public void setEncryptedPassword(String ep) {
    this.encryptedPassword = ep;
  }

  @Column(name = "login_name")
  public String getLoginName() {return loginName;}
  public void setLoginName(String loginName) {
    this.loginName = loginName;
  }
```

```
@Column(name = "password", nullable=false)
  public String getPassword() {return password;}
  public void setPassword(String password) {
    this.password = password;
  }

  public String getEmailAddress() {return emailAddress;}

@Temporal(TemporalType.TIMESTAMP)
  public java.util.Date getLastAccessTime() {
    return lastAccessTime;
  }

  @Temporal(TemporalType.DATE)
  public java.util.Calendar getRegistrationDate() {
    return registrationDate;
  }

  @Basic
  public Boolean isVerified() {return verified;}

  public void setEmailAddress(String emailAddress) {
    this.emailAddress = emailAddress;
  }
  public void setLastAccessTime(java.util.Date lastAccessTime) {
    this.lastAccessTime = lastAccessTime;
  }
  public void setRegistrationDate(java.util.Calendar registrationDate){
    this.registrationDate = registrationDate;
  }
  public void setVerified(Boolean verified) {
    this.verified = verified;
  }

  public String toString() {
    return getId() + " : " +
      getLoginName() + " : " +
        getPassword() + " : " +
            getEmailAddress();
  }

}
```

A User Management Application?

So far, we've been giving the User class a pretty solid workout. It's a good class, and it's pretty representative of the type of component you'll see in just about any enterprise application.

Now, just imagine a standard application that managed instances of the User class. You'd probably have some type of search function that allows the end user to search for a user based on a login_name, or based on the id, or the email address. You may even want to see everyone that hasn't verified their email address, or perhaps, everyone that has logged in during the previous day. These are all reasonable searches that a simple User management application might require. So, how many SQL, or should I say, *HQL queries*, would be required to implement such a system? Well, if you're using the Criteria API, the answer is <u>none</u>!

The User Management Application

The User management application is something we will build in the following chapters, but the Criteria API concepts that we learn here will be a central part of its creation. Here's a sneak peak of what our User management application will look like:

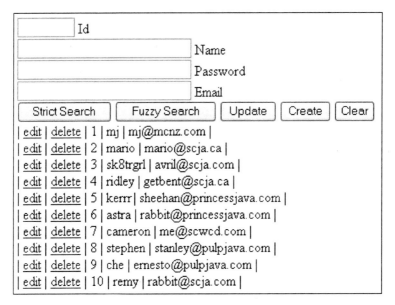

Welcome to the Criteria API

If you want to use the Criteria API to perform queries based on the User, all you have to do is create an instance of the User class, populate the properties on which you wish to search, and pass the populated instance to Hibernate. Behind the scenes, Hibernate will generate all of the required SQL, execute the query, and package the results up into a list of very handsome User objects. The Criteria API is the most elegant and flexible way to query your database in an object-oriented way.

So, say you wanted to find all of the Users in your database that hadn't verified their email address. All you'd have to do is follow a few, simple steps.

The first thing you do is create an instance of the User class. For our current use case, we just want users that are not verified, so we create a new User instance, and initialize the verified property to false:

```
User user = new User();
user.setVerified(false);
```

From there, we create something called an Example object based on the initialized User. It's easily done by passing the recently created User instance to the static create method of the Example class:

```
Example example = Example.create(user);
```

And from there, you just ask the Hibernate Session to create a special Criteria object based on your User class. You then add the Example to the criteria instance. When the list() method is invoked on the criteria instance, the calling program will be returned a list of User instances that match the criteria query. Look at the code, it's quite elegant:

```
Criteria criteria = session.createCriteria(User.class);
criteria.add(example);
List results = criteria.list();
```

Can you believe it? That's all you have to do. This very simple snippet of Java code will result in a query executing against the database that returns all of the users who have a *verified* property of false. You don't have to write a single lick of SQL or HQL– the Criteria API takes care of it all for you!

The Complete FindVerifiedUsers Class

```java
package com.examscam.criteria;
import java.util.List;import org.hibernate.Criteria;
import org.hibernate.Session;
import org.hibernate.criterion.Example;
import com.examscam.HibernateUtil;import com.examscam.model.User;
public class FindVerifiedUsers {
  public static void main(String[] args) {
    User user = new User();
    user.setVerified(false);
    Example example = Example.create(user);
    Session session = HibernateUtil.beginTransaction();
    Criteria criteria = session.createCriteria(User.class);
    criteria.add(example);
    List results = criteria.list();
    HibernateUtil.commitTransaction();
    for (int i = 0; i<results.size(); i++) {
      System.out.println(results.get(i).toString());
    }
  }
}
```

When I run the FindVerifiedUsers class, I can see Hibernate kicking out the following SQL query:

```
Hibernate: select this_.id as id0_0_, this_.emailAddress as
emailAdd2_0_0_, this_.lastAccessTime as lastAcce3_0_0_,
this_.login_name as login4_0_0_, this_.password as
password0_0_, this_.registrationDate as registra6_0_0_,
this_.verified as verified0_0_ from examscam.user this_
where (this_.verified=?)
```

When the code runs, the query finds that six of the ten users in the database have not verified their email address. The application actually spits out the following data (formatted nicely due to the new toString() method defined on a previous page in the User class):

```
1 : mj : abc123 : mj@mcnz.com
3 : sk8trgrl : password : avril@scja.com
5 : kerrr : pwd : sheehan@princessjava.com
6 : astra : pwd : rabbit@princessjava.com
8 : stephen : low : stanley@pulpjava.com
10 : remy : password : rabbit@scja.com
```

Expanding You Criteria Queries

But wait – it gets even better. Let's say you wanted to find all of the people who registered today, *and* have not verified their email accounts? Well, you just create another User instance, initialize the *verified* property to false, and initialize the *registrationDate* property to today's date. Again, create an org.hibernate.criterion.Example object based on the User instance, create a Hibernate Criteria query object based on the User.class, add the Example object to the Criteria Query object, and then have the Criteria query object list the results. It's just that easy!

```
User user = new User();
user.setVerified(false);
user.setRegistrationDate(new GregorianCalendar());
Example example = Example.create(user);

Session session = HibernateUtil.beginTransaction();
Criteria criteria = session.createCriteria(User.class);
criteria.add(example);
List results = criteria.list();
HibernateUtil.commitTransaction();
for (int i = 0; i<results.size(); i++) {
  System.out.println(results.get(i).toString());
}
```

As this query runs, one record is returned. Apparently, Astra is the only person to register today and not verify her email:

```
6 : astra : pwd : rabbit@princessjava.com
```

> *Note that the User class, provided at the beginning of this chapter, has **a new toString()** method that formats a user's details in the form of:* **id : loginName : password : email.**

Returning a Single Row of Results

If you know for a fact that a given query will only return a single row, you can use the uniqueResult() method of the Criteria class. This will return a single, lazy, java.lang.Object instance that you will need to cast into the appropriate type.

If we wanted to do a query, based on a loginName and a password (*you know,* a basic query to facilitate the process of a client logging into our application) we could simply initialize the loginName and password properties of a User instance appropriately, and use the Example and Criteria objects to process the query. A username and password combination should be unique across the application, so we can use the uniqueResult method to process the results:

```
public static void main(String[] args) {

  User user = new User();
  user.setLoginName("mj");
  user.setPassword("abc123");
  Example example = Example.create(user);
  Session session = HibernateUtil.beginTransaction();
  Criteria criteria =
                session.createCriteria(User.class);
  criteria.add(example);

  User u = (User)criteria.uniqueResult();
  System.out.println(u);
}
```

Running this main method generates the following result:

```
1 : mj : abc123 : mj@mcnz.com
```

204

Helpful Methods of the Example Class

Sometimes, your database will contain a variety of entries that have been initialized to zero by default, even though a field initialized to zero is pretty much meaningless. By default, the Example class will match on zero valued properties, but you can reverse this behavior by invoking the excludeZeroes() method on the Example instance:

example.excludeZeroes();

```
Example example = Example.create(new User());
example.excludeZeroes();
```

example.excludeNone()

On the flipside, criteria queries ignore matching null values. However, you may actually want to pull records where a given property has been initialized to a null value. For example, you might want to retrieve every record where the loginName wasn't initialized properly, and has been assigned a null value. To enable matches on null values, you just call the excludeNone() method on your Example instance. The excludeNone() method has the added functionality of enabling matching on fields initialized to zero as well.

```
Example example = Example.create(new User());
example.excludeNone();
```

example.excludeProperty(String property)

Furthermore, you can also exclude a particular named property with the aptly named excludeProperty method. This will ensure that matches on this particular property will not be used to decide whether or not a particular record is returned.

```
Example example = Example.create(new User());
example.excludeProperty("verified");
```

Like Queries with the Criteria API

I'm always amazed when the database gurus I know get in front of the awful DB2 Control Console and start whipping out all sorts of crazy SQL statements that use weird escape characters to do nutty like and matching queries. Those skills are simply beyond my grasp. That's why I was so excited to see that the Example class in the criteria API makes it incredibly easy to issue 'like' or 'fuzzy matching' queries by simply invoking a few methods of the API.

For example, say I wanted to find all of the users whose email address ended with .com? It'd be easy! All I'd have to do is create a criteria query that uses an example User instance, and have that instance's email property initialized to *.com*. Of course, simply initializing the email property to *.com* won't return any results, because there is no email address in my database that is exclusively *.com*. However, if I invoke the *enableLike()* method, and set the **MatchMode** to **END**, the criteria query will return all of the results where the end of the email address is *.com* Pretty neat, eh?

```
public static void main(String[] args) {
  User user = new User();
  user.setEmailAddress(".com");
  Example example = Example.create(user);
  example.enableLike(MatchMode.END);
  Session session = HibernateUtil.beginTransaction();
  Criteria criteria = session.createCriteria(User.class);
  criteria.add(example);  List results = criteria.list();
  for (int i = 0; i<results.size(); i++) {
    System.out.println(results.get(i).toString());
  }
  HibernateUtil.commitTransaction();
}
```

When I run the main method coded above, I get the following results, which are correctly filtered based on the .com suffix at the end of each user's email address:

```
1 : mj : abc123 : mj@mcnz.com
3 : sk8trgrl : password : avril@scja.com
5 : kerrr : pwd : sheehan@princessjava.com
6 : astra : pwd : rabbit@princessjava.com
8 : stephen : low : stanley@pulpjava.com
10 : remy : password : rabbit@scja.com
```

org.hibernate.criterion.MatchMode

The MatchMode class has four properties that allow you to set the fuzzy matching facilities for an Example instance. The default is EXACT, while ANYWHERE is the most generous. END and START are bookend properties that only allow matches at the front or at the end of a given property.

```
static MatchMode   ANYWHERE
   Match the pattern anywhere in the string
static MatchMode   END
   Match the end of the string to the pattern
static MatchMode   EXACT
   Match the entire string to the pattern
static MatchMode   START
   Match the start of the string to the pattern
```

Really Fuzzy Matches: example.ignoreCase()

Obviously, the ANYWHERE property will generate the fuzziest matches out of the four MatchMode options, but to get *really* fuzzy matches, you might also want to ignore character casing. That is easily achieved by calling the ignoreCase() method on the example object before executing the query. Here's a sample of the ignoreCase() method in use, followed by the results of running the code snippet in question:

```
User user = new User();
user.setPassword("PASS");
Example example = Example.create(user);
example.enableLike(MatchMode.ANYWHERE);
example.ignoreCase();
example.excludeProperty("verified");
```

```
2 : mario : pass : mario@scja.ca
3 : sk8trgrl : password : avril@scja.com
4 : ridley : mypassword : getbent@scja.ca
9 : che : password : ernesto@pulpjava.com
10 : remy : password : rabbit@scja.com
```

FindAll Query using the Criteria API

As you can see, the Criteria API is amazing at generating an SQL statement on the fly that filters out results based upon an example instance. However, what happens if you don't pass an Example instance to your criteria query? Well, if the query doesn't have any information on which to filter the results, which is essentially what the Example object provides, then the criteria query will bring back *all* of the records based on the class the criteria instance is based upon.

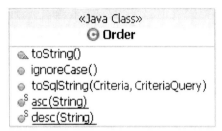

So, to find all of the User instances in your database, a criteria query would be as simple as this:

```
public class FindAll {
  public static void main(String args[]) {
    User user = new User();
    Session session = HibernateUtil.beginTransaction();
    Criteria criteria=
            session.createCriteria(User.class);
    /*Notice that there is no Example object!!!*/
    List results = criteria.list();
    HibernateUtil.commitTransaction();
    for (int i = 0; i<results.size(); i++) {
        System.out.println(results.get(i).toString());
    }
  }
}
```

Running the main method of the FindAll class brings back the following results, which is essentially, the entire database:

```
1  : mj        : abc123      : mj@mcnz.com
2  : mario     : pass        : mario@scja.ca
3  : sk8trgrl  : password    : avril@scja.com
4  : ridley    : mypassword  : getbent@scja.ca
5  : kerrr     : pwd         : sheehan@princessjava.com
6  : astra     : pwd         : rabbit@princessjava.com
7  : cameron   : 90210       : me@scwcd.com
8  : stephen   : low         : stanley@pulpjava.com
9  : che       : password    : ernesto@pulpjava.com
10 : remy      : password    : rabbit@scja.com
```

Pagination & Limiting the Results

Now, if your database has any size to it at all, you don't want to be executing too many findAll queries; actually, you don't want to be executing any. Not only is it a ridiculous load on your database, but end users typically have a hard time sifting through more than ten or twenty results at a time. So, it's no surprise to find out that the Criteria API makes it incredibly easy to limit the number of results that get delivered back from a query.

The Criteria object has two very helpful methods for facilitating the paging of results. The setFirstResult(int) method allows you to determine the index number at which the first result should be returned. The setMaxResults(int) method allows you to determine how many results will actually be returned from the query.

So, to get the first five results from the database, you would first pass the number zero to the setFirstResult(int) method, and pass 5 to the setMaxResults(int) method. This would return to you five results, with the first result being the first record in the database, and the last instance returned would map to the fifth record in the database. To get the next five records, you would issue a setFirstResults(5) invocation on the criteria object, and again, setMaxResults(int) to five, setMaxResults(5). It's all very simple ☺. Here's how it looks in code:

```
Criteria criteria =
        session.createCriteria(User.class);

criteria.setFirstResult(0);
criteria.setMaxResults(5);

List results = criteria.list();
```

The FindFirstFive Class

```
package com.examscam.criteria;
import java.util.List;
import org.hibernate.Criteria;import org.hibernate.Session;
import org.hibernate.criterion.Example;
import com.examscam.HibernateUtil; import com.examscam.model.User;

public class FindFirstFive {
 public static void main(String args[]) {
   User user = new User();
   Session session = HibernateUtil.beginTransaction();
   Criteria criteria = session.createCriteria(User.class);
   criteria.setFirstResult(0);
   criteria.setMaxResults(5);
   List results = criteria.list();
   HibernateUtil.commitTransaction();
   for (int i = 0; i<results.size(); i++) {
     System.out.println(results.get(i).toString());
   }
 }
}
```

Running this class against the sample database defined at the beginning of this chapter generates the following results, which as you can see, is the first five records in the database:

```
1 : mj : abc123 : mj@mcnz.com
2 : mario : pass : mario@scja.ca
3 : sk8trgrl : password : avril@scja.com
4 : ridley : mypassword : getbent@scja.ca
5 : kerrr : pwd : sheehan@princessjava.com
```

Ordering Results: The Order Class

A common requirement for any application is to have the results that are generated sorted by a particular column or attribute. Again, the Criteria API makes sorting your results extremely easy by providing you with an addOrder method in the Criteria class.

The addOrder method takes something called an Order object as an argument, which itself is a pretty straight forward component.

An Order object is created by using one of the two static methods in the Order class, namely the static asc(String) and desc(String) methods. Basically, you just chose whether you want your list to be sorted in ascending order, or descending order, and pass to the appropriate method the name of the field on which you want to sort. So, to sort all of my User's based on their loginName, in a ascending order, I would create an Order object like so:

```
Order order = Order.asc("loginName");
```

Then, you just pass the order object to the Criteria object's addOrder method, and your results will come back ordered in exactly the manner that you have specified. The full class and query results are provided on the following page.

```
User user = new User();
Session session = HibernateUtil.beginTransaction();
Criteria criteria = session.createCriteria(User.class);
Order order = Order.asc("loginName");
criteria.addOrder(order);
List results = criteria.list();
HibernateUtil.commitTransaction();
for (int i = 0; i<results.size(); i++) {
    System.out.println(results.get(i).toString());
}
```

The FindAllOrderedByLoginName Class

```
package com.examscam.criteria;
import java.util.List;
import org.hibernate.Criteria;
import org.hibernate.Session;
import org.hibernate.criterion.Order;
import com.examscam.HibernateUtil;
import com.examscam.model.User;
public class FindAllOrderedByLoginName {
  public static void main(String args[]) {

    User user = new User();
    Session session = HibernateUtil.beginTransaction();
    Criteria criteria = session.createCriteria(User.class);
    Order order = Order.asc("loginName");
    criteria.addOrder(order);
    List results = criteria.list();
    HibernateUtil.commitTransaction();
    for (int i = 0; i<results.size(); i++) {
        System.out.println(results.get(i).toString());
    }
  }
}
```

Executing the main method of this class generates the following output, ordered ascending by the loginName field, using the Canadian format of alphabetization.

6	:	**a**stra	:	pwd	:	rabbit@princessjava.com
7	:	**c**ameron	:	90210	:	me@scwcd.com
9	:	**c**he	:	password	:	ernesto@pulpjava.com
5	:	**k**errr	:	pwd	:	sheehan@princessjava.com
2	:	**ma**rio	:	pass	:	mario@scja.ca
1	:	**m**j	:	abc123	:	mj@mcnz.com
10	:	**r**emy	:	password	:	rabbit@scja.com
4	:	**r**idley	:	mypassword	:	getbent@scja.ca
3	:	**s**k8trgrl	:	password	:	avril@scja.com
8	:	**st**ephen	:	low	:	stanley@pulpjava.com

Using the Restrictions Class

Personally, I love the ability to do queries by using the Criteria API's Example class. Equally powerful is the Criteria API's Restrictions class.

As you know by now, simply passing the class type to the Criteria API, and executing a query, will return all of the database rows associated with that particular class. So, for example, the following code is basically a select all query from the table associated with the User class:

```
Criteria criteria = session.createCriteria(User.class);
List results = criteria.list();
```

Now, instead of grabbing all of the User objects, you can use an instance of the Restrictions class to limit the results. So, let's just say you wanted to get all of the users who have an id that is greater than 5. To do that, you just create a Restrictions class, set a gt (greater than) restriction on the id field to the value of 5, and then add the restriction to the Criteria object. Once you execute your query, you'll only get records with an id that is greater than 5. ☺

So, the following code generates the *restricted* results below:

```
Session session = HibernateUtil.beginTransaction();
Criteria criteria =
      session.createCriteria(User.class);
criteria.add(Restrictions.gt("id", 5));
List results = criteria.list();
HibernateUtil.commitTransaction();
for (int i = 0; i<results.size(); i++) {
  System.out.println(results.get(i).toString());
}
```

Notice the results are restricted to users with ids > 5.

```
6 : astra : pwd : rabbit@princessjava.com
7 : cameron : 90210 : me@scwcd.com
8 : stephen : low : stanley@pulpjava.com
9 : che : password : ernesto@pulpjava.com
10 : remy : password : rabbit@scja.com
```

213

The Restrictions Class Diagram

```
                «Java Class»
              ⊕ Restrictions
─────────────────────────────────────
▲ᵗ Restrictions()
⚙ˢ idEq(Object)
⚙ˢ eq(String, Object)
⚙ˢ ne(String, Object)
⚙ˢ like(String, Object)
⚙ˢ like(String, String, MatchMode)
⚙ˢ ilike(String, String, MatchMode)
⚙ˢ ilike(String, Object)
⚙ˢ gt(String, Object)
⚙ˢ lt(String, Object)
⚙ˢ le(String, Object)
⚙ˢ ge(String, Object)
⚙ˢ between(String, Object, Object)
⚙ˢ in(String, Object[])
⚙ˢ in(String, Collection)
⚙ˢ isNull(String)
⚙ˢ eqProperty(String, String)
⚙ˢ neProperty(String, String)
⚙ˢ ltProperty(String, String)
⚙ˢ leProperty(String, String)
⚙ˢ gtProperty(String, String)
⚙ˢ geProperty(String, String)
⚙ˢ isNotNull(String)
⚙ˢ and(Criterion, Criterion)
⚙ˢ or(Criterion, Criterion)
⚙ˢ not(Criterion)
⚙ˢ sqlRestriction(String, Object[], Type[])
⚙ˢ sqlRestriction(String, Object, Type)
⚙ˢ sqlRestriction(String)
⚙ˢ conjunction()
⚙ˢ disjunction()
⚙ˢ allEq(Map)
⚙ˢ isEmpty(String)
⚙ˢ isNotEmpty(String)
⚙ˢ sizeEq(String, int)
⚙ˢ sizeNe(String, int)
⚙ˢ sizeGt(String, int)
⚙ˢ sizeLt(String, int)
```

```
⚙ˢ isNull(String)
⚙ˢ eqProperty(String, String)
⚙ˢ neProperty(String, String)
⚙ˢ ltProperty(String, String)
⚙ˢ leProperty(String, String)
⚙ˢ gtProperty(String, String)
⚙ˢ geProperty(String, String)
⚙ˢ isNotNull(String)
⚙ˢ and(Criterion, Criterion)
⚙ˢ or(Criterion, Criterion)
⚙ˢ not(Criterion)
⚙ˢ sqlRestriction(String, Object[], Type[])
⚙ˢ sqlRestriction(String, Object, Type)
⚙ˢ sqlRestriction(String)
⚙ˢ conjunction()
⚙ˢ disjunction()
⚙ˢ allEq(Map)
⚙ˢ isEmpty(String)
⚙ˢ isNotEmpty(String)
⚙ˢ sizeEq(String, int)
⚙ˢ sizeNe(String, int)
⚙ˢ sizeGt(String, int)
⚙ˢ sizeLt(String, int)
⚙ˢ sizeGe(String, int)
⚙ˢ sizeLe(String, int)
⚙ˢ naturalId()
```

The Criterion Interface

When we invoke some of the more helpful static methods of the Restrictions class, such as gt, le, iLike or isNull, the objects returned from these methods all implement the Criterion interface. It is these types of objects, objects that implement the Criterion interface, that can be passed to the Criteria class' add method. And while all of our examples have really only added a single Restriction, or a single Example, the fact is, you can create very complex queries by passing multitudes of Criterion objects to the Criteria's add method. Take a look at the following query, and notice how many different Criterion objects are being used to create the custom query:

```
public static void main(String args[]) {
  Session session = HibernateUtil.beginTransaction();
  Criterion c1 = Restrictions.gt("id", (long)2);
  Criterion c2 = Restrictions.lt("id", (long)8);
  Criterion c3 = Restrictions.isNotNull("emailAddress");
  User user = new User();
  user.setEmailAddress(".com");
  Example c4 = Example.create(user);
  c4.enableLike(MatchMode.END);
  c4.ignoreCase();
  Criteria criteria = session.createCriteria(User.class);
  criteria.add(c1);
  criteria.add(c2);
  criteria.add(c3);
  criteria.add(c4);
  List results = criteria.list();
  HibernateUtil.commitTransaction();
  for (int i = 0; i<results.size(); i++) {
    System.out.println(results.get(i).toString());
  }
}
```

Running the query in this main method returns the following:

```
3 : sk8trgrl : password : avril@scja.com
5 : kerrr : pwd : sheehan@princessjava.com
6 : astra : pwd : rabbit@princessjava.com
7 : cameron : 90210 : me@scwcd.com
```

The Criterion Interface and Some Implementing Classes

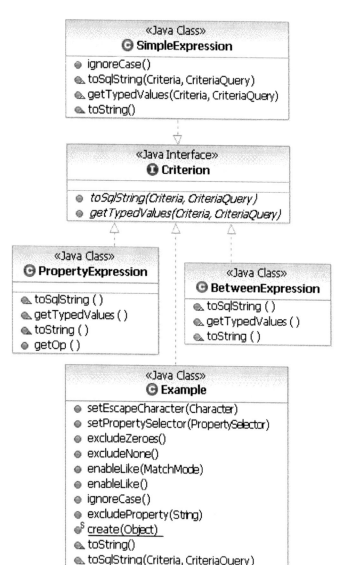

findByCriterion(Criterion... criterion)

Because the Criterion object is so adaptable and comprehensive, it is very common to see a findByCriterion method defined in DAO (Data Access Object) classes and in custom Helper class. A very elegant implementation of this method that leverages the *varargs* and *for:each loop* features of Java 5 is as follows:

```
package com.examscam.criteria;
import java.util.List;import org.hibernate.*;
import org.hibernate.criterion.*; import com.examscam.model.User;
import com.examscam.HibernateUtil;
public class UserHelper {
public static List findByCriterion(Criterion... criterion){
   Session session = HibernateUtil.getSession();
   Criteria criteria=session.createCriteria(User.class);
   for (Criterion crit : criterion) {
      criteria.add(crit);
   }
   return criteria.list();
 }
}
```

So, with such a method, an application could obtain a very specific List of Users by passing many criterion instances to the UserHelper's findByCriterion method:

```
List specificUsers = UserHelper.findByCriterion(
        Restrictions.gt("id", (long)2),
        Restrictions.lt("id", (long)8),
            Restrictions.isNotNull("emailAddress") );
```

A findAll using findByCriterion()

Furthermore, a user could find all of the User instances in the database by invoking the findByCriterion method, but without passing in any criterion objects at all:

```
List allUsers = UserHelper.findByCriterion();
```

Indeed, leveraging the Criteria API in your applications will greatly improve your ability to create and manage all of your query centric applications. Use it. You'll love it!!! ☺

Chapter 10
Data Access Objects

There's no debating the fact that Hibernate greatly simplifies the job of managing the persistent state of the classes in your domain model. With access to a Hibernate Session, it's pretty easy to perform a quick query, save a POJO, or update a record in the database.

However, as elegant and powerful as Hibernate is, it's sometimes polite to hand over some very simple Data Access Objects(DAOs) to your application integrators so they can more easily, and consistently, interact with the underlying datasource. Furthermore, Data Access Objects can hide the underlying implementation of the persistence framework from the end user, making it easier to implement future changes to the database layer. In fact, the concepts of creating Data Access Objects for you application integrators is so commonly accepted that it considered one of the most fundamental of all of the design patterns.

In this chapter, we'll take a first pass at creating Data Access Objects that will help developers interact with the underlying datastore, subsequently shielding developers and application integrators from the implementation logic in the Hibernate layer.

The UserDAO Interface

At the heart of the DAO design pattern is the idea that client applications will be provided simple Java interfaces for accessing data, with the actual implementation of those interfaces being performed by classes that can be easily switched in and out of the application if the need ever arises. As such, it is necessary to define all of the methods that will be used for mitigating access to the back end database in a DAO interface.

Our UserDAO interface will define six methods: create, update, delete, findAll, findByPrimaryKey and finally, the findByExample method which will leverage our newfound knowledge of the Criteria API.

```
package com.examscam.dao;
import java.util.List;
import com.examscam.model.User;


public interface UserDAO {

  public User create(User user);
  public boolean update(User user) ;
  public boolean delete(User user) ;
  public User findByPrimaryKey(Long primaryKey);
  public List findByExample(User user, boolean fuzzy);
  public List findAll();


}
```

Generic Data Access Object (DAO) Methods

Factoring out common behavior into reusable methods is always a fundamental goal. Our domain model currently only has one class defined in it, the User class, but we could easily imagine more and more classes being added over time. As such, when we create our DAOs, we should bear in mind that additional classes will eventually make it into our framework. With this thought in mind, any Hibernate based implementation of the DAO pattern should factor out CRUD related commonality into a reusable, abstract, inheritable, parent class.

```
           «Java Class»
         ⊙ ExamScamDAO

   ◇ getSession()
   ◇ save(Object)
   ◇ delete(Object)
   ◇ findByPrimaryKey(Class, Long)
```

For our purposes, we will code and implement four important methods in an abstract class called the ExamScamDAO. Those methods will be: getSession, save, delete and the findByPrimaryKey method.

Methods of the ExamScamDAO Class

The getSession() method of the ExamScamDAO is simply a helper method that encapsulates the call to the getSession() method of the HibernateUtil class. There's nothing very interesting to see here. ☹

```
protected Session getSession() {
   return HibernateUtil.getSession();
}
```

The delete and save methods are also relatively simple, simply taking any JPA annotated POJO and either saving or deleting the state of that POJO to the database. Since Hibernate does introspection on the bean being passed to the Hibernate Session's delete, save or update methods, we don't need to explicitly specify the object type in the argument list of the ExamScamDAO's save or delete methods. All we require is that the subclassing DAOs pass in a JPA annotated JavaBean.

```
protected void save(Object pojo) {
   Session hibernateSession = this.getSession();
   hibernateSession.saveOrUpdate(pojo);
}
protected void delete(Object pojo) {
   Session hibernateSession = this.getSession();
   hibernateSession.delete(pojo);
}
```

Finally, given a valid primary key that is passed in as an argument, the findByPrimaryKey method simply grabs an instance of a JPA annotated POJO from the underlying database. The *class of the type* must be passed into the method as well, as Hibernate cannot ascertain the object type of interest based solely on a numeric primary key. The findByPrimaryKey method must be passed both a primary key, and a definition of the class type of the object being queried.

```
protected Object
        findByPrimaryKey(Class c, Long primaryKey){
   Object pojo;
   Session hibernateSession = this.getSession();
   pojo = hibernateSession.get(c, primaryKey);
   return pojo;
}
```

The Abstract ExamScamDAO Class

```java
package com.examscam.dao;

import java.util.List;
import org.hibernate.Criteria;
import org.hibernate.HibernateException;
import org.hibernate.Session;
import com.examscam.ExamScamException;
import com.examscam.HibernateUtil;

public abstract class ExamScamDAO {

  protected Session getSession() {
    return HibernateUtil.getSession();
  }

  protected void save(Object pojo) {
    Session hibernateSession = this.getSession();
    hibernateSession.saveOrUpdate(pojo);
  }

  protected void delete(Object pojo) {
    Session hibernateSession = this.getSession();
    hibernateSession.delete(pojo);
  }

  protected Object
        findByPrimaryKey(Class c, Long primaryKey){
    Object pojo;
    Session hibernateSession = this.getSession();
    pojo = hibernateSession.get(c, primaryKey);
    return pojo;
  }
}
```

The HibernateUserDAO

The key component in our DAO implementation will be the HibernateUserDAO class, which will provide the concrete implementation of the UserDAO interface. Taking advantage of the methods coded in the parent class, the HibernateUserDAO will extend the ExamScamDAO class, and of course, implement the UserDAO interface.

```
package com.examscam.dao;
import java.util.List;
import org.hibernate.Criteria;
import org.hibernate.Query;
import org.hibernate.Session;
import org.hibernate.criterion.Example;
import org.hibernate.criterion.MatchMode;
import com.examscam.model.User;

public class HibernateUserDAO
        extends ExamScamDAO implements UserDAO {
      /* class implementation will go here */
}
```

One of the key benefits to creating a DAO is that it makes interactions with your database, or for that matter, your Hibernate framework, a bit easier for application integrators. As such, it's not a bad idea to provide your DAO users with methods that make sense to them. For example, we have seen how Hibernate provides a saveOrUpdate method that will update a record if it already exists, or create a new database record if the object being passed into it does not have a primary key. That's fine for us, because we're intelligent Hibernate developers. But lower life forms such as Servlet and JSP developers might have a hard time with that concept. To help make life easier for our web developers, we can provide very simple methods, such as create and update, with which our DAO users are likely more familiar and more comfortable. Behind the scenes, we will just call saveOrUpdate in both methods. ☺

More Benefits of Using DAOs

Another benefit of using a DAO is the fact that it is a great place to provide extra little initializations or business logic that your domain model components require. For example, in the create method, we'll be passed in a User object with the basic properties that an end user will type in, such as loginName, emailAddress and password. But, it's our job to set the verified flag to false, and set the registrationDate and lastAccessTime properties to the current time and date. We can hide these details in the create method of the UserDAO class, simplifying the creation process, while at the same time, giving us more control over how new User records are inserted into the database. Data Access Objects really are a great way to mitigate database access for your end users. ☺

Class Diagram for the HibernateUserDAO

To implement the UserDAO interface, we will create a concrete class named HibernateUserDAO that will extend the abstract ExamScamDAO.

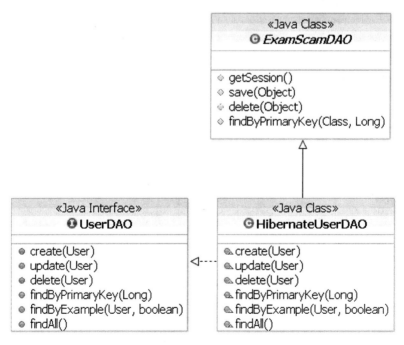

Coding the HibernateUserDAO: create

As you can see, the create method of the UserDAO has some funky programming logic in it, helping out with the initialization of the User instance.

```
public User create(User user) {
  if (user.getId() != null && user.getId() != 0) {
    user = null;
  }
  else {
    user.setLastAccessTime(new java.util.Date());
    user.setRegistrationDate
              (new java.util.GregorianCalendar());
    user.setVerified(false);
    super.save(user);
  }
  return user;
}
```

At a very high level, we can see that the create method takes an instance of a user and tries to persist that user to the database. The persisted user, with all of the various fields appropriately initialized, is then returned from the method upon successful completion.

Looking more closely at the code, we will notice a little bit of validation logic at the beginning. If someone passes to the create method a user with an id that is not null and/or not zero, then the create method shouldn't work; after all, if a User instance has a positive, non-zero id, that tells us that the user must already have a representation in the database. If we are indeed passed a user that has an id, we simply nullify the user, bypass the creation logic, and return the nulled out user instance to the calling program.

```
  if (user.getId() != null && user.getId() != 0)
```

Of course, if the user instance does pass the id inspection, we initialize the lastAccessTime, registrationDate and verified properties, and then pass the appropriately initialized user instance to the parent class' save method.

The HibernateUserDAO update Method

In contrast to the create method, the update method of our DAO checks to ensure that the user instance being passed into the method does *indeed* have an id associated with it. If a user instance does not have an id, be it null or zero, then Hibernate doesn't know which row to update, and will instead try to create a new record, which sorta goes against the whole idea of an *update* operation. So, to be safe, the update method checks for an id, and if it can't find one, it sets the success flag to false, bypassing the update operation.

```
if (user.getId() == null || user.getId() == 0)
```

Furthermore, the update method catches any exceptions that are thrown, and if the operation fails due to an exception being thrown, the success flag is set to false, and the calling program is informed that the update operation has failed.

```
public boolean update(User user) {
  boolean successFlag = true;
  try {
    if (user.getId() == null || user.getId() == 0) {
      successFlag = false;
    }else {
      super.save(user);
    }
  }
  catch (Throwable th) {
    successFlag = false;
  }
  return successFlag;
}
```

The HibernateUserDAO delete Method

Even the delete method of the HibernateUserDAO has some programmatic hanky-panky going on. The delete method is passed a User instance to be deleted; an operation that should be relatively straight forward so long as the instance passed in has a valid id field. However, the password field of the User is annotated as being non-null, so if the password field isn't initialized, even though we're deleting the darned record, Hibernate will choke worse than the NHL's Ottawa Senators. To avoid any problems, we just initialize the password field to a blank String, and then pass the instance of the user to the parent's delete method.

```
public boolean delete(User user) {
  boolean successFlag = true;
  try {
    user.setPassword("");
    super.delete(user);
  } catch (Throwable th) {successFlag = false;}
  return successFlag;
}
```

HibernateUserDAO findByPrimaryKey Method

As far as finder methods go, it doesn't get much simpler than the findByPrimaryKey method. The method is simply passed a primary key of type Long, which is then passed to the parent implementation of findByPrimaryKey. The only curve ball is the fact that we must also pass in *User.class*, just to let the parent know the class type for which we are searching.

```
public User findByPrimaryKey(Long primaryKey) {
  User user = (User)
      super.findByPrimaryKey(User.class, primaryKey);
  return user;
}
```

You should also notice that a quick cast, (User), is required on the return of the findByPrimaryKey method. This is because the parent simply returns a lazy little Object. We need to remind that lazy little Object that it is intended to be a hard working User.

The HibernateUserDAO findAll Method

The findAll method is relatively straight forward, using the "from User" HQL statement that we've seen several times before to generate a java.util.List of User instances:

```
public List findAll() {
  String queryString = "from User";
  java.util.List allUsers;
  Query queryResult =
        this.getSession().createQuery(queryString);
  allUsers = queryResult.list();
  return allUsers;
}
```

The HibernateUserDAO: findByExample

The findByExample method represents an interesting use of the Criteria API. Essentially, an instance of the User class is passed into the method, and a query is performed based on the initialized fields of that object. However, there is also a boolean, fuzzy parameter passed into the method as well, and if the value is true, very weak matches will be returned, as the MatchMode is set to ANYWHERE and the casing of fields is ignored.

```
public List findByExample(User user, boolean fuzzy) {
  List users = null;
  Session session = this.getSession();
  Criteria criteria =
            session.createCriteria(User.class);
  Example example = Example.create(user);
  if (fuzzy) {
    example.enableLike(MatchMode.ANYWHERE);
    example.ignoreCase();
    example.excludeZeroes();
  }
  criteria.add(example);
  users = criteria.list();
  return users;
}
```

```
package com.examscam.dao;

import java.util.List; import org.hibernate.*;
import org.hibernate.criterion.*;
import com.examscam.model.User;

public class HibernateUserDAO
        extends ExamScamDAO implements UserDAO {

 public User create(User user) {
  if (user.getId() != null && user.getId() != 0){
   user = null;
  }
  else {
   user.setLastAccessTime(new java.util.Date());
   user.setRegistrationDate(
            new java.util.GregorianCalendar());
   user.setVerified(false);
   super.save(user);
  }
  return user;
 }

 public boolean update(User user) {
  boolean successFlag = true;
  try {
   if (user.getId() == null || user.getId() == 0) {
    successFlag = false;
   } else {
    super.save(user);
   }
  }
  catch (Throwable th) {
   successFlag = false;
  }
  return successFlag;
 }
}
```

```
public boolean delete(User user) {
  boolean successFlag = true;
  try {
   user.setPassword("");
   super.delete(user);
  }catch (Throwable th) {
   successFlag = false;
  }
  return successFlag;
 }
public User findByPrimaryKey(Long primaryKey) {
  User user=(User)super.findByPrimaryKey(
                      User.class, primaryKey);
  return user;
 }
 public List findByExample(
                    User user, boolean fuzzy) {
  List users = null;
  Session session = this.getSession();
  Criteria criteria =
      session.createCriteria(User.class);
  Example example = Example.create(user);
  if (fuzzy) {
   example.enableLike(MatchMode.ANYWHERE);
   example.ignoreCase();
   example.excludeZeroes();
  }
  criteria.add(example);
  users =  criteria.list();
  return users;
 }
 public List findAll() {
   String queryString = "from User";
   Query queryResult =
    this.getSession().createQuery(queryString);
   return queryResult.list();
 }
}
```

The HibernateUserDAO in Action

Having fully implemented the UserDAO, let's create a simple little stand-alone Java application that uses the UserDAO to persist new User objects to the database.

I'm just going to create a basic class called AddUsers that has a main method, and in that main method, I'll initialize the loginName, emailAddress, and password fields of a User instance based on console input. The rather mundane, non-hibernate part of the class will look like this:

```
package com.examscam.app;
import org.hibernate.HibernateException;
import com.examscam.HibernateUtil;
import com.examscam.dao.*;
import java.util.Scanner;
import com.examscam.model.User;
public class AddUsers {
 public static void main (String args[]) {
  int keepAdding = 1;
  while (keepAdding == 1) {
   Scanner keyboard = new Scanner(System.in);
   User user = new User();
   System.out.println("What is the user's login name?");
   user.setLoginName(keyboard.next());
   System.out.println("What is the email address?");
   user.setEmailAddress(keyboard.next());
   System.out.println("What is the password?");
   user.setPassword(keyboard.next());
    ✂✂✂
  }
  ✂✂✂
 }
}
```

As you can see, the main method simply uses the Scanner class and the System.in stream to take input from the user, initializing the loginName, emailAddress, and password properties of a newly instantiated User instance.

Calling the DAO within a Transaction

Once the basic properties of the user instance are initialized, it's time to begin a transaction, create an instance of our DAO, and pass the User instance to the UserDAO's create method. That is the only database interaction needed for this program, so once the create method has finished executing, we ask the HibernateUtil class to commit the transaction.

```
✂✂✂
user.setPassword(keyboard.next());
try {
  HibernateUtil.beginTransaction();
  UserDAO userDAO = new HibernateUserDAO();
  userDAO.create(user);
  HibernateUtil.commitTransaction();
  System.out.println("User successfully added.");
} catch (HibernateException e) {
  e.printStackTrace();
  System.out.println("Database Insert Failed");
  System.out.println(e.getClass() + e.getMessage());
}
System.out.println("Would you like to continue? (1=y / 0=n)");
keepAdding = keyboard.nextInt();
✂✂✂
```

If the transaction commits successfully, we let the user know that the record was successfully added to the database. On the other hand, if a HibernateException is thrown, we must catch it, and tell the user that the insert has failed.

You'll also notice that the whole main method is insulated within a nice little while loop that keeps adding records to the database until the data entry person decides not to continue by entering a zero.

```
int keepAdding = 1;
while (keepAdding == 1) {  ✂✂✂    ✂✂✂
  System.out.println("Continue? ✂(1=y / 0=n)");
  keepAdding = keyboard.nextInt();
}
```

The Whole AddUser Class

```java
package com.examscam.app;
import java.util.Scanner; import org.hibernate.HibernateException;
import com.examscam.HibernateUtil;
import com.examscam.dao.*; import com.examscam.model.User;
public class AddUsers {
 public static void main (String args[]) {

  int keepAdding = 1;
  while (keepAdding == 1) {

   Scanner keyboard = new Scanner(System.in);
   User user = new User();
   System.out.println("New user's login name?");
   user.setLoginName(keyboard.next());
   System.out.println("New user's email address?");
   user.setEmailAddress(keyboard.next());
   System.out.println("New user's password?");
   user.setPassword(keyboard.next());

   try {

    HibernateUtil.beginTransaction();
    UserDAO userDAO = new HibernateUserDAO();
    userDAO.create(user);
    HibernateUtil.commitTransaction();
    System.out.println("User successfully added.");

   } catch (HibernateException e) {
    e.printStackTrace();
    System.out.println("Database Insert Failed");
    System.out.println(e.getClass() + e.getMessage());
   }
   System.out.println("Continue? (1=y / 0=n)");
   keepAdding = keyboard.nextInt();
  }
 }
}
```

Debriefing the AddUsers Class

Although the AddUsers class is intended as a very simple test case, there are a few important points to take out of how it uses the UserDAO.

First off, you should notice that while we are using a DAO, the developer writing the application is still tasked with the job of beginning and ending the database transaction. That's not an oversight in this application, but instead, a very typical programming construct.

In the AddUsers class, we only really hit the database once when inside the loop, which happens when we add a new user. But if there were multiple things going on, such as an update to one table, a delete from another, and a query to a third, all of which must happen as a single unit of work, then the developer using the DAO, or a multitude of DAOs for that matter, must be able to control when a transaction begins, when a transaction ends, and for that matter, which database centric components take part in that transaction. Transaction demarcation is not something you want to perform inside of a DAO, lest you fall into the 'one transaction per database interaction' anti-pattern. The developers using your DAO should be given the ability to start and end their own database transactions.

```
HibernateUtil.beginTransaction();
UserDAO userDAO = new HibernateUserDAO();
userDAO.create(user);
HibernateUtil.commitTransaction();
```

Now, in this case, the developer uses the HibernateUtil class to begin the transaction. It might have been kind to hide the call to the HibernateUtil's beginTransaction method within a wrapper method of the UserDAO, or the ExamScamDAO for that matter. I have no objections to that at all, so long as the DAO always knows what type of transaction mechanism is being used. However, depending upon where the DAO is deployed, the client may be using a different transaction mechanism than the one wrapped within the DAO. For example, in a J2EE environment, developers may want to do a JTA lookup to obtain a transactional context through the UserTransaction object, as opposed to going through your Hibernate code. In that case, using a DAO method that wraps the Hibernate Session's beginTransaction() method might not be the correct implementation strategy.

Much of this gets down to various important application design decisions, namely, how to make the transactional context available to the people using your data access objects. But regardless of what transactional context your applications use, it is important to emphasize that the developer or integrator using the DAOs will be tasked with *beginning* and *ending* their transactions in the same manner in which the HibernateUtil class is used in the main method of the AddUsers class.

Working Around the HibernateException

The other ugly aspect of the AddUsers class is the fact that the client application is forced to handle the HibernateException. The HibernateException is a runtime exception, and as such, the Java compiler does not force a developer to catch this exception in their code. If this exception is thrown at runtime, well, I guess it sucks to be you, but if you never catch it in your code, it's going to cause a runtime error. Here's how we handled the HibernateException in the AddUsers class:

```
try {
    HibernateUtil.beginTransaction();
    UserDAO userDAO = new HibernateUserDAO();
    userDAO.create(user);
    HibernateUtil.commitTransaction();
    System.out.println("User successfully added.");

} catch (HibernateException e) {
    /* Handle? Re-throw? Log? It's your call! */
    e.printStackTrace();
    System.out.println("Database Insert Failed");
    System.out.println(e.getClass() +
                         e.getMessage());
}
```

Now, dealing with the HibernateException really isn't that big of a problem. If there's a database problem, I mean a real database problem, like the darn thing isn't plugged in, well, there's not much a stand-alone, JSF, or any other web based application can do about it other than provide a polite message to the end user. So, the applications using our DAOs should be wise enough to trap any exceptions that come to them, and respond appropriately.

How to handle the HibernateException is really another one of those application design questions on which development teams must come to a general agreement. I've seen some environments allow the HibernateException to bubble up to other application layers, and I've seen other development teams catch the HibernateException and rethrow it as a custom, checked application exception. Both strategies have merit, and more importantly, both approaches can work.

The Merits of Using DAOs

Overall, providing application developers or integrators Data Access Objects, as opposed to asking them to code directly against the Hibernate API, can greatly simplify application development, while at the same time, help to decouple and insulate changes that may occur in the database from other layers in an application. So long as DAO users know how to begin transactions, and handle the exceptions that might be thrown when accessing a DAO, interacting with the database layer will become easier, and long term maintainability of your application is greatly improved.

Chapter 11
Hibernate and JSPs

The whole idea behind creating Data Access Objects is to deliver them to other application developers, such as JSF or Struts developers, and allow those developers to interact with the back end database without any great deal of knowledge of how the back end is implemented. Seeing that we just spent some time implementing the DAO design pattern around our User class, it only makes sense that we demonstrate how to really take advantage of that DAO and integrate it into a web based application.

The focus of this chapter will be to create a relatively simple and straight-forward web based application that leverages JSPs, JSTL custom tags, and a few intelligently placed scriptlets that will mitigate database access through the use of the UserDAO class.

Please....Cut Me Some Slack

Now I just want to point out the fact that the goal here is not to develop the worlds greatest MVC application. At the very least, a production environment should be using Servlets and JSPs, if not Struts, JSF or Seam. But this book isn't about web design – it's about *Hibernate*. This example will show you a very interesting, exciting, and simple web site that leverages the Hibernate code we have written so far. However, it does not employ the most elegant Model-View-Controller ethics. Furthermore, this chapter won't try and explain JSP development and deployment. I'm sorry, but that's a 500 page book in itself. This chapter is here to provide a simple idea of how the Hibernate code we have written might fit into a very simple, web-based application. If you have no idea of what HTML is, or how a Java Server Page works, or how to deploy a JSP to a Servlet engine like Tomcat or WebSphere, you might be better off skipping this chapter and going right into the sections on mappings and advanced DAOs. ☺

The user.jsp User Interface

The goal of this chapter is to create a very simple, user friendly, web based application that allows a user to add, update, delete, and do custom searches against the user table in the database. The finished product will look something like this:

```
┌─────────────────────────────────────────────────────────┐
│  ┌──────────┐  Id                                         │
│  └──────────┘                                             │
│  ┌─────────────────────────┐  Name                        │
│  └─────────────────────────┘                              │
│  ┌─────────────────────────┐  Password                    │
│  └─────────────────────────┘                              │
│  ┌─────────────────────────┐  Email                       │
│  └─────────────────────────┘                              │
│  [ Strict Search ] [ Fuzzy Search ] [ Update ] [ Create ] [ Clear ] │
│  | edit | delete | 1 | mj | mj@mcnz.com |                  │
│  | edit | delete | 2 | mario | mario@scja.ca |             │
│  | edit | delete | 3 | sk8trgrl | avril@scja.com |         │
│  | edit | delete | 4 | ridley | getbent@scja.ca |          │
│  | edit | delete | 5 | kerri | sheehan@princessjava.com |  │
│  | edit | delete | 6 | astra | rabbit@princessjava.com |   │
│  | edit | delete | 7 | cameron | me@scwcd.com |            │
│  | edit | delete | 8 | stephen | stanley@pulpjava.com |    │
│  | edit | delete | 9 | che | ernesto@pulpjava.com |        │
│  | edit | delete | 10 | remy | rabbit@scja.com |           │
└─────────────────────────────────────────────────────────┘
```

To help describe how this application will work, I'm going to quickly go over all of the command buttons and action links you see on this user interface, and briefly describe their purpose.

The Clear Command Button

At various times, incorrect data will be typed into the textfields that needs to be cleared by the end user. If someone clicks on the Clear command button, the four textfields are cleared.

> **NOTE:** on some screenshots on the next few pages, the Clear button may be cropped off, just to get the content formatted on the page a little bit better. My apologies if it catches you off guard. ☺

Adding Records: The Create Command Button

If an end user types in a name, password and email address, clicking on Create will add a new record to the database. The id field is read-only in this application, so a user cannot type in an id. Instead, Hibernate will generate a unique id for new records.

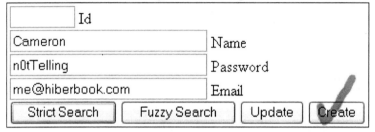

Updating & Deleting Records

Below the command buttons such as Update and Create, a summary of each record in the database will be listed. To the left of each record listed are two separate command links, one named **edit** and the other named **delete**. Clicking the **delete** link will delete the record in question. However, clicking on the **edit** link will have the textfields populated with information pertinent to that record. From there, if the Update button is pressed, the corresponding record in the database is updated.

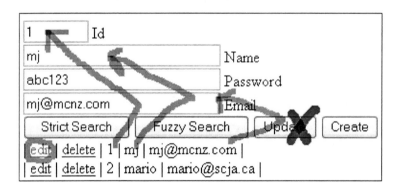

Notice that when a record is selected for editing, the id textfield gets populated. This is a read-only field that cannot be edited, but it can be used for display purposes.

Search Functionality

The search functionality is probably the neatest part of the application. The application client can type text into any of the editable text fields and perform a search. If they click the Strict Search command button, they will be returned a list of records that match exactly on what was typed into the textfields:

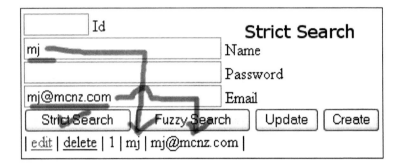

The Fuzzy Search

In contrast to the Strict Search, if a user types values into the textfields and clicks on the Fuzzy Search command button, then records that match the entered text, *anywhere* in their corresponding properties, are returned and listed:

	Id	
e		Name
p		Password
a.com		Email

[Strict Search] [Fuzzy Search] [Update] [Create]

edit	delete	5	kerri	sheehan@princessjava.com
edit	delete	9	che	ernesto@pulpjava.com
edit	delete	10	remy	rabbit@scja.com

The Basic HTML for the JSP Page

To develop this web based application, the first thing you need to do is create a very simple JSP page, named *user.jsp*, with an open and closed form tag that links its action back to itself, the *user.jsp* page

```
<html>
<body>
<form action="user.jsp">  </form>
</body>
</html>
```

Adding the Textfields

The JSP page will have four input fields for displaying the user's id, loginName, emailAddress and password properties, with the id being read-only. So, the HTML grows:

```
<html><body><form action="user.jsp">
<!-- Here are our four textfields  -->
<input type="text" size="7" readonly name="id"
value="${user.id}"> Id
<BR/>
<input type="text" size="30" name="loginName"
value="${user.loginName}"> Name
<BR/>
<input type="text" size="30" name="password"
value="${user.password}"> Password
<BR/>
<input type="text" size="30" name="emailAddress"
value="${user.emailAddress}"> Email
<BR/></form></body></html>
```

Notice how the value of each field uses an expression, such as **${user.id}**. These expressions will automatically populate the text fields with data if a user instance has been selected for display. They'll make life significantly easier for us, that's for sure!

Note that *the names of the textfields match the properties of the User class.* This is not by accident. If the names of the textfields do not **match the case sensitive names** of the properties in the User class, the JSP will not work properly.

Adding the Command Buttons

When a client using our application clicks on a button or a link, it will issue what we will call a 'command,' such as Update, Edit, Delete or Search, and that *command* needs to be executed. Our application will have seven commands, five of which will be triggered by buttons, the other two of which will be triggered by links.

The five *buttons* our application uses will include: Strict Search, Fuzzy Search, Update, Create and Clear. Edit and delete commands will be triggered by *links* on the page.

Here is the HTML code for the five buttons, which will go under the textfields, and inside the <form ...> </form> tags.

```
<!-- Here are all of our buttons!!! -->
<input type="submit" name="command" value="Strict Search">
<input type="submit" name="command" value="Fuzzy Search">
<input type="submit" name="command" value="Update">
<input type="submit" name="command" value="Create">
<input type="submit" name="command" value="Clear">
```

Notice that each button, while displaying a different *value* on the JSP page, has the same name: *command*. This is important, as the logic in the JSP page will inspect the name of the command button and subsequently execute logic based on which button was clicked. The logic for responding to the client clicking on a particular button looks something like this:

```
String command=request.getParameter("command");
if (command != null) {
        if (command.equals("Create")) {
            userDAO.create(user);
        }
        }<}<}<     }<}<}<
}
```

244

JSTL forEach and the Taglib Directive

Along with all of the handsome buttons, the JSP will also display a listing of users. If a search has been performed, the JSP will display the results of that search. If no search has been performed, *performance concerns aside*, the JSP will list all of the users in the database.

To achieve this listing of users, the JSP will always ensure that a java.util.List, containing instances of the User class, is placed in the request scope with the identifying name of *users*. As such, a simple JSTL custom tag can easily loop through that list, and display basic information about each user, one record at a time. Here's how the JSTL loop would look:

```
<c:forEach items="${users}" var="user">
|  <c:out value="${user.id}" />
|  <c:out value="${user.loginName}" />
|  <c:out value="${user.emailAddress}" />
|  <br/>
</c:forEach>
```

The Required JSTL Taglib Directive

It should also be noted that in order to use the JSTL tag libraries, you need a taglib directive at the top of the JSP. You can place it right before the <HTML> tag.

```
<%@ taglib prefix="c"
      uri="http://java.sun.com/jsp/jstl/core" %>
<html>
<head>
><><>< ><><><
```

Creating the Edit URL

The JSTL forEach tag is used to loop through every entity in the list of users that is placed in the request scope. However, what would be really nice is to have a little link that says *edit* right before the first data field is displayed, so that if the end user clicks on it, the details of the user in question will be displayed in the JSP's textfields. To do this, we need to create a link that displays the word **edit**, is associated with a command named edit, and of course, has the id of the user being edited so that our JSP knows which user will have its data displayed.

This becomes a bit mucky. Inside the forEach loop, you need to create a new URL named editurl that links back to the user.jsp page. Here's how it looks initially:

```
<c:url  var="editurl" value="user.jsp" >
</c:url>
```

Of course, we want the link to trigger a *command* named *edit*, and we also want the link to be associated with the id of the user being displayed on the given row. This requires the following two param tags to be added within the url tag:

```
<c:url  var="editurl" value="user.jsp" >
  <c:param name="command" value="edit" />
  <c:param name="id" value="${user.id}"/>
</c:url>
```

Of course, this only builds a URL that can be referenced by the variable name editurl. To actually have this information display as a clickable link, we need to use the anchor tag and reference the editurl.

```
| <a href="${editurl}">edit</a>
```

Creating the Delete URL

In almost the same way that we created the edit URL inside of the JSTL forEach loop, we need to create a link that will trigger the delete command.

You will notice that the deleteurl is almost identical to the editurl, except the var has changed from editurl to deleteurl, and the value of the first param tag is delete, associating the link with the delete command.

```
<c:url  var="deleteurl" value="user.jsp" >
  <c:param name="command" value="delete" />
  <c:param name="id" value="${user.id}"/>
</c:url>

| <a href="${deleteurl}">delete</a>
```

After all of the crazy URLs are created and prepared for page display, the messy forEach JSTL loop looks like this:

```
<c:forEach items="${users}" var="user">
<c:url  var="editurl" value="user.jsp" >
  <c:param name="command" value="edit" />
  <c:param name="id" value="${user.id}"/>
</c:url>
<c:url  var="deleteurl" value="user.jsp" >
  <c:param name="command" value="delete" />
  <c:param name="id" value="${user.id}"/>
</c:url>
  | <a href="${editurl}">edit</a>
  | <a href="${deleteurl}">delete</a>
  | <c:out value="${user.id}" />
  | <c:out value="${user.loginName}" />
  | <c:out value="${user.emailAddress}" /> |<br/>
</c:forEach>
```

```
<%@ taglib prefix="c" uri="http://java.sun.com/jsp/jstl/core" %>
<html><body>
<form action="user.jsp">

<!--  Here are our four textfields  -->
<input type="text" size="7" readonly name="id"
    value="${user.id}"> Id <BR/>
<input type="text" size="30" name="loginName"
    value="${user.loginName}"> Name <BR/>
<input type="text" size="30" name="password"
    value="${user.password}"> Password <BR/>
<input type="text" size="30" name="emailAddress"
    value="${user.emailAddress}"> Email <BR/>

<!-- Here are all of our buttons!!! -->
<input type="submit" name="command" value="Strict Search">
<input type="submit" name="command" value="Fuzzy Search">
<input type="submit" name="command" value="Update">
<input type="submit" name="command" value="Create">
<input type="submit" name="command" value="Clear"> <BR>

<c:forEach items="${users}" var="user">

  <c:url  var="editurl" value="user.jsp" >
    <c:param name="command" value="edit" />
    <c:param name="id" value="${user.id}"/>
  </c:url>

  <c:url  var="deleteurl" value="user.jsp" >
    <c:param name="command" value="delete" />
    <c:param name="id" value="${user.id}"/>
  </c:url>

 | <a href="${editurl}">edit</a>
 | <a href="${deleteurl}">delete</a>
 | <c:out value="${user.id}" />
 | <c:out value="${user.loginName}" />
 | <c:out value="${user.emailAddress}" /> | <BR/>
</c:forEach>

</form>
</body></html>
```

Directives, UseBeans and Property Setters

We've actually got three more JSP related tags that we need to add to our JSP page before we start in on the actual logic. The first is a page directive, which will provide all of the required package imports. We can place this anywhere on the page, although towards the top, right next to the taglib directive, is perhaps the most handsome spot.

```
<%@page
    import="com.examscam.dao.*,com.examscam.model.*,
                    com.examscam.*,org.hibernate.*;"
        contentType="text/html;   %>
```

After the @page directive, we want a useBean and a setProperty tag to manage an instance of the User class. This instance will be creatively named *user*. Here's how it looks:

```
<jsp:useBean class="com.examscam.model.User"
                    id="user" scope="request"/>

<jsp:setProperty name="user" property="*" />
```

The useBean tag is just a simple way of declaring an instance variable to be used on the page. Essentially, at runtime, it instructs the JSP to look for an instance of the User class, which will be named *user*, in the request scope. If there isn't one in the request scope, the JSP engine will create one by calling the default constructor of the User class and placing it in there. Basically, it ensures that an instance of the User class, with the variable name of *user*, is always available when the JSP runs.

The setProperty tag has the effect of initializing all of the properties of the User instance, named *user*, with like-named textfields when the JSP page is submitted. So, if someone types "Cameron" into the loginName textfield, and "passw0rd" into the password textfield, then the jsp:setProperty will see to it that the loginName and password fields of the User instance named *user* are initialized accordingly. It's all really neat. ☺

```
<%@page import="com.examscam.dao.*,com.examscam.model.*,
com.examscam.*,org.hibernate.*;" contentType="text/html;%>

<jsp:useBean class="com.examscam.model.User"
id="user" scope="request"/>

<jsp:setProperty name="user" property="*" />

<%@ taglib prefix="c" uri="http://java.sun.com/jsp/jstl/core" %>

<html><body>
<form action="user.jsp">
<!-- Here are our four textfields -->
<input type="text" size="7" readonly name="id"
    value="${user.id}"> Id <BR/>
<input type="text" size="30" name="loginName"
    value="${user.loginName}"> Name <BR/>
<input type="text" size="30" name="password"
    value="${user.password}"> Password <BR/>
<input type="text" size="30" name="emailAddress"
    value="${user.emailAddress}"> Email <BR/>
<!-- Here are all of our buttons!!! -->
<input type="submit" name="command" value="Strict Search">
<input type="submit" name="command" value="Fuzzy Search">
<input type="submit" name="command" value="Update">
<input type="submit" name="command" value="Create">
<input type="submit" name="command" value="Clear"> <BR>
<c:forEach items="${users}" var="user">
  <c:url var="editurl" value="user.jsp" >
    <c:param name="command" value="edit" />
    <c:param name="id" value="${user.id}"/>
  </c:url>
  <c:url var="deleteurl" value="user.jsp" >
    <c:param name="command" value="delete" />
    <c:param name="id" value="${user.id}"/>
  </c:url>
 | <a href="${editurl}">edit</a>
 | <a href="${deleteurl}">delete</a>
 | <c:out value="${user.id}" />
 | <c:out value="${user.loginName}" />
 | <c:out value="${user.emailAddress}" /> | <BR/>
</c:forEach>
</form>
</body></html>
```

250

The Java Scriptlet Logic

With the HTML and custom tags all added into the JSP, we can start concentrating on the logic required to implement our multi-faceted JSP page.

Immediately following our jsp:setProperty tag, we will add a JSP scriptlet, which is delineated with the following tag: <% %>. Basically, every piece of Java code we write that is part of this scriptlet must be contained within the two percentage signs.

Our scriptlet will start off simple enough, with the simple initiation of a transaction using the HibernateUtil class. From there, we will declare and initialize the UserDAO instance. Then we will declare a java.util.List object named users, and initialize this list to null. This list will eventually be populated, and the contents of the list will be displayed by the JPS's forEach JSTL loop.

```
<%
HibernateUtil.beginTransaction();
UserDAO userDAO = new UserDAO();
java.util.List users = null;
%>
```

Which Button Was Pressed?

After beginning a transaction, and doing a little declaration and initializations with the UserDAO and java.util.List classes, we go to the request object and ask it which button or link the user has pressed to trigger this page to appear. Each button or link on the page is associated with the word *command*, so to find out which action was invoked, we simply ask the request object to return the value associated with the parameter "command".

```
<%
HibernateUtil.beginTransaction();
UserDAO userDAO = new UserDAO();
java.util.List users = null;
String command=request.getParameter("command");
%>
```

251

Responding to the Client Request

Our JSP is pretty much focused around responding to which one of the seven command actions were invoked. Correspondingly, the bulk of the JSP scriptlet will involve reacting to one of the seven commands. A skeleton of the scriptlet, without any logic placed in the body of the if blocks, would look like this:

```
<%
HibernateUtil.beginTransaction();
UserDAO userDAO = new UserDAO();
java.util.List users = null;
String command=request.getParameter("command");
if (command != null) {
  if (command.equals("Create")) {/*do something*/}
  if (command.equals("Update")) {/*do something*/}
  if (command.equals("edit"))   {/*do something*/}
  if (command.equals("delete")) {/*do something*/}
  if (command.equals("Fuzzy Search")) {/*do something*/}
  if (command.equals("Strict Search")) {/*do something*/}
  if (command.equals("Clear"))  {/*do something*/}
}
%>
```

Notice that the first if statement is a check for null. The command will be null if the page is being invoked for the first time, or simply being refreshed. Not checking for a null command will trigger a potential NullPointerException. ☹

Harking back to the buttons that were added to the page, you can see that the command names being used map back to the values associated with the various buttons that were added to the page:

```
<input type="submit" name="command" value="Strict Search">
<input type="submit" name="command" value="Fuzzy Search">
<input type="submit" name="command" value="Update">
<input type="submit" name="command" value="Create">
<input type="submit" name="command" value="Clear">
```

The buttons represent five of the possible commands. The other two commands, edit and delete, are similarly triggered by anchor links coded in the JSTL forEach loop.

Your Wish is my Command

So, what do we do when we encounter a *Create* command? Well, the useBean tag has already initialized a User instance, named user, and the setProperty tag has initialized the values of that User instance to whatever the application client typed into the loginName, emailAddress and password textfields. So, with a fully initialized User instance at our fingertips, all we need to do is pass that instance to the create method of the already declared and initialized UserDAO:

```
if (command.equals("Create")) {
  userDAO.create(user);
}
```

And what do we do if the client has triggered an update command? Well, it's the same thing, except it's different. ☺ With the update command, we pass the initialized User instance to the UserDAO's update method:

```
if (command.equals("Update")) {
  userDAO.update(user);
}
```

Do you want to guess what you do for the Delete command? Yeah, it's pretty similar. ☺

```
if (command.equals("delete")) {
  userDAO.delete(user);
  request.setAttribute("user", null);
}
```

One thing to notice about the delete command implementation is that it actually nulls out the user instance sitting in the request scope. We need to do this, because if the user instance stays in the request scope, the JSP engine will try to repopulate the textfields on the page with the user instance's values the next time the page renders. Nulling out the user instance in the request scope will stop any textfield rendering of the deleted user's properties.

We're in the Clear

The clear method is intended just to clear the textfields of their current values. As such, the Clear command does not actually involve the UserDAO at all, but instead, just pulls the same trick the delete method pulled when it nulled out the User instance in the request scope:

```
if (command.equals("Clear")) {
    request.setAttribute("user", null);
}
```

The edit Command

The edit command shakes things up a little bit by invoking a finder method. The edit command will give us access to the id of the user for which the application client wants to see more information. Given the id, we can use the findByPrimaryKey method of the UserDAO to obtain the unique user. From there, we do the opposite of nulling out the user in the request scope by instead, stuffing the user we just found **into** the request scope. Thus, when the JSP re-renders, the JSP engine will display the properties of this user in the appropriate textfields.

```
if (command.equals("edit")) {
  user = userDAO.findByPrimaryKey(user.getId());
  request.setAttribute("user", user);
}
```

Strict and Fuzzy Searches

The search commands, Fuzzy Search and Strict Search, are both very similar, but different from the other commands in the fact that they pass the singular user instance into their finder methods, but get a collection, or List, of user instances in return. Notice that the findByExample method returns a collection of user instances that are used to initialize the java.util.List variable named *users*, which was originally initialized to null at the beginning of the JSP scriptlet.

```
if (command.equals("Fuzzy Search")) {
  userS = userDAO.findByExample(user, true);
}
if (command.equals("Strict Search")) {
  userS = userDAO.findByExample(user, false);
}
```

The fuzzy and strict searches differ only by the Boolean value passed into the findByExample method. When the Boolean value is true, a fuzzy search is performed, while a strict search is performed when the Boolean value is set to false.

Making Sure the Users List is Initialized

We have seen the java.util.List named users initialized by the fuzzy and strict search commands. However, if the client has invoked a different command, the users List remains null after we have run through all of the command logic. So, after all the commands have executed, it's prudent to check to see if the users List is null, and if it is, we call the findAll method of the UserDAO to provide a fruitful initialization. We then place the users List into the request scope for future retrieval by other parts of the application.

```
if (users == null) {
  users = userDAO.findAll();
}
request.setAttribute("users", users);
```

HibernateUtil.commitTransaction

When all is said and done, the scriptlet ends with a termination of the database transaction that made all of this wonderful JSP coding experience possible. Here's the full scriptlet:

```
<%
HibernateUtil.beginTransaction();
UserDAO userDAO = new UserDAO();
java.util.List users = null;
String command = request.getParameter("command");
  if (command != null) {
    if (command.equals("Create")) {
      userDAO.create(user);
    }
    if (command.equals("Update")) {
      userDAO.update(user);
    }
    if (command.equals("edit")) {
      user = userDAO.findByPrimaryKey(user.getId());
      request.setAttribute("user", user);
    }
    if (command.equals("delete")) {
      userDAO.delete(user);
      request.setAttribute("user", null);
    }
    if (command.equals("Fuzzy Search")) {
      users = userDAO.findByExample(user, true);
    }
    if (command.equals("Strict Search")) {
      users = userDAO.findByExample(user, false);
    }
    if (command.equals("Clear")) {
      request.setAttribute("user", null);
    }
  }
  if (users == null) { users = userDAO.findAll(); }

request.setAttribute("users", users);
HibernateUtil.commitTransaction();
%>
```

The Whole JSP, DONE!!!

```
<%@page
import="com.examscam.dao.*,com.examscam.model.*,
com.examscam.*,org.hibernate.*;" contentType="text/html; %>
<%@ taglib prefix="c" uri="http://java.sun.com/jsp/jstl/core" %>
<jsp:useBean class="com.examscam.model.User" id="user"
                                    scope="request"/>
<jsp:setProperty name="user" property="*" />
<%
HibernateUtil.beginTransaction();
UserDAO userDAO = new UserDAO();
java.util.List users = null;
String command = request.getParameter("command");
if (command != null) {
if (command.equals("Create")) {
userDAO.create(user);
}
if (command.equals("Update")) {
userDAO.update(user);
}
if (command.equals("edit")) {
user = userDAO.findByPrimaryKey(user.getId());
request.setAttribute("user", user);
}
if (command.equals("delete")) {
userDAO.delete(user);
request.setAttribute("user", null);
}
if (command.equals("Fuzzy Search")) {
users = userDAO.findByExample(user, true);
}
if (command.equals("Strict Search")) {
users = userDAO.findByExample(user, false);
}
if (command.equals("Clear")) {
request.setAttribute("user", null);
}
}
if (users == null) {
users = userDAO.findAll();
}
request.setAttribute("users", users);
HibernateUtil.commitTransaction();
%> <!-- Continued on the next page... -->
```

```
<html>
<body><form action="user.jsp">
<!-- Here are our four textfields -->
<input type="text" size="7" readonly name="id"
value="${user.id}"> Id
<BR/>
<input type="text" size="30" name="loginName"
value="${user.loginName}"> Name
<BR/>
<input type="text" size="30" name="password"
value="${user.password}"> Password
<BR/>
<input type="text" size="30" name="emailAddress"
value="${user.emailAddress}"> Email
<BR/>
<!-- Here are all of our buttons!!! -->
<input type="submit" name="command" value="Strict Search">
<input type="submit" name="command" value="Fuzzy Search">
<input type="submit" name="command" value="Update">
<input type="submit" name="command" value="Create">
<input type="submit" name="command" value="Clear">
<BR>
<c:forEach items="${users}" var="user">
<c:url  var="editurl" value="user.jsp" >
  <c:param name="command" value="edit" />
  <c:param name="id" value="${user.id}"/>
</c:url>
<c:url  var="deleteurl" value="user.jsp" >
  <c:param name="command" value="delete" />
  <c:param name="id" value="${user.id}"/>
</c:url>
 | <a href="${editurl}">edit</a>
 | <a href="${deleteurl}">delete</a>
 | <c:out value="${user.id}" />
 | <c:out value="${user.loginName}" />
 | <c:out value="${user.emailAddress}" />
 |
<BR/>
</c:forEach>
</form>
</body>
</html>
```

Deploying the user.jsp

The user.jsp has to be the simplest of all web based applications that might leverage the Hibernate framework. To deploy the user.jsp page, you must place the user.jsp page in a working deployment directory of a Servlet engine such as Tomcat. Furthermore, you must make sure that all of the Hibernate libraries and the custom Java code use by the JSP, such as the HibernateUtil class and the User class, are on the classpath of the Servlet engine.

Typically, web based applications are deployed as Web Application Archive files, also known as WAR files. If a WAR file was being deployed, the user.jsp page would be placed in the root of the WAR file, while the required libraries would go in the WAR file's WEB-INF\lib directory, and compiled source code would be placed in the WEB-INF\classes directory.

When deployed to the open source Tomcat Servlet engine, the user.jsp page creates a very handsome and easy to use, user management dashboard type of application, demonstrating how a web based application can take advantage of the Hibernate framework in order to perform database persistence.

```
[          ] Id
[                              ] Name
[                              ] Password
[                              ] Email
[ Strict Search ] [ Fuzzy Search ] [ Update ] [ Create ] [ Clear ]
| edit | delete | 1 | mj | mj@mcnz.com |
| edit | delete | 2 | mario | mario@scja.ca |
| edit | delete | 3 | sk8trgrl | avril@scja.com |
| edit | delete | 4 | ridley | getbent@scja.ca |
| edit | delete | 5 | kerri | sheehan@princessjava.com |
| edit | delete | 6 | astra | rabbit@princessjava.com |
| edit | delete | 7 | cameron | me@scwcd.com |
| edit | delete | 8 | stephen | stanley@pulpjava.com |
| edit | delete | 9 | che | ernesto@pulpjava.com |
| edit | delete | 10 | remy | rabbit@scja.com |
```

Mappings

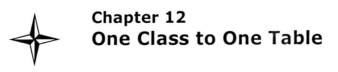

Chapter 12
One Class to One Table

The simplest mapping of them all is the *one Java class to one database table* mapping. We saw this type of mapping with the User class in the first couple of chapters, where the User class mapped directly to the user table, and *properties* of the User class were mapped pretty directly to corresponding table *columns*.

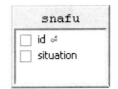

Just to liven things up a bit, I'm going to create a new class called Snafu, and similarly, map that Snafu class to a single database table named snafu. It's the same old *one class to one table mapping* that we have seen before, but with a different class and table just to keep things fresh.

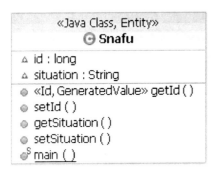

Looking at the Snafu Class Code

Looking at the code for the Snafu class, you'll notice the basic elements of a JPA annotated class, namely the required @Entity tag above the class declaration, along with the @Id tag before the getId() method. The getId() method is also decorated with the @GeneratedValue annotation to allow the database to create unique ids when new records are added to the Snafu table.

Adding the Class to the Configuration

With the @Entity, @Id and @GeneratedValue tags added, the SNAFU class has all of the annotations required for it to have its persistence managed by Hibernate. We have even added a runnable main method that leverages the HibernateUtil class to begin a transaction and provide access to the Hibernate Session.

Be aware of the fact that in order for Hibernate to understand how to manage the persistent state of the Snafu class, the Snafu class must be added to the AnnotationConfiguration, which is done in the getInitializedConfiguration() method of our HibernateUtil class. Failing to add the Snafu class to the configuration will result in the following runtime exception:

```
Exception in thread "main"
org.hibernate.MappingException:
Unknown entity: com.examscam.mappings.Snafu at
org.hibernate.impl.SessionFactoryImpl.getEntityPersister
```

Seeing that we've already mentioned it a few times, the full HibernateUtil class, with the added annotation for the Snafu class, can be found at the end of this chapter.

```
public class HibernateUtil {×××
 public static Configuration getInitializedConfiguration(){
     AnnotationConfiguration config =
             new AnnotationConfiguration();
  /* all of your JPA annotated classes go here!!! */
     config.addAnnotatedClass(User.class);
     config.addAnnotatedClass(Snafu.class);
     config.configure();
     return config;
   }×××
}
```

One Class to One Table Hibernate Mapping

```
package com.examscam.mappings;
import javax.persistence.*;
import org.hibernate.Session;
import com.examscam.HibernateUtil;

@Entity
public class Snafu {

  long id;
  String situation;

  @Id
  @GeneratedValue
  public long getId() {return id;}
  public void setId(long id) {this.id = id;}

  public String getSituation(){
    return situation;
  }
  public void setSituation(String situation) {
    this.situation = situation;
  }

  /* main not required - just for testing */
  public static void main(String args[]) {
    HibernateUtil.recreateDatabase();
    Snafu snafu = new Snafu();
    snafu.setSituation("normal");
    Session session = HibernateUtil.beginTransaction();
    session.save(snafu);
    HibernateUtil.commitTransaction();
  }
}
```

Creating the snafu Database Table

Notice how the first line of code in the Snafu class' main method is a call to HibernateUtil.recreateDatabase(). This method call is required in order to create the underlying snafu table. Of course, if the snafu table is already created, you can comment out this line of code. If the snafu table is not created and you try to run this code, you will get the following error:

```
SEVERE: Table 'examscam.snafu' doesn't exist
Exception in thread "main"
org.hibernate.exception.SQLGrammarException: could not
insert: [com.examscam.mappings.Snafu] at
org.hibernate.exception.SQLStateConverter.convert(SQLStateC
onverter.java:67) at
org.hibernate.exception.JDBCExceptionHelper.convert(JDBCExc
eptionHelper.java:43)
```

If you wanted to create the snafu table by throwing some SQL at your database, here's the script; it's pretty simple:

```
DROP TABLE IF EXISTS `examscam`.`snafu`;
CREATE TABLE `examscam`.`snafu` (
  `id` bigint(20) NOT NULL auto_increment,
  `situation` varchar(255) default NULL,
  PRIMARY KEY  (`id`)
);
```

SNAFU is an acronym meaning roughly, "things are in a mess — as usual".
The most commonly accepted rendering is "Situation Normal: All F*c*ed Up". It is sometimes given as "Situation Normal: All Fouled Up" or similar, in circumstances where profanity is discouraged or censored. In modern usage, "snafu" is often used as an interjection, as a shorthand for the sentiment expressed by the phrase. "Snafu" is also sometimes used as a noun or verb, referring to a situation that suddenly went awry, or the cause of the trouble. The acronym is believed to have originated in the US Army during World War II.

-SNAFU, Wikipedia.org

Inspecting the Results of the Snafu's main

When the Snafu class runs, you'll likely see a statement in your log files such as **Hibernate: *insert into Snafu (situation) values (?).*** Furthermore, if you inspect your database, you should see a new record containing an autogenerated id, along with a value of 'normal' in the situation column.

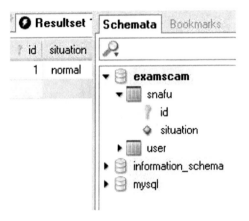

The Full HibernateUtil Class

I know some people may be jumping directly to this chapter, and may not have read the chapter that created the HibernateUtil class. As a convenience, I'm going to reprint the HibernateUtil class in its entirety. Just part of my attempt to make this book as readable and useable as possible. ☺

```
package com.examscam;
import org.hibernate.Session;
import org.hibernate.SessionFactory;
import org.hibernate.cfg.AnnotationConfiguration;
import org.hibernate.cfg.Configuration;
import org.hibernate.tool.hbm2ddl.SchemaExport;
import com.examscam.model.User;
import com.examscam.mappings.Snafu;


public class HibernateUtil {

 private static SessionFactory factory;

 public static Configuration
                getInitializedConfiguration() {
   AnnotationConfiguration config =
                new AnnotationConfiguration();
/* add all of your JPA annotated classes here!!! */
   config.addAnnotatedClass(User.class);
   config.addAnnotatedClass(Snafu.class);
   config.configure();
   return config;
 }

 public static Session getSession() {
   if (factory == null) {
   Configuration config =
      HibernateUtil.getInitializedConfiguration();
   factory = config.buildSessionFactory();
   }
   Session hibernateSession =
                factory.getCurrentSession();
   return hibernateSession;
 }

 public static void closeSession() {
   HibernateUtil.getSession().close();
 }
        /*** continued on next page ***/
```

```
    /*** continued from previous page ***/

public static void recreateDatabase() {
  Configuration config;
  config =
     HibernateUtil.getInitializedConfiguration();
  new SchemaExport(config).create(true, true);
}

public static Session beginTransaction() {
  Session hibernateSession;
  hibernateSession = HibernateUtil.getSession();
  hibernateSession.beginTransaction();
  return hibernateSession;
}

public static void commitTransaction() {
  HibernateUtil.getSession()
               .getTransaction().commit();
}

public static void rollbackTransaction() {
  HibernateUtil.getSession()
               .getTransaction().rollback();
}
}
```

Remember, any type that uses the HibernateUtil class, and is not in the *com.examscam* package, needs the following import:

import com.examscam.HibernateUtil;

It would appear that I left the import out in a few places of this books first printing. ☹ Hopefully, I've fixed up all of the omissions.

The @GeneratedValue JPA Annotation

Quite often in this book, we have used the @GeneratedValue annotation to get the database to generate a unique primary key. We have used the default *GenerationType* in each of our examples, although there are actually four different primary key generation strategies available to us through Hibernate. Those four strategies are:

«Java Enum»

🄴 GenerationType
(from javax.persistence)

§ᶠ AUTO
§ᶠ IDENTITY
§ᶠ SEQUENCE
§ᶠ TABLE

☞ *AUTO*

☞ *IDENTITY*

☞ *TABLE*

☞ *SEQUENCE*

javax.persistence.GenerationType.AUTO

The AUTO generation strategy is the default, and this setting simply chooses the primary key generation strategy that is the default for the database you are using, which quite typically is IDENTITY, although it might be TABLE or SEQUENCE depending upon how the database is configured. The AUTO strategy is typically recommended, as it makes your code and your applications most portable.

AUTO is the default strategy, and it is the strategy that has been used so far throughout this book.

javax.persistence.GenerationType.IDENTITY

The IDENTITY option simply allows the database to generate a unique primary key for your application. No sequence or table is used to maintain the primary key information, but instead, the database will just pick an appropriate, unique number for Hibernate to assign to the primary key of the entity. With MySQL, the first, *lowest numbered,* id key available in the table in question is chosen, although this behavior may differ from database to database.

javax.persistence.GenerationType.SEQUENCE

Some database vendors support the use of a database sequence object for maintaining primary keys. To use a sequence, you set the GenerationType strategy to SEQUENCE, specify the name assigned to the SequenceGenerator annotation by using the *generator* attribute, and then provide the @SequenceGenerator annotation that has attributes for defining both the name of the sequence annotation, and the name of the actual sequence object in the database.

Here's what the getId() method of the Snafu class would look like if we used a SEQUENCE GenerationType:

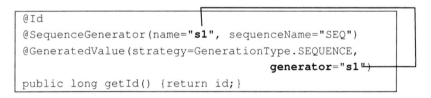

```
@Id
@SequenceGenerator(name="s1", sequenceName="SEQ")
@GeneratedValue(strategy=GenerationType.SEQUENCE,
                                  generator="s1")
public long getId() {return id;}
```

javax.persistence.GenerationType.TABLE

The TABLE GenerationType allocates a separate database table to keep track of the generation of unique ids. To facilitate the description of the table to be used, the TABLE strategy works hand in hand with the @TableGenerator annotation. So, if our Snafu class was to use a separate table, named *pk_table*, for managing primary keys, the getId() method annotation would look like this:

```
@Id
@TableGenerator(name="tg", table="pk_table",
 pkColumnName="name", valueColumnName="value",
                            allocationSize=10)
@GeneratedValue(strategy=GenerationType.TABLE,
                            generator="tg")
public long getId() {return id;}
```

With this @TableGenerator annotation, a separate table in the database, named pk_table, would be created with two columns, one called *name*, and the other called *value*. For each entity using this table, there will be a row entry, with the *name* being the name of the class, and the *value* being the current iteration of key generation. The allocationSize attribute of the @TableGenerator annotation determines the increment size of the generated primary keys *for a new thread*.

Using the @TableGenerator Annotation

So, if we recreated the database using the @TableGenerator annotation, and then added three Snafu objects to the database in separate threads, a pk_table would maintain a database column with the name of Snafu, indicating through the value column that three iterations of primary key generations would have occurred. Furthermore, the Snafu table would have three records, with the primary keys all incrementing to the nearest hundred value.

pk_table	
name	value
Snafu	3

snafu	
id	situation
1	normal
100	normal
200	normal

Chapter 13
One Class to Two Tables

From time to time, you'll run into a scenario where your application defines a single class, but the database maintains the corresponding information in two separate tables. Well, with Hibernate, that's not a problem. All you have to do to map one Java class to two database tables is to define the first table mapping as you normally would, and then specify the name of the second table your class uses with the very intelligently named @SecondaryTable annotation. From there, when you get to a field that is supposed to be stored in the second table, well, you just mention the second table's name in the @Column annotation. It's all very simple and straight forward.

This section will look at how we map one Java class to two database tables using the @SecondaryTable and @Column JPA annotations. In doing so, we will create a single class named **FooBar**, and map it to two database tables, named **foo** and **bar**.

«Java Class, Entity, Table, SecondaryTable»
⊕ FooBar
⌂ id : int
⌂ fooName : String
⌂ barCode : String
◉ «Id, GeneratedValue» getId ( )
◉ setId ( )
◉ getBarCode ( )
◉ setBarCode ( )
◉ «Column» getFooName ( )
◉ setFooName ( )
◉ˢ main ( )

foo
☐ fooName
☐ id ⚷

bar
☐ id ⚷
☐ barCode

FooBar Class to Foo and Bar Tables

To demonstrate the idea of a single class mapping to two different database tables, we're going to create a single class named FooBar.The FooBar class will define an id field of type int, and two String properties named *fooName* and *barCode*. As you could imagine, the two String fields in this FooBar class will map to two different database tables, with one table being named foo, and the other table being named bar.

As far as the property mappings go, we'll throw the fooName field in the foo table, and we'll map the barcode field to a column in the bar table. But, how do we do this with Hibernate and JPA annotations?

Well, first, we need to figure out which table will be the main, primary table. For our purposes, the foo table will be the primary mapping table, and the bar table will be the secondary table. As such, we decorate the class declaration of the FooBar class as so:

```
@Entity
@Table(name="bar")
@SecondaryTable(name="foo")
public class FooBar {
        int id;
        String fooName;
        String barCode;
        ><><><    ><><><
}
```

The UnAnnotated, Un-*main*ed FooBar Class

Here's the FooBar class before we add any annotations, or for that matter, a main method. The key question you should be asking yourself is *'what will this code look like when we map the fields in this single class across two database tables?'*

```
package com.examscam.mappings;
import javax.persistence.*;
import org.hibernate.Session;
import com.examscam.HibernateUtil;


public class FooBar {

      int id;
      String fooName; /* maps to foo table */
      String barCode; /* maps to bar table */

      public int getId() {return id;}

      public void setId(int id) {this.id = id;}

      public String getBarCode() {
            return barCode;
      }
      public void setBarCode(String barCode) {
            this.barCode = barCode;
      }


      public String getFooName() {
            return fooName;
      }
      public void setFooName(String fooName) {
            this.fooName = fooName;
      }
}
```

Primary Keys and Secondary Tables

After mapping the FooBar class to its default and secondary database tables, standard @Id and @GeneratedValue annotations must be used to decorate the getId() method.

```
@Entity
@Table(name="bar")
@SecondaryTable(name="foo")
public class FooBar {
  int id;
  String fooName;
  String barCode;
  @Id
  @GeneratedValue
  public int getId() { return id; } ✂✂✂    ✂✂✂
}
```

Now, the @Id annotation appears to be fairly innocuous, but there is a very significant and easily overlooked detail with regards to how the primary key is mapped behind the scenes. In this case, a primary key named id will appear in both the foo table *and* the bar table. After all, both tables need a unique identifier for all record entries, and since a single Java instance branches across two tables, records in those two tables must share the same, unique, yet common, identifier. Without a common, shared primary key, recreating the state of a single instance persisted across two database tables would be impossible.

Just looking at the create statements for the two tables, you can see that both have a defined primary key, although only the default table, bar, defines the auto_increment property.

```
CREATE TABLE `examscam`.`bar` (
  `id` int(11) NOT NULL auto_increment, `barCode`
varchar(255) default NULL,PRIMARY KEY (`id`) );

CREATE TABLE `examscam`.`foo` (
  `fooName` varchar(255) default NULL,`id` int(11) NOT
NULL, PRIMARY KEY (`id`), KEY `FK18CC6E9F1224B` (`id`) );
```

rsists the pertinent fields to the appropriate database tables.

Mapping Columns to Secondary Tables

With the @Table(name="bar") annotation pointing at the bar table, any column not explicitly mapped to another table will, by default, be persisted to the bar table. Of course, that's fine for the barCode field, but we need to ensure that the fooName field is persisted to the secondary, foo table. This is easily accomplished by adding a (table="foo") attribute to the @Column annotation decorating the getFooName() method.

```
><><><
@Column(table="foo")
public String getFooName() {
   return fooName;
} ><><><
```

Testing FooBar with a main Method

With all of the annotations in place, we're free to code a simple main method that creates a new FooBar object, and subsequently persists the pertinent fields to the appropriate database tables. Here's how the runnable main method looks:

```
><><><
public static void main(String args[]) {
/* HibernateUtil needs FooBar.class in AnnotationConfiguration*/
   HibernateUtil.recreateDatabase();
   FooBar fb = new FooBar();
   fb.setBarCode("90210");
   fb.setFooName("ManChu");
   Session session =HibernateUtil.beginTransaction();
   session.save(fb);
   HibernateUtil.commitTransaction();
}><><><
```

The following page shows the FooBar class in its entirety.

The Complete & Annotated FooBar Class

```java
package com.examscam.mappings;
import javax.persistence.*;import org.hibernate.Session;
import com.examscam.HibernateUtil;

@Entity
@Table(name="bar")
@SecondaryTable(name="foo")
public class FooBar {
  int id;
  String fooName;
  String barCode;

  @Id
  @GeneratedValue
  public int getId() {return id;}
  public void setId(int id) {this.id = id;}

  @Column(table="foo")
  public String getFooName() {return fooName;}
  public void setFooName(String fooName) {
    this.fooName = fooName;
  }

  /* no need for mapping-goes to default bar table */
  public String getBarCode() {return barCode;}
  public void setBarCode(String barCode) {
    this.barCode = barCode;
  }

  public static void main(String args[]) {
/*HibernateUtil needs FooBar.class in AnnotationConfiguration*/
    HibernateUtil.recreateDatabase();
    FooBar fb = new FooBar();
    fb.setBarCode("90210");
    fb.setFooName("ManChu");
    Session session = HibernateUtil.beginTransaction();
    session.save(fb);
    HibernateUtil.commitTransaction();
  }
}
```

Adding the Annotated FooBar.class

As with any newly JPA annotated persistence class, you must ensure that it is added to the AnnotationConfiguration object. The custom class we have coded to maintain the configuration of our environment is the HibernateUtil class. The code below contains the getInitializedConfiguration() method of the HibernateUtil class with the FooBar.class being added to the AnnotationConfiguration object.

```
public class HibernateUtil {✂✂✂
 public static Configuration getInitializedConfiguration(){
    AnnotationConfiguration config =
                     new AnnotationConfiguration();
    /* add all of your JPA annotated classes here!!! */
    config.addAnnotatedClass(User.class);
    config.addAnnotatedClass(Snafu.class);
    config.addAnnotatedClass(FooBar.class);
    config.configure();
    return config;
 }✂✂✂
}
```

foo and bar Table Creation

Furthermore, you must make sure the bar and foo tables exist in the examscam database. You can have Hibernate create these tables for you by using the SchemaExport class in conjunction with the updated Configuration object that can be generated by the HibernateUtil's getInitializedConfiguration method. Of course, if you're more into running ddl scripts, here's a little bit of SQL that will create the required tables through a scripting tool:

```
CREATE TABLE  `examscam`.`bar`  (
 `id` int(11) NOT NULL auto_increment, `barCode`
varchar(255) default NULL, PRIMARY KEY  (`id`));

CREATE TABLE  `examscam`.`foo`  (
 `fooName` varchar(255) default NULL,`id` int(11) NOT
NULL, PRIMARY KEY  (`id`),  KEY `FK18CC6E9F1224B` (`id`));
```

Running the FooBar's main Method

After running the FooBar's main method, you'll find that the following two SQL queries have been executed by Hibernate against the database:

```
Hibernate: insert into bar (barCode) values (?)
Hibernate: insert into foo (fooName, id) values (?,?)
```

Of course, the FooBar class' main method set the barCode property to "90210" and the fooName property to "Manchu", so inspecting the database after the main method has run shows the "90210" and "Manchu" properties saved to the appropriate database tables, with both records sharing a common id.

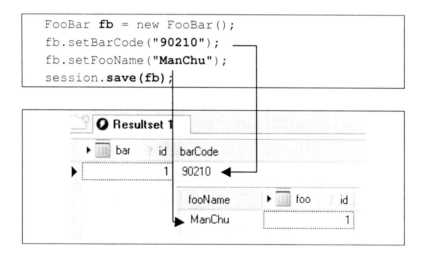

Chapter 14
Two Classes to One Table

The previous chapter examined how to annotate a single JavaBean whose properties were mapped to two separate database tables. The converse of that scenario is what we will be looking at in this chapter. We will look at how we can map two Java classes to a single, common, database table.

One of the most common object-oriented design constructs is the idea that objects are typically *things*, and those things can be associated with all sorts of extra information that can be factored out into a *detail* class. In fact, Peter Coad asserts in his groundbreaking book, UML Modeling in Color that all objects in a problem domain will fall into one of four categories, with the first two being *things* and *thing-details*. (Roles and moment-intervals are the other two object types that find their way into a domain model.)

In an object model, a thing is typically associated with its detail object through a one to one mapping. Of course, database administrators don't always see the philosophical benefits of breaking objects mapped together in a one-to-one type of manner into two separate database tables. So, a common need we see in enterprise applications is the need to map two classes that are related in a one to one manner, into a single, monolithic, database table.

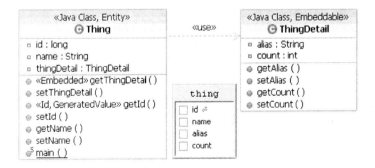

The Thing and the ThingDetail

Keeping the example fairly simple so we can concentrate on the Hibernate and JPA implementation, as opposed to other more esoteric, Java based concepts, I'm going to create two classes, a Thing class, and a ThingDetail class.

The Thing class maintains a primary key, named id, of type long.

The Thing class also has property of type String called name, and an instance variable of type ThingDetail. Essentially, we can say that *a Thing has-a ThingDetail.*

The ThingDetail will have two additional properties, an alias of type String, and a count of type int. What are we counting? Who cares, it's just an example. ☺

The Unannotated Thing Class

```java
package com.examscam.mappings; import com.examscam.*;
public class Thing {

  private long id;
  private String name;

/*A Thing has-a ThingDetail as an instance variable*/

  private ThingDetail thingDetail;

  public ThingDetail getThingDetail() {
    return thingDetail;
  }
  public void setThingDetail(ThingDetail detail) {
    this.thingDetail = detail;
  }
/* The primary key id is defined only in the Thing class*/

  public long getId() {return id;}
  public void setId(long id) {this.id = id;}
  public String getName() {return name;}
  public void setName(String n) {this.name = n; }
}
```

The Unannotated ThingDetail Class

The ThingDetail class is a really simple class with only two instance variables, and curiously, no property to represent a primary key. In fact, since the ThingDetail is entirely contained within the encapsulating Thing class, there is no need for the ThingDetail class to worry about a primary key at all.

```java
package com.examscam.mappings;
import com.examscam.*;

public class ThingDetail {

    private String alias;
    private int count;

    public String getAlias() {
        return alias;
    }
    public void setAlias(String alias) {
        this.alias = alias;
    }
    public int getCount() {
        return count;
    }
    public void setCount(int count) {
        this.count = count;
    }
}
```

The Annotated ThingDetail Class

Annotating the ThingDetail class really couldn't be easier. The ThingDetail class is an encapsulated property of the Thing class, and the Thing class will be mapped to a database table named Thing. As a result, we simply need to place an annotation at the top of the ThingDetail class that tells Hibernate that the ThingDetail is going to be *embedded* inside of another class, and when it comes time to persist the Thing and the ThingDetail, just flatten all of the properties out, and smush them all into a common *thing* table. A simple @Embeddable tag does the trick here. Look how simple it is:

```
package com.examscam.mappings;
import javax.persistence.Embeddable;

@Embeddable
public class ThingDetail {

    private String alias;
    private int count;

    public String getAlias() {return alias;}
    public void setAlias(String alias) {
        this.alias = alias;
    }

    public int getCount() {return count;}
    public void setCount(int count) {
        this.count = count;
    }
}
```

The only difference between the annotated and unannotated ThingDetail class is the introduction of the @Embeddable tag before the class declaration, along with the import statement that makes it possible to reference the @Embeddable annotation.

@Embedded vs. @Embeddable Annotations

The Thing class is the main entity here, with the ThingDetail being nothing more than a single, simple, embedded property. The Thing class, which I guess you could call the *encapsulating* class, defines all of the usual tag suspects, including the @Entity tag at the beginning of the class, and the @Id and @GeneratedValue tags before the getId() method.

However, the big distinction with the Thing class, which has an encapsulated property of type ThingDetail, is the fact that the getter for the ThingDetail instance must be decorated with the **@Embedded** tag. So, the ThingDetail class itself defines a top level @Embeddable annotation, while the getter for the instance variable of type ThingDetail in the encapsulating Thing class must be marked with the **@Embedded** annotation.

```
package com.examscam.mappings;
import javax.persistence.*;import org.hibernate.Session;
import com.examscam.HibernateUtil;

@Entity
public class Thing {
  private long id;
  private String name;

  private ThingDetail thingDetail;

  @Embedded
  public ThingDetail getThingDetail(){return thingDetail;}
  public void setThingDetail(ThingDetail detail) {
    this.thingDetail = detail;
  }

  @Id
  @GeneratedValue
  public long getId() {return id;}
  public void setId(long id) {this.id = id;}

  public String getName() {return name;}
  public void setName(String name) {this.name = name;}
}
```

Testing the Embedded & Embeddable Code

With all of the required annotations in place, a main method can be coded in the Thing class to test how well the application will work. And remember, what we have is *two* Java classes, but only *one* database table. While we will create two separate classes in our test method, the state of the two JavaBeans will be persisted to a single database table, with a database column defined for each property, all of which is mapped to a single database row with a single, unique, primary key.

```
public static void main(String args[]) {
  HibernateUtil.recreateDatabase();

  ThingDetail detail = new ThingDetail();
  detail.setAlias("Joey Shabidoo");
  detail.setCount(10);

  Thing thing = new Thing();
  thing.setName("Homer");
  thing.setThingDetail(detail);

  Session session = HibernateUtil.beginTransaction();
  session.save(thing);
  HibernateUtil.commitTransaction();
}
```

Notice that in the main method, only the instance of type Thing, sensibly named *thing*, is passed to the save method of the Hibernate Session. However, since the ThingDetail is associated with the *thing* being saved through the *thing.setThingDetail(detail)* method call, well, all of the data in both the instance of the *Thing* and the encapsulated instance of the *ThingDetail* will be persisted to the database.

Again, to run the main method, the *Thing* table must exist in the database, and the AnnotationConfiguration object must be configured with the Thing.class added.

```
AnnotationConfiguration config = new AnnotationConfiguration();
config.addAnnotatedClass(Thing.class);
config.configure();
```

The Whole Thing ☺

```
package com.examscam.mappings;
import javax.persistence.*;import org.hibernate.Session;
import com.examscam.HibernateUtil;

@Entity
public class Thing {
  private long id;
  private String name;
  private ThingDetail thingDetail;

  @Embedded
  public ThingDetail getThingDetail(){return thingDetail;}
  public void setThingDetail(ThingDetail thingDetail) {
    this.thingDetail = thingDetail;
  }

  @Id
  @GeneratedValue
  public long getId() {return id;}
  public void setId(long id) {this.id = id;}

  public String getName() {return name;}
  public void setName(String name) {this.name = name;}

  public static void main(String args[]) {
/* recreateDatabase is need to ensure the Thing table is created */
    HibernateUtil.recreateDatabase();

    ThingDetail detail = new ThingDetail();
    detail.setAlias("Joey Shabidoo");
    detail.setCount(10);

    Thing thing = new Thing();
    thing.setName("Homer");
    thing.setThingDetail(detail);

    Session session = HibernateUtil.beginTransaction();
/*only the instance of Thing is explicitly saved*/
    session.save(thing);
    HibernateUtil.commitTransaction();
  }
}
```

Thing, ThingDetail &AnnotationConfigurations

One of the questions that often gets asked at this point in time is whether or not I've accidentally left out any mention of the ThingDetail class when adding JPA annotated POJOs to the Hibernate Configuration. Well, actually, I haven't forgotten anything.

Certainly, we need to add the Thing.class:

```
config.addAnnotatedClass(Thing.class);
```

But you'll notice that we don't have to add the ThingDetail.class. This is true for any Embedded class. When using the @Embedded annotation, only the class that has the actual @Embedded annotation needs to be added to the configuration. The encapsulated class that had the @Embeddable annotation, which in this case is the ThingDetail, does not get added to the configuration. Simply adding the encapsulating class to the configuration is all the information Hibernate needs to go and inspect that embedded class and create columns for the properties the class defines.

```
public static Configuration getInitializedConfiguration() {
    AnnotationConfiguration config = new AnnotationConfiguration();
    /* add all of your JPA annotated classes here!!! */
    config.addAnnotatedClass(User.class);
    config.addAnnotatedClass(Snafu.class);
    config.addAnnotatedClass(FooBar.class);
    config.addAnnotatedClass(Thing.class);
    config.configure();
    return config;
}
```

By the way, just in case you were looking for it, here's the SQL for the creation of the Thing table. Notice the thing table contains fields for the alias and count properties, along with the name and the id.

```
DROP TABLE IF EXISTS `examscam`.`thing`;
CREATE TABLE  `examscam`.`thing` (
 `id` bigint(20) NOT NULL auto_increment,`name`
varchar(255) default NULL,`alias` varchar(255)
default NULL,`count` int(11) NOT NULL,PRIMARY KEY
(`id`))
```

Running the Executable main Method

After running the executable main method of the Thing class, Hibernate kicks out an informative little snippet of SQL:

```
Hibernate: insert into Thing
           (name, alias, count) values (?, ?, ?)
```

A quick inspection of the database indicates that a new record exists in the thing table, with a generated id of 1, a meaningless count of 10, a name of Homer and an alias of Joey Shabidoo.

And that's pretty much it! As you can see, the values written to the thing table are what we would expect from the Thing and ThingDetail objects that were created in the main method of the Thing class:

```
ThingDetail detail = new ThingDetail();
detail.setAlias("Joey Shabidoo");
detail.setCount(10);

Thing thing = new Thing();
thing.setName("Homer");
thing.setThingDetail(detail);
```

The Updated HibernateUtil Again

With all of the work we've been doing, I just thought I'd print out the HibernateUtil class in its entirety again. ☺

```java
package com.examscam;
import org.hibernate.Session; import org.hibernate.SessionFactory;
import org.hibernate.cfg.AnnotationConfiguration;
import org.hibernate.cfg.Configuration;
import org.hibernate.tool.hbm2ddl.SchemaExport;
import com.examscam.model.User;
public class HibernateUtil {
  private static SessionFactory factory;
  public static Configuration
              getInitializedConfiguration() {
    AnnotationConfiguration config =
                new AnnotationConfiguration();
    config.addAnnotatedClass(User.class);
    config.addAnnotatedClass(Snafu.class);
    config.addAnnotatedClass(FooBar.class);
    config.addAnnotatedClass(Thing.class);
    config.configure();
    return config;
  }
  public static Session getSession() {
    if (factory == null) {
    Configuration config =
      HibernateUtil.getInitializedConfiguration();
    factory = config.buildSessionFactory();
    }
    Session hibernateSession =
                    factory.getCurrentSession();
    return hibernateSession;
  }

  public static void closeSession() {
    HibernateUtil.getSession().close();
  }
          /*** continued on next page ***/
```

```
      /*** continued from previous page ***/

public static void recreateDatabase() {
  Configuration config;
  config =
  HibernateUtil.getInitializedConfiguration();
  new SchemaExport(config).create(true, true);
}

public static Session beginTransaction() {
  Session hibernateSession;
  hibernateSession =
          HibernateUtil.getSession();
  hibernateSession.beginTransaction();
  return hibernateSession;
}

public static void commitTransaction() {
  HibernateUtil.getSession()
              .getTransaction().commit();
}

public static void rollbackTransaction() {
  HibernateUtil.getSession()
              .getTransaction().rollback();
}

  public static void main(String args[]) {
    HibernateUtil.recreateDatabase();
  }

}
```

Chapter 15
Compound Primary Keys

A common requirement of many data driven applications is to define tables that use composite primary keys, which essentially means that instead of having one column in a database table to uniquely identify a record, the table uses two columns that together, represent a unique combination.

Compound primary keys are very common, and to be honest, I feel just a tad guilty about getting this far in a book about Hibernate without addressing the concept, but I assure you, there is a very good reason for the delay. You see, when a database table uses a composite primary key, the Hibernate layer is forced to create a separate class that maps directly to that primary key, and then that class must become an embedded property of the JPA annotated class that maps to the database table of interest. Since the @Embeddable annotation wasn't covered until the previous chapter, any earlier discussion of compound primary keys would have been a bit premature. ☺

In this chapter, we will explore the creation of compound primary key classes, and discover how those classes can be embedded within a JPA annotated class. In doing so, we will examine at the following concepts:

☞ *Using the @Embedded tag to define compound primary keys*

☞ *Using the @IdClass JPA annotation*

☞ *Using the @EmbeddedId JPA annotation*

☞ *The importance of overriding .hashCode() and the .equals method in both primary key and entity classes*

293

Compound Keys & the Interest Table

I have a sweet little database table named interest, that has one numeric property called rate, and two non-unique, numeric properties called userId and bankId, which together, uniquely represent a record in the interest table.

So, how do we map compound primary keys in Hibernate using JPA annotations? Well, when we run into compound primary keys, the Java developer is forced to create a separate, unique class that will represent the primary key combination. For the interest table, we will create a separate class called CompoundKey to manage the compound primary key.

```
package com.examscam.mappings;
import javax.persistence.Embeddable;
     /* First Iteration of the CompoundKey Class */
@Embeddable
public class CompoundKey implements
                              java.io.Serializable{
  private Long userId;
  private Long bankId;
  public CompoundKey() {}
  public CompoundKey(Long user, Long bank) {
    userId = user;
    bankId = bank;
  }

  public Long getBankId() {return bankId;}
  public void setBankId(Long bankId) {
    this.bankId = bankId;
  }
  public Long getUserId() {return userId;}
  public void setUserId(Long userId) {
    this.userId = userId;
  }
}
```

Basic Requirements of Compound Key Classes

There are a couple of quick notes that you should make about the CompoundKey class. First of all, the class is not decorated with the @Entity annotation, but instead, the class uses the @Embeddable annotation, emphasizing that this primary key class will actually be used by, or embedded into, another JPA annotated class that is responsible for defining the database table mappings.

The other important addition to the CompoundKey class is the implementation of the java.io.Serializable interface. All compound keys must implement this interface, otherwise, when Hibernate maps the compound key to the database, you'll get the following exception:

```
org.hibernate.MappingException:
composite-id class must implement Serializable
```

Primary Key Comparisons

Our CompoundKey class has a two argument constructor that allows you to create instances in the following manner:

```
CompoundKey key01 =
    new CompoundKey(new Long(1), new Long(2));
CompoundKey key02 =
    new CompoundKey(new Long(1), new Long(2));
```

Now, from looking at that code, are key01 and key02 equal to each other? Think about it from a Hibernate perspective; if we have two instances of the primary key class, perhaps generated by two separate Hibernate Sessions calling load or get, and both of them have the exact same values for userId and bankId, are those two instances logically and comparably the same?

Well, it's not really up for debate – two primary keys with two identical key values MUST BE EQUAL, but, as it stands right now, the **key01.equals(key02);** method call will return *false*, and that is disastrous to our Hibernate applications.

Comparing Instances with .equals(Object o)

In Hibernate, all compound primary key classes must override the .equals() and the .hashCode() methods inherited from the Object class. Actually, all Hibernate Entity classes should override .equals() and .hashCode() with their own, custom .equals() and .hashCode() methods so that the same persistent object loaded from separate Hibernate Sessions will equate to true. You see, when objects are created, they are given a unique memory location, and the default implementation of the .equals() method is to compare the memory locations of two instances. As a result, the following code generates an output of *false*.

```
CompoundKey key01 =
   new CompoundKey(new Long(1), new Long(2));
CompoundKey key02 =
   new CompoundKey(new Long(1), new Long(2));
boolean flag = key01.equals(key02):
System.out.println(flag);   // prints out false
```

However, we can override the default implementation of the .equals() method, and generate a boolean value based on the comparison of the various instance variables within the class. With this in mind, we can override the .equals() method of the CompoundKey class by returning a true value if the two instances being compared have the same value for the userId and bankId properties:

```
public boolean equals(Object key) {
  boolean result = true;
  if (!(key instanceof CompoundKey)) {return false;}
    Long otherUserId = ((CompoundKey)key).getUserId();
    Long otherBankId = ((CompoundKey)key).getBankId();
    if (bankId == null || otherBankId == null) {
      result = false;
    }else {
      result = bankId.equals(otherBankId);
    }
    if (userId == null || otherUserId == null) {
      result = false;
    }else {
      result = userId.equals(otherUserId);
    }
  return result;
}
```

Overriding .equals() and hashCode()

```
package com.examscam.mappings;import javax.persistence.Embeddable;
          /* Final Iteration of the CompoundKey Class */
@Embeddable
public class CompoundKey implements java.io.Serializable{
  private Long userId;  private Long bankId;
  public CompoundKey() { }
  public CompoundKey(Long user, Long bank) {
    userId = user;  bankId = bank;
  }
  public Long getBankId() {return bankId;}
  public void setBankId(Long bankId) {
    this.bankId = bankId;
  }
  public Long getUserId() {return userId;}
  public void setUserId(Long userId) {
    this.userId = userId;
  }

  public boolean equals(Object key) {
    boolean result = true;
    if (!(key instanceof CompoundKey)) {return false;}
    Long otherUserId = ((CompoundKey)key).getUserId();
    Long otherBankId = ((CompoundKey)key).getBankId();
    if (bankId == null || otherBankId == null) {
      result = false;
    }else {
      result = bankId.equals(otherBankId);
    }
    if (userId == null || otherUserId == null) {
      result = false;
    }else {
      result = userId.equals(otherUserId);
    }
   return result;
  }

  public int hashCode() {
    int code = 0;
    if (userId!=null) {code +=userId;}
    if (bankId!=null) {code +=bankId;}
    return code;
  }
}
```

Overriding the hashCode() Method

Any time you override the .equals() method, you must override the .hashCode() method in a way that ensures that two objects whose .equals() comparison generates a true result will also generate a common .hashCode() value.

I'm going to simply leverage the values of the userId and bankId properties as I override the hashCode() method. This is obviously an oversimplified implementation hashCode(), as it will produce duplicates for instances that have keys that add up to the same value, but for this very simplified example, it will suffice.

```
public int hashCode() {
    int code = 0;
    if (userId!=null) {code +=userId;}
    if (bankId!=null) {code +=bankId;}
    return code;
}
```

Once the .hashCode() and .equals() methods are properly implemented and overridden, the following code, which uses .equals() to compare two CompoundKey instances that share common attribute values, but are stored in different memory locations, will generate a boolean comparison result of *true*.

```
CompoundKey key01 =
    new CompoundKey(new Long(1), new Long(2));
CompoundKey key02 =
    new CompoundKey(new Long(1), new Long(2));
boolean flag = key01.equals(key02):
System.out.println(flag);  // now returns true!!!
```

Using the CompoundKey Class

So, once you have a primary key class that implements Serializable, is decorated with the @Embeddable tag, and has overridden the .equals() and the .hashCode() methods, you are ready to embed your compound key class within a JPA annotated entity class. For this example, we will create a class called Interest, with two properties, one of type double to represent an interest rate, and a property of type CompoundKey that we will name id. With the @Id annotation over the getter for the id field, our Interest class would look like this:

```
package com.examscam.mappings;
import javax.persistence.*; import org.hibernate.Session;
import com.examscam.HibernateUtil;
@Entity
public class Interest {

  private CompoundKey id;
  private double rate;

  @Id
  public CompoundKey getId() {return id;}
  public void setId(CompoundKey id) {this.id=id;}
  public double getRate() {return rate;}
  public void setRate(double rate) {this.rate=rate;}

  public static void main(String args[]) {
    Interest rate = new Interest();
    rate.setRate(18.5);

    Long wayne=new Long(99); Long mario=new Long(88);
    CompoundKey key = new CompoundKey(wayne, mario);
    rate.setId(key);

    HibernateUtil.recreateDatabase();
    Session session = HibernateUtil.beginTransaction();
    session.save(rate);
    HibernateUtil.commitTransaction();
  }
}
```

Running the Interest Class

Running the main method of the Interest class successfully adds a new record to the interest table, with the appropriate fields being initialized according to the code.

```
public static void main(String args[]) {
   Interest rate = new Interest();
   rate.setRate(18.5);

   Long wayne=new Long(99); Long mario=new Long(88);
   CompoundKey key = new CompoundKey(wayne, mario);
   rate.setId(key);

   HibernateUtil.recreateDatabase();
   Session session = HibernateUtil.beginTransaction();
   session.save(rate);
   HibernateUtil.commitTransaction();
}
```

bankId	userId	rate
88	99	18.5

Of course, to have Hibernate recognize the Interest class, it must be added to the AnnotationConfiguration object in the HibernateUtil class. Notice that the CompoundKey class does not need to be added. As the CompoundKey class is marked as being **@Embeddable**, only the embedding class, Interest, needs to be explicitly added to the AnnotationConfiguration object.

```
public static Configuration getInitializedConfiguration() {
   AnnotationConfiguration config =
                new AnnotationConfiguration();
   /* add all of your JPA annotated classes here!!! */
   config.addAnnotatedClass(Interest.class);
   config.configure();
   return config;
}
```

More Compound Key Mappings

Personally, I like the idea of implementing compound primary keys by simply creating a compound key class, marking it as being @Embeddable, and then creating an instance variable in the embedding class that simply gets marked with an @Id tag. To me, it's fairly simple, fairly straight forward, intuitive, and easy. However, there are alternatives, one of which is to use the @IdClass annotation in your persistent entity class, and then simply provide setters and getters for the properties defined in the primary key class.

Using the @IdClass JPA Annotation

With the @IdClass annotation, you simply point to the class implementing your compound primary key. The @IdClass is placed right after the @Entity tag, just before the class declaration. We'll create a new class called Fracture to demonstrate:

```
@Entity
@IdClass(com.examscam.mappings.CompoundKey.class)
public class Fracture {   }
```

With the @IdClass annotation, you don't declare an instance variable of type CompoundKey, but instead, just define instance variables for each of the primary key fields. You then mark the corresponding getter tags with standard @Id annotations.

```
@Entity
@IdClass(com.examscam.mappings.CompoundKey.class)
public class Fracture {
  Long bankId; Long userId; String bone;
  @Id
  public Long getBankId() {return bankId;}
  @Id
  public Long getUserId() {return userId;}
  public void setBankId(Long bankId){this.bankId = bankId;}
  public void setUserId(Long userId){this.userId = userId;}
  public String getBone() {return bone;}
  public void setBone(String bone) {this.bone = bone;}
}
```

The Compound Fracture: Using @IdClass

```
package com.examscam.mappings;

import javax.persistence.Entity;
import javax.persistence.Id;
import javax.persistence.IdClass;
import org.hibernate.Session;
import com.examscam.HibernateUtil;

@Entity
@IdClass(com.examscam.mappings.CompoundKey.class)
public class Fracture {
  Long bankId; Long userId; String bone;

  @Id
  public Long getBankId() {return bankId;}

  @Id
  public Long getUserId() {return userId;}
  public void setBankId(Long bankId){this.bankId = bankId;}
  public void setUserId(Long userId){this.userId = userId;}
  public String getBone() {return bone;}
  public void setBone(String bone) {this.bone = bone;}

  public static void main(String args[]) {
    Fracture bone = new Fracture();
    bone.setBone("arm");
    bone.setBankId( new Long(99));
    bone.setUserId(new Long(88));
    HibernateUtil.recreateDatabase();
    Session session=HibernateUtil.beginTransaction();
    session.save(bone);
    HibernateUtil.commitTransaction();
  }

}
```

Running the main Method

Running the main method of the Fracture class successfully gets the Hibernate framework to write a record to the Fracture table, with the appropriate key fields populated.

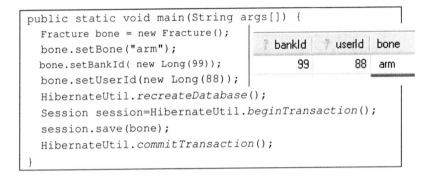

```
public static void main(String args[]) {
  Fracture bone = new Fracture();
  bone.setBone("arm");
  bone.setBankId( new Long(99));
  bone.setUserId(new Long(88));
  HibernateUtil.recreateDatabase();
  Session session=HibernateUtil.beginTransaction();
  session.save(bone);
  HibernateUtil.commitTransaction();
}
```

bankId	userId	bone
99	88	arm

Making Sure HibernateUtil is Updated

As we run these main methods that test the Fracture and the Interest classes, we must remember that all classes marked with the @Entity tag must be added to the AnnotationConfiguration object. The getInitializedConfiguration() method of the HibernateUtil class is where we typically perform this initialization.

```
public static Configuration getInitializedConfiguration() {
    AnnotationConfiguration config =
                new AnnotationConfiguration();
    /* add all of your JPA annotated classes here!!! */
    //config.addAnnotatedClass(ClientDetail.class);
    //config.addAnnotatedClass(Address.class);
    //config.addAnnotatedClass(Skill.class);
    config.addAnnotatedClass(Interest.class);
    config.addAnnotatedClass(Fracture.class);
    config.configure();
    return config;
}
```

The @EmbeddedId JPA Annotation

The third way I know of managing a compound primary key, and perhaps the easiest, is through the @EmbeddedId annotation. With the compound primary key class properly implemented, all you have to do in your persistent entity class is declare an instance variable in the type of your compound primary key class, and then mark the getter for the id field with the @EmbeddedId tag. Here's how it looks with the Prison class:

The Prison Compound: Using @EmbeddedId

```
package com.examscam.mappings;
import javax.persistence.EmbeddedId;
import javax.persistence.Entity;
import org.hibernate.Session;
import com.examscam.HibernateUtil;

@Entity
public class Prison {
  private String city;
  private CompoundKey id;

  public String getCity() {return city;}
  public void setCity(String city) {this.city=city;}

  @EmbeddedId
  public CompoundKey getId() {return id;}
  public void setId(CompoundKey id) {this.id = id;}

  public static void main(String args[]) {
    Prison jail = new Prison();
    jail.setCity("Milhaven");
    Long wayne = new Long(99);
    Long mario = new Long(88);
    CompoundKey key = new CompoundKey(wayne, mario);
    jail.setId(key);
    HibernateUtil.recreateDatabase();
    Session session = HibernateUtil.beginTransaction();
    session.save(jail);
    HibernateUtil.commitTransaction();
  }
}
```

Running the Prison Class

After adding the Prison.class to the AnnotationConfiguration in the HibernateUtil class, the main method can be executed, and as we would expect, the prison table in the database, which contains a compound primary key, is updated successfully.

```
public static void main(String args[]) {

    Prison jail = new Prison();
    jail.setCity("Milhaven");
    Long wayne = new Long(99);
    Long mario = new Long(88);

    CompoundKey key = new CompoundKey(wayne, mario);
    jail.setId(key);

    HibernateUtil.recreateDatabase();
    Session session = HibernateUtil.beginTransaction();
    session.save(jail);
    HibernateUtil.commitTransaction();
}
```

bankId	userId	city
88	99	Milhaven

Chapter 16
Mapping Inheritance

In no other place in J2EE development does the divide between application design and database persistence become quite so pronounced as it does when we attempt to map an inheritance hierarchy to a relational database. Inheritance mapping is a difficult thing to do, because databases don't really have any concept that is equivalent to inheritance, while at the same time, inheritance is a central part of every object-oriented domain model.

There are a number of different ways to map inheritance hierarchies to a database, with some options being better than others, and each option having its own set of drawbacks.

This chapter will explore and contrast the three key mechanisms for mapping an object-oriented, inheritance hierarchy, into a relational database and its tables. The three mapping strategies that we will explore will include:

☞ *One table per class Inheritance Mapping*

☞ *Inheritance mapping through joined tables*

☞ *The default, single table inheritance mapping*

The Inheritance Model

To demonstrate inheritance mapping, I'm going to use a very simple hierarchy of three classes, with the Ancestor class being at the top, the Parent class being in the middle, and the Child class being at the bottom.

The Ancestor-Parent-Child Class Diagram

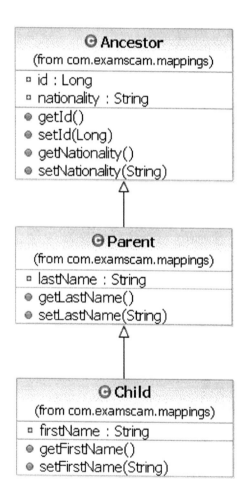

The Ancestor class will declare a property of type id, along with a nationality property of type String:

```
package com.examscam.mappings; import javax.persistence.*;
@Entity
public class Ancestor {
  private Long id;
  private String nationality;
  @Id
  @GeneratedValue
  public Long getId() {return id;}
  public void setId(Long id) {this.id = id;}
  public String getNationality() {return nationality;}
  public void setNationality(String nationality) {
    this.nationality = nationality;
  }
}
```

The Parent class inherits all of the properties of the Ancestor, and declares a new String property called lastName:

```
package com.examscam.mappings;import javax.persistence.*;
@Entity
public class Parent extends Ancestor{
  private String lastName;
  public String getLastName() {return lastName;}
  public void setLastName(String lastName) {
        this.lastName = lastName;
  }
}
```

The Child class will extend the Parent class, thus inheriting all of the properties defined in both the Parent and Ancestor classes. Furthermore, the Child class will declare one new String property called firstName:

```
package com.examscam.mappings;import javax.persistence.*;
@Entity
public class Child extends Parent {
  private String firstName;
  public String getFirstName() {return firstName;}
  public void setFirstName(String firstName) {
    this.firstName = firstName;
  }
}
```

Inheritance Strategies

Hibernate provides three separate options for mapping inheritance hierarchies:

☞ *TABLE_PER_CLASS*

☞ *JOINED*

☞ *SINGLE_TABLE (default)*

```
«Java Enum»
🅔 InheritanceType
(from javax.persistence)
📭 JOINED
📭 SINGLE_TABLE
📭 TABLE_PER_CLASS
```

To specify a strategy, you simply place the @Inheritance annotation after the @Entity tag on the class at the top of your class hierarchy, which in this case, would be the Ancestor class. From there, you specify the strategy attribute, which can be set to any one of the three values the InheritanceType enum can take. So, to specify a TABLE_PER_CLASS inheritance strategy, the Ancestor class declaration would look like this:

```
@Entity
@Inheritance(strategy=InheritanceType.TABLE_PER_CLASS)
public class Ancestor {   ✂✂✂   }
```

Using the TABLE_PER_CLASS inheritance strategy, Hibernate expects three separate tables to be defined in the database, with each table containing the aggregate of all of the declared *and* inherited properties of the associated class. As a result, the ancestor table would only have two properties, namely the id and nationality fields, whereas the child table duplicates these properties, adds in columns for the Parent's lastName property, and then adds fields for the locally declared firstName.

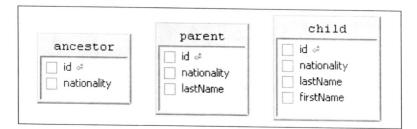

Joined Table Inheritance

One of the ugly aspects of the TABLE_PER_CLASS inheritance type is the fact that properties get duplicated down the class hierarchy. For example, why should the child table declare columns of type id and nationality when they are already defined in the ancestor table? The JOINED inheritance type addresses this problem by having tables only maintain data that maps directly to the properties in the associated class. Subclasses are then linked to their inherited properties through common primary key fields in the tables, linking as UNION joins at runtime.

To use a JOIN for mapping inheritance, all we have to do is edit the @Inheritance annotation of the Ancestor class, and set the strategy attribute to InheritanceType.JOINED:

```
@Entity
@Inheritance(strategy=InheritanceType.JOINED)
public class Ancestor {   }
```

When using a JOINED strategy for our problem domain, Hibernate expects three database tables, with each table mapping to the various properties defined in each class. The id field then forms a union between tables. So, if an Ancestor instance is saved, a record will be created in only the ancestor table, whereas if a Child instance is created, the fields of the instance will be saved in all three tables, with the records in each table associated, or joined, through a common value for the id field. In essence, the class hierarchy of an instance is JOINED together from all of the individual tables.

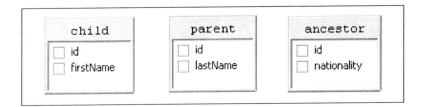

The Single Table Inheritance Strategy

So, one of the problems with the TABLE_PER_CLASS inheritance strategy was that sub-classes re-defined properties in their corresponding database tables that were already defined in tables that mapped to parent classes. The JOINED table strategy addresses this deficiency by having the database tables that map to classes only define columns that map to properties for that particular class. A join between the primary key column of tables making up an object's class hierarchy makes it possible to re-create a given entity at runtime. However, the JOINED strategy does have its own set of problems, not the least of which is its inefficiency.

Imagine you wanted to get a list of all of the Child objects? In that case, the database would have to issue a select * statement against the child, parent *and* ancestor tables, as properties of a Child instance are spread out over all three tables. This isn't an efficient process at all. Furthermore, three classes tightly joined together by a common primary key, mapped between tables with a one-to-one relationship, could just as easily be flattened out into a single table without any complex primary key joins at all. That is exactly what the third, and often preferential method for mapping class hierarchies, utilizes. The third and final strategy for mapping inheritance is the SINGLE_TABLE strategy.

For our problem domain, in order to use the SINGLE_TABLE strategy, we must change the *strategy* attribute of the @Inheritance annotation to the value of *InheritanceType.SINGLE_TABLE.* With this inheritance strategy, all of the properties on the entire class hierarchy are defined in a single table, along with an extra field, named DTYPE, that keeps track of the Java class type associated with the given record.

ancestor
☐ DTYPE
☐ id
☐ nationality
☐ lastName
☐ firstName

```
@Entity
@Inheritance(strategy=InheritanceType.SINGLE_TABLE)
public class Ancestor {  ✄✄✄  }
```

Benefits of the Single Table Inheritance Type

The single table inheritance type is often the best choice for performing inheritance mapping. First of all, it minimizes the number of tables that need to be queried, which can be significant for large class hierarchies. Furthermore, mapping associations can be very difficult with other strategies. For example, imagine we were using a single class per table strategy, and we decided an Ancestor could be associated in a one to one manner with another type, say a Location type. Since this relationship would be true for all subclasses, and given the fact that associations are implemented at the database level by foreign keys, we would have to add a new foreign key column to every table that was based on a sub-class of Ancestor. In a large class hierarchy, adding those foreign key fields would be extremely onerous. On the other hand, with the single table inheritance strategy, only one column would need to be added to one table, which would be a much, much simpler process.

Testing the InheritanceType.*SINGLE_TABLE*

Here's a little main method you can use to test the single table inheritance type with the Ancestor, Parent and Child classes:

```
public static void main(String args[]) {
  Ancestor a = new Ancestor();
  a.setNationality("Korean");

  Parent p = new Parent();
  p.setNationality("Jewish");  p.setLastName("Steinberg");

  Child c = new Child();
  c.setNationality("Irish");
  c.setLastName("McKenzie");
  c.setFirstName("Cameron");

  Session session = HibernateUtil.beginTransaction();
  session.save(a); session.save(p); session.save(c);
  HibernateUtil.commitTransaction();
}    /* make sure you import com.examscam.HibernateUtil; */
```

Saving an Inheritance Hierarchy

When we run the main method that saves an instance of an Ancestor, Parent and Child class, we see the following output in the Hibernate log files:

```
Hibernate: insert into Ancestor (nationality, DTYPE)
values (?, 'Ancestor')

Hibernate: insert into Ancestor (nationality,
lastName, DTYPE) values (?, ?, 'Parent')

Hibernate: insert into Ancestor (nationality,
lastName, firstName, DTYPE) values (?, ?, ?, 'Child')
```

As you can see, each record gets saved into the table named after the top of the class hierarchy, which in this case is Ancestor. However, in the actually SQL, Hibernate hard-codes the class type, be it Ancestor, Parent or Child, into the SQL statement, so that the DTYPE field can be used to positively identify the Java type the given records is associated with. So, to get all records associated with the Ancestor class, you would perform a single query against the Ancestor table for records where the DTYPE is Ancestor, Parent or Child, as all share an is-a relationship with the Ancestor class. On the other hand, to find all records associated with Child instances, Hibernate would simply query the Ancestor table for records where the DTYPE is set to Child. Overall, this data access strategy tends to be fairly simple, fairly efficient, and the most manageable.

Looking at the database after running our main method, we can see three records, all differentiated by the DTYPE column, as being associated with either the Ancestor, Child or Parent class.

DTYPE	id	nationality	lastName	firstName
Ancestor	1	Korean	NULL	NULL
Parent	2	Jewish	Steinberg	NULL
Child	3	Irish	McKenzie	Cameron

Chapter 17

Mapping Associations: One to One

On a few of my websites, I provide some online, multiple choice exams to help people test their portal skills, or Java skills, hopefully helping people evaluate whether or not they're ready to write an IBM or Sun certification exam. I have a few different exams that people can take, so a very regular request from my application is a listing of all of the exams that I've made available. That triggers a quick query against the Exam table in my database.

Less frequently requested, but equally important, is detailed information on a particular exam, namely, information about the number of question on an exam, the passing score, and even the full, official, name of the exam. These pieces of information are stored in a separate database table that is queried much less frequently, and as such, the table is optimized accordingly.

In my online exam application, my *class to database table mapping* is pretty direct, with a class named Exam mapping to the exam table, and a class named ExamDetail mapping to the exam_detail table.

In this chapter, my goal is to use the Exam and ExamDetail classes as an example, and demonstrate how to map a one to one association between Java classes using Hibernate and JPA annotations, just as I have done on my own websites that provide free, online, mock certification exams.

One to One Hibernate Mappings

By the way, in an earlier chapter, we mapped a philosophically similar one to one mapping between a User and a UserDetail. You may be asking yourself how the Exam and the ExamDetail scenario is different from the User and the UserDetail scenario. Well, if you recall, the User and UserDetail had all of their fields assembled into one, single, monolithic table named User. However, I'm actually not a huge fan of that type of branching, so for the **Exam** and the **ExamDetail**, I'm going to map the Java classes to *two independent tables* in the examscam database named ***exam*** and ***exam_detail.***

The ExamDetail Class

The ExamDetail class is fairly anemic, simply maintaining extra information about an exam. The properties of the ExamDetail class include an id of type int, an int property to keep track of the number of questions on the exam, and an int property that tells you what the passing score is for the exam. There is also a String property named fullName to keep track of the actual, full name of the exam. For example, SCJA is the short name for the entry level Java certification exam from Sun, whereas the full name is "Sun Certified Java Associate."

The Exam Class

The Exam class isn't necessarily chock full of properties either, with a simple id of type int to maintain the primary key, and a String property called shortName to keep track of the abbreviated description of the exam. However, each Exam instance must keep track of its associated ExamDetail instance, so the Exam class defines a property of type ExamDetail, simply named detail. The ExamDetail instance defined in the Exam class also comes with the requisite setters and getters.

Also, since the Exam maintains a reference to the ExamDetail, we call this a unidirectional association, as the Exam knows about its associated detail, but the detail does not have any knowledge of its encapsulating exam.

⊖ Exam	⊖ ExamDetail
▫ id : int	▫ id : int
▫ shortName : String	▫ fullName : String
▫ detail : ExamDetail	▫ numberOfQuestions : int
◉ getId ( )	▫ passingPercentage : int
▣ setId ( )	◉ getId ( )
◉ «Basic» getShortName ( )	▣ setId ( )
◉ setShortName ( )	◉ getFullName ( )
◉ getDetail ( )	◉ setFullName ( )
◉ setDetail ( )	◉ getNumberOfQuestions ( )
	◉ setNumberOfQuestions ( )

Unidirectional Association: Exam has an ExamDetail

1

◉ getPassingPercentage ( )
◉ setPassingPercentage ( )

The Un-Annotated Exam

```
package com.examscam.hib.exam;

public class Exam {

  private int id;
  private String shortName;
  private ExamDetail detail;

  public int getId() {
    return id;
  }
  private void setId(int id) {
    this.id = id;
  }
  public String getShortName() {
    return shortName;
  }
  public void setShortName(String shortName) {
    this.shortName = shortName;
  }

  /* Notice that the Exam maintains an instance
          of the ExamDetail class. */

  public ExamDetail getDetail() {
    return detail;
  }
  public void setDetail(ExamDetail detail) {
    this.detail = detail;
  }

}
```

Exam
- id : int
- shortName : String
- detail : ExamDetail
- getId ( )
- setId ( )
- getShortName ( )
- setShortName ( )
- getDetail ( )
- setDetail ( )

The Un-Annotated ExamDetail Class

```java
package com.examscam.hib.exam;

public class ExamDetail {
 private int id;
 private String fullName;
 private int numberOfQuestions;
 private int passingPercentage;

  public int getId() {
    return id;
  }
  private void setId(int id){
    this.id = id;
  }
  public String getFullName() {
    return fullName;
  }
  public void setFullName(String fullName) {
    this.fullName = fullName;
  }
  public int getNumberOfQuestions() {
    return numberOfQuestions;
  }
  public void setNumberOfQuestions(int numberOfQuestions) {
    this.numberOfQuestions = numberOfQuestions;
  }
  public int getPassingPercentage() {
    return passingPercentage;
  }
  public void setPassingPercentage(int passingPercentage) {
    this.passingPercentage = passingPercentage;
  }
}
```

UML class diagram box:

ExamDetail
- id : int
- fullName : String
- numberOfQuestions : int
- passingPercentage : int
- getId ( )
- setId ( )
- getFullName ( )
- setFullName ( )
- getNumberOfQuestions ( )
- setNumberOfQuestions ( )
- getPassingPercentage ( )
- setPassingPercentage ( )

New Tables: exam and exam_detail

So, we have defined two classes, the Exam and the ExamDetail classes, with the Exam class maintaining a reference to the ExamDetail class through an instance variable that is very uncreatively named *detail*. Now, the goal of this chapter is to map these two associated classes to two database tables named exam and exam_detail. Here's the ddl for the exam and the exam_detail tables if you'd like to create them from scratch.

exam table ddl

```
CREATE TABLE `examscam`.`exam` (
  `id` int(11) NOT NULL auto_increment,
  `shortName` varchar(255) default NULL,
  `detail_id` int(11) default NULL,
  PRIMARY KEY (`id`),
  KEY `FK2FB81FB83A97F5` (`detail_id`),
  CONSTRAINT `FK2FB81FB83A97F5` FOREIGN KEY (`detail_id`)
REFERENCES `exam_detail` (`id`)
)
```

exam_detail table ddl

```
DROP TABLE IF EXISTS `examscam`.`exam_detail`;
CREATE TABLE `examscam`.`exam_detail` (
  `id` int(11) NOT NULL auto_increment,
  `fullName` varchar(255) default NULL,
  `numberOfQuestions` int(11) NOT NULL default '0',
  `passingPercentage` int(11) NOT NULL default '0',
  PRIMARY KEY (`id`)
)
```

Entity Mappings: The Basics

We need to add the appropriate JPA annotations to properly describe the mapping between our Java classes to Hibernate and the underlying database tables. Starting off, our Java classes require the standard @Entity, @Table and @Id annotations that describe their basic database mapping semantics. Note that the ExamDetail class is mapped to a table named exam_detail.

```
✂✂✂
@Entity
@Table(name = "exam", schema = "examscam")
public class Exam {
✂✂✂
```

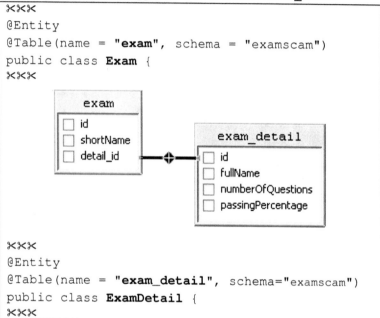

```
✂✂✂
@Entity
@Table(name = "exam_detail", schema="examscam")
public class ExamDetail {
✂✂✂
```

Annotating the getId() Methods

Remember that both classes need the getId() method to be decorated with the appropriate JPA annotations, as below:

```
/* this will be identical for the getId() method in
    BOTH the Exam and ExamDetail classes*/
✂✂✂
@Id
@GeneratedValue
@Column(name = "id")
public int getId() {return id;}   ✂✂✂
```

The @OneToOne JPA Annotation

We have defined a unidirectional association between the Exam and the ExamDetail object by declaring an instance variable of type ExamDetail, named detail, in the Exam class. To tell Hibernate about this association, we mark the getter method, getDetail(), with the special @OneToOne annotation.

```
@OneToOne
public ExamDetail getDetail(){ return detail; }
```

The @OneToOne annotation essentially tells Hibernate to enforce the assertion that one Exam object is associated with one, and only one, ExamDetail object.

Mapping the Foreign Key

Now, in order to map and manage the @OneToOne relationship between database tables, Hibernate expects the table for which the enclosing class is mapped, which in this case is the Exam, to have a foreign key that maps to a primary key in the enclosed table, which in this case would be the ExamDetail class, which maps to the exam_detail table.

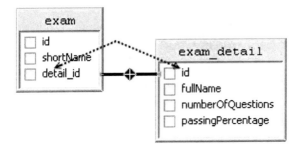

The @JoinColumn Annotation

Something to note is that by default, Hibernate uses the name of the instance variable in the enclosing class when looking for a mapped foreign key to the enclosed class. So, even though the enclosed instance in the Exam class is of type ExamDetail, the instance is simply *named* detail, which causes Hibernate to look for a foreign key in the Exam table which will be named **detail_id**, as opposed to examdetail_id. Note, that *there is no property in the Exam Java class called detail_id* – detail_id only exists in the exam table in the database as a foreign key, not in the object model.

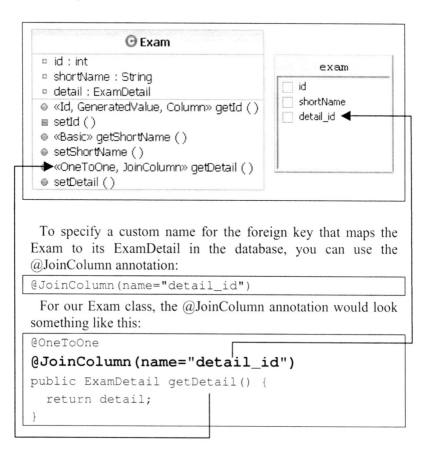

To specify a custom name for the foreign key that maps the Exam to its ExamDetail in the database, you can use the @JoinColumn annotation:

```
@JoinColumn(name="detail_id")
```

For our Exam class, the @JoinColumn annotation would look something like this:

```
@OneToOne
@JoinColumn(name="detail_id")
public ExamDetail getDetail() {
    return detail;
}
```

Saving a @OneToMany Mapped Record

So, let's say you've created your Exam and ExamDetail POJOs, and you've added the @OneToMany annotation to the getExamDetail() method of the Exam class. How would you go about saving an instance of your Exam class? Well, first off, you would create and initialize an instance of the Exam:

```
Exam exam = new Exam();
exam.setShortName("SCJA");
```

Then, you would create and initialize an instance of the ExamDetail class:

```
ExamDetail detail = new ExamDetail();
detail.setFullName("Sun Certified Associate");
detail.setNumberOfQuestions(50);
detail.setPassingPercentage(60);
```

Then, you need to associate the ExamDetail instance with the Exam, so the instance of the ExamDetail is passed to the setDetail() method of the exam.

```
exam.setDetail(detail);
```

This would successfully create an instance of an Exam, along with an ExamDetail instance that is associated with the Exam.

☉ Exam	☉ ExamDetail
◻ id : int	◻ id : int
◻ shortName : String	◻ fullName : String
◻ detail : ExamDetail	◻ numberOfQuestions : int
◉ getId ( )	◻ passingPercentage : int
▣ setId ( )	◉ getId ( )
◉ «Basic» getShortName ( )	▣ setId ( )
◉ setShortName ( )	◉ getFullName ( )
◉ getDetail ( )	◉ setFullName ( )
◉ setDetail ( )	◉ getNumberOfQuestions ( )
	◉ setNumberOfQuestions ( )
Unidirectional Association:	◉ getPassingPercentage ( )
Exam has an ExamDetail	◉ setPassingPercentage ( )

With "1" label between the two class boxes.

Saving Associated Objects with Hibernate

So, now you've got the Exam and ExamDetail instances initialized appropriately, and you have the ExamDetail instance associated with the Exam. Assuming you've gone through all the plumbing code to appropriately initialize the Hibernate Session, how would you save your data? Well, you have two JPA annotated instances floating around, and as such, both must touch the Hibernate Session. So, to properly save the instance of the Exam, and the associated instance of the ExamDetail, your code would look like this:

Saving the Exam and the ExamDetail

```
session.save(exam);
session.save(detail);
```

A Common Mistake with Default Settings

A common mistake when persisting entities to the database, when default settings are in effect, is to assume that since you are persisting the enclos**ing** entity by passing it to the save method of the Hibernate Session, that all of the enclos**ed** or associated entities will be persisted as well. This is not the case. Since both the ExamDetail and Exam are separately defined JPA annotated Java classes, the ***default behavior*** of Hibernate is to require all instances to *touch* the Hibernate Session at some point in order to have their state persisted to the database. Failure to do so will generate a TransientObjectException, and a little message such as ***"object references an unsaved transient instance."***

Of course, if your application has associated entities, you'd probably *like* the ability to pass an enclosing entity, such as an instance of the Exam class, to the save method of the Hibernate Session, and have all of the associated entities persisted as well. To do this, all you have to do is provide a cascade attribute to the @OneToOne annotation, and set the cascade attribute to one of the five CascadeType values.

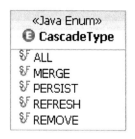

```
«Java Enum»
  CascadeType

  ALL
  MERGE
  PERSIST
  REFRESH
  REMOVE
```

The JPA CascadeType Enumeration

When we decorate our Java code with the @OneToOne annotation, we really should put in a special attribute named cascade, and explicitly set it to at least one of the five possible CascadeType values.

For example, if we wanted **session.save(exam);** to save not only the properties of the exam instance, but also the properties of all of the associated mapped instances, which would include the associated ExamDetail, we could use the cascade setting of CascadeType.PERSIST.

```
@OneToOne(cascade=CascadeType.PERSIST)
@JoinColumn(name="detail_id")
public ExamDetail getDetail() {return detail;}
```

CascadeType.PERSIST

So, with the getDetail() method of the Exam class annotated with the cascade attribute being set to CascadeType.PERSIST, whenever the Hibernate framework saves an exam, all of the associated ExamDetail data will be persisted as well. But be warned, that only works for saving – it doesn't help you out with refreshes, deletes and merges. There are other CascadeType options for that. ☺

The javax.persistence.CascadeType Enum

The CascadeType is an enumeration type that defines five possible states:

```
public enum CascadeType{
    ALL,
        PERSIST,
            MERGE,
                REMOVE,
                    REFRESH
}
```

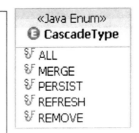

javax.persistence.CascadeType.REMOVE

Setting the cascade attribute on the @OneToOne annotation to CascadeType.PERSIST helps you out during the creation of a database record, but it doesn't cover you when you want to delete a record. If, when you delete an record in the Exam table, you also want to delete the associated ExamDetail record, well, you have to add another CascadeType option to your annotation. The CascadeType associated with a deletion is appropriately named CascadeType.REMOVE.

```
@OneToOne(cascade={CascadeType.PERSIST,
                   CascadeType.REMOVE})
@JoinColumn(name="detail_id")
public ExamDetail getDetail() {return detail;}
```

With a setting of CascadeType.REMOVE set on the getDetail() method in the Exam class, when an Exam record is deleted from the database, the associated ExamDetail record will be deleted as well.

javax.persistence.CascadeType.REFRESH

Along with cascading the persistence and removal functions, you can also ensure that an associated, or linked property, is *refreshed* at the same time the associating object is refreshed. To ensure that our ExamDetail is refreshed from the database every time our Exam is refreshed, we can add the CascadeType.REFRESH attribute to the @OneToOne annotation.

```
@OneToOne(cascade={CascadeType.PERSIST,
                   CascadeType.REMOVE,
                   CascadeType.REFRESH})
@JoinColumn(name="detail_id")
public ExamDetail getDetail() {return detail;}
```

Updating: The JPA CascadeType.MERGE

For reassociating a detached object with the Hibernate Session, there is the CascadeType.MERGE setting you can place on your @OneToOne relationships. Basically, the MERGE option ensures that when an encapsulating instance, such as the Exam, is reattached to its persistent storage, any changes or updates to the encapsulated class, which would be the ExamDetail, would be merged as well.

```
@OneToOne(cascade={CascadeType.PERSIST,
                   CascadeType.REMOVE,
                   CascadeType.REFRESH,
                   CascadeType.MERGE})
@JoinColumn(name="detail_id")
public ExamDetail getDetail() {return detail;}
```

javax.persistence.CascadeType.All

Finally, if you want to take advantage of all of the PERSIST, REMOVE, REFRESH and MERGE cascade options, you can eliminate alot of code by simply adding in the ALL option for the CascadeType. In fact, CascadeType.ALL is probably the most commonly used type in a Hibernate/JPA based application.

```
@OneToOne(cascade={CascadeType.ALL)
@JoinColumn(name="detail_id")
public ExamDetail getDetail() {return detail;}
```

The FetchType and Lazy Loading

Another important attribute you can set for an association is the fetch attribute, which determines how an associated property is loaded. The fetch attribute can be set to one of two values, *FetchType.LAZY* or *FetchType.EAGER.*

Essentially, if the FetchType is set to EAGER, when an encapsulating object is loaded, all of the EAGERly associated objects will be loaded into memory as well. When the FetchType is set to LAZY, when an encapsulating object is loaded, only the attributes defined directly in the class itself are loaded into memory, and any properties mapped through LAZY associations will *not* be loaded into memory until they are explicitly requested; essentially, the associated properties will be detached.

Default Fetch Settings

For performance reasons, it's always preferential to minimize the load placed on a system's memory. As such, most associations are set to a FetchType of LAZY. This is especially true for **one to many** and **many to many** relationships, where the impact of loading a large number of associated properties can be significant.

For one-to-many and many-to-many relationships, the default FetchType is LAZY. However, *for one-to-one mappings, the default is EAGER,* meaning that a class, and all of its one-to-one associations, are loaded into memory when it is invoked by the client. If this is not the behavior you want, you can set the FetchType to LAZY in your @OneToOne annotations.

```
@OneToOne(cascade=CascadeType.ALL,
                         fetch=FetchType.LAZY)
@JoinColumn(name="detail_id")
public ExamDetail getDetail() {
   return detail;
}
```

The @OneToOne Owned Entity

In our application, the Exam is considered the own**ing** entity, and the ExamDetail is considered the own**ed** entity.

Our Exam class keeps track of its associated ExamDetail through the definition of an instance variable. From a database perspective, this association manifests itself as a foreign key named detail_id in the exam table.

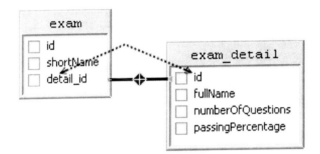

Unidirectional vs. Bi-Directional Associations

From the standpoint of our Java code so far, the Exam and the ExamDetail have a uni-directional relationship, where the Exam knows about its associated ExamDetail, but an ExamDetail does not know about its associated Exam. But what if this uni-directional relationship wasn't enough?

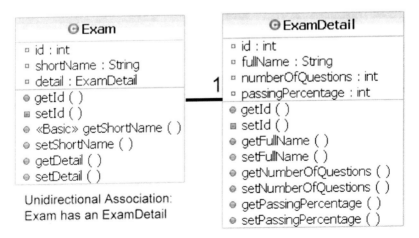

Implementing Bi-Directional Relationships

To implement a bi-directional relationship between the Exam and the ExamDetail, we simply add an instance variable of type Exam, along with the corresponding setters and getters, in the ExamDetail class, and then decorate that getExam() method with the @OneToOne annotation, using a special *mappedBy* attribute to link the enclosed class back to the instance variable used to link to it in the enclosing class. So, since the Exam class defines an instance variable of type ExamDetail named *detail*, the ExamDetail's @OneToOne annotation would include a mappedBy attribute set to *detail*.

Here's how it would look in code:

```
public class ExamDetail { XXX  XXX
/* an instance variable of type Exam is needed  */
  private Exam exam;

/*detail is the instance variable name in the Exam */

  @OneToOne(mappedBy="detail", cascade=CascadeType.ALL)
  public Exam getExam(){return exam;}
  public void setExam(Exam exam){this.exam=exam;}
XXX
}
```

The Fully Annotated Exam Class

```
package com.examscam.hib.exam;
import javax.persistence.Basic; import javax.persistence.CascadeType;
import javax.persistence.Column; import javax.persistence.Entity;
import javax.persistence.FetchType; import javax.persistence.GeneratedValue;
import javax.persistence.Id; import javax.persistence.JoinColumn;
import javax.persistence.OneToOne; import javax.persistence.Table;


@Entity
@Table(name = "exam", schema = "examscam")
public class Exam {
/* @Basic annotation has been added to all basic fields*/
  private int id;
  private String shortName;

  private ExamDetail detail;

  @Id
  @GeneratedValue
  @Column(name = "id")
  public int getId() { return id; }
  private void setId(int id) {this.id = id;}

  @OneToOne(cascade=CascadeType.ALL, fetch=FetchType.LAZY)
  @JoinColumn(name="detail_id")
  public ExamDetail getDetail() {return detail; }
  public void setDetail(ExamDetail detail) {
    this.detail = detail;
  }

  @Basic
  public String getShortName() { return shortName; }
  public void setShortName(String shortName) {
    this.shortName = shortName;
  }
}
```

The Fully Annotated ExamDetail Class

```
package com.examscam.hib.exam;
import javax.persistence.Basic;import javax.persistence.CascadeType;
import javax.persistence.Column;import javax.persistence.Entity;
import javax.persistence.GeneratedValue;import javax.persistence.Id;
import javax.persistence.OneToOne;import javax.persistence.Table;

@Entity
@Table(name = "exam_detail", schema = "examscam")
public class ExamDetail {
/* @Basic annotation has been added to all basic fields*/
  private int id;
  private String fullName;
  private int numberOfQuestions;
  private int passingPercentage;
  private Exam exam;

  @Id
  @GeneratedValue
  @Column(name = "id")
  public int getId() {return id;}
  private void setId(int id) {this.id = id;}

  @OneToOne(cascade=CascadeType.ALL, mappedBy="detail")
  public Exam getExam(){return exam;}
  public void setExam(Exam exam){this.exam=exam;}

  @Basic
  public String getFullName() {return fullName;}
  public void setFullName(String fullName) {
    this.fullName = fullName;
  }

  @Basic
  public int getNumberOfQuestions() {return numberOfQuestions;}
  public void setNumberOfQuestions(int numberOfQuestions) {
    this.numberOfQuestions = numberOfQuestions;
  }

  @Basic
  public int getPassingPercentage() {return passingPercentage;}
  public void setPassingPercentage(int passingPercentage) {
    this.passingPercentage = passingPercentage;
  }
}
```

Testing the Exam & ExamDetail

Let's take a final look at how instances of the bi-directionally related Exam and ExamDetail classes could be created in a Java application, and subsequently persisted to the database:

Notice that the last iteration of the Exam and ExamDetail classes changed the CascadeType to CascadeType.**ALL**. With a CascadeType of ALL, when an instance of the Exam class is saved to the database, the associated ExamDetail will be persisted as well.

```
public static void main(String args[]){
  HibernateUtil.recreateDatabase();
  Exam exam = new Exam();
  exam.setShortName("SCJA");

  ExamDetail detail = new ExamDetail();
  detail.setFullName("Sun Certified Java Associate");
  detail.setPassingPercentage(62);
  detail.setNumberOfQuestions(55);
  exam.setDetail(detail);

  Session session = HibernateUtil.beginTransaction();
  //possible due to CascadeType.ALL
  session.save(exam);
  HibernateUtil.commitTransaction();
}   /* make sure this class imports com.examscam.HibernateUtil */
```

As you can see from a quick inspection of the database after running this code, the exam and exam_detail tables have been populated appropriately, as the detail_id column of the exam table points to the corresponding record in the exam_detail table.

exam

id	shortName	detail_id
1	SCJA	1

exam_detail

id	fullName	numberOfQuestions	passingPercentage
1	Sun Certified Java Associate	55	62

333

Class Diagram for Exam and ExamDetail

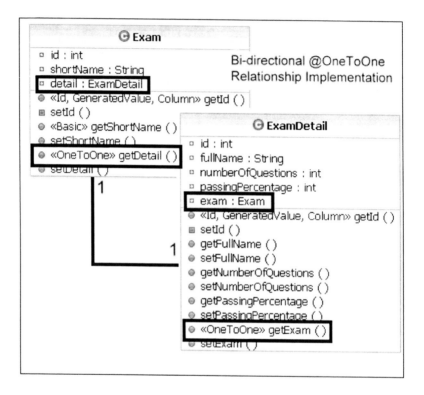

ERD for Exam and ExamDetail Tables (Again)

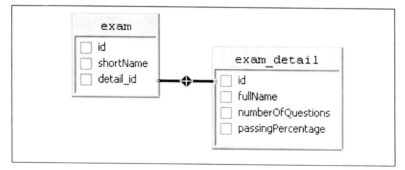

Chapter 18: Mapping One-to-Many Associations

Chapter 18
One to Many Associations

Of all the mappings you're going to see in a Java application, a one to many mapping has to be the most common. Just think about it: an Order has many LineItems; a Bank has many BankAccounts; a Record has many Songs; an Exam has many Questions. The one to many association really has to be the most common multiplicity we see in our Java apps.

For this chapter, I'm going to model the idea that a Team has many Players. So, given a team, you will be able to obtain a List of the Players that are associated with that Team. Furthermore, given a Player, you can find out with which Team that Player is associated. I guess you could say that it's a bi-directional relationship, as the Player is navigable through the Team object, and the Team is navigable through the Player.

«Java Class, Entity»	«Java Class, Entity»
Team	**Player**
△ id : long	△ id : long
△ name : String	△ team : Team
△ players : List<Player>	△ nickName : String
● «Id, GeneratedValue» getId ( )	● getNickName ( )
● setId ( )	● setNickName ( )
● getName ( )	● «ManyToOne, JoinColumn» getTeam ( )
● setName ( )	● setTeam ( )
● «OneToMany» getPlayers ( )	● «Id, GeneratedValue» getId ( )
● setPlayers ( )	● setId ( )
●ˢ main ( )	

335

A Team Has Many Players

Since both the Team and Player objects will map to their own, individual, database tables, both the Team and Player classes will have their own primary key to keep track of a record's uniqueness. In both classes, we will maintain the primary key field using a primitive of type long which will be uncreatively named id.

As far as the interesting properties of the Team class goes, well, every team has a name of type String. So, a team might be named the "*Soo Greyhounds*," or the "*Pickering Atoms*." As far as the Player class goes, every player has a nickName of type String, so "*Lefty*" and "*Pork Chop*" might play for the Pickering *Atoms*.

Phase 1 of the Player Class (No Association Yet)

```
package com.examscam.mappings;
public class Player {

    private long id;
    private String nickName;


    public long getId() {return id;}
    public void setId(long id) {this.id = id;}
    public String getNickName() {return nickName;}
    public void setNickName(String n) {this.nickName = n;}
}
```

«Java Class»
 Team

▫ id : long
▫ name : String
● getId ( )
● setId ( )
● getName ( )
● setName ( )

Phase 1 of the Team Class (No Association Yet)

```
package com.examscam.mappings;
public class Team {

    private long id;
    private String name;


    public long getId() {return id;}
    public void setId(long id) {this.id = id;}
    public String getName() {return name;}
    public void setName(String name) {this.name = name;}
}
```

«Java Class»
 Player

▫ id : long
▫ nickName : String
● getId ( )
● setId ( )
● getNickName ( )
● setNickName ( )

Coding an Association in Java

Phase 1 of the Team and the Player classes define the basic properties of each object, without doing anything to imply the relationship between the two. Of course, the association between the two is the fact that a Player is associated with a Team, and a Team is associated with many Players. These relationships will be expressed in our Java code through instance variables.

To express the fact that a Player is associated with a Team, we need to add an instance variable of type *Team* in the Player class.

Phase 2 of the Player Class (Java Associations)

```
package com.examscam.mappings;
public class Player {
 private long id;private String nickName;

 private Team team;          /* A Player is on a Team */
 public Team getTeam() {return team;}
 public void setTeam(Team t) {this.team = t;}

 public long getId() {return id;}
 public void setId(long id) {this.id = id;}
 public String getNickName() {return nickName;}
 public void setNickName(String n) {this.nickName = n;}
}
```

Phase 2 of the Team Class (Java Associations)

To express the fact that a Team has many players, we add a variable of type *java.util.List,* named *players,* to the Team class.

```
package com.examscam.mappings;
import java.util.List;
public class Team {
 private long id;private String name;

 private List<Player> players; /*A Team Has Players*/
 public List<Player> getPlayers() {return players;}
 public void setPlayers(List<Player> p) {players=p;}

 public long getId() {return id;}
 public void setId(long id) {this.id = id;}
 public String getName() {return name;}
 public void setName(String name) {this.name = name;}
}
```

Adding the Standard Hibernate Annotations

Of course, instance variables only describe an association between classes at a Java bytecode level. Simply adding instance variables in your Java classes doesn't give Hibernate any information about how to manage the association. To have Hibernate persist and manage any associations between classes, those Java classes need to be annotated.

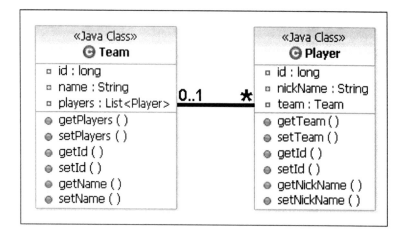

Both the Team and the Player classes need the standard JPA annotations that describe the fact that they are to be Hibernate managed entities. We also need annotations that describe the fact that the id field will be the primary key whose values will be auto-generated by the database. That means adding the @Entity, @Id and @GeneratedValue JPA tags at the appropriate places in the Player and Team classes.

Phase 3 of the Player Class (Basic Annotations)

```
package com.examscam.mappings; import javax.persistence.*;
@Entity
public class Player {
 private long id;
 private String nickName;

 private Team team;
 public Team getTeam() {return team;}
 public void setTeam(Team t) {this.team = t;}

 @Id
 @GeneratedValue
 public long getId() {return id;}
 public void setId(long id) {this.id = id;}
 public String getNickName() {return nickName;}
 public void setNickName(String n) {nickName = n;}
}
```

Phase 3 of the Team Class (Basic Annotations)

```
package com.examscam.mappings;
import java.util.List; import javax.persistence.*;
@Entity
public class Team {
 private long id;
 private String name;

 private List<Player> players;
 public List<Player> getPlayers() {return players;}
 public void setPlayers(List<Player> p){players=p;}

 @Id
 @GeneratedValue
 public long getId() {return id;}
 public void setId(long id) {this.id = id;}
 public String getName() {return name;}
 public void setName(String name) {this.name = name;}
}
```

339

@OneToMany & @ManyToOne Annotations

After the basic JPA annotations identifying the Team and Player classes as managed entities have been added, along with the annotations to decorate the id fields of the two classes, it's time to add the @OneToMany and @ManyToOne JPA annotations. These annotations help Hibernate understand the purpose of the instance variables that implement the Java based association between the Team and Player classes.

Let's first concentrate on the Player class that maintains a single instance variable of type Team to help identify the team with which a player is associated. Since many players can be associated with a single team, the relationship is many-to-one, and as such, the getTeam() method in the Player class gets decorated with the @ManyToOne annotation.

Now, it is the responsibility of each Player to keep track of the single Team with which they are associated. In Java, this is achieved through an instance variable, but databases don't understand instance variables. Instead, databases use foreign keys in much the same way a Java program uses an instance variable. For a database, each row on the many side of a one to many relationship must maintain a foreign key that maps the row back to the associated row on the many side of the relationship.

So, each row in the Player table must define a column to map the Player back to the associated team. We'll call that column, which will be defined in the player table, *team_id.*

The team_id maps a Player back to the encapsulating Team.

It is worth mentioning that while the *many side* in a one to many relationship must define a field that maps back to the encapsulating *one side,* the reverse is not true. With the player and team tables, the player table (the many table) uses the team_id column to map back to the team table (the one table), but no column is needed in the team table to map to the player.

@JoinColumn & @ManyToOne Annotations

When using JPA annotations to map the *many side* of a relationship to the encapsulating *one side*, we not only use the @ManyToOne annotation, but we further decorate the class with the @JoinColumn annotation.

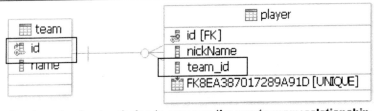

A unique foreign key helps to express the one to many relationship.

Again, the player database table must define a column to map rows back to the encapsulating team table, and this fact manifests itself through the *name* attribute of the very important @JoinColumn annotation. These annotations will appear immediately before the getTeam() method of the Player class:

```
@Entity
public class Player {        ⋉⋉⋉

   @ManyToOne
   @JoinColumn(name="team_id")
   public Team getTeam() {return team;}     ⋉⋉⋉
}
```

Of Databases and Java Programs

So, from the perspective of a Java program, the only thing that is needed to express a relationship between classes is the existence of an instance variable; but since databases don't quite work the same way, we need to inform the Hibernate framework as to how it should manage the association at the database layer. This is where the @ManyToOne and @JoinColumn JPA annotations come in. ☺

@OneToMany JPA Annotation

The getTeam() method in the Player class was decorated with the @ManyToOne JPA annotation, so it'll probably come as no surprise to find out that the Team side of this bi-directional relationship requires a @OneToMany annotation decorating the getPlayers() method.

```
public class Team { ⋇⋇⋇
@OneToMany(mappedBy="team",
                targetEntity=Player.class,
                fetch=FetchType.EAGER,
                cascade=CascadeType.ALL)
public List<Player> getPlayers() {return players;} ⋇⋇⋇
}
```

The @OneToMany annotation has a few important attributes that need to be included. First of all, it needs to have the *mappedBy* attribute. And what is the mappedBy attribute? Well, this actually maps to the variable name the encapsulating class (Team) takes in the encapsulated entity (Player). So, if you looked at the Player class, you'd see that there is an instance variable of type Team named *team*, in all lower case letters. This variable named *team* maps the Player back to their Team, and as such, becomes the value of the mappedBy attribute.

```
public class Player {
  private long id;
  private String nickName;
/* The Player class has an instance variable named team */
  private Team team; ⋇⋇⋇ ⋇⋇⋇
}
```

Along with the mappedBy attribute, the @OneToMany annotation needs a *targetEntity* attribute. Since any generic Object can be placed into a List, Vector, or other collection class that implements the many part of the association, it is important to explicitly state in the annotation what type of object class will be contained in the collection. This should be done even when the contained object type is defined using generics syntax. Since our team contains players, Player.class is the value of the targetEntity attribute of the Team's @OneToMany annotation.

Final Phase of the Player Class

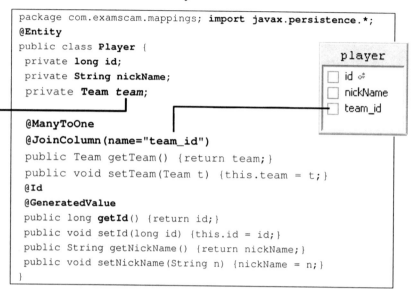

```
package com.examscam.mappings; import javax.persistence.*;
@Entity
public class Player {
  private long id;
  private String nickName;
  private Team team;

  @ManyToOne
  @JoinColumn(name="team_id")
  public Team getTeam() {return team;}
  public void setTeam(Team t) {this.team = t;}
  @Id
  @GeneratedValue
  public long getId() {return id;}
  public void setId(long id) {this.id = id;}
  public String getNickName() {return nickName;}
  public void setNickName(String n) {nickName = n;}
}
```

Final Phase of the Team Class

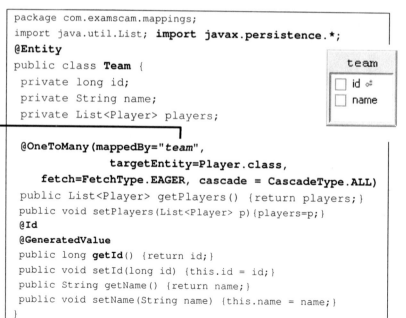

```
package com.examscam.mappings;
import java.util.List; import javax.persistence.*;
@Entity
public class Team {
  private long id;
  private String name;
  private List<Player> players;

  @OneToMany(mappedBy="team",
             targetEntity=Player.class,
       fetch=FetchType.EAGER, cascade = CascadeType.ALL)
  public List<Player> getPlayers() {return players;}
  public void setPlayers(List<Player> p){players=p;}
  @Id
  @GeneratedValue
  public long getId() {return id;}
  public void setId(long id) {this.id = id;}
  public String getName() {return name;}
  public void setName(String name) {this.name = name;}
}
```

343

FetchType & CascadeType Revisited

Notice that the @OneToMany annotation uses the *fetch* and *cascade* attributes. While optional, it is always important to think about the potential negative impact of doing an eager fetch on associated classes. If loading associated classes will have a negative impact on performance, you might want to leave the fetch type to the default value of LAZY. Just be sure that with a lazy fetch setting you don't try and access associated classes outside of a transaction, as you will ended up getting a blank proxy, not the actual data, resulting in a very frustrating, and often perplexing, LazyInitializationException at runtime.

Furthermore, it is important to think about how saves to a containing object, such as Team, will effect the contained objects, in this case, the Players. If you want changes to the owning entity to cascade to the owned entities when a change occurs, you should set your CascadeType to ALL. Other available options for the CascadeType include: MERGE, PERSIST, REFRESH and REMOVE.

«Java Enum»
🅔 CascadeType

🔗 ALL
🔗 MERGE
🔗 PERSIST
🔗 REFRESH
🔗 REMOVE

«Java Class, Entity» 🅖 Team	«Java Class, Entity» 🅖 Player
△ id : long	△ id : long
△ name : String	△ team : Team
△ players : List<Player>	△ nickName : String
● «Id, GeneratedValue» getId ( )	● getNickName ( )
● setId ( )	● setNickName ( )
● getName ( )	● «ManyToOne, JoinColumn» getTeam ( )
● setName ( )	● setTeam ( )
● «OneToMany» getPlayers ( )	● «Id, GeneratedValue» getId ( )
● setPlayers ( )	● setId ( )
●ˢ main ( )	

Testing the Implementation

Let's test our one-to-many JPA annotated classes. ☺

To test the @OneToMany and @ManyToOne mappings, you must first add both the Team and Player classes to the Hibernate configuration.

```
AnnotationConfiguration config = new AnnotationConfiguration();
config.addAnnotatedClass(Player.class);
config.addAnnotatedClass(Team.class);
config.configure();
```

After making sure the Player and Team classes are added to the configuration, you must make sure the corresponding tables actually exist in the database. I like to get Hibernate to do this for me by using my HibernateUtil.recreateDatabase() method, but you can also do it by running the following SQL script:

```
CREATE TABLE `examscam`.`player` (`id` bigint(20)
NOT NULL auto_increment, `nickName` varchar(255)
default NULL, `team_id` bigint(20) default NULL,
PRIMARY KEY (`id`),
KEY `FK8EA387017289A91D` (`team_id`));
```

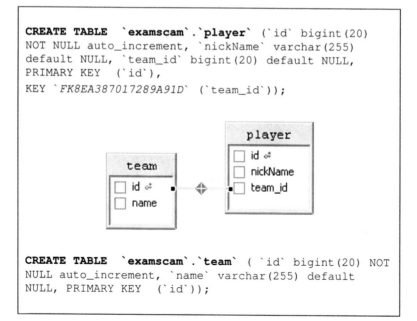

```
CREATE TABLE `examscam`.`team` ( `id` bigint(20) NOT
NULL auto_increment, `name` varchar(255) default
NULL, PRIMARY KEY (`id`));
```

345

Testing the Team and Players

Because both the Team and Player classes are marked with the @Entity tags, any time a Team or Player class is created, it is a good practice to have the entity touch the Hibernate Session in order for its persistence to be managed.

```
Session session = HibernateUtil.beginTransaction();
Team team = new Team();
Player p1 = new Player();
Player p2 = new Player();
session.save(team);
session.save(p1);
session.save(p2);
```

After 'touching' the Hibernate Session, any subsequent changes, updates or associations that are made are managed by Hibernate and persisted to the database.

```
team.setName("Pickering Atoms");
p1.setNickName("Lefty");
p1.setTeam(team);
p2.setNickName("Blinky");
p2.setTeam(team);
HibernateUtil.commitTransaction();
```

After committing the transaction to the database, there are two players, Lefty and Blinky, who are both associated with the Pickering Atoms, giving them both a team_id of 1.

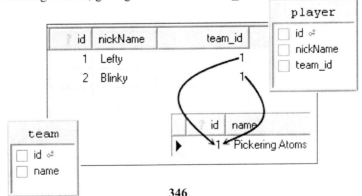

Full Team Class with the Testable main

```java
package com.examscam.mappings;
import java.util.*; import javax.persistence.*;
import org.hibernate.Session; import com.examscam.HibernateUtil;
@Entity
public class Team {
 private long id;
 private String name;
 private List<Player> players;

@OneToMany(mappedBy="team",
            targetEntity=Player.class,
   fetch=FetchType.EAGER, cascade = CascadeType.ALL)
 public List<Player> getPlayers() {return players;}
 public void setPlayers(List<Player> p){players=p;}
@Id
@GeneratedValue
 public long getId() {return id;}
 public void setId(long id) {this.id = id;}
 public String getName() {return name;}
 public void setName(String name) {this.name = name;}
}
 public static void main(String args[]){
     HibernateUtil.recreateDatabase();
     Session session=HibernateUtil.beginTransaction();

     Team team = new Team();
     Player p1 = new Player();
     Player p2 = new Player();

     session.save(team);
     session.save(p1);
     session.save(p2);

     team.setName("Pickering Atoms");
     p1.setNickName("Lefty");
     p1.setTeam(team);
     p2.setNickName("Blinky");
     p2.setTeam(team);
     HibernateUtil.commitTransaction();
   }
}
```

Hibernate and SQL Execution

When committing the transaction to the database, Hibernate logs the following very interesting SQL statements, reflecting the flow of object creation and updates to the instance variables of the Player and Team classes as the code progresses.

```
Session session = HibernateUtil.beginTransaction();
Team team = new Team();
Player p1 = new Player();
Player p2 = new Player();
session.save(team);
session.save(p1);
session.save(p2);
team.setName("Pickering Atoms");
p1.setNickName("Lefty");
p1.setTeam(team);
p2.setNickName("Blinky");
p2.setTeam(team);
HibernateUtil.commitTransaction();
H: insert into Team (name) values (?)
H: insert into Player (nickName, team_id) values (?, ?)
H: insert into Player (nickName, team_id) values (?, ?)
H: update Team set name=? where id=?
H: update Player set nickName=?, team_id=? where id=?
H: update Player set nickName=?, team_id=? where id=?
```

Looking at the results in the database, you can see that Lefty and Blinky are both players on the Pickering Atoms team. The single Team, the Pickering Atoms, has many players, namely Lefty and Blinky – making this a *one to many*, and inversely, a *many to one,* relationship mapping.

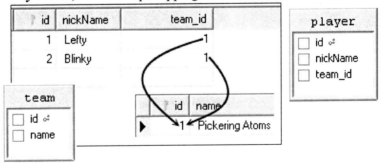

Chapter 19
Many to Many
Associations

Of all of the possible association mappings, probably the most difficult and confusing is the bi-directional, many to many relationship that we are going to look at now. Don't fret though, Hibernate makes mapping a bi-directional, many to many relationship about as easy as it could possibly get. This is a big step forward for database persistence, as only a few years ago, many of the big vendor's container mapping tools actually ran out of steam when it came to properly managing complex many to many relationships.

Many to many relationships happen fairly frequently in enterprise applications, making it a fairly common pattern. For this chapter, I'm going to rather glibly model the relationship between a *Student* and a college or university *Course*.

Conceptually, the student-course, many to many relationship, is fairly easy to conceptualize. For example, a single student named Bart could be in several college courses, such as Java-101, English-101 and UML-101. So, a student can be in many courses.

At the same time, a course, such as Java-101, can also have many students. Not only could Bart be enrolled in Java-101, but so could Kerri and Samantha and Leslie, etc. So, since the many relationship goes both ways, we call this a many to many relationship.

One of the challenges of dealing with many to many relationships is the fact that they manifest themselves in such a specific way at the database level, as compared to their implementation at the Java programming level. In a Java program, two classes maintaining a many to many relationship with each other simply maintain a list or collection of the corresponding class. So, with an example such as *the Student has a many to many relationship with a Course*, a student would maintain a collection listing the courses in which they are

349

enrolled, and a course would maintain a collection or a list of attending students. However, at the database level, the implementation is much different.

At the database level, a many to many relationship between two classes is maintained with a third table that is known as a join table. Each table participating in the many to many relationship, which in this case would be a course and a student table, maintains its own primary key. However, any relationships between the two tables are maintained by a third, join table, where matching, or intersecting primary keys of course-student matches, are maintained. Again, the contrast between how many to many relationships are implemented in Java code, as opposed to how they are implemented at the database level, is a complicating factor. However, Hibernate does a pretty good job at simplifying the situation, allowing Java developers to concentrate on their code, while allowing the underlying database structure to elute naturally from the Java domain model.

A Left and Right Simplification

When mapping and working with a many to many relationship, one class in the relationship needs to make reference to the other, and vice-versa. This back and forth referencing can often be confusing. I always find it easier to conceptualize a many to many relationship with one class being on the left, one class being on the right, and the third, join class, placed in the middle. For this chapter, I am going to graph the class and table relationships in a left-right-middle manner; I'm even going to name the classes accordingly. The class names I will use in this chapter are LeftManyStudent and RightManyCourse, and the join table will simply be named join_table.

Also, it should be noted that there is no Java class that represents the join table, although there will be a leftmanystudent and rightmanycourse table to map to the LeftManyStudent and RightManyCourse Java classes.

Tables and Joins

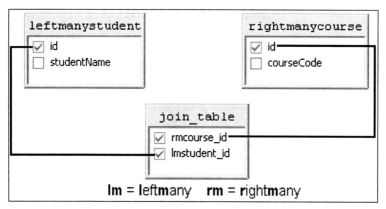

Class Diagram

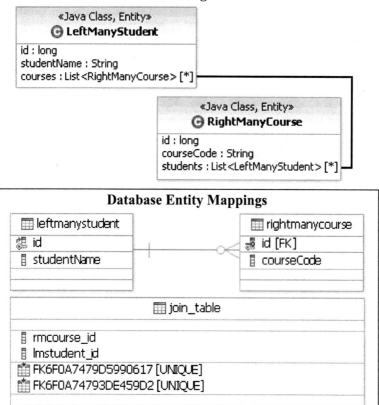

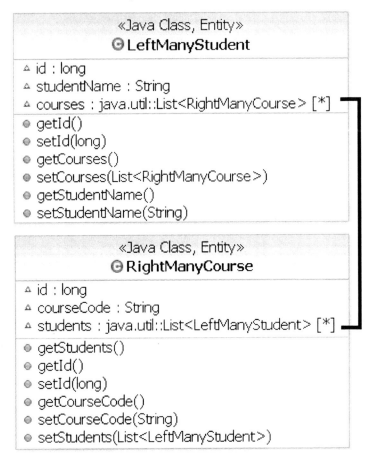

LeftManyStudent & RightManyCourse Classes

Because the annotation used for mapping a many to many relationship is probably the most complicated of them all, I'm going to keep the two classes we have here as simple as possible.

The LeftManyStudent class will have an id field of type long to track the primary key of the class, along with a simple String property called studentName. Furthermore, the LeftManyStudent class will have a property of type List named courses that keeps track of the many courses in which a student might be enrolled.

Similarly, the RightManyCourse class will have an id of type long, a String property called courseCode, and an object of type List to keep track of the many students enrolled in the course.

LeftManyStudent with the Initial Annotations

```
package com.examscam.mappings;   import com.examscam.*;
import java.util.*; import javax.persistence.*;;
@Entity
public class LeftManyStudent {

  long id;
  String studentName;
  List<RightManyCourse> courses = new Vector();

  @Id
  @GeneratedValue
  public long getId() {return id;}
  public void setId(long id) {this.id = id;}

  public List<RightManyCourse> getCourses(){return courses;}
  public void setCourses(List<RightManyCourse> righties) {
    this.courses = righties;
  }
  public String getStudentName() {return studentName;}
  public void setStudentName(String s) {studentName = s;}
}
```

RightManyCourse with the Initial Annotations

```
package com.examscam.mappings; import com.examscam.*;
import java.util.*;import javax.persistence.*;
@Entity
public class RightManyCourse {
  long id;
  String courseCode;
  List<LeftManyStudent> students = new Vector();
  public List<LeftManyStudent> getStudents() {return students;}
  @Id
  @GeneratedValue
  public long getId() {return id;}
  public void setId(long id) {this.id = id;}
  public String getCourseCode() {return courseCode;}
  public void setCourseCode(String courseCode) {
    this.courseCode = courseCode;
  }
  public void setStudents(List<LeftManyStudent> lefties) {
    this.students = lefties;
  }
}
```

353

Student and Course Classes as Entities

Both the LeftManyStudent and RightManyCourse classes are individual entities whose state will be mapped back to respective database tables. As a result, both the Student and Course classes must have the required @Entity decoration before the class declaration, and the standard @Id and @GeneratedValue annotations before the getId() method. Of course, these are the standard annotations that we've been throwing on just about every JPA annotated POJO that we have created. What makes the Student and Course relationship interesting is the bi-directional many-to-many mapping that exists between them.

The fact that a Student can be enrolled in many Courses manifests itself in the form of a java.util.List named courses in the LeftManyStudent class. Subsequently, the getCourses() method in the LeftManyStudent class that returns the List of RightManyCourse instances must be decorated with the @ManyToMany annotation. Of course, this is a bi-directional, many to many relationship, with a join table that needs to be used to keep track of the relationship in the database. As a result, the getCourses() method not only needs the @ManyToMany annotation, but it needs the @JoinTable annotation to describe the mapping of the details of the Student and Course instances into the join table. The @JoinTable is a little intimidating the first time you see it in a bi-directional, many-to-many join. For now, just take a look at how the getCourses() method is decorated; an explanation will follow. ☺

```
public class LeftManyStudent { ✗✗✗  ✗✗✗
 @ManyToMany
 @JoinTable(name = "join_table",
 joinColumns = { @JoinColumn(name = "lmstudent_id")},
 inverseJoinColumns={@JoinColumn(name="rmcourse_id")}
 )
  public List <RightManyCourse> getCourses() {
    return courses;
  } ✗✗✗  ✗✗✗
}
```

Documenting the Join Table

The manner in which the @JoinTable uses two nested @JoinColumn tags within the annotation is a little scary, but when you think about it, it actually makes a lot of sense.

To map a many to many relationship in a database, you need a join table. The join table we are going to use is simply named join_table, thus the sensible beginning of the @JoinTable annotation:

@JoinTable(name = "join_table", ⅗<⅗<⅗<   ⅗<⅗<⅗<)

Of course, we are currently coding this annotation in the LeftManyStudent class, and the @JoinTable tag wants to know the name of the column in the join_table that will be used to store the primary key of the LeftManyStudent instance. We'll use the letters 'l' and 'm' plus the word student, followed by an _id as the name of the column to store the LeftManyStudent id. Put it together, and you get lmstudent_id, and the first @JoinColumn part of the @JoinTable tag looks like this:

```
@JoinTable(name = "join_table",
joinColumns={@JoinColumn(name= "lmstudent_id")},
⅗<⅗<  ⅗<⅗<)
```

Of course, the first @JoinColumn annotation only tells Hibernate how to save the primary key of the LeftManyStudent class, not how to find out the name of the column that maps the Student to its associated RightManyCourse. So, to help Hibernate process the inverse, Course to Student relationship, we add a second @JoinColumn annotation, but associate it with the inverseJoinColumns attribute of the @JoinTable annotation:

```
@ManyToMany
@JoinTable (name = "join_table",
  joinColumns={ @JoinColumn(name="lmstudent_id")},
    inverseJoinColumns
      ={ @JoinColumn (name = "rmcourse_id") } )
```

Mapping Both Side of the Many To Many

After mastering the @JoinTable annotation on the left hand side of the many-to-many relationship, understanding the right hand side of the relationship is a lead pipe cinch. Basically, it's the same, while at the same time, it's a little different. ☺

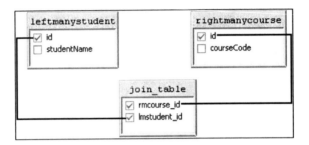

Let's look at the LeftManyStudent mapping for its side of the many to many relationship:

```
public class LeftManyStudent { ✂✂✂
  @ManyToMany
  @JoinTable(name = "join_table",  joinColumns = {
@JoinColumn(name = "lmstudent_id")},
inverseJoinColumns={@JoinColumn(name="rmcourse_id")})
    public List<RightManyCourse> getCourses(){return courses;}
}
```

Now, take a look at the RightManyCourse side of the many to many relationship.

```
public class RightManyCourse {✂✂✂
  @ManyToMany
  @JoinTable(name = "join_table",
joinColumns={@JoinColumn(name="rmcourse_id")},
  inverseJoinColumns={@JoinColumn(name="lmstudent_id")})
   public List<LeftManyStudent> getStudents(){return students;}
}
```

Comparing the *Many* Sides

You will notice that the @JoinTable annotation in the RightManyCourse class only differs from the @JoinTable annotation in the LeftManyStudent class in the ordering of the **lmstudent_id** and the **rmcourse_id** fields from the **inverseJoinColumns** and **joinColumns** attributes of the @JoinTable annotation. This obvious similarity makes sense, as both the LeftManyStudent and RightManyCourse classes, while on opposite sides, are participating in the same many to many relationship.

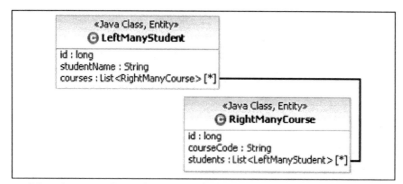

It's also worth noting that the values of lmstudent_id and rm_courseid, which are used in the @JoinTable annotation, do not actually manifest themselves as instance variables anywhere in the Java code. The JoinColumns are purely a manifestation of how a database, not a Java program, manages a many to many relationship.

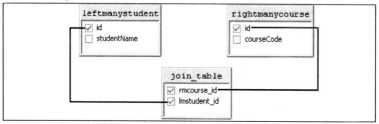

Completed LeftManyStudent with Full Annotations

```
package com.examscam.mappings;
import java.util.*;
import javax.persistence.*;

@Entity
public class LeftManyStudent {

  long id;
  String studentName;
  List<RightManyCourse> courses = new Vector();


  @ManyToMany
  @JoinTable(name = "join_table",
  joinColumns = { @JoinColumn(name = "lmstudent_id")},
  inverseJoinColumns={@JoinColumn(name="rmcourse_id")}
  )
  public List<RightManyCourse> getCourses(){
    return courses;
  }
  public void setCourses(List<RightManyCourse> righties){
    this.courses = righties;
  }

  @Id
  @GeneratedValue
  public long getId() {return id;}
  public void setId(long id) {this.id = id;}

  public String getStudentName() {
    return studentName;
  }
  public void setStudentName(String s){
    studentName=s;
  }

}
```

Completed RightManyCourse with the Full Annotations

```
package com.examscam.mappings;

import java.util.*;
import javax.persistence.*;

@Entity
public class RightManyCourse {
  long id;
  String courseCode;
  List<LeftManyStudent> students = new Vector();

 @ManyToMany
 @JoinTable(name = "join_table",
 joinColumns={@JoinColumn(name="rmcourse_id")},
inverseJoinColumns={@JoinColumn(name="lmstudent_id")})
  public List<LeftManyStudent> getStudents() {
    return students;
  }
  public void setStudents(List<LeftManyStudent> lefties){
    this.students = lefties;
  }

  @Id
  @GeneratedValue
  public long getId() {
    return id;
  }
  public void setId(long id) {
    this.id = id;
  }

  public String getCourseCode() {
    return courseCode;
  }
  public void setCourseCode(String courseCode) {
    this.courseCode = courseCode;
  }

}
```

Testing the Many to Many Mapping

As with all Hibernate mappings that leverage JPA annotations, the classes in question must be added to Hibernate's AnnotationConfiguration object in the central spot where the Hibernate Configuration is initialized.

```
AnnotationConfiguration config =
                new AnnotationConfiguration();
config.addAnnotatedClass(LeftManyStudent.class);
config.addAnnotatedClass(RightManyCourse.class);
config.configure();
```

Testing the Many to Many Mapping

To test the many to many mappings, we need to create instances of Student and Course objects. So, a Student object might be created like this:

```
LeftManyStudent student01 = new LeftManyStudent();
student01.setStudentName("Jim Jump");
```

A course object would be created like this:

```
RightManyCourse java101 = new RightManyCourse();
java101.setCourseCode("Java-101");
```

And once a student and a course exists, we can associate them with each other. So, we can have student01 enrolled in java101 by executing the following code:

```
java101.getStudents().add(student01);
```

To save this relationship to the database, we need to have each entity 'touch' the Hibernate Session within the scope of a transaction. Using our HibernateUtil class, here's how we'd persist the fact that *student01* is enrolled in *java101*.

```
Session session = HibernateUtil.beginTransaction();
session.save(student01);
session.save(java101);
HibernateUtil.commitTransaction();
```

A Full Many-to-Many Test Method

The following main method, when executed, will create many students, and have them associated with various courses. See if you can keep track of who is enrolled in which course – the initials of the student's first and last name is a big hint. ☺

```
public static void main (String args[]) {
 HibernateUtil.recreateDatabase();

 LeftManyStudent student01 = new LeftManyStudent();
 student01.setStudentName("Jim Jump");
 LeftManyStudent student02 = new LeftManyStudent();
 student02.setStudentName("Julie Camp");
 LeftManyStudent student03 = new LeftManyStudent();
 student03.setStudentName("Cam Johnson");
 LeftManyStudent student04 = new LeftManyStudent();
 student04.setStudentName("Marcus McKenzie");
 RightManyCourse java101 = new RightManyCourse();
 java101.setCourseCode("Java-101");
 RightManyCourse cplus101 = new RightManyCourse();
 cplus101.setCourseCode("C++ - 101");
 RightManyCourse math101 = new RightManyCourse();
 math101.setCourseCode("Math - 101");

 java101.getStudents().add(student01);
 java101.getStudents().add(student02);
 java101.getStudents().add(student03);
 cplus101.getStudents().add(student02);
 cplus101.getStudents().add(student03);
 math101.getStudents().add(student04);

 Session session = HibernateUtil.beginTransaction();
 session.save(student01);
 session.save(student02);
 session.save(student03);
 session.save(student04);
 session.save(java101);
 session.save(cplus101);
 session.save(math101);
 HibernateUtil.commitTransaction();
} /* make sure this class imports com.examscam.HibernateUtil */
```

Running the Test Method

When Hibernate commits the transaction in the main method that tests the many to many mapping, it will spit out some interesting SQL, so long as you have enabled the hibernate.show_sql property in your hibernate.cfg.xml file. Here's the SQL that Hibernate generates:

```
Hibernate: insert into LeftManyStudent (studentName) values (?)
Hibernate: insert into LeftManyStudent (studentName) values (?)
Hibernate: insert into LeftManyStudent (studentName) values (?)
Hibernate: insert into LeftManyStudent (studentName) values (?)
Hibernate: insert into RightManyCourse (courseCode) values (?)
Hibernate: insert into RightManyCourse (courseCode) values (?)
Hibernate: insert into RightManyCourse (courseCode) values (?)
Hibernate: insert into join_table (rmcourse_id,
lmstudent_id) values (?, ?)
Hibernate: insert into join_table (rmcourse_id,
lmstudent_id) values (?, ?)
Hibernate: insert into join_table (rmcourse_id,
lmstudent_id) values (?, ?)
Hibernate: insert into join_table (rmcourse_id,
lmstudent_id) values (?, ?)
Hibernate: insert into join_table (rmcourse_id,
lmstudent_id) values (?, ?)
Hibernate: insert into join_table (rmcourse_id,
lmstudent_id) values (?, ?)
```

Simply by annotating our Java classes with the appropriate @ManyToMany annotations, and corresponding @JoinTable tags, Hibernate knows how to manage the primary keys of the classes participating in a many to many join, and it knows how to subsequently map those primary keys to a corresponding join table in order to permanently persist the relationship between instances.

Viewing the Results

After running the test method, viewing the contents of the database reveals three tables that have been populated with data, namely the leftmanystudent, rightmanycourse and the join_table.

leftmanystudent		join_table		rightmanycourse	
id	studentName	lmstudent_id	rmcourse_id	id	courseCode
1	Jim Jump	1	1	1	Java-101
2	Julie Camp	2	1	2	C++ - 101
3	Cam Johnson	3	1	3	Math - 101
4	Marcus McKenzie	2	2		
		3	2		
		4	3		

As you can see, individual students are still saved in the leftmanystudent table, and courses are stored in the rightmanycourse table. However, the fact that Julie Camp (id of 2)` is enrolled in Java (id of 1) 101 and C++ 101 (id of 2) is maintained by the join table, as it maintains the matching primary keys of entities in the student and course tables. The key lines of code that map Julie to the Java 101 and C++ 101 courses is below:

```
LeftManyStudent student02 = new LeftManyStudent();
student02.setStudentName("Julie Camp");

RightManyCourse java101 = new RightManyCourse();
java101.setCourseCode("Java-101");
RightManyCourse cplus101 = new RightManyCourse();
cplus101.setCourseCode("C++ - 101");

java101.getStudents().add(student02);
cplus101.getStudents().add(student02);

session.save(student02);
session.save(java101);
session.save(cplus101);
```

Chapter 20
Advanced Mappings

Having looked at a number of fairly simple and straight forward examples of how Hibernate can be used to implement persistent data mappings, I thought that it would be nice to take a look at a slightly more complex example that combines all of the most common mapping patterns.

The goal of this chapter, and section, is to work towards the implementation of a fairly typical *Human Resources* or *Job Placement* application. In this application, clients will register, provide their primary home address, along with any work or business addresses, and finally, from a provided list of skills, the client must select the ones that most closely match their personal competencies. Basically, we're going to be working towards the implementation of a skills management type of application.

The design model will place central focus on a **Client** class, with the client having a one-to-one relationship with a **ClientDetail** class, a one-to-many relationship with an **Address** class, and finally, a many to many relationship with a **Skill** class. Furthermore, all of the relationships will be bi-directional.

Discovering the Solution

As you could imagine, the mappings contained in the Client class will get pretty hairy, but as with all J2EE applications, if you break things down into their individual components and tackle the problem one step at a time, the whole solution will quickly and seamlessly fall into place.

Implementing the Domain Model

The first step towards putting together a solution for the Skills Manager application is to create a basic skeleton for each of the classes involved in the domain model. The Client class will reference each of the other classes in the domain, so without a compiled class definition for each component, you'll end up with a bunch of compile errors as you begin to build the Client class.

Here are the basic, codeless, class declarations for the POJOs we'll be using to create the Skills Manager application:

```
package com.examscam.model;

public class Client {

}
```

```
package com.examscam.model;

public class ClientDetail {

}
```

```
package com.examscam.model;

public class Address {

}
```

```
package com.examscam.model;

public class Skill {

}
```

Each public class must be defined in its own .java file, all of which should be saved in a directory structure consistent with the package name of com.examscam.model.

Class Diagram for the Skills Manager App

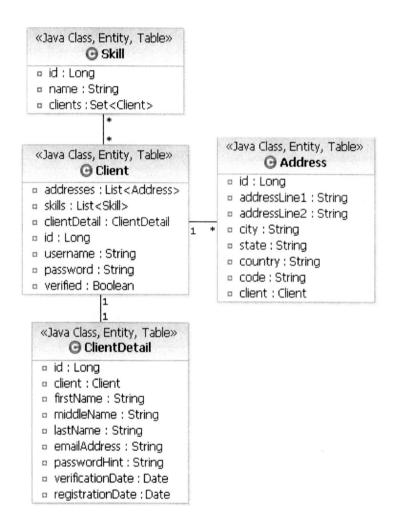

Adding Properties and Methods

After the basic class files have been created and compiled, it's time to take a look at the object model that has been developed, and start coding the basic properties and methods required to implement the domain. For this iteration, we will just concentrate on adding the appropriate properties and setter/getter methods. When the basic class structures have been coded, we will begin to add the appropriate and required JPA annotations.

Properties of the Client Class

Without any JPA annotations, the Client class will define four internal properties of its own:

☞ *two String properties for the username and password*

☞ *a Boolean value to indicate whether the client is verified or not*

☞ *an id field of type Long*

Implementing Associations with the Client

As for implementing the associations between the Skill, Address and Client Detail classes, the Client class will define:

☞ *an instance variable of type ClientDetail*

☞ *an instance variable of type java.util.List to contain the many Address objects a client might have*

☞ *an instance variable of type java.util.List to maintain the many Skill objects a client might have*

```
package com.examscam.model;
import java.util.List;import java.util.Vector;
public class Client {

  private List<Address> addresses = new Vector<Address>();
  private List<Skill> skills = new Vector<Skill>();
  private ClientDetail clientDetail;

  private Long id;

  private String username;
  private String password;
  private Boolean verified;

  public Long getId() {return id;}
  public void setId(Long id) {this.id = id;}

  public List<Skill> getSkills() {return skills;}
  public void setSkills(List<Skill> skills) {
    this.skills = skills;
  }

  public List<Address> getAddresses() {return addresses;}
  public void setAddresses(List<Address> addresses) {
    this.addresses = addresses;
  }

  public ClientDetail getClientDetail(){return clientDetail;}
  public void setClientDetail(ClientDetail clientDetail) {
    this.clientDetail = clientDetail;
  }
  public String getPassword() {return password;}
  public void setPassword(String password) {
    this.password = password;
  }
  public String getUsername() {return username;}
  public void setUsername(String username) {
    this.username = username;
  }
  public Boolean getVerified() {return verified;}
  public void setVerified(Boolean verified) {
    this.verified = verified;
  }
}
```

The ClientDetail Class

All of the really yummy information about a client is held in the ClientDetail class. The ClientDetail class defines five properties of type String, namely:

☞ *a firstName*

☞ *a middleName*

☞ *a lastName*

☞ *an emailAddress*

☞ *a password*

☞ *a password hint*

Furthermore the ClientDetail class will define two java.sql.Date objects to maintain the registrationDate and the verificationDate. The id will quite unspectacularly be maintained as an instance variable of type Long.

Implementing the Association in Java

Of course, the ClientDetail class is associated with a Client in a bi-directional manner, so, the ClientDetail class defines an instance variable of type Client, which will quite logically be named: *client*.

Unannotated Code for the ClientDetail Class

```
package com.examscam.model; import java.sql.*;

public class ClientDetail {

  private Long id;
  private Client client;
  private String firstName, middleName, lastName;
  private String emailAddress, passwordHint;
  private Date registrationDate, verificationDate;

  public Client getClient(){return client;}
  public void setClient(Client client){this.client=client;}

  public Long getId() {return id;}
  public void setId(Long id) {this.id = id;}

  public String getEmailAddress() {return emailAddress;}
  public void setEmailAddress(String emailAddress) {
    this.emailAddress = emailAddress;
  }
  public String getFirstName() {return firstName;}
  public void setFirstName(String firstName) {
    this.firstName = firstName;
  }
  public String getLastName() {return lastName;}
  public void setLastName(String lastName) {
    this.lastName = lastName;
  }
  public String getMiddleName() {return middleName;}
  public void setMiddleName(String middleName) {
    this.middleName = middleName;
  }
  public String getPasswordHint() {return passwordHint;}
  public void setPasswordHint(String passwordHint) {
    this.passwordHint = passwordHint;
  }
  public Date getRegistrationDate() {return registrationDate;}
  public void setRegistrationDate(Date registrationDate) {
    this.registrationDate = registrationDate;
  }
  public Date getVerificationDate() {return verificationDate;}
  public void setVerificationDate(Date verificationDate) {
    this.verificationDate = verificationDate;
  }

}
```

The Address Class

The address class looks somewhat like a unified theory of the sub-particle universe, as it's just loaded with Strings. With the exception of the id of type Long, and the ever important reference to the associated Client, the Address class contains the following six variables of type String:

☞ *addressLine1*

☞ *addressLine2*

☞ *city*

☞ *state*

☞ *country*

☞ *code (for the zip code or postal code)*

It's worth mentioning again that the relationship between the Address and the Client is bidirectional, so the Client class maintains a collection of Address objects in a java.util.List, while the Address class links back to the owning class through an instance variable of type Client.

```
package com.examscam.model;
public class Address {

  private Long id;
  private Client client;

  private String addressLine1;
  private String addressLine2;
  private String city;
  private String state;
  private String country;
  private String code;

  public Long getId() {return id;}
  public void setId(Long id) {this.id = id;}

  public Client getClient() {return client;}
  public void setClient(Client c) {this.client = c;}

  public String getAddressLine1() {return addressLine1;}
  public void setAddressLine1(String addressLine1) {
    this.addressLine1 = addressLine1;
  }

  public String getAddressLine2() {return addressLine2;}
  public void setAddressLine2(String addressLine2) {
    this.addressLine2 = addressLine2;
  }

  public String getCity() {return city;}
  public void setCity(String city) {this.city = city;}

  public String getCountry() {return country;}
  public void setCountry(String c) {this.country = c;}

  public String getCode() {return code;}
  public void setCode(String code) {this.code = code;}

  public String getState() {return state;}
  public void setState(String state) {
    this.state = state;
  }

}
```

The Skill Class

The Skill class, which shares a many-to-many relationship with the Client class, is the simplest Java class we have in this problem domain. The Skill class simply defines an id of type Long, and a name for the Skill in question of type String.

The collection of Skills itself is implemented as a java.util.Set, as opposed to a java.util.List. The nice thing about a Set, as opposed to a List, is that it can't contain duplicate entries, which makes sense for the unique set of Skills that our application will maintain.

Unannotated Code for the Skill Class

```java
package com.examscam.model;

import java.util.Set;

public class Skill {

  private Long id;
  private String name;

  private Set<Client> clients;

  public Set<Client> getClients() {
    return clients;
  }
  public void setClients(Set<Client> clients) {
    this.clients = clients;
  }

  public Long getId() {
    return id;
  }
  public void setId(Long id) {
    this.id = id;
  }

  public String getName() {
    return name;
  }
  public void setName(String name) {
    this.name = name;
  }

}
```

The Client to ClientDetail Relationship

With the problem domain classes coded with instance variables and public setter and getter methods, it's time to start adding in some JPA annotations.

The simplest of all the relationships is the one-to-one, bidirectional relationship between the Client and the ClientDetail. Preparing the Client class to participate in Java Persistence, we must first add the appropriate @Entity and @Table annotations, followed by the correct decorations needed for the getter of the primary key.

```
import java.util.*;
import javax.persistence.*;
@Entity
@Table(name = "client", schema = "examscam")
public class Client {
}<}<}<   }<}<}<
@Id
@GeneratedValue
@Column(name = "id")
public Long getId() { return id; }
}<}<}<   }<}<}<
}
```

Of course, the most pertinent annotation of interest happens when we place the @OneToOne annotation above the getClientDetail() method:

```
@OneToOne(cascade=CascadeType.ALL, fetch=FetchType.LAZY)
@JoinColumn(name="detail_id")
public ClientDetail getClientDetail() {
   return clientDetail;
}
```

Notice that the owning class, the Client, defines the name of the join column, which turns into a foreign key in the client database table, allowing the Client to be able to link to the corresponding ClientDetail class. The @OneToOne annotation describes the fact that every class has one, *and only one*, ClientDetail object. Furthermore, the fetch type, which defaults to active, is over-ridden, as it has been set to *LAZY*.

The ClientDetail to Client Relationship

The ClientDetail class maps the opposite end of the one-to-one relationship owned by the Client class. Notice in the ClientDetail's @OneToOne annotation that the *mappedBy* attribute references the name of the instance variable of type ClientDetail that is used by the Client class. The ClientDetail side of the relationship does not need to define the @JoinColumn, as that is defined in the Client class through the getter for the instance variable named clientDetail. However, on ClientDetail side of the relationship, we need to specify the name of that ClientDetail instance on the owning side through the mappedBy attribute, as shown below:

```
import javax.persistence.*;
@Entity
@Table(name = "client_detail", schema = "examscam")
public class ClientDetail {

><><><   ><><><
 @Id
 @GeneratedValue
 @Column(name = "id")
 public Long getId() {return id;}
 public void setId(Long id) {this.id = id;}

 @OneToOne(cascade=CascadeType.ALL,
                 mappedBy="clientDetail")
 public Client getClient() {return client;}
 public void setClient(Client c) {client=c;}
><><><   ><><><
}
```

It is also worth pointing out that the database table name will not be simply mapped by the name of the class, but instead, true to database naming conventions, an underscore will separate the word client and detail, making the table name "client_detail," as seen in the @Table annotation.

The Client Has Many Address Objects

After getting the one-to-one Client to ClientDetail association implemented with JPA annotations, it's time to move onto the OneToMany relationship between the Client and Address object. A client can have many address objects, which means the getAddress() method in the client class must be decorated with the @OneToMany annotation:

```
@Entity
@Table(name = "client", schema = "examscam")
public class Client {
XXX  XXX
  @OneToMany(mappedBy="client",
             targetEntity=Address.class,
             fetch=FetchType.EAGER,
             cascade = CascadeType.ALL)
  public List<Address> getAddresses() {
    return addresses;
  }
XXX  XXX
}
```

The @OneToMany mapping from the owning class (Client) to the owned class (Address) is relatively straight forward, with the standard fetch and cascade attributes defined as EAGER and ALL respectively. As for the mappedBy attribute, this is the name of the instance variable used by the Address class to define an instance variable of type Client. Since the Address class will define the @JoinColumn, the Client class will need to specify the name of the instance variable in the Address class in order to navigate the opposite end of the mapping.

Additionally, the @OneToMany mapping defines a targetEntity attribute which explicitly defines the type of the class (*Address.class*) that represents the many side of the OneToMany relationship.

```
package com.examscam.model;
import javax.persistence.*;
@Entity
@Table(name = "address", schema = "examscam")
public class Address {
  private Long id;
  private Client client;
  private String addressLine1;
  private String addressLine2;
  private String city, state, country, code;

  @Id
  @GeneratedValue
  @Column(name = "id")
  public Long getId() {return id;}
  public void setId(Long id) {this.id = id;}

  @ManyToOne
  @JoinColumn(name="client_id")
  public Client getClient() {return client;}
  public void setClient(Client c) {this.client = c;}

  @Column(name = "addr1", nullable=true)
  public String getAddressLine1() {return addressLine1;}
  public void setAddressLine1(String addressLine1) {
    this.addressLine1 = addressLine1;
  }

  @Column(name = "addr2", nullable=true)
  public String getAddressLine2() {return addressLine2;}
  public void setAddressLine2(String addressLine2) {
    this.addressLine2 = addressLine2;
  }
  public String getCity() {return city;}
  public void setCity(String city) {this.city = city;}
  public String getCountry() {return country;}
  public void setCountry(String c) {this.country = c;}
  public String getCode() {return code;}
  public void setCode(String code) {this.code = code;}
  public String getState() {return state;}
  public void setState(String state) {
    this.state = state;
  }
}
```

The Address Class Annotations

The Address class implements the many side of the relationship between the Client and the Address, and as such, it is decorated with the @ManyToOne annotation.

The many side of a relationship is also responsible for defining a foreign key that maps back to the primary key of the owning class. The name of this field is defined through the name attribute of the @JoinColumn annotation, as evidenced below:

```
@ManyToOne
@JoinColumn(name="client_id")
public Client getClient() {return client;}
public void setClient(Client c) {this.client = c;}
```

It should also be pointed out that the addressLine1 and the addressLine2 properties are mapped to database columns with slightly different names, namely *addr1* and *addr2* respectively. This is evidenced by the @Column annotations above the corresponding getter methods:

```
@Column(name = "addr1", nullable=true)
public String getAddressLine1() {return addressLine1;}
public void setAddressLine1(String addressLine1) {
    this.addressLine1 = addressLine1;
}
@Column(name = "addr2", nullable=true)
public String getAddressLine2() {return addressLine2;}
public void setAddressLine2(String addressLine2) {
    this.addressLine2 = addressLine2;
}
```

Completing the annotations for the Address class are the decorations above the class declaration and the getId() method:

```
import javax.persistence.*;
@Entity
@Table(name = "address", schema = "examscam")
public class Address {  XXX  XXX

    @Id
    @GeneratedValue
    @Column(name = "id")
    public Long getId() {return id;}
    XXX  XXX
}
```

The Client Has Skills

ManyToMany relationships always tend to be the most annotation intensive associations to map. On the Client side of the relationship, we will define the @ManyToMany annotation above the getSkills() method.

Further detail about the ManyToMany relationship is described in the @JoinTable annotation. This annotation describes the fact that a new table, named client_skill, will be used to keep track of the primary keys of instances of both the Client and Skill classes that are associated with each other. Furthermore, the embedded @JoinColumn tells us that the primary key of the client will be held in a column named client_id, and the inverse side of the relationship will be maintained by storing the primary key of the instance of the associated Skill class in a column of the client_skill table named skill_id.

```
@ManyToMany          /***** From the Client Class *****/
@JoinTable( name = "client_skill",
 joinColumns = { @JoinColumn(name = "client_id") },
  inverseJoinColumns={ @JoinColumn(name = "skill_id")
})
public List<Skill> getSkills() {
return skills;
}
```

It can all seem somewhat intimidating, but really, the @JoinTable annotation is simply defining the name of the join table, along with the names of the two columns in that join table.

A Skill is Associated with Many Clients

Of course, the same type of ManyToMany mapping needs to be made in the Skill class, mapping the Skill back to the many Clients with which it might be associated. As you can see, the mapping is very similar:

```
                    /***** From the Skill Class *****/
@ManyToMany(cascade = CascadeType.PERSIST)
@JoinTable(name = "client_skill",
   joinColumns={@JoinColumn(name="skill_id")},
       inverseJoinColumns={
           @JoinColumn(name = "client_id") })
public Set<Client> getClients() {return clients;}
```

The Skill Class

Along with the @ManyToMany annotation above the getClients() method, which is essentially the exact reverse of the @ManyToMany annotation defined above the getSkills() method in the Client class, the Skill class also requires the requisite annotations to describe the class as an entity, and to define the id field as the primary key for the class. Here's the fully annotated code for the Skill class:

```
package com.examscam.model;
import java.util.Set;
import javax.persistence.*;

@Entity
@Table(name = "skill", schema = "examscam")
public class Skill {
  private Long id;
  private String name;
  private Set<Client> clients;

  @ManyToMany(cascade = CascadeType.PERSIST)
  @JoinTable ( name = "client_skill",
  joinColumns = { @JoinColumn ( name = "skill_id") },
    inverseJoinColumns = {
       @JoinColumn ( name = "client_id" )
    })
  public Set<Client> getClients() {return clients;}
  public void setClients(Set<Client> c) {clients=c;}

  @Id
  @GeneratedValue
  @Column(name = "id")
  public Long getId() {return id;}
  public void setId(Long id) {this.id = id;}
  public String getName() {return name;}
  public void setName(String name) {this.name = name;}

}
```

The Completely Annotated Client Class

```
package com.examscam.model;
import java.util.*;import javax.persistence.*;
@Entity
@Table(name = "client", schema = "examscam")
public class Client {
 private List<Address> addresses = new Vector<Address>();
 private List<Skill> skills = new Vector<Skill>();
 private ClientDetail clientDetail;
 private Long id;private String username;
 private String password;private Boolean verified;
 @Id
 @GeneratedValue
 @Column(name = "id")
 public Long getId() {return id;}
 public void setId(Long id) {this.id = id;}
 @ManyToMany
 @JoinTable(name = "client_skill",
   joinColumns = { @JoinColumn(name = "client_id") },
    inverseJoinColumns = { @JoinColumn(name = "skill_id") })
 public List<Skill> getSkills() {return skills;}
 public void setSkills(List<Skill> skills){this.skills=skills;}
 @OneToMany(mappedBy="client", targetEntity=Address.class,
        fetch=FetchType.EAGER, cascade = CascadeType.ALL)
 public List<Address> getAddresses() {return addresses;}
 public void setAddresses(List<Address> addresses) {
  this.addresses = addresses;
 }
 @OneToOne(cascade=CascadeType.ALL,fetch=FetchType.LAZY)
 @JoinColumn(name="detail_id")
 public ClientDetail getClientDetail(){return clientDetail;}
 public void setClientDetail(ClientDetail clientDetail) {
  this.clientDetail = clientDetail;
 }
 public String getPassword() {return password;}
 public void setPassword(String password){this.password = password;}
 public String getUsername() {return username;}
 public void setUsername(String username) {
  this.username = username;
 }
 public Boolean getVerified() {return verified;}
 public void setVerified(Boolean verified){this.verified=verified;}
}
```

Creating the Required Database Tables

Finally, with all of the classes, coded, you must make sure that any Hibernate Session that is used to manage the persistence of these objects has the various classes added to the configuration. The best place to do this is in the HibernateUtil class that we defined in an earlier chapter. The initialization of the AnnotationConfiguration would look something like this:

```
public static Configuration getInitializedConfiguration(){

    AnnotationConfiguration config =
                new AnnotationConfiguration();

    /* add all of your JPA annotated classes here!!! */
    //config.addAnnotatedClass(User.class);
    //config.addAnnotatedClass(Snafu.class);
    //config.addAnnotatedClass(FooBar.class);
    //config.addAnnotatedClass(Thing.class);
    //config.addAnnotatedClass(LeftManyStudent.class);
    //config.addAnnotatedClass(RightManyCourse.class);

    config.addAnnotatedClass(Client.class);
    config.addAnnotatedClass(ClientDetail.class);
    config.addAnnotatedClass(Address.class);
    config.addAnnotatedClass(Skill.class);
    config.configure();
    return config;
}
```

Recreating the Database

Adding these four new classes to the AnnotationConfiguration object, and then running the *recreateDatabase()* method of the HibernateUtil class would then create the underlying tables needed to support this JPA annotated domain model. ☺

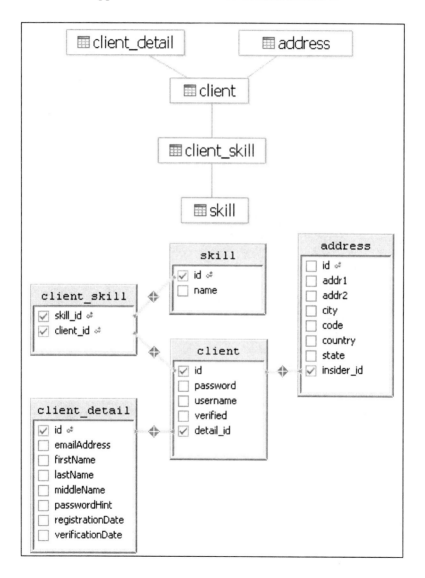

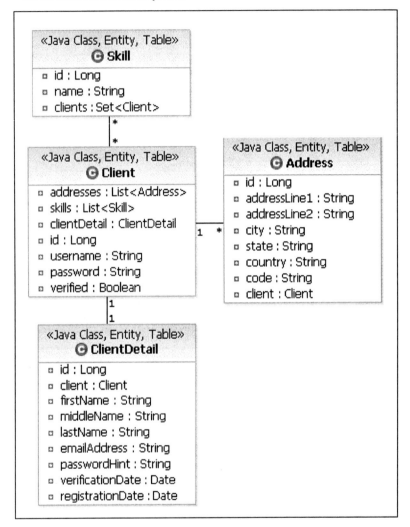

Chapter 21
Advanced DAOs

Earlier in this book, we created a simple DAO that was designed to facilitate the persistence of a User object. The UserDAO did the trick, and it was certainly simple enough to implement, but I have to admit that in its simplicity, it sorta sidestepped many of the reasons we use DAOs in the first place.

The DAO, or Data Access Object, is an important design pattern, not simply because it makes the process of persisting data a bit easier; no, the DAO pattern is important because it provides a very, very abstract interface that hides both the underlying database implementation and the mechanism or framework that is being used to persist data to the database. The UserDAO, created in an earlier chapter, wasn't very transparent with regards to how the underlying persistence mechanism was implemented. The UserDAO leaves plenty of room for improvement, that's for sure.

Now, the thing I would eventually like to do in this section is implement a little web based application that leverages the object model that was created in the previous chapter. This web based application will gather personal information from the end user, and persist that information to the database. Since the *to be developed* web based application will be using the object model developed in the previous tutorial, why not use those same Client, ClientDetail, Address and Skill classes to demonstrate the proper, and a very elegant, implementation of the DAO design pattern? Well, I can't think of any reasons not to, so that's exactly what we will do this chapter.

The Highest Level of DAO Abstraction

I'm going to do a little something here that will totally blow your mind. I'm going to create the most abstract DAO you've ever seen, namely a GenericDAO interface, which all DAOs in the enterprise application will implement.

Part of the magic here is going to be the use of the much loved, Java 5 generics. The interface declaration of the GenericDAO will not only include the name of the interface, which is obviously *GenericDAO*, but it will also specify that all implementing classes will use two object types, one of which is very generically defined (thus the term *generics*) with the uppercase letter T, and the other type being named ID, which is further described as a Serializable object.

As we code, the T will represent the class the DAO manages, so the type T for the *Skill*DAO will be the *Skill* class, and the type T for the *Client*DAO will be the *Client* class. This syntax might seem a little weird if you're new to generics, but once you see it all in action, it's all very elegant, and it all makes a lot of sense.

The GenericDAO interface defines seven important methods, three of which are finder methods:

☞ *T findByPrimaryKey(ID id);*

☞ *List<T> findAll(int startIndex, int fetchSize);*

☞ *List<T> findByExample(T exampleInstance,*
String[] excludeProperty);

There are also two persistence related methods:

☞ *T save(T entity);*

☞ *void delete(T entity);*

And finally, there are two transaction related methods:

☞ *void beginTransaction();*

☞ *void commitTransaction();*

The Amazing GenericDAO Interface

```
package com.examscam.dao;
import java.io.Serializable;
import java.util.List;

interface GenericDAO < T, ID extends Serializable >{

  T findByPrimaryKey( ID id);
  List< T > findAll(int startIndex, int fetchSize);
  List< T > findByExample( T exampleInstance,
                          String[] excludeProperty);
  T save( T entity);
  void delete( T entity);

  void beginTransaction();
  void commitTransaction();
}
```

The fabulous thing about the GenericDAO is that it defines the most important methods and functionality that our applications need, namely the ability to save, delete and retrieve entities from our persistence layer.

For specific DAOs, such as the ClientDetailDAO, or the SkillDAO, you really don't need to define too many new methods, as the important ones are already defined in the parent GenericDAO interface. For the most part, DAOs inheriting from the GenericDAO interface will generally contain little else other than custom create methods, and extra finder methods that might make sense for the associated class.

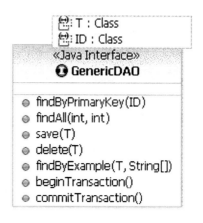

DAOs for the SkillsManagement Application

So, the SkillsManagement application has four Java classes, namely the Client, ClientDetail, Address and Skill classes. As a rule of thumb, we create a DAO for each class defined in the problem domain, which for us, would equate to a ClientDAO, ClientDetailDAO, AddressDAO and SkillDAO.

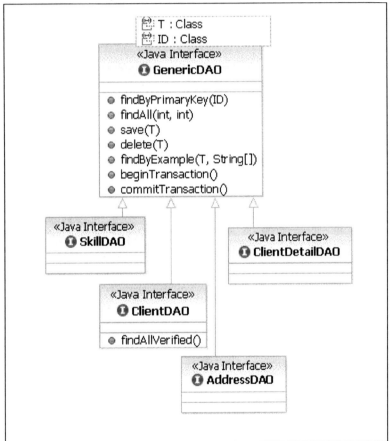

Really, the methods defined in the parent GenericDAO interface will suffice for our application. Nevertheless, an additional finder method was added to the ClientDAO to demonstrate how you can enhance your DAOs with additional methods. You can see the additional findAllVerified() method in the ClientDAO on the class diagram.

Code for the Child DAOs

What follows is the code for the four DAO interfaces, all of which inherit directly from the GenericDAO. While these are currently unimplemented interfaces, a Hibernate based implementation will soon be developed. However, these interfaces are the only things a JSF or Struts or any other application developer will use when persisting their JavaBeans. As a result, it would be possible to replace the Hibernate implementation with any other technology or framework; The client won't be affected, as they will continue to use the interfaces defined here.

Notice how each interface *concretely* defines the **generic T type** and **generic Serializable ID type** that was part of the top level definition in the GenericDAO interface.

```
package com.examscam.dao;
import com.examscam.model.Client;
public interface ClientDAO
          extends GenericDAO <Client, Long> {
   public java.util.List<Client> findAllVerified();
}
```

```
package com.examscam.dao;
import com.examscam.model.ClientDetail;
public interface ClientDetailDAO
          extends GenericDAO <ClientDetail, Long> {
}
```

```
package com.examscam.dao;
import com.examscam.model.Address;
public interface AddressDAO
          extends GenericDAO <Address, Long> {
}
```

```
package com.examscam.dao;
import com.examscam.model.Skill;
public interface SkillDAO
          extends GenericDAO<Skill, Long>{
}
```

Providing the Abstract HibernateDAO

The client applications interacting with our persistence layer will be completely buffered from the back end implementation by using nothing other than the DAO interfaces provided. However, there does need to be a concrete implementation of the DAO interfaces *somewhere*. The place we'll put most of the implementation code is in an abstract HibernateDAO class. The **Hibernate**DAO will implement as many of the inherited, unimplemented methods of the **Generic**DAO as possible.

We're going to have a number of classes in our domain that will inherit from the HibernateDAO class, namely:

☞ *the HibernateClientDAO*

☞ *the HibernateClientDetailDAO*

☞ *the HibernateAddressDAO*

☞ *the HibernateSkillDAO*

Of course, when a **Skill**DAO returns an entity, it must return an entity of type **Skill**, and when a **Client**DAO returns an entity, it must return an entity of type **Client**. So, one of the things that needs to be defined when an inheriting child DAO is created, is the *type* of entity with which the child DAO is intended to work. This will be done through a single argument constructor that defines the model class, such as *Skill.class*, with which the DAO is associated. So, the HibernateDAO, with its single-argument constructor, would look like this:

```
public abstract class HibernateDAO <T, ID extends Serializable>
                  implements GenericDAO <T, ID> {
    private Class<T> persistentClass;
    public HibernateDAO(Class c)  { persistentClass = c; }
}
```

And a concrete, child DAO, inheriting from HibernateDAO would look like this:

```
public class HibernateSkillDAO  extends HibernateDAO
                <Skill, Long> implements SkillDAO {
    public HibernateSkillDAO() { super(Skill.class); }
}
```

HibernateDAO: Iteration 1

With the property of type Class defined, and a constructor provided to initialize that property, implementing the save, delete, findByPrimaryKey, and even the transactional methods, is just a matter of writing some basic Hibernate implementation code:

```
package com.examscam.dao;
import java.io.*; import java.util.*;
import org.hibernate.*; import org.hibernate.criterion.*;
import com.examscam.HibernateUtil;
public abstract class HibernateDAO
                <T, ID extends Serializable>
                    implements GenericDAO <T, ID> {

  private Class<T> persistentClass;

  public HibernateDAO(Class c) {persistentClass = c;}

  public T findByPrimaryKey(ID id) {
     return (T) HibernateUtil.getSession()
                    .load(persistentClass, id);
  }
  public T save(T entity) {
    HibernateUtil.getSession().saveOrUpdate(entity);
    return entity;
  }
  public void delete(T entity) {
    HibernateUtil.getSession().delete(entity);
  }

  public void beginTransaction() {
    HibernateUtil.beginTransaction();
  }
  public void commitTransaction() {
    HibernateUtil.commitTransaction();
  }
}
```

The findByExample Method

The findByExample method is relatively straight forward, as it simply leverages the Criteria API, along with the generic <T> return type, to implement a findByExample method that would work for any class that extends the HibernateDAO.

```
public List<T> findByExample(T exampleInstance,
                         String[] excludeProperty) {
  Criteria crit = HibernateUtil.getSession()
                  .createCriteria(persistentClass);
  Example example = Example.create(exampleInstance);
  if (excludeProperty!=null){
    for (int i=0; i< excludeProperty.length; i++) {
      example.excludeProperty(excludeProperty[i]);
    }
  }
  crit.add(example);
  return crit.list();
}
```

The findAll Method

Again, because the HibernateDAO class doesn't exactly know the type of POJO the subclass will be using, the generic type notation, < T >, is used to define the return type for the findAll method. But, other than that little twist, the findAll method simply leverages the criteria API, the persistentClass instance variable of the HibernateDAO, and the setFirstResult and setFetchSize methods of the Criteria object, to implement a very elegant findAll method:

```
public List<T> findAll(int startIndex, int fetchSize){
  Criteria crit =
          HibernateUtil.getSession()
                  .createCriteria(persistentClass);
  crit.setFirstResult(startIndex);
  crit.setFetchSize(fetchSize);
  return crit.list();
}
```

HibernateDAO – Iteration 2

```
package com.examscam.dao;import java.io.*; import java.util.*;
import org.hibernate.*; import org.hibernate.criterion.*;
import com.examscam.HibernateUtil;
public abstract class HibernateDAO
   <T,ID extends Serializable>implements GenericDAO <T,ID>{
   private Class<T> persistentClass;
   public HibernateDAO(Class c) {persistentClass = c;}
   public T findByPrimaryKey(ID id) {
      return (T) HibernateUtil.getSession()
                       .load(persistentClass, id);
   }
   public List<T> findByExample(T exampleInstance,
                          String[] excludeProperty) {
     Criteria crit = HibernateUtil.getSession()
                    .createCriteria(persistentClass);
     Example example = Example.create(exampleInstance);
     if (excludeProperty!=null){
       for (int i=0; i< excludeProperty.length; i++) {
         example.excludeProperty(excludeProperty[i]);
       }
     }
     crit.add(example);
     return crit.list();
   }
   public List<T> findAll(int startIndex, int fetchSize){
     Criteria crit = HibernateUtil.getSession()
                       .createCriteria(persistentClass);
     crit.setFirstResult(startIndex);
     crit.setFetchSize(fetchSize);
     return crit.list();
   }
   public T save(T entity) {
     HibernateUtil.getSession().saveOrUpdate(entity);
     return entity;
   }
   public void delete(T entity) {
     HibernateUtil.getSession().delete(entity);
   }
   public void beginTransaction(){HibernateUtil.beginTransaction();}
   public void commitTransaction() {
     HibernateUtil.commitTransaction();
   }
}
```

The Concrete DAO Classes

With the abstract HibernateDAO providing concrete implementations for all of the key DAO methods, implementing the actual, concrete, DAO subclasses is a lead pipe cinch. Child DAOs simply need to extend the HibernateDAO class, implement the appropriate DAO interface, and provide concrete class names for the generic types defined by the GenericDAO interface. Here they all are, including the ClientDAO with the additional, implemented, *findAllVerified* method:

```
package com.examscam.dao;
import com.examscam.HibernateUtil;import com.examscam.model.Client;
public class HibernateClientDAO extends HibernateDAO
                    <Client, Long> implements ClientDAO {
  public HibernateClientDAO() { super(Client.class); }
  public java.util.List<Client> findAllVerified(){
    Client client = new Client(); client.setVerified(true);
    return super.findByExample(client, null);
  }
}
```

```
package com.examscam.dao;
import com.examscam.model.ClientDetail;
public class HibernateClientDetailDAO extends HibernateDAO
      <ClientDetail, Long> implements ClientDetailDAO {
 public HibernateClientDetailDAO(){super(ClientDetail.class);}
}
```

```
package com.examscam.dao;
import com.examscam.model.Address;
public class HibernateAddressDAO extends HibernateDAO
                    <Address, Long> implements AddressDAO {
  public HibernateAddressDAO() {super(Address.class);}
}
```

```
package com.examscam.dao;
import com.examscam.model.Skill;
public class HibernateSkillDAO  extends
        HibernateDAO <Skill, Long> implements SkillDAO {
  public HibernateSkillDAO() {super(Skill.class);}
}
```

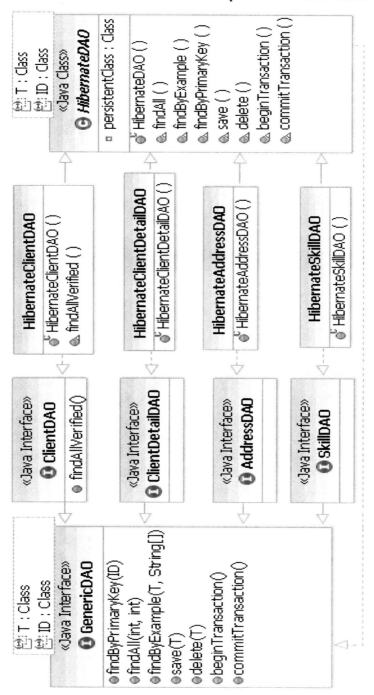

Mitigating Client Access to DAOs

Okay, so we've done all of this crazy coding with interfaces, abstract classes and DAO objects, all with the promise of completely and totally obfuscating the back end implementation of the persistence layer from the client. I mean, that's the whole point, right? We have created these simple DAO interfaces that the client will use, all the while, behind the scenes, we can *swap in* or *swap out* just about any persistence layer implementation we want.

But at this point, we've got DAO interfaces, like the ClientDAO, and we have a Hibernate based implementation through such classes as the concrete HibernateClientDAO. Right now, if a web developer wants to use the ClientDAO, they need to write some code that looks like this:

```
ClientDAO clientDAO = new HibernateClientDAO();
```

Now, I'm no genius, but just looking at that line of code, it seems pretty clear to me that Hibernate is being used to implement the ClientDAO interface. The goal of the DAO pattern is to hide the back end implementation of the persistence layer. That's not being done very well if the actual word *HIBERNATE* is peppered throughout the client's application.

So, how do we solve the dilemma of not adequately hiding information about the how the persistence layer is implemented? Well, that's easy – we just make sure the client never sees the HibernateClientDAO() class, and instead, when they need an instance of the ClientDAO, they have to go through a DAO *factory* instead. Yes, the GOF (Gang of Four) *Factory* design pattern is an integral part of any good DAO design pattern implementation. The Factory is how we hide the actual DAO implementation from the client.

The Abstract DAOFactory Class

To gain access to the DAO of interest, our clients will be given an abstract class called DAOFactory, which contains abstract methods for accessing each of the DAO classes of interest, namely the ClientDAO, ClientDetailDAO, SkillDAO and AddressDAO.

The abstract DAOFactory class will have one, single, static, *invocable* method that will return an instantiated instance of the DAOFactory itself. It is through this instance that clients will be able to gain access to the DAOs of interest.

Now one thing that you should note is that the concrete class that implements the DAOFactory will be named HibernateDAOFactory. This class is referenced inside the DAOFactory through the constant variable FACTORY_CLASS. Since this class hasn't been created yet, attempting to compile the code below would fail, as the compiler would not be able to find the HibernateDAOFactory. Don't worry, creating the HibernateDAOFactory is the next class we'll create (after this one, of course!).

```
/*this won't compile until you also create the HibernateDAOFactory*/
package com.examscam.dao;
public abstract class DAOFactory {

public static final Class FACTORY_CLASS =
          com.examscam.dao.HibernateDAOFactory.class;

/*public static final Class FACTORY_CLASS = JDBCDAOFactory.class;*/
/*public static final Class FACTORY_CLASS =JDODAOFactory.class;*/

  public static DAOFactory getFactory() {
    try {
      return (DAOFactory)FACTORY_CLASS.newInstance();
    } catch (Exception e) {
      throw new RuntimeException("Couldn't create Factory");
    }
  }
}
public abstract ClientDAO getClientDAO();
public abstract ClientDetailDAO getClientDetailDAO();
public abstract AddressDAO getAddressDAO();
public abstract SkillDAO getSkillDAO();
}
```

DAO Access through the DAOFactory

The DAOFactory is the class that client developers will use to gain access to the DAO objects needed to persist their Java components to the database. So, for a client to gain access to the ClientDAO, they'd simply code something like this:

```
DAOFactory factory = DAOFactory.getFactory();
ClientDAO clientDAO = factory.getClientDAO();
```

As you can see, there is absolutely no reference here to the fact that the underlying persistence layer is implemented through Hibernate. And what's more, the underlying implementation could be changed from Hibernate to JDO or to JDBC quite easily, so long as the same DAO interfaces, such as the ClientDAO or SkillDAO interfaces, are implemented. So, we gain infinite flexibility on the data side with regards to how the persistence layer is managed, and we get complete persistence layer independence on the client side of the application as well. The DAO pattern, in cahoots with the factory pattern, really demonstrates the actualization of the separation of concerns to which all enterprise architects and developers aspire.

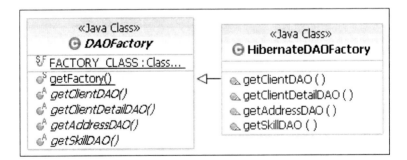

The DAOFactory's getFactory() Method

One of the most important aspects of this design is the manner in which the static getFactory method of the DAOFactory is implemented.

As you can see, the getFactory method returns an instance of a class that implements the abstract methods that are defined in the DAOFactory class. The class *type* is coded as a static final class variable in the DAOFactory, and instantiated and returned from the getFactory method. Now, this is all hidden from the client, so they don't know that the implementation of the DAOFactory is actually the yet to be coded **HibernateDAOFactory** class. In fact, we could switch that factory class with perhaps a **JDBCDAOFactory** class, or a **JDODAOFactory** class, or whatever factory class implementation we wanted, and the client would be none the wiser! Really, this is an extremely elegant design, bringing to fruition a true separation of concerns.

```
public static final Class FACTORY_CLASS =
        com.examscam.dao.HibernateDAOFactory.class;

/*public static final Class FACTORY_CLASS = JDBCDAOFactory.class;*/
/*public static final Class FACTORY_CLASS =JDODAOFactory.class;*/

 public static DAOFactory getFactory() {
   try {
     return (DAOFactory)FACTORY_CLASS.newInstance();
   } catch (Exception e) {
     throw new RuntimeException("Couldn't create Factory");
   }
 }
```

The HibernateDAOFactory

In order for the application integrators to gain access to the data access objects they need to persist Client, ClientDetail, Address and Skill objects, all they need is the DAOFactory, as it defines the various methods used to access the corresponding DAO objects. However, the methods defined in the DAOFactory are abstract, and we need a class to provide a concrete implementation of the getClientDAO(), getClientDetailDAO(), getSkillDAO() and the getAddressDAO() methods. Of course, Hibernate has been providing all of our concrete implementations thus far, so it just makes sense that it will deliver to us a concrete implementation of the abstract DAOFactory class as well.

As you can see, there's really nothing too earth shattering about the HibernateDAOFactory. All it really does is implement the getxxxDAO methods by returning the corresponding HibernateDAO that implements the interface required. So, for example, with the getClientDAO() method, the HibernateDAOFactory simply returns an instance of the HibernateClientDAO, which itself implements the ClientDAO interface.

```
public ClientDAO getClientDAO() {
     return new HibernateClientDAO();
}
```

The HibernateDAOFactory Class

```
package com.examscam.dao;
public class HibernateDAOFactory
                    extends DAOFactory {

  public ClientDAO getClientDAO() {
    return new HibernateClientDAO();
  }
  public ClientDetailDAO getClientDetailDAO() {
    return new HibernateClientDetailDAO();
  }

  public AddressDAO getAddressDAO() {
    return new HibernateAddressDAO();
  }

  public SkillDAO getSkillDAO() {
    return new HibernateSkillDAO();
  }

}
```

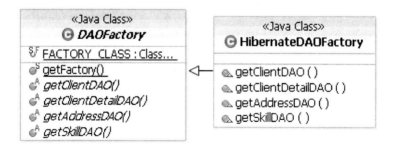

A Simple, Stand-Alone, Skills Manager App

So, the promise of the DAO and Factory patterns was the idea that the persistence framework and the back-end database implementation could be completely shielded from the client applications interacting with the DAOs. Well, let's put that theory into practice.

Take a look at the code for the SkillManagerApp. It's a simple class with nothing more than a runnable main method that creates a Client, a ClientDetail, an Address, and a few Skill objects:

```
Client client = new Client();
✂✂✂  ✂✂✂
ClientDetail detail = new ClientDetail();
✂✂✂  ✂✂✂
client.setClientDetail(detail);
Address address = new Address();  ✂✂✂  ✂✂✂
address.setClient(client);
client.getAddresses().add(address);
Skill basting = new Skill();
basting.setName("turkey basting");
client.getSkills().add(basting);✂✂✂  ✂✂✂
```

However, by using the DAO interfaces and abstract classes that are involved in the implementation of the DAO and factory patterns, saving the state of these JavaBean instances becomes very simple, and there is no indication that Hibernate is doing the work under the covers:

```
DAOFactory factory = DAOFactory.getFactory();
ClientDAO clientDAO = factory.getClientDAO();
ClientDetailDAO clientDetailDAO = factory.getClientDetailDAO();
SkillDAO skillDAO = factory.getSkillDAO();
AddressDAO addressDAO = factory.getAddressDAO();
✂✂✂  ✂✂✂
clientDAO.save(client);
clientDetailDAO.save(detail);
addressDAO.save(address);
skillDAO.save(basting);
```

The Stand-Alone SkillManagerApp

```
package com.examscam.dao;  import com.examscam.model.*;
public class SkillManagerApp {
  public static void main(String args[]) {
    DAOFactory factory = DAOFactory.getFactory();
    factory.getClientDAO().beginTransaction();
    ClientDAO clientDAO = factory.getClientDAO();
    ClientDetailDAO clientDetailDAO =
                        factory.getClientDetailDAO();
    SkillDAO skillDAO = factory.getSkillDAO();
    AddressDAO addressDAO = factory.getAddressDAO();
    Client client = new Client();
    client.setUsername("me");
    client.setPassword("passw0rd");
    ClientDetail detail = new ClientDetail();
    detail.setEmailAddress("mail@scja.com");
    detail.setFirstName("Cameron");
    detail.setLastName("McKenzie");
    client.setClientDetail(detail);
    Address address = new Address();
    address.setAddressLine1("390 Queens Quay");
    address.setAddressLine2("apt 2301");
    address.setCity("Toronto");
    address.setCountry("Canada");
    address.setClient(client);
    client.getAddresses().add(address);
    Skill basting = new Skill();
    basting.setName("turkey basting");
    client.getSkills().add(basting);
    Skill kicking = new Skill();
    kicking.setName("tire kicking");
    /* kicking not added as a skill */
    Skill polishing = new Skill();
    polishing.setName("shoe polishing");
    client.getSkills().add(polishing);
    clientDAO.save(client);
    clientDetailDAO.save(detail);
    addressDAO.save(address);
    skillDAO.save(basting);
    skillDAO.save(kicking);
    skillDAO.save(polishing);
    factory.getClientDAO().commitTransaction();
  }
}
```

Inspecting the Database

After running the SkillManagerApp, we can quickly inspect the database to ensure that all of the tables have been populated with the appropriate data fields.

id	password	username	verified	detail_id
1	passw0rd	me	NULL	1

id	emailAddress	firstName	lastName	middleName	passwc
1	mail@scja.com	Cameron	McKenzie	NULL	NULL

id	addr1	addr2	city	country	client_id
1	390 Queens Quay	apt 2301	Toronto	Canada	1

id	name	skill_id	client_id
1	turkey basting	1	1
2	tire kicking	3	1
3	shoe polishing		

As you can see from the collage of screen captures generated by the *MySQL GUI Browser* tool, data has been populated in all of the tables used by this application, namely the client, client_detail, address, skill, and even the client_skill table. Primary keys and foreign keys all map back to one another to maintain the associations set up in the runnable main method of the SkillManagerApp class.

Chapter 22
The Web Wizard

Having worked so hard on our SkillsManager object model, and having put so much effort into creating a data access object design implementation that effectively shields the client application from the back end Hibernate implementation, it would be a shame not to at least create some type of web based, Java application that leverages the facilities of our JPA annotated object model and our data access pattern implementation. So, that's exactly what we're going to do in this chapter. We're going to create a wizard type application that allows a client to provide their personal information, add addresses, and finally, choose from a list of skills the ones that most accurately reflect their own personal skillset

Simple Development: *No Deployment Tutorials*

To develop this, I will again use nothing but Java Server Pages. I know, JSF is much sexier, and at the very least, using Servlets as a controller is a much more sound MVC type of architecture, but the thing I'm striving for here is simplicity, and you don't get much simpler than JSPs. And besides, this isn't a book on Servlets, Struts or JSP development. However, I assure you that if you are familiar with Servlets or JSPs, you'll find it extremely simple to take the Java code inside of these JSPs and copy and paste them into your own Servlets or JSF command objects.

Web Application Flow

Before we jump into coding the JSP pages , let's take a look at the basic flow of the web based, SkillsManager web application. The first page will be a very simple form that asks the end user to fill out some personal information.

First Name:	Cameron
Middle Name:	Wallace
Last Name:	McKenzie
Email Address:	mail@scja.com
Login Name:	scameron
Password:	passw0rd
Password Hint:	0 not o

[Next]

The astute observer will notice that the fields in the form above map to fields in both the client and the client_detail tables of the database.

The address.jsp Page

After filling out their personal details and clicking the *Next* button, the end user will move to the address.jsp page, which asks a user to fill in their address information:

Address Line 1:	85 Clover Ridge Dr
Address Line 2:	EAST
City:	Ajax
State:	ON
Country:	Canada
Code:	L1S1G8

Add Address

Continue to Add Skills ++

After the end user has filled out all of the fields on the address page, they must click the **Add Address** button. This will store the address they just submitted and redisplay the address.jsp page, with the address they just entered being redisplayed at the bottom of the page.

The end user keeps adding addresses until they are satisfied and ready to move on to the skills selection page. This is done by clicking on the **"Continue to Add Skills++"** link on the address.jsp page.

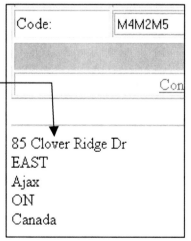

Code:	M4M2M5

Con

85 Clover Ridge Dr
EAST
Ajax
ON
Canada

The skills.jsp Page

When the end user clicks on the **Continue to Add Skills ++** link, the skills.jsp page will display, showing a list on the left hand side containing all of the possible skills from which the user can select. The end user then selects the skills that are most appropriate and then clicks the **Update Skills** button. After clicking on this button, the selected skills from the list of skills on the left appear in the list of selected skills on the right.

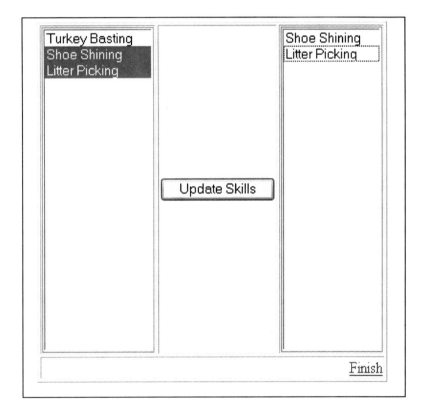

Summing It All Up!

When the user clicks on the **Finish** button on the skills.jsp page, all of the data they have provided is saved to the database, and a summary is displayed back to the user. It isn't pretty, but it's sufficient for our purposes. ☺

Congratulations! You have registered! Here is a summary of your information.

Personal Info:	Address Info:	Skills:
4 scameron passw0rd 0 not o Cameron Wallace McKenzie mail@scja.com	85 Clover Ridge Dr EAST Ajax ON Canada	Shoe Shining Litter Picking
	390 Queens Quay Apt 2003 Toronto ON Canada	

Let's Get Coding!

That should give you a good overview of where I want to take this web based, JSP application. With that quick tour of the application, let's start building the first page – the index.jsp.

The index.jsp – Obtaining Client Data

First Name:	Cameron
Middle Name:	Wallace
Last Name:	McKenzie
Email Address:	mail@scja.com
Login Name:	scameron
Password:	passw0rd
Password Hint:	0 not o

Next

«Java Class, Entity, Table»
ⓖ **Client**
- addresses : List<Address>
- skills : List<Skill>
- clientDetail : ClientDetail
- id : Long
- username : String
- password : String
- verified : Boolean

«Java Class, Entity, Table»
ⓖ **ClientDetail**
- id : Long
- client : Client
- firstName : String
- middleName : String
- lastName : String
- emailAddress : String
- passwordHint : String
- verificationDate : Date
- registrationDate : Date

Client & ClientDetail Class Diagram

Fields on the index.jsp form map directly to some of the properties defined in the Client and ClientDetail classes.

Adding Client Information – index.jsp

The first page of the SkillsManagerWebApp will simply ask the user for their personal details, namely their firstName, lastName, middleName, emailAddress, username, password and passwordHint.

```html
<html><head><title>index</title></head><body>

<form action="address.jsp" method="get">
First Name:
<input type="text" name="firstName" size="30"><br/>
Middle Name:
<input type="text" name="middleName" size="30"><br/>
Last Name:
<input type="text" name="lastName" size="30"><br/>
Email Address:
<input type="text" name="emailAddress" size="30"><br/>
Login Name:
<input type="text" name="username" size="30"><br/>
Password:
<input type="text" name="password" size="30"><br/>
Password Hint:
<input type="text" name="passwordHint" size="30"><br/>
<input type="submit" name="command" value="Next">
</form>

</body></html>
```

Furthermore, notice that the *action* of the JSP page's form is the address.jsp, which will read the information provided through these textfields, and subsequently save the data to the database. Since the address.jsp is going to use some nifty setProperty tags to initialize the needed Client and ClientDetail objects, we must make sure the names of the parameters in the input fields match the *names* and *casing* of the corresponding properties defined in the Client and ClientDetail classes.

Note that the name of the submit button is *command*, and the value associated with someone clicking the button on the Client details page is *Next*. This will become important in the address.jsp page as it differentiates between requests to add a new client, and requests to add a new address.

The address.jsp Page

Address Line 1:	85 Clover Ridge Dr
Address Line 2:	EAST
City:	Ajax
State:	ON
Country:	Canada
Code:	L1S1G8

Add Address

Continue to Add Skills ++

The Client Can Have Many Address Objects

«Java Class, Entity, Table»
ⓒ **Client**
- addresses : List<Address>
- skills : List<Skill>
- clientDetail : ClientDetail
- id : Long
- username : String
- password : String
- verified : Boolean

«Java Class, Entity, Table»
ⓒ **Address**
- id : Long
- addressLine1 : String
- addressLine2 : String
- city : String
- state : String
- country : String
- code : String
- client : Client

The address.jsp Java Server Page

The key visual element to the address.jsp page is the HTML
form that allows a user to type in their address information:

```
<form action="address.jsp" method="get">
Address Line 1:
<input type="text" name="addressLine1" size="30"><br/>
Address Line 2:
<input type="text" name="addressLine2" size="30"><br/>
City:<input type="text"    name="city" size="30"><br/>
State:<input type="text"   name="state" size="30"><br/>
Country:<input type="text" name="country" size="30"><br/>
Code:<input type="text"    name="code" size="30"><br/>
<input type="submit" name="command" value="Add Address">
</form>
```

Note, that like the index.jsp, the submit button is named
command, but the value associated with a user clicking the
button to add an address is actually the String "Add Address".

The address.jsp page is very interesting in how it might be
invoked. You see, a user can add multiple addresses, so when a
user adds an address, the address.jsp page must be designed to
handle the submission of the form, store the address data
provided by the user, and subsequently redisplay itself so the
user can add more addresses. It is not until the users clicks on the
link at the bottom of the page that says "Continue to Add Skills"
that the user will move away from the address.jsp page and to
the skills.jsp page, allowing a user to select the skills that most
appropriately match their competencies.

However, the address.jsp page is also invoked when the initial
form, asking for all of the Client and ClientDetail data, is
submitted. So the address.jsp page must not only handle the
submission of address data for the client, it must also be able to
handle the submission of all of the Client's basic information as
well. Essentially, the kloogyness of the address.jsp page
demonstrates why frameworks like JSF and Struts were invented
– to help offload the job of controlling application flow to more
appropriate command components. Nevertheless, with a little
hard work, and a tad of Haitian Voodoo thrown in for good
measure, we can get our address.jsp page to do everything that it
needs to do.

Controller Login in the address.jsp

Since the address.jsp can potentially be handing the submission of Client data **and** the submission of Address data, there needs to be three getProperty and setProperty tags defined for the page, namely tags for the ClientDetail, Client, and Address objects that need to be created and populated based on form data being submitted to the page. Furthermore, since the page will be requiring a number of imports, along with the use of the JSTL core tag libraries, the address.jsp page will need a solid page directive, and a JSTL taglib directive:

```
<%@page
  import="com.examscam.dao.*,com.examscam.model.*;"%>
<%@ taglib prefix="c"
         uri="http://java.sun.com/jsp/jstl/core" %>

<jsp:useBean class="com.examscam.model.Client"
             id="client" scope="session"/>
<jsp:useBean class="com.examscam.model.ClientDetail"
             id="clientDetail" scope="request"/>
<jsp:useBean class="com.examscam.model.Address"
             id="address" scope="request"/>

<jsp:setProperty name="client"       property="*" />
<jsp:setProperty name="clientDetail" property="*" />
<jsp:setProperty name="address"      property="*" />
```

Of course, this simply sets up the page for the Java logic that we must implement. Remember, this page can be invoked in one of two ways, either by the clicking of the command button on the index.jsp page, which submits a Client's personal information, or by the clicking of the command button on the address.jsp page. So, an important part of the logic of our address.jsp page is seeing which button, either the one on the index.jsp page or the one on the address.jsp page, triggered the page to be displayed. To figure out which button was pressed, the code looks like this:

```
String command = request.getParameter("command");
```

Once we know which command button was clicked, we can implement the appropriate logic.

```
/* Find out which button was pressed */
String command = request.getParameter("command");

/*This means client information has been submitted */
if ((command!=null) && command.equals("Next")){
/* Perform the logic to add a Client and ClientDetail to
the database */
}


/* This means the client is adding an address */
if ((command!=null) &&
                 command.equals("Add Address")){
/* Do the logic to add a new Address object for the given
client to the database*/
}
```

Handling the Submission of Client Info

Of course, with the setProperty tags defined at the top of the JSP page, handling the "Next" command, where a client has submitted their personal details, is fairly easy. All we have to do is grab the already populated Client and ClientDetail objects, make sure they are associated with one another, and then use the DAOs to persist the Client and the ClientDetail instances to the database.

```
String command = request.getParameter("command");
if ((command!=null) && command.equals("Next")){
  client.setClientDetail(clientDetail);
  clientDetail.setClient(client);
  DAOFactory factory = DAOFactory.getFactory();
  factory.getClientDAO().beginTransaction();
  factory.getClientDetailDAO().save(clientDetail);
  factory.getClientDAO().save(client);
  factory.getClientDAO().commitTransaction();
}
```

Handling Address Information Submission

Clients can add as many addresses as they like, such as a home address, work address, cottage address, etc. So, when they add addresses, the address information they have submitted gets saved, and the address.jsp page gets redisplayed so they can add more addresses. This creates the scenario where the address.jsp page ends up handing its own form submission.

When someone adds an address, the value of the command button is "Add Address". And of course, the setProperty tags on the page have ensured that an address object has already been populated for us, based on what the user has typed into the various textfields. So, with an address object already created and populated for us, it's just a matter of saving to the database, which with our DAOs, should be easy as 3.14.

```
if ((command!=null)&& command.equals("Add Address")){
    address.setClient(client);
    client.getAddresses().add(address);
    DAOFactory factory = DAOFactory.getFactory();
    factory.getAddressDAO().beginTransaction();
    factory.getAddressDAO().save(address);
    factory.getClientDAO().save(client);
    factory.getAddressDAO().commitTransaction();
}
```

One thing you should notice is that the client object is still hanging around, despite that fact that the address.jsp page does not actually contain any html fields that relate to client properties. The existence of the client instance is not magic, though. The Client is still hanging around due to the fact that it was placed in the session scope, as opposed to the request scope:

```
<jsp:useBean class="com.examscam.model.Client"
                id="client" scope="session"/>
```

As a result, once the client instance is placed in the session, it will be available to the end-user until they either log out, close their browser, or have the server time their session out.

With the client instance available, we can make sure the client and the address objects are associated with each other, and then we can call on the friendly AddressDAO and ClientDAO objects to ensure that our POJOs are properly persisted to the database.

```jsp
<%@page import="com.examscam.dao.*,com.examscam.model.*;"%>
<%@ taglib prefix="c" uri="http://java.sun.com/jsp/jstl/core" %>
<jsp:useBean class="com.examscam.model.Client" id="client"
scope="session"/>
<jsp:useBean class="com.examscam.model.ClientDetail"
id="clientDetail" scope="request"/>
<jsp:useBean class="com.examscam.model.Address"
id="address" scope="request"/>
<jsp:setProperty name="client" property="*" />
<jsp:setProperty name="clientDetail" property="*" />
<jsp:setProperty name="address" property="*" />
<%
String command = request.getParameter("command");
if ((command!=null) && command.equals("Next")){
  client.setClientDetail(clientDetail);
  clientDetail.setClient(client);
  DAOFactory factory = DAOFactory.getFactory();
  factory.getClientDAO().beginTransaction();
  factory.getClientDetailDAO().save(clientDetail);
  factory.getClientDAO().save(client);
  factory.getClientDAO().commitTransaction();
}
if ((command!=null)&& command.equals("Add Address")){
  address.setClient(client);
  client.getAddresses().add(address);
  DAOFactory factory = DAOFactory.getFactory();
  factory.getAddressDAO().beginTransaction();
  factory.getAddressDAO().save(address);
  factory.getClientDAO().save(client);
  factory.getAddressDAO().commitTransaction();
}
%>
<html><head><title>address</title></head><body>
<form action="address.jsp" method="get">
Address Line 1:
<input type="text" name="addressLine1" size="30"><br/>
Address Line 2:
<input type="text" name="addressLine2" size="30"><br/>
City:<input type="text" name="city" size="30"><br/>
State:<input type="text" name="state" size="30"><br/>
Country:<input type="text" name="country" size="30"><br/>
Code:<input type="text" name="code" size="30"><br/>
<input type="submit" name="command" value="Add Address">
</form>
<a href="skills.jsp">Continue to Add Skills ++ </a>
</body></html>
```

Displaying a Client's Address Objects

Now, a user can add as many address objects as they like. Obviously, when they come to the address page for the first time, they haven't added any addresses at all. However, as they do add addresses, we should redisplay them on the page when the address.jsp re-renders. That way, they'll know if the address information they just provided was actually accepted by the server.

To do this, we're simply going to add a JSTL for loop to loop through the Client's collection of addresses. Since the Client instance is already stored in the session, and made available to the page through the corresponding getProperty tag, the for:each JSTL custom tag can be implemented by effectively using *expression language* semantics. Here's how the custom tag would look:

```
<c:forEach items="${client.addresses}" var="a">
<hr/>
<c:out value="${a.addressLine1}"></c:out><BR/>
<c:out value="${a.addressLine2}"></c:out><BR/>
<c:out value="${a.city}"></c:out><BR/>
<c:out value="${a.state}"></c:out><BR/>
<c:out value="${a.country}"></c:out><BR/>
</c:forEach>
```

Displaying the Client's Address Objects

Essentially, the *items* attribute of the *forEach* tag points to the collection of addresses to which the client is associated. The forEach loop then loops through all of the address instances, using the variable named '*a*' to represent the current address in each iteration. Also, notice that a little <hr/> tag was used so that each address would be separated by a horizontal rule.

```
Code:                M4M2M5

                              Con

85 Clover Ridge Dr
EAST
Ajax
ON
Canada
```

The last thing to pay attention to on the address.jsp page is the anchor tag that allows the user to finish adding addresses, and subsequently jump to the skills.jsp page.

```
<a href="skills.jsp">Continue to Add Skills ++ </a>
```

```
<%@page import="com.examscam.dao.*,com.examscam.model.*;"%>
<%@ taglib prefix="c" uri="http://java.sun.com/jsp/jstl/core" %>
<jsp:useBean class="com.examscam.model.Client" id="client" scope="session"/>
<jsp:useBean class="com.examscam.model.ClientDetail" id="clientDetail" scope="request"/>
<jsp:useBean class="com.examscam.model.Address" id="address" scope="request"/>
<jsp:setProperty name="client" property="*" />
<jsp:setProperty name="clientDetail" property="*" />
<jsp:setProperty name="address" property="*" />
<%
String command = request.getParameter("command");
if ((command!=null) && command.equals("Next")){
  client.setClientDetail(clientDetail);
  clientDetail.setClient(client);
  DAOFactory factory = DAOFactory.getFactory();
  factory.getClientDAO().beginTransaction();
  factory.getClientDetailDAO().save(clientDetail);
  factory.getClientDAO().save(client);
  factory.getClientDAO().commitTransaction();
}
if ((command!=null)&& command.equals("Add Address")){
  address.setClient(client);
  client.getAddresses().add(address);
  DAOFactory factory = DAOFactory.getFactory();
  factory.getAddressDAO().beginTransaction();
  factory.getAddressDAO().save(address);
  factory.getClientDAO().save(client);
  factory.getAddressDAO().commitTransaction();
}
%>
<html><head><title>address</title></head><body>
<form action="address.jsp" method="get">
Address Line 1:<input type="text" name="addressLine1" size="30"><br/>
Address Line 2:<input type="text" name="addressLine2" size="30"><br/>
City:<input type="text" name="city" size="30"><br/>
State:<input type="text" name="state" size="30"><br/>
Country:<input type="text" name="country" size="30"><br/>
Code:<input type="text" name="code" size="30"><br/>
<input type="submit" name="command" value="Add Address">
</form>
<a href="skills.jsp">Continue to Add Skills++</a>
<c:forEach items="${client.addresses}" var="a">
<hr/>
<c:out value="${a.addressLine1}"></c:out><BR/>
<c:out value="${a.addressLine2}"></c:out><BR/>
<c:out value="${a.city}"></c:out><BR/>
<c:out value="${a.state}"></c:out><BR/>
<c:out value="${a.country}"></c:out><BR/>
</c:forEach>
<a href="skills.jsp">Continue to Add Skills ++ </a>
</body></html>
```

Adding Skills: The Skills.jsp

The skills.jsp works by displaying a list of all of the available skills in a multi-select list on the left hand side of the page. The end-user then presses the CRTL key and uses their cursor to select multiple skills from the list box. When they have highlighted all of the skills that match their own personal competencies, they click the command button named "Update Skills." The action of this command button is to call the skills.jsp again, and have the page process each skill that was selected in the list of all skills, and subsequently associated those chosen skills with the client.

Of course, the skills.jsp will require the usual suspect of characters, namely the page directive containing the appropriate imports, a taglib directive making the JSTL core custom tag library available to the page, and of course, the requisite jsp:getProperty tag for the client instance that has been stuffed into the session. Furthermore, the page will need the DAOFactory and an initiated transaction if we're going to be hitting the database. The skills.jsp will start off looking like this:

```
<%@taglib prefix="c" uri="http://java.sun.com/jsp/jstl/core"%>
<%@page import="com.examscam.dao.*,com.examscam.model.*;"%>
<jsp:useBean class="com.examscam.model.Client"
id="client" scope="session"/>

<%
DAOFactory factory = DAOFactory.getFactory();
factory.getClientDAO().beginTransaction();
✄✄✄ more code to come ☺ ✄✄✄
%>
```

The Skills.jsp and Skill Class Diagram

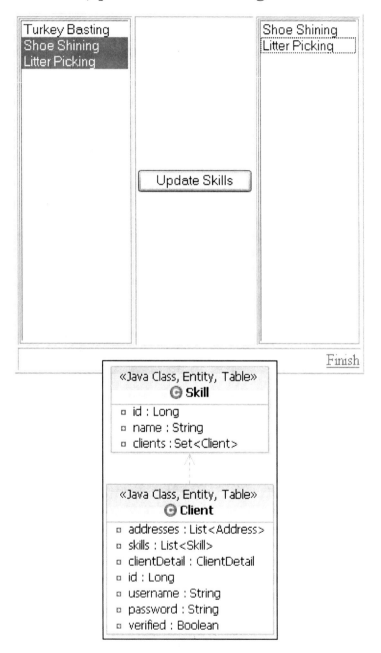

Logic of the skills.jsp

The multi-select box that the client chooses skills from is named **allskills**. So, to find out which skills the user selected from the multi-select box, we simply execute the following piece of code:

```
String[] clientSkills =
        request.getParameterValues("allskills");
```

Again, this code doesn't get all the skills, it simply asks the multi select box that displays all of the skills, *which of the skills in the list has the client actually selected*. The selected skills are returned in an array of String objects that we call **clientSkills**.

So long as there are indeed selected skills, we grab the client instance and clear out the old list of client skills, and then, one at a time, we grab one of the items in the list box that was selected, find the value associated with the selected item, which we will set up to be the primary key of the skill in question, grab that corresponding skill instance from the database using the SkillDAO's findByPrimaryKey method, and then, finally, associate that selected skill with the client. Once we have looped through each of the skills that the client has selected, we can save the client, and rest assured that all of the client's associated skills have been saved as well. ☺

```
<%
DAOFactory factory = DAOFactory.getFactory();
factory.getClientDAO().beginTransaction();
String[] clientSkills =
        request.getParameterValues("allskills");
if(clientSkills!=null) {
  client.getSkills().clear();
  for (int i = 0; i< clientSkills.length; i++) {
    Long id = new Long(clientSkills[i]);
    Skill skill=(Skill)factory.
                getSkillDAO().findByPrimaryKey(id);
    client.getSkills().add(skill);
  }
  factory.getClientDAO().save(client);
}
%>
```

Displaying all the Available Skills

When the skills.jsp page first displays, all of the skills in the database will be displayed in a multi-select list box. This requires a hardy combination of the HTML select tag, the JSTL forEach custom tag, and a quick interaction with the SkillDAO to retrieve all of the skills in the database. The code for the allSkills multi-select list box is as follows:

```
<select size="20" name="allskills" multiple>

<c:forEach
    items="<%=factory.getSkillDAO().findAll(0,100)%>"
        var="skill" >
<option value="${skill.id}" id="${skill.id}">
  <c:out value="${skill.name}"></c:out>
</option>
</c:forEach>

</select>
```

As you can see, displaying all of the skills really tests your Java, Hibernate, expression language and JSTL tag library talents.

Notice that the select box has the name **allskills**. This is why, when we want to know which skills a user has selected, we issue the command:

```
String[] clientSkills =
        request.getParameterValues("allskills");
```

Also notice that for each option element in the select list, that the value that is displayed is the name of the skill, ${skill.name}, but the value associated with the option element is actually the primary key of the skill, ${skill.id}. Knowing the primary key of the skill the client has selected, we can use the findByPrimaryKey method of the SkillDAO to pull the corresponding Skill instance from the database, and add that skill to the collection of skills that are associated with the client.

```
Long id = new Long(clientSkills[i]);
Skill skill=(Skill)factory.
getSkillDAO().findByPrimaryKey(id);
client.getSkills().add(skill);
```

Displaying the Client's Skills

The code for displaying the client's set of skills is fairly similar to that of the allSkills list, with the exception being the fact that we can simply use the instance of the client that has been pulled out of the session scope to find the skills to display.

```
<select size="20" name="allskills" multiple>
<c:forEach
    items="<%=client.getSkills()%>" var="skill">

<option value="${skill.id}" id="${skill.id}">
<c:out value="${skill.name}"></c:out>
</option>

</c:forEach>
</select>
```

Rounding off the HTML form, we need a command button between the two lists so users can actually commit their selections. All of this must be contained within an HTML <form> tag that points to the skills.jsp page as the value of the action attribute.

```
<form action="skills.jsp" method="post">
<select size="20" name="allskills" multiple>
<c:forEach items="<%=factory.getSkillDAO().findAll(0,100)%>" var="skill" >
<option value="${skill.id}" id="${skill.id}"><c:out value="${skill.name}"></c:out></option>
</c:forEach></select>
<input type="submit" name="command" value="Update Skills">
<select size="20" name="allskills" multiple>
<c:forEach items="<%=client.getSkills()%>" var="skill" >
<option value="${skill.id}" id="${skill.id}"><c:out value="${skill.name}"></c:out></option>
</c:forEach></select>
</form>
```

Finally, we need a link that takes the user to the final, summary page, of the SkillsManager Web Wizard.

```
<a href="summary.jsp"> Finish  </a>
```

427

Ending the Transaction

If you look at the skills.jsp, you'll notice that we kick off a transaction right at the start of the Java logic:

```
<%
DAOFactory factory = DAOFactory.getFactory();
factory.getClientDAO().beginTransaction();
✂✂✂ ✂✂✂
%>
```

However, we never actually commit that transaction within that same scriptlet. Strange, isn't it?

Well, actually, it's not very strange at all. Not only do we need the transaction to be open within the logic of the scriptlet, but when the select lists are initialized, we're using a SkillDAO to pull all of the skills out of the database, and if the skills of the client are set to lazy-loading, trying to access them outside of the scope of a transaction will create a LazyInitializationException. To avoid this, we start a transaction right at the beginning of the page, and end that transaction as the page has finished rendering.

```
</body>
</html>
<%
factory.getClientDAO().commitTransaction();
%>
```

To finish the skills.jsp page, we need a little scriptlet at the end of the page to finally commit the transaction that we started earlier. Now, one thing that should be mentioned is that since we're using JSPs, we are starting a transaction at the beginning of the page, and committing it at the end of the page. However, it would be more accurate to say that the transaction should be started when the request comes in, and committed when the request has been completely handled, and a response is being sent back to the client. Such an approach is effective, and commonly referred to as the one transaction per request pattern.

```jsp
<%@ taglib prefix="c" uri="http://java.sun.com/jsp/jstl/core"%>
<%@page import="com.examscam.dao.*,com.examscam.model.*;"%>
<jsp:useBean class="com.examscam.model.Client" id="client"
scope="session"></jsp:useBean>
<%
DAOFactory factory = DAOFactory.getFactory();
factory.getClientDAO().beginTransaction();
String[] clientSkills =
request.getParameterValues("allskills");
if(clientSkills!=null) {
  client.getSkills().clear();
    for (int i = 0; i< clientSkills.length; i++) {
      Long id = new Long(clientSkills[i]);
      Skill skill=(Skill)factory
                        .getSkillDAO().findByPrimaryKey(id);
      client.getSkills().add(skill);
    }
  factory.getClientDAO().save(client);
}
%>
<html><head><title>skills</title></head><body>
<form action="skills.jsp" method="post">
<select size="20" name="allskills" multiple>
<c:forEach
items="<%=factory.getSkillDAO().findAll(0,100)%>"
var="skill" >
<option value="${skill.id}" id="${skill.id}">
<c:out value="${skill.name}"></c:out></option>
</c:forEach>
</select>
<input type="submit" name="command" value="Update Skills">
<select size="20" name="allskills" multiple>
<c:forEach items="<%=client.getSkills()%>" var="skill" >
<option value="${skill.id}" id="${skill.id}">
<c:out value="${skill.name}"></c:out></option>
</c:forEach>
</select>
</form>
<a href="summary.jsp">Finish  </a>
</body></html>
<%
factory.getClientDAO().commitTransaction();
%>
```

The Summary Page: summary.jsp

The summary.jsp page is just that – a simple summary of all of the information that has been saved about the client who has just completed the wizard. The page simply regurgitates all of the information that the client has just provided.

Of course, the page will begin with the standard useBean tags, taglibs and page directives.

```
<%@page import="com.examscam.dao.*,com.examscam.model.*;"%>
<%@ taglib prefix="c" uri="http://java.sun.com/jsp/jstl/core" %>
<jsp:useBean class="com.examscam.model.Client" id="client"
scope="session"/>
```

Of course, there is still a client object floating around in the session. Now, I want to make sure that I have the absolutely most up to date information, so I'll use the id of the client in the session to actually do a lookup directly against the database, using the findByPrimaryKey method of the ClientDAO. This means going through the DAO factory, and beginning a database transaction in the process:

```
<%
DAOFactory factory = DAOFactory.getFactory();
factory.getClientDAO().beginTransaction();
client = (Client)factory.getClientDAO()
            .findByPrimaryKey(client.getId());
%>
```

And like the skills.jsp before it, the transaction that is started at the beginning of the request is ended as the full JSP page has completed, and content is ready to be delivered to the client:

```
</body>
</html>
<%factory.getClientDAO().commitTransaction();%>
```

As far as accessing data, client information is accessed simply by using the client instance, and expression language in the JSP is used to access the pertinent fields:

```
${client.id}
${client.clientDetail.lastName}
${client.addresses}
${client.skills}
```

The Summary Page: summary.jsp

Along with the basic properties defined in the Client and ClientDetail classes, the summary.jsp page must also loop through all of the skills and all of the addresses that are associated with the Client. This is achieved by using the client instance that was obtained through the ClientDAO, and passing the associated collection, be it the collection of skills or the collection of addresses, to a JSTL forEach custom tag.

Looping through the Client's Skills

```
<p>Skills:</p>
<c:forEach items="${client.skills}"  var="skill" >
<c:out value="${skill.name}"/><br/>
</c:forEach>
```

Looping through the Client's Addresses

```
<p>Address Info</p>
<c:forEach items="${client.addresses}" var="addr">
<c:out value="${addr.addressLine1}"/><br/>
<c:out value="${addr.addressLine2}"/><br/>
<c:out value="${addr.city}"/><br/>
<c:out value="${addr.state}"/><br/>
<c:out value="${addr.country}"/><br/><hr/>
</c:forEach>
```

The following page shows what the summary.jsp page might look like after a user goes through the application, and of course, a full listing of the code that makes up the summary.jsp page.

The summary.jsp Page

When the end user has finished providing data to the web wizard, a summary page is finally displayed back to them.

Congratulations! You have registered! Here is a summary of your information.

Personal Info:	Address Info:	Skills:
4		
scameron	85 Clover Ridge Dr	Shoe Shining
passw0rd		Litter Picking
0 not o	EAST	
Cameron	Ajax	
Wallace	ON	
McKenzie	Canada	
mail@scja.com		
	390 Queens Quay	
	Apt 2003	
	Toronto	
	ON	
	Canada	

Full Code for the summary.jsp

```
<%@page import="com.examscam.dao.*,com.examscam.model.*;"%>
<%@ taglib prefix="c" uri="http://java.sun.com/jsp/jstl/core" %>
<jsp:useBean class="com.examscam.model.Client" id="client"
scope="session"/>
<%
DAOFactory factory = DAOFactory.getFactory();
factory.getClientDAO().beginTransaction();
client = (Client)factory.getClientDAO()
            .findByPrimaryKey(client.getId());
%>
<html><head><title>summary</title></head><body>
<p>Congratulations! You have registered!</p>
<c:out value="${client.id}" /><br/>
<c:out value="${client.username}" /><br/>
<c:out value="${client.password}" /><br/>
<c:out value="${client.clientDetail.passwordHint}" /><br/>
<c:out value="${client.id}" /><br/>
<c:out value="${client.clientDetail.firstName}" /><br/>
<c:out value="${client.clientDetail.middleName}" /><br/>
<c:out value="${client.clientDetail.lastName}" /><br/>
<c:out value="${client.clientDetail.emailAddress}" /><br/>
<c:out value="${client.clientDetail.registrationDate}" /><br/>
<c:out value="${client.clientDetail.verificationDate}" /><br/>
<c:out value="${client.clientDetail.middleName}" /><br/>

<p>Skills:</p>
<c:forEach items="${client.skills}"  var="skill" >
<c:out value="${skill.name}"/><br/>
</c:forEach>

<p>Address Info</p>
<c:forEach items="${client.addresses}" var="addr">
<c:out value="${addr.addressLine1}"/><br/>
<c:out value="${addr.addressLine2}"/><br/>
<c:out value="${addr.city}"/><br/>
<c:out value="${addr.state}"/><br/>
<c:out value="${addr.country}"/><br/><hr/>
</c:forEach>
</body></html>
<%factory.getClientDAO().commitTransaction();%>
```

Successful Completion and Deployment

And that completes the code for the SkillsManager web application. With the JSP pages packaged in a web application archive file (WAR file), the supporting Java classes compiled and placed in the classes folder of the WAR files WEB-INF directory, and all of the required JAR files placed in the \lib directory of the WAR file's WEB-INF directory, this web application could successfully be deployed to any web container that runs on a 1.5 or better Java Runtime Environment (JRE).

I really do consider it an honor for you to have taken the time to read these four hundred or so pages. Even though it's just a technical book, I like to think that anyone who reads one of my works, gets to know me just a little bit.

Thanks so much for your time and your support.

-Cameron McKenzie-

www.hiberbook.com

(I'd love to hear from you.)

Index

Breinigsville, PA USA
18 January 2010
230967BV00004B/19/P